COUNSELING IN THE REHABILITATION PROCESS

Second Edition

COUNSELING IN THE REHABILITATION PROCESS

Community Services for Mental and Physical Disabilities

Authored/Edited by

GERALD L. GANDY, PH.D., CRC, NCC

E. DAVIS MARTIN, JR., ED.D., CRC, NCC

RICHARD E. HARDY, ED.D., ABP

Charles C Thomas
PUBLISHER • LTD.
SPRINGFIELD • ILLINOIS • U.S.A.

Published and Distributed Throughout the World by

CHARLES C THOMAS • PUBLISHER, LTD.
2600 South First Street
Springfield, Illinois 62794-9265

ISBN 0-398-06969-7 (cloth)
ISBN 0-398-06970-0 (pbk.)

Library of Congress Catalog Card Number: 99-19788

With THOMAS BOOKS *careful attention is given to all details of manufacturing and design. It is the Publisher's desire to present books that are satisfactory as to their physical qualities and artistic possibilities and appropriate for their particular use.* THOMAS BOOKS *will be true to those laws of quality that assure a good name and good will.*

Printed in the United States of America
CR-R-3

Library of Congress Cataloging in Publication Data

Gandy, Gerald L.
Counseling in the rehabilitation process : community services for mental and physical disabilities / authored/edited by Gerald L. Gandy, E. Davis Martin, Richard E. Hardy. -- 2nd ed.
p. cm.
Rev. ed. of: Rehabilitation counseling and services / Gerald L. Gandy ... [et al.]. c1897.
Includes bibliographical references and index.
ISBN 0-398-06969-7 (cloth). -- ISBN 0-398-06970-0 (pbk.)
1. Rehabilitation counseling. 2. Vocational rehabilitation. I. Martin, E. Davis. II. Hardy, Richard E. III. Rehabilitation counseling and services. IV. Title.
HD7255.5.R38 1999
361'.06--dc21 99-19788
CIP

AUTHORS AND EDITORS

GERALD L. GANDY, Ph.D., CRC, NCC: Professor Emeritus, Department of Rehabilitation Counseling, School of Allied Health Professions (SAHP), Medical College of Virginia (MCV), Virginia Commonwealth University (VCU), Richmond. Formerly, Professor, Department of Rehabilitation Counseling, SAHP, MCV/VCU; President of the Faculty, School of Community and Public Affairs, VCU; Director, Rehabilitation Services Education Program, VCU; Chief, Counseling and Rehabilitation Services, Veterans Administration Regional Office, Columbia, South Carolina; Counselor, University of South Carolina Counseling Center; and Captain, United States Army Medical Service Corps. Dr. Gandy has either authored or co-authored/co-edited five major textbooks and contributed numerous articles to the professional literature. He has been active in local, national, and international professional activities and has received various awards and recognition for his service. Dr. Gandy is a Licensed Professional Counselor (Virginia), Licensed Counseling Psychologist (South Carolina), Certified Rehabilitation Counselor, and National Certified Counselor. He is registered with the National Register of Health Service Providers in Psychology and holds the Association of State and Provincial Psychology Boards Certificate of Professional Qualification in Psychology. Dr. Gandy is also a Fellow and Diplomate in Professional Counseling of the International Academy of Behavioral Medicine, Counseling and Psychotherapy.

E. DAVIS MARTIN, Jr., Ed.D., CRC, NCC: Professor, Department of Rehabilitation Counseling, School of Allied Health Professions (SAHP), Medical College of Virginia (MCV), Virginia Commonwealth University (VCU), Richmond. Formerly, Interim Chair, Department of Rehabilitation Counseling, SAHP, MCV/VCU; Professor of Special Education, School of Education, VCU; Acting Dean, School of Community and Public Affairs (SCPA), VCU; Associate and Assistant Dean, SCPA, VCU; Director of Continuing Studies, SAHP, MCV/VCU, and served in various positions in the state-federal rehabilitation program. Dr. Martin has co-authored/co-edited three major textbooks and been a frequent contributor to the rehabilitation literature. He has consulted with local, state, and federal agencies as well as with organizations in the private sector. Dr. Martin has been repeatedly recognized for his outstanding leadership and service by the receipt of many awards and commendations from professional, governmental, and private organizations including appointment to significant Boards and Councils by the past five Governors of the Commonwealth of Virginia. Considered to be a leading forensic disability expert, he has served as a Vocational Expert to the Office of Hearings and Appeals, Social

Security Administration for more than twenty years as well as provided Vocational Expert testimony in numerous civil suits involving occupational injury, accidental injury, disability retirement, and issues of product liability involving injury. He is a Licensed Professional Counselor (Virginia), Certified Rehabilitation Provider (Virginia), Certified Rehabilitation Counselor, and National Certified Counselor.

RICHARD E. HARDY, Ed.D., ABP: Chairman and Professor Emeritus, Department of Rehabilitation Counseling, School of Allied Health Professions, Medical College of Virginia, Virginia Commonwealth University, Richmond. Dr. Hardy was named for this Emeritus status after 26 years of service in this capacity. In 1997, he was named Outstanding Alumnus of the Department of Rehabilitation Counseling from which he graduated in 1962. A scholarship was also established in his name. Formerly, Chief Psychologist and Supervisor of Professional Training, South Carolina Department of Rehabilitation; Rehabilitation Advisor with the Rehabilitation Services Administration, Washington, D.C.; and Rehabilitation Counselor with the Virginia Commission for the Visually Handicapped. He also served on the South Carolina Board of Examiners of Psychology and taught part time in the psychology department at the University of South Carolina. Dr. Hardy has consulted extensively internationally on mental health and rehabilitation. He has published many books and articles used worldwide, and over one hundred reviews of them have been published thus far in the professional journals of other countries. Several national organizations have named him a Fellow, and he has received both national and international awards. Dr. Hardy is practicing as a licensed clinical psychologist in Richmond, Virginia, and is a Diplomate in both Psychotherapy and Hypnotherapy of the American Board of Psychotherapy.

CONTRIBUTING AUTHORS

JOHN G. CULL, PH.D.: Director of Operations, CODA, Ltd, San Antonio, Texas and Clinical Professor, Department of Rehabilitation Counseling, School of Allied Health Professions, Medical College of Virginia, Virginia Commonwealth University (VCU), Richmond.. Formerly, Private Practice of Clinical Psychology and Professor, St Mary's University and Our Lady of the Lake University, San Antonio, Texas; Professor and Director, Regional Continuing Education Program for Rehabilitation Personnel, Department of Rehabilitation Counseling, VCU; Director of Research and Program Development, Virginia Department of Vocational Rehabilitation; and Rehabilitation Counselor, Texas Commission for the Blind and Texas Division of Vocational Rehabilitation. Dr. Cull has contributed numerous articles, book chapters, and books to the rehabilitation literature and has received national and international recognition. Dr. Cull is a licensed clinical psychologist (Texas) and Fellow and Diplomate in Professional Psychotherapy of the International Academy of Behavioral Medicine, Counseling and Psychotherapy.

MURIEL GRAY, Ph.D., LCSW, CADAC, CEAP: Associate Professor and Chair, Substance Abuse Concentration, School of Social Work, University of Maryland at Baltimore and Co Director, Employee Assistance Program HealthCare Institute, Mitchellville, Maryland. Formerly, Regional Representative, United Airlines Employee Assistance Program; Group Facilitator, U.S. Department of the Navy; Clinical Social Worker, Children's Aid Society, La Plata, Maryland; Acting Director, Catholic Counseling Center School Program, Seattle, Washington; and Clinical Social Worker, Ryther Child Center, Seattle, Washington. Dr. Gray has numerous publications and has made national and international presentations. She has been a member of several national boards, review panels, and committees. Dr. Gray is a Licensed Clinical Social Worker (Maryland, District of Columbia, and Virginia), Certified Alcohol and Drug Addiction Counselor, and Certified Employee Assistance Professional.

GEORGE R. JARRELL, Ph.D.: Professor Emeritus, Department of Rehabilitation Counseling, School of Allied Health Professions, Medical College of Virginia, Virginia Commonwealth University (VCU), Richmond. Formerly, Professor and Coordinator of the Work-Study Program, Department of Rehabilitation Counseling, VCU; Assistant Dean, School of Community and Public Affairs, VCU; Rehabilitation Counselor, South Carolina Department of Vocational Rehabilitation. Dr. Jarrell is currently a Vocational Expert Consultant with the Office of Hearings and Appeals, Social Security Administration. He has written a number of articles on the role of the vocational expert. He is widely known in the legal profession and is frequently asked to lecture on utilization of vocational experts in personal injury cases. Dr. Jarrell has been a Licensed Professional Counselor (Virginia), Certified Rehabilitation Counselor, and National Certified Counselor.

MARTHA HUGHES LASSITER, Ed.D.: Retired from Chesterfield County Schools as a Vision Specialist after a career as an educator spanning 25 years, the areas ranging from Kindergarten to Graduate School. Dr. Lassiter was Coordinator of the Independent Living Center and later Education Specialist for the Virginia Department for the Visually Handicapped; Adjunct Faculty, Department of Rehabilitation Counseling, Virginia Commonwealth University, Richmond, Virginia; and continues to be active in community and professional organizational activities both in the education and rehabilitation fields. Dr. Lassiter was co-editor of a textbook on vocational evaluation, work adjustment, and independent living. She has also made other contributions to the rehabilitation literature.

ROBERT A. LASSITER, Ph.D.: Professor Emeritus, Department of Rehabilitation Counseling, School of Allied Health Professions, Medical College of Virginia, Virginia Commonwealth University (VCU), Richmond. Formerly, Professor and Coordinator of the Work-Study Program, Department of Rehabilitation Counseling, VCU; Founder and Chairman, Department of Rehabilitation Counseling, University of North Carolina; State Administrator of the North Carolina Department of Vocational Rehabilitation; Executive Director, North Carolina Easter Seals and the Project Director for the camp for people with severe disabilities at Southern Pines and the evaluation and adjustment center in Asheville; and served as a rehabilitation counselor and supervisor in the Florida Vocational Rehabilitation Program. Dr. Lassiter has made numerous contributions to national, regional, and state programs in vocational rehabilitation. He co-edited a book on vocational evaluation, work adjustment, and independent living and has contributed several articles and book chapters to the rehabilitation literature. Dr. Lassiter has been a Licensed Professional Counselor (Virginia) and Certified Rehabilitation Counselor. He is also an Associate Fellow recipient of the Institute for Rational-Emotive Therapy and a Fellow of the National Rehabilitation Counseling Association.

MARCIA J. LAWTON, Ph.D.: Associate Professor Emeritus of Rehabilitation Counseling, Department of Rehabilitation Counseling, School of Allied Health Professions (SAHP), Medical College of Virginia (MCV), Virginia Commonwealth University (VCU), Richmond. Formerly, Associate Professor and Director, Alcohol and Drug Education/Rehabilitation Program (ADERP), Department of Rehabilitation Counseling, SAHP, MCV/VCU and President and Supervisor, Growth and Recovery Opportunities, Richmond, Virginia. She was a licensed clinical psychologist in private practice in Denver, Colorado and has held other institutional as well as university adjunct faculty appointments in Virginia, Colorado,

Illinois, and Nebraska. Dr. Lawton is a recipient of the Mel Schulstad Award by the National Association of Alcoholism and Drug Abuse Counselors as well as numerous other awards and forms of recognition at the local, regional, and national level for her community service in the field of alcohol and drug rehabilitation. She is also the recipient of an outstanding university teaching award for innovative curricular development and clinical classroom instruction at VCU. Dr. Lawton is a Licensed Clinical Psychologist and Certified Alcohol and Drug Abuse Counselor in Virginia.

RICHARD S. LUCK, Ed.D., CRC, NCC: Associate Professor, Director, Alcohol and Drug Education Program, Director, Professional Counseling Advanced Certificate Program, and Vice Chair, Department of Rehabilitation Counseling, School of Allied Health Professions, Medical College of Virginia, Virginia Commonwealth University (VCU), Richmond. Formerly, Acting Director, Doctor of Public Administration, School of Community and Public Affairs, VCU; Director of the Regional Continuing Education Program for Rehabilitation Personnel, Department of Rehabilitation Counseling, VCU; and Rehabilitation Counselor, Virginia Department of Vocational Rehabilitation. Dr. Luck has served as Vice Chair and Chair of the Virginia Board of Professional Counselors and Marriage and Family Therapists and as President of the American Association of State Counseling Boards. He is a Certified Rehabilitation Provider (Virginia), Licensed Professional Counselor (Virginia), Licensed Clinical Psychologist (Virginia), Certified Rehabilitation Counselor, and National Certified Counselor. Dr. Luck is also a National Certified Clinical Hypnotherapist and Diplomate in Mental Health Managed Care and holds the Certificate of Proficiency in the Treatment of Alcohol and other Psychoactive Substances.

JAMES A. ROTHROCK, M.S.: President of Rothrock Group, Ltd., Richmond, Virginia, a consulting firm working with business and government on the Americans with Disabilities Act. Formerly, Director of the Department for the Rights of Virginians with Disabilities; Executive Director of Handicaps Unlimited of Virginia; served in positions in both the public and private sector of rehabilitation in Virginia; and was a Counselor with the Woodrow Wilson Rehabilitation Center. Mr. Rothrock has been quite active for a number of years in community service and professional organizational activity related to the rehabilitation field. He has contributed to the rehabilitation literature. Mr. Rothrock is also a Licensed Professional Counselor (Virginia).

WARREN R. RULE, Ph.D, CRC: Professor, Department of Rehabilitation Counseling, School of Allied Health Professions, Medical College of Virginia, Virginia Commonwealth University, Richmond. Formerly, Adjunct Faculty Member, University of South Carolina, a Counselor in higher education institutions, and a Rehabilitation Counselor with the South Carolina Vocational Rehabilitation Department. Dr. Rule has developed a course on Adlerian lifestyle counseling related to rehabilitation and has conducted numerous Adlerian oriented seminars and workshops. He is a nationally prominent researcher and writer focusing on Adlerian concepts related to rehabilitation counseling. He has edited two major textbooks, written numerous book chapters, and contributed many articles to refereed journals in counseling, rehabilitation, and psychology. He has served in different editorial capacities for Adlerian and rehabilitation journals and publications. Dr. Rule is also a Licensed Professional Counselor (Virginia) and Certified Rehabilitation Counselor.

CONSTANCE CORLEY SALTZ, Ph.D., LCSW: Associate Professor and Co-Chair, Aging Specialization, School of Social Work, University of Maryland at Baltimore, and Adjunct Faculty, University of Maryland College Park Center of Aging, College Park. Formerly, Associate Professor, School of Social Work, Virginia Commonwealth University, Richmond; Assistant Professor and Chair, Health Specialization, Department of Social Work, School of Social Work and Human Services, Southern Connecticut State University, New Haven; and various faculty affiliations with several other universities including the Department of Psychiatry, Yale University School of Medicine, New Haven, Connecticut, Division of Psychiatric Social Work, Duke University Medical Center, Durham North Carolina, and School of Social Work and School of Public Health, University of North Carolina–Chapel Hill. Dr. Saltz has numerous publications spanning the fields of social work, health care, aging, and addictions and several honors and awards. She is a member of the U.S. Committee to the United Nations International Year of Older Persons' Kitchen Cabinet. Her current responsibilities include mentoring students in related disciplines as well as social work particularly in interdisciplinary research/team building in rehabilitation and health promotion/disease prevention. Dr. Saltz is a Licensed Clinical Social Worker (Maryland).

LARRY L. SINSABAUGH, Ph.D., CRC, NCC, CDMS, CCM, CEAP, PHR. Private consultant in Richmond, Virginia, specializing in private sector rehabilitation and forensic practice. Dr. Sinsabaugh has extensive rehabilitation counseling experience in both state (Virginia and Ohio) and federal (Veterans Administration and Department of Labor) rehabilitation programs. He has served for many years as an Adjunct Faculty member teaching career development and occupational analysis and placement courses in the Department of Rehabilitation Counseling, School of Allied Health Professions, Medical College of Virginia, Virginia Commonwealth University, Richmond. Dr. Sinsabaugh is a Licensed Professional Counselor (North Carolina, Virginia, and West Virginia; and a Certified Professional Counselor in Maryland); Certified Rehabilitation Counselor, National Certified Counselor, Certified Disability Management Specialist, Certified Case Manager, Certified Employee Assistance Professional, and Certified Professional in Human Resources. He is also a Diplomate of the American Board of Vocational Experts.

KEITH C. WRIGHT, M.A: Professor Emeritus, Department of Rehabilitation Counseling, School of Allied Health Professions, Medical College of Virginia, Virginia Commonwealth University (VCU), Richmond. Formerly, Professor, Department of Rehabilitation Counseling, VCU; Research Analyst, West Virginia

Division of Vocational Rehabilitation and Counselor and Research Analyst with the United States Public Health Service. Mr. Wright served for many years as Chair of the Board of Professional Counselors for the Virginia Department of Health Regulatory Boards. He also served as President of the Virginia Rehabilitation Association, President of the Virginia Easter Seal Society, and President of the Faculty of the School of Community and Public Affairs at VCU. He has received several awards and honors for his distinguished community service. Professor Wright has contributed numerous articles and book chapters on a variety of topics to the rehabilitation literature. He has been a Licensed Professional Counselor (Virginia), Certified Rehabilitation Counselor, and National Certified Counselor.

To

Patrick Gandy, my brother (in memory); and Tamiko Gandy, his daughter and my niece.

Ruth Mackey Martin, beloved wife and best friend.

Jason Elliott Hardy, beloved son.

PREFACE

This text represents a complete revision and update of *Rehabilitation Counseling and Services: Profession and Process* published in 1987. This text will provide the reader with a comprehensive overview and introduction to the field of rehabilitation counseling and services but will also have applicability to the growing field of community counseling. The relationship to the latter field not only reflects a broadening of focus but also the fact that community counseling and rehabilitation counseling have begun to merge and overlap in many respects. We believe that this text will be particularly useful in graduate introductory rehabilitation or community counseling courses and may be readily adaptable to undergraduate courses in rehabilitation or general human services related areas. Additionally, this book should prove to be a useful and current source for the rehabilitation or community counselor practitioner.

The new *Counseling in the Rehabilitation Process: Community Services for Mental and Physical Disabilities* (Second Edition) contains some material from the previous edition but for the most part has been completely revised and updated. Philosophical considerations of the rehabilitation process have been expanded and incorporated into a new foundations of rehabilitation chapter. A new historical aspects chapter has been developed that includes updated material on the modern rehabilitation enterprise in America including implications for the private as well as public rehabilitation sector. Educational considerations have been expanded and incorporated into a chapter on the development of the rehabilitation counseling discipline. Adjustments and modifications have been made that have enhanced the previous historical chapters. Material on the rehabilitation process and occupational analysis and placement have been reorganized and includes new material on job development and placement. The social and psychological aspects of acceptance and adjustment to disability have been updated, expanded, and reorganized in order to combine counseling approaches with psychosocial aspects. New material has been included on counseling credentialing and substance use disabilities and material on international and multicultural perspectives has been reorganized and updated.

As before, we have selected an outstanding group of contributors. They have achieved an excellent balance in regard to their academic training, professional experience, community service, publications, and credentialed status. Their collective achievements have included agency executive leadership; university professorships; national and international committee and consultation activities; extensive publications in the form of books, articles, and other media, and the highest level of professional training, experience, and credentials.

Considerable thought was put into the organization of this book to ensure a consistent and integrated frame of reference as reflected in the following description of each section:

Part One, the introductory section, lays the foundation. Professor Martin discusses and describes the basic foundations of the rehabilitation process. Doctors R. Lassiter and M. Lassiter describe the historical antecedents of the modern rehabilitation enterprise in America. They then detail the early development of this enterprise. Professors Martin and Gandy continue with a more recent history of the modern rehabilitation enterprise in America discussing implications for both the public and private rehabilitation sectors. Doctors Gandy and Martin then describe the educational and professional organizational development of the discipline of rehabilitation counseling.

Part Two, The Rehabilitation Process, provides the reader with an insightful appreciation and understanding of the rehabilitation process. Professor Wright's and Martin's chapter provides a description of the rehabilitation process from the unique perspective of the counselor-client relationship. Doctors Martin, Sinsabaugh, Jarrell, and Hardy overview the methodology of occupational analysis, job development, and placement and include several case abstracts that relate to the public and private sector in rehabilitation. Professors Martin and Wright conclude the section with a very meaningful discussion of ethical issues in rehabilitation counseling.

In Part Three, the counseling and psychosocial aspects of disability are traced from multiple points of view–both theoretical and practical. Psychodynamic, Adlerian, Rational Emotive Behavioral, and Gestalt perspectives are explored and examined by Professors Hardy and Cull, Rule, Gandy, and Hardy respectively. Doctors Gandy and Martin then provide an integration of these perspectives including reference to existential and humanistic views as this material relates to acceptance and adjustment to disability. A unique aspect of this section is Mr. Rothrock's personal account of his experience in adjusting to disability. The psychodynamic chapter is a classic and has been included in several previous publications and expanded over the years; its contribution to acceptance and adjustment to disability is timeless.

Part Four discusses some special topics in rehabilitation appropriate for an introductory textbook but more suitable for an in-depth examination. Doctor Luck provides a study of the development and current status of rehabilitation counseling credentialing as a professional counseling specialty. Doctors Saltz, Lawton, and Gray describe the pervasive problem of substance use in America with implications for treatment and rehabilitation on both the practice and policy levels. Professors Gandy and Hardy conclude with some personal perspectives on rehabilitation as an international and multicultural phenomenon.

We wish to take this opportunity to thank those who have provided us with professional and personal support during the past several years of planning, researching, and writing. We would especially like to thank Mrs. Patricia Gandy, a management analyst (as well as Doctor Gandy's wife), for her administrative and computer technology expertise in the final preparation of the manuscript.

We would also like to thank Ms. Kelley G. Kramer, a graduate student in our master's degree program for her technical assistance with the figure illustrations.

Gerald L. Gandy
E. Davis Martin, Jr
Richard E. Hardy

CONTENTS

Part One
INTRODUCTION TO REHABILITATION

Part Two
THE REHABILITATION PROCESS

Part Three
COUNSELING AND PSYCHOSOCIAL ASPECTS OF REHABILITATION

COUNSELING IN THE REHABILITATION PROCESS

Part One
INTRODUCTION TO REHABILITATION

Chapter 1

FOUNDATIONS OF REHABILITATION

E. DAVIS MARTIN, JR.

Rehabilitation as a concept is, perhaps, one of the better ideas set forth by human beings. It is idealistic yet most pragmatic. The ideal of assisting a person with a disability reclaim lost productivity or to become productive in the first instance fulfills the basic purpose of rehabilitation. The goal set forth by the National Council on Rehabilitation in 1942 to return the person with a disability "...to the fullest physical, mental, social, vocational and economic usefulness of which they are capable" (Wright, 1980, p.5) is, in today's world, just as valid.

Former Secretary of Health, Education and Welfare John Gardner (1967) defined the concept of rehabilitation as:

> By rehabilitation I mean giving people the chance and the challenge to develop their own resources, inner and outer, to become independent and responsible as possible. I mean giving people the chance and the challenge to make the most of their talents and their lives and to find personal satisfaction and fulfillment through participation to live their lives with some measure of dignity.

The 1987 amendments to the Developmental Disabilities Assistance and Bill of Rights Act, while not specifically concerned with vocational rehabilitation, did nonetheless significantly enhance the concept of habilitation/rehabilitation by introducing into legislation the values of independence, productivity, and integration. This legislation sought to:

> . . . assure that all persons . . . receive the services and other assistance and opportunities necessary to enable such persons to achieve their maximum potential through increased independence, productivity, and integration into the community.

The passage of the Americans with Disabilities Act, PL101-336, in 1990 was an acknowledgment that discrimination in all spheres of life must end if the concept of rehabilitation was to measure up to the ideals stated by the National Council on Rehabilitation nearly five decades earlier. President George Bush's words as he lifted the pen to sign the Act must continue to echo in the consciousness of all Americans as we enter the new millennium:

> . . . let the shameful wall of exclusion finally come tumbling down.

Parker and Szymanski (1998, p. 2) noted that rehabilitation, in the context of rehabilitation counseling, may be defined as ". . . a comprehensive sequence of services, mutually planned by the consumer and rehabilitation counselor to maximize employability, independence, integration, and participation of people with disabilities in the workplace and community." Moreover, they observed that the concepts underlying the principles of service delivery models such as zero exclusion, ecology, supported employment, empowerment, and independent living have contributed greatly to the emergence of rehabilitation counseling philosophy over the last three decades. In sum, then, rehabilitation as a concept or as an ideal is one that is never quite completed; it offers a continuing challenge to the individual rehabilitation professional, to the rehabilitation agency (whether public or private), and to the person with a disability. Rehabilitation is a dynamic concept.

A distinction between rehabilitation and habilitation is often discussed by many authors, the distinction being, in most instances, related to the onset or manner in which a person acquired a disability. Disabilities that are present from birth or early childhood such as cerebral palsy, mental retardation, or epilepsy comprise a categorization of disability that is distinct from disabilities which are the result of disease, accident, or other environmental trauma. In the latter, rehabilitation refers to a restoration of function. In the former, however, there is no return to a former state of function; therefore usage of the term seems somewhat inappropriate. Wright, similarly, has stated that rehabilitation " . . . implies 'putting back to a former state of unimpairment'; consequently, strictly speaking, the term is inappropriate for congenital conditions (e.g. mental retardation). Thus, the substitute **habilitation** is often favored by persons associated with early childhood development" (1980, p.4). These two terms while not exactly alike are, nevertheless, differing aspects of the same concept. The two terms, rehabilitation and habilitation, convey essentially the same meaning; that is, " . . . making a person aware of his [*sic*] potential and providing him [*sic*] with the means of attaining that potential" (Allen, p. 1). The term rehabilitation, both from a traditional and historical perspective, is often the preferred mode of usage even through technically incorrect at times (Wright, 1980).

George Wright (1980) noted that " . . . three fundamental courses of action (are) available when a disability imposes limitations that handicap the individual: (1) one can remedy the cause of the person's handicap by restoring ability, (2) compensate for the handicap by enhancing other characteristics of the person, or (3) change the environmental circumstances so that the impact of the disability is avoided or negated" (p. 2). Wright further observed that " . . . the best foundation for rehabilitation incorporates all of these approaches, utilizing and developing all needed resources of the community and embracing all professions that can contribute to the process" (p.5). In other words, if rehabilitation is to be effective for the individual with a disability, then it must be pursued with vigor and enthusiasm borne out of an assertive knowledge that the full measure of potential for a person is at stake. All professions represented as well as all workers who come into contact with the person with a disability have an obligation and responsibility to contribute to this sense of vitality . . . of becoming.

Accordingly, the goal of rehabilitation when viewed from the perspective of the individual may be expressed as (1) taking an individual with a disability to their maximum potential in terms of remunerative employment as the ultimate outcome, or (2) when remunerative employment is not feasible, taking an individual with a disability to their maximum potential in terms of daily living as the ultimate outcome. In both instances, the rehabilitation process is designed to allow the person to achieve a maximal level of independence, productivity, and inclusion. Both as outcomes of the rehabilitation process, whether remunerative employment or independent living, fulfill the basic concept of rehabilitation: to assist the person with a disability to achieve his or her maximum potential.

Disability and Handicap: A Definition

The terms disability and handicap are often used interchangeably and often incorrectly. There have been many definitions posited for each; each shaded perhaps from the perspective of the profession or agency that proffered the definition. From a medical point of view, disability as a concept is more than the existence of a medical impairment. McBride (1963) stated that disability:

> . . . is not a purely medical condition. A patient is "permanently disabled" [*sic*] when his actual or presumed ability to engage in gainful activity is reduced or absent because of "impairment" and no fundamental or marked change in the future can be expected. (p. 36)

McBride further observed that an impairment:

> . . . is a purely medical condition. Permanent impairment is any anatomic or functional abnormality or loss after maximal medical rehabilitation has been achieved and which abnormality or loss the physician considers stable or non-progressive at the time evaluation is made. It is always a basic consideration in evaluation of permanent disability. It should be remembered, however, that permanent impairment is a contributing factor to but not necessarily an indication of, the extent of a patient's permanent disability. (pp. 36-37)

Disability, then, from this point of view is concerned with the establishment or confirmation of a medically determinable condition or impairment that affects the person's ability to perform certain physical or mental functions. Blindness, for example, is a visual impairment that fits this definition. A person who has visual acuity of 20/200 or less is considered to be legally blind. The physician diagnoses the medical impairment. The extent of disability imposed by the medical impairment is known, in general, from a functional standpoint. Disability from this perspective incorporates handicap (the resulting functional limitation) into the basic concept of disability. James Bitter (1979) simply defined disability in this way: "A disability is either a physical or mental condition which limits a person's activities or functioning" (p. 9). Similarly, Beatrice Wright (1983) reported that the concept of disability: " . . . refers to limitation of function that results directly from an impairment at the level of a specific organ or body system" (p. 11). George Wright (1980) also defined disability as a medically determinable impairment that limits the individual's ability to function but with more precision:

> . . . a disability is any physical, mental or emotional condition that is chronic or long-lasting (not acute or temporary) which is severe enough to limit the individuals's functioning, and which results in, or threatens to be, a handicap to productive activity. (p. 9)

Accordingly, if a medical condition or impairment is to be considered a disability, it must be of a (1) chronic or permanent nature which (2) limits the person's ability to function in ways that differ from the general population. To illustrate, examine the following medical impairments.

1. Amputation of the left arm
2. Muscular dystrophy
3. Peptic ulcer
4. Dsythmic disorder
5. Diabetes
6. Fracture of the pelvis

7. Epilepsy
8. Bronchitis
9. Cerebral palsy
10. Alcoholism

Each of these medical impairments meet the criterion of being a physical, mental or emotional condition. The second criterion of chronicity is met by numbers 1, 2, 4, 5, 7, 9, and 10. Peptic ulcer disease may be an acute condition but frequently evolves to a chronic state. Similarly, a fractured pelvis or bronchitis are conditions which are generally of an acute nature but may or do have the potential to become chronic health problems. The criterion of limiting the person's ability to function is met in varying degrees by all of these impairments. When then does an impairment or medical condition become a disability? It is the cumulative and progressive impact of each criterion that determines disability: (a) physical, mental, or emotional condition; (b) chronic nature of the impairment; and (c) the effects of a and b to a level of severity that limits or threatens to limit the person's ability to function that differs significantly from the general population. When these criteria are applied (and dependent upon the individual circumstances of each) each of the above noted medical impairments could result in disability for a given individual.

Given the individual nature of disability, at what point do the effects of a disability impose a barrier to functioning? This depends on a number of variables. Stolov (1981) has made the following observations regarding the characteristics of disability:

> 1. There is no one-to-one correlation between a disease and the spectrum of associated disability problems. The same disease can produce separate sets of disability problems in different individuals.
> 2. There is no one-to-one relationship between a disease and the amount of residual disability. Disability problems can be removed even though the disease is unchanged.
> 3. The ability of a patient and the total health care team to remove disability in the face of chronic disease is dependent upon the patient's residual capacity for physiological and psychological adaptation. Residual strength must be evaluated and enhanced to "work around" an impairment in order to remove disability. (p. 2)

The presence of a disability and the effects of a particular disability vary depending on the individual. In some persons the effects of a disability may, from both a physiological and/or psychological basis, be completely devastating or may have relatively few effects. Two persons, for example, may have the same disability–an amputation–and each react in completely different ways. Even though the effect of the injury was comparable, each individual reacts to the event differently. The medical aspects may or may not be comparable: One person may develop phantom limb pain while the other does not; residual functional capacity may differ considerably in the two persons; and circulation and/or healing of the stump may vary significantly from one person to the other. Psychological overlay may pose a significant barrier to one person and may be of little consequence to the other. In essence, the effects of a disability will vary with the individual; generalizations regarding the effects of a particular disability must always note this caveat.

Not all disabilities pose a barrier to functioning. When a disability does present a barrier to functioning or to performance, the person may be described as having a handicap. Rubin and Roessler (1983) reported in *Foundations of the Vocational Rehabilitation Process* that Hamilton defined handicap as " . . . the cumulative result of the obstacles which disabilities interposes between the individual and maximum functional level. The handicap is the measure of the loss of the individual's capacity, wherever evident" (p. 66). Beatrice Wright (1983) described handicap in this way: " . . . the actual obstacles the person encounters in the pursuit of goals in real life, no matter what their source" (p. 11). A handicap, then, results from the disability, not so much from the impairment as from the effects that the impairment may have on the person's ability to function in a particular way or in a particular setting. Burgdof (1980) observed that:

> . . . handicaps are perceived to be a result of a person's environment and not of the physical or mental impairment itself. Consequently, in an appropriate environment, with proper societal attitudes and supportive services, the disabled [*sic*] person, it is argued, need not be handicapped. There is nothing inherent in disability to produce handicap. (p. 4)

Simply put, a handicap results from the limitations imposed by the disability. The individual circumstances, both physiological and/or psychological, will determine if the disability will be a handicap. Recently, the term impediment has been equated to handicap. This term, most notably, appeared in the 1992 amendments to the Rehabilitation Act in the revised eligibility criteria for receipt of vocational rehabilitation services. The term impediment is more descriptive, and, perhaps, more pertinent and precise from a linguistic perspective.

An individual who has epilepsy that is well controlled by medication may or may not experience handicaps or impediments as a result of the disability; this person may experience handicaps or impediments in some situations. The limitations imposed by the disability–the unexpected occurrence of a seizure and the resultant effects of a seizure–will be expressed, in general, through the environment and/or through the attitudes of others. Environmentally, the impediment or barrier to performance is revealed in a prohibition (from a safety perspective) of climbing and balancing and/or the operation of moving machinery. These restrictions would preclude persons with epilepsy from seeking employment that may require activities or tasks that would involve climbing and balancing or the operation of certain machines. Similarly, these restrictions would preclude recreational and other types of activities that involve climbing or balancing or operation of certain machinery. The handicap or impediment presented in these situations, of course, may vary considerably given the individual circumstances that a disability has upon a particular person.

A handicap or impediment is always situational. A handicap results from the complex interaction among the variables of environment, attitudinal perception, and actual physical/mental limitation. Consequently, disability and its potential handicaps are highly individualized and rest upon the unique interactions of environment, attitudinal perception, and residual functional capacity. What is thought to be completely devastating to one person (or those close to that person) may be just a "bump in the road of life" for another person. Assistive technology, however, has the capability to completely eliminate or lessen the impact of a particular handicap. Figure 1-1 contains a schematic illustration of the relationship between disability and handicap. The degree of handicap or impediment depends on the resulting physical/mental limitations, environmental conditions, and attitudinal perceptions. Disability is a dynamic, not static, process.

The attitudes of others regarding a disability are often formed from beliefs and opinions that are, in fact, misperceptions of reality. As such, attitudinal handicaps are very pervasive in our society and, in most instances, are much more devastating than handicaps or impediments imposed as a result of the environment. Henderson and Bryan (1997) reported the following perceptions held by the general public regarding the abilities and capabilities of persons with disabilities:

- People with disabilities are inferior.
- People with disabilities are totally impaired.
- People with disabilities are less intelligent.
- People with disabilities need charity.
- People with disabilities prefer the company of others with disabilities. (pp. 79-86)

Figure 1-1. The Relationship Among the Concepts of Disability and Handicap Regarding Functional Capacity

Type of Disability or Impairment	Functional Capacity Related to Activities of Daily Living/Employment
Cardiovascular	
Cognitive	Interaction of
Endocrine/Metabolic	a) Environment
Gastrointestinal	
Genitourinary	
Integumentary	
Musculoskeletal/Connective Tissue	b) Attitudinal Perceptions
Neurological	
Psychiatric	
Pulmonary	c) Residual Functional Capacity
Sensory	

Degree of Handicap

none---total

These misperceptions about persons with disabilities are not held in some abstract manner by the general public but are very subtly incorporated in the very fabric of society. The net result of these attitudinal handicaps imposed upon persons with disabilities has been the loss of educational, employment, transportation, housing, and recreational opportunities. Much of the recent rehabilitation legislation has been directed toward the development of viable public policies regarding the issue of equality of opportunity in employment, transportation, and housing.

Usage of Terms Relating to Disability

The terms that are commonly used to refer to a person with a disability–disabled, handicapped, or a reference to the medical condition (e.g., an epileptic)–have tended to create a negative image of the person with a disability in the minds of many persons. When one thinks of the phrase "disabled person," one thinks, as the language suggests, that the person is not able. This clearly is not the case. The presence of a disability does not totally incapacitate a person. As noted earlier, a disability is a medical condition which is characterized by chronicity and limits or threatens to limit a person's ability to perform. A disability does not always impose an impediment or barrier to performance. Thus, the blanket usage of the terms "disabled" and/or "handicapped" person is inappropriate and inaccurate to refer to persons who have disabilities.

These terms have been employed by the lay public as well as by professionals and justified on the basis that these terms have very precise and scientific meanings. In brief, these terms have been utilized as short-cuts by professionals to convey conceptual information with the resultant economy of fewer words. Beatrice Wright (1983) has very eloquently written on the dangers of using short-cuts to describe persons with disabilities:

> Is a "disabled person" one who is unable to do anything? "Of course not," is the retort–the phrase is assuredly meant to be applicable to varying degrees of disability and not just to the extreme where a person is helping or virtually moribund. More accurately, then, a "disabled person" is also an able person. There are things that the person can do as well as things that the person cannot do. In fact the person is atypically more able than disabled. Then why call the person "disabled"? We may conclude that the designations "disabled person" or "the disabled" are short-cuts to psychologically more valid formulations such as "the person (or individual) with a disability," or "people who have a disability." A tolerant concurrence, combined with the feeling that this is much ado about nothing much, may greet this proposal; however, . . . it is precisely the preception of a person with a physical disability as a disabled person that reduces the person to the disabling aspect of his or her functioning. (p. 8)

The usage of these terms, disabled and handicapped and other derivatives of these two words, to refer to people or persons with disabilities, is considered by many to be pejorative and dehumanizing. Beatrice Wright has advocated for many years that persons with disabilities not be referred to as disabled, handicapped, or by their medical condition; that to do so is clearly a devaluation of the person. She conducted a study (1983) of persons with disabilities' preference regarding terminology and found that the more involved term "person with a disability" rather than a general reference to the "disabled" or "handicapped" or a reference to a medical condition was preferred.

Increasingly, many organizations and groups which represent persons with disabilities have begun to advocate the usage of "person/individual with a disability" as preferred language. Perhaps one of the best and earliest illustrations of this were the guidelines produced by the National Easter Seal Society (1980): *Portraying People with Disabilities in Print.* These guidelines are, as well, equally applicable to speech. In part, these guidelines are reproduced below:

> 1. Out of respect for the uniqueness and worth of the whole individual and because a disabling condition may or may not be handicapping, use the word *disability* rather than the word *handicap*, but give reference to the person first. Make it *person/individual* with a disability or *person/individual* who has a disability. In the plural case, *persons, individuals* and *people* may all the used. Avoid using the derivative word disabled as a labeling adjective, which implies that the person as a person is *disabled*, as in the expression *disabled person* or *person who is disabled*. Also avoid using *disabled*, which implies a state of separateness or total disability, as in *the disabled*.
> 2. Because the person is not the condition, reference to the person in terms of the condition he or she has is inaccurate as well as demeaning. Avoid, then, reference to the person as a *postpolio, a c/p., a stroke, an epileptic, a hemophilic*, etc. Say, instead, the person who . . . *had/has polio, has cerebral palsy or c.p., had/ experienced a stroke, has hemiplegia*, etc.
> 3. Some categorical terms are used correctly only when communicating technical information--for example, *hard of hearing, deaf, partially sighted* and *blind*. More accurate choices when referring generally to persons who have disabilities of these kinds are *person/individual who has a partial hearing loss, person with a total/severe hearing loss, person who has limited/partial vision, person with total/severe loss of vision*.
> 4. Avoid all terms carrying negative or judgmental connotations and replace them with objective descriptions..

These guidelines when used do, indeed, lessen the very subtle and negative impact that the words disabled and/or handicapped have upon many people.

The subtle effects of words can be especially devastating. For example, the following is a listing of commonly used words or phrases that are encountered in daily newspapers, in our school systems, and in our daily speech:

Disabled
Handicapped
Confined to a wheelchair
Afflicted with . . .
Suffers with . . .
Victim of . . .
Cripple/crippled by . . .
Special Education labels: EMR (educable mentally retarded), TMR (trainable mentally retarded, ED (emotionally disturbed), SPH (severely and profoundly handicapped), etc.
Physically challenged, Mentally challenged
Able bodied, Nondisabled

Usage of such language is generally not intended to devalue the person, yet that is exactly what occurs. The rationale set forth for usage of such language is that it's quicker, easier, and more accurate to use these terms. Yes, it may be quicker and it's certainly easier to say these words rather than using person first language, but it is not more accurate. Quite to the contrary, the phrase "confined to a wheelchair," for example, is quite inaccurate. A wheelchair for a person who uses one represents freedom of movement, mobility not confinement. Euphemistic language such as "physically challenged" or "mentally challenged" should as well be avoided. What do these phrases really mean–are not most of us physically or mentally challenged? Should not we all strive to be mentally challenged? Physically challenged? The usage of words such as "able-bodied" or "nondisabled" to refer to people without disabilities is also a reference to people who are "disabled" and is often used gratuitously. Newspaper articles about a person with a disability, for example, will often distinguish other persons in the story who do not have a disability with a reference to being "able bodied" or "nondisabled." What does this bit of information add to the story? What it does do, however, is to further separate or segregate people with disabilities from the mainstream of society. The perceived meaning of such words, phrases, or labels is not good for a person's sense of self or worth. Two questions should be asked when tempted to used language other than person first:

1. What effect does usage of language do to the self concept or image of the child or person who is repeatedly referred to in terms of their disability?

2. What effect does usage of language of this type have on the perceptions of the child's or person's parents, loved ones, peers, teachers, and human service workers?

The President's Committee on Employment of People with Disabilities in the *Profit From Our Experience* (1995) education kit outlined the "Ten

Commandments of Etiquette for Communicating with People with Disabilities" (three sources are acknowledged in this booklet: The President's Committee on Employment of People with Disabilities, Media Project; Research and Training Center on Independent Living, University of Kansas; and the National Center for Access Unlimited) which is quite instructive:

1. When talking with a person with a disability, speak directly to that person rather than through a companion or sign language interpreter.
2. When introduced to a person with a disability, it is appropriate to offer to shake hands. People with limited hand use or who wear an artificial limb can usually shake hands. (Shaking hands with the left hand is an acceptable greeting.)
3. When meeting a person who is visually impaired, always identify yourself and others who may be with you. When conversing in a group, remember to identify the person to whom you are speaking.
4. If you offer assistance, wait until the offer is accepted. Then listen to or ask for instructions.
5. Treat adults as adults. Address people who have disabilities by their first names only when extending the same familiarity to all others. (Never patronize people who use wheelchairs by patting them on the head or shoulder.)
6. Leaning on or hanging onto a person's wheelchair is similar to learning or hanging onto a person and is generally considered annoying. The chair is part of the personal body space of the person who uses it.
7. Listen attentively when you're talking with a person who has difficulty speaking. Be patient and wait for the person to finish, rather than correcting or speaking for the person. If necessary, ask short questions that require short answers, a nod or shake of the head. Never pretend to understand if you are having difficulty doing so. Instead, repeat what you have understood and allow the person to respond. The response will clue you in and guide your understanding.
8. When speaking with a person who uses a wheelchair or a person who uses crutches, place yourself at eye level in front of the person to facilitate the conversation.
9. To get the attention of a person who is deaf, tap the person on the shoulder or wave your hand. Look directly at the person and speak clearly, slowly and expressively to determine if the person can read lips. For those who do lip read, be sensitive to their needs by placing yourself so that you face the light source and keep hands, cigarettes, and food away from your mouth when speaking.
10. Relax. Don't be embarrassed if you happen to use accepted, common expressions such as "See you later," or "Did you hear about that?" that seem to relate to a person's disability. Don't be afraid to ask questions when you're unsure of what to do.

Professional written communication, as well, should heed these general principles. *The Publication Manual of the American Psychological Association* (1994, p. 53) noted that the "... guiding principle for 'nonhandicapping' language is to maintain the integrity of individuals as human beings." Moreover, the *Publication Manual* provided the following three guidelines regarding language (pp. 59-60):

1. Put people first, not their disability.
Comment: Preferred expressions avoid the implication that the person as a whole is disabled.
2. Do not label people by their disability or overextend its severity.
Comment: Because the person is not the disability, the two concepts should be separate.
3. Use emotionally neutral expressions.
Comment: Problematic expressions have excessive, negative overtones and suggest continued helplessness.

Some persons–whether professionals, the general public, and/or aspiring professionals–will question the need to use person first language indicating that it has been inspired by the notion to be politically correct or by dismissing person first language because a person with a disability used the previously noted pejorative words, labels, or phrases to describe themselves or others who have a disability. Person first language is not inspired by a need to be politically correct; it is language that conveys information without the excess baggage of emotionally laden words and stereotypical images of, generally, what a person cannot do. People without disabilities, in general, do not refer to themselves in negative and limiting ways. Why should reference to people with disabilities be presented in such a manner? It does not make good sense. Because some persons refer to themselves in a pejorative manner does not give others license to use pejorative language to refer to other persons with similar attributes. If one person refers to him or herself as a *bastard* or *bitch*, does that give others the right to call all males or females by these terms because of the attribute of gender? Similarly, if a person who uses a wheelchair refers to him or herself as a *cripple*, does that legitimatize referring to other persons who use wheelchairs as cripples? Of course not! In the instance of using the words *bastard* or *bitch*, it is recognized by most persons as an exception that related to one particular person while the word *cripple* is generalized as a rule to all persons who may have a similar attribute. A major reason for this response may be due to our tendency as human beings to "pigeon hole" or to stereotype and to generalize situations that we are unfamiliar with or uncomfortable around.

It should be noted that some persons wish to be referred to in terms of their disability and not in strict person first language. Most notable are persons with sensory disabilities. Some persons who are deaf wish to be referred to as "deaf" or "hard of hearing" or prefer all who have hearing disabilities to be collectively referred to as the "deaf community." Similarly, some persons who are blind prefer to be referred to as "blind" and not as visually impaired or as having a visual disability. When communicating with persons with disabilities, it is always a good idea to ascertain that person's preferences regarding language usage. In all situations, courtesy and tact are appropriate regardless of the presence or absence of a disability. Reference to the presence or absence of a disability when it adds nothing material to the conversation or written material is superfluous and serves only to send a confused and perhaps erroneous message. In a very powerful cartoon, Morrie Turner (Field Enterprises, Inc., 1981) displays in two scenes the essence of this section on language usage and the effects words have on our self concept: In scene one, two young girls are asking a third young girl who is sitting in a wheelchair "Do we call you handicapped or disabled?" In the next scene, the young girl in the wheelchair says "Call me Charlotte." Perhaps we spend too much time trying to be too precise and correct that we miss the essence of the encounter. We need to pay attention to the person, not the disability.

It must, however, be noted that the terms disability and/or disabled may be and are often used in a legal or quasi-legal manner. Insurance carriers, medical practitioners, and various governmental departments or units attach very specific and precise meanings to the usage of these words. In the instance of governmental units, definitions are found in regulations which carry the weight of law. The Social Security Administration's definition of disability, for example, is the basis for the entire Social Security Disability Insurance Program. Note the specificity and precision in this particular definition:

> The ability to engage in any substantial gainful activity by reason of any medically determinable physical or mental impairment which can be expected to last for a continuous period of not less than twelve months. A person must be not only unable to do his/her previous work or work commensurate with work in the amount of earnings and utilization of capacities but cannot, considering age, education and work experience, engage in any other kind of substantial gainful work which exists in the national economy. (Social Security Handbook)

Similarly, the terms developmental disability and severe disability were legislatively defined as noted:

A. PL 100-146, The Developmental Disabilities Assistance and Bill of Rights Act Amendments of 1987, defines a *developmental disability* as a severe chronic disability of a person which:

a) is attributable to a mental or physical impairment or combination of mental and physical impairments;
b) is manifested before the person attains age 22;
c) is likely to continue indefinitely;
d) results in substantial functional limitations in three or more of the following areas of major life activity;

- self-care
- receptive and expressive language
- learning
- mobility
- self-direction
- economic self sufficiency, and

e) reflects the person's need for a combination and sequence of special interdisciplinary, or generic care, treatment, or other service which are of lifelong or extended duration and are individually planned and coordinated.

B. The 1992 Amendments to the Rehabilitation Act

1. Disability is defined as an individual who:
   a) has a physical or mental impairment which substantially limits one or more of such a person's major life activities;
   b) has a record of such an impairment; or
   c) is regarded as having such an impairment.
2. Severe disability is defined as an individual who:
   a) has a physical or mental impairment which substantially limits one or more functional capacities (such as mobility, communication, self-care, self-direction, interpersonal skills, work tolerance, or work skills) in terms of an employment outcome;
   b) whose vocational rehabilitation can be expected to require multiple vocational rehabilitation services over an extended period of time; and
   c) who has one or more physical or mental disabilities resulting from amputation, arthritis, autism, blindness, brain injury, cancer, cerebral palsy, cystic fibrosis, deafness, head injury, heart disease, hemiplegia, hemophilia, respiratory or pulmonary dysfunction, mental retardation, mental illness, multiple sclerosis, muscular dystrophy, musculoskeletal disorders, neurological disorders (including stroke and epilepsy), paraplegia, quadriplegia, and other spinal cord injuries, sickle cell anemia, specific learning disability, end-stage renal disease or another disability or combination of disabilities . . . ."
3. Most severe disability is defined as an individual:
   a) for whom competitive employment has not traditionally occurred, or
   b) for whom competitive employment has been interrupted or intermittent as a result of severe disability, and intensive supported services or extended services in order to perform much work (such term includes transitional employment for persons who are individuals with the most severe disabilities due to mental illness).

These definitions when employed to describe the characteristics of a severe or developmental disability vis-a-vis the provision of a particular service or to establish eligibility for a service or services are appropriate. It should be emphasized that the derivative terms, developmentally disabled or severely disabled used to refer to persons who have a developmental, severe or most severe disability is, as noted earlier, an incorrect and inaccurate usage of the words which have a definite tendency to devalue the person with a disability. The 1998 amendments substitute the qualifier "significant" in place of the term "severe."

Magnitude of Disability

The various source documents regarding disability statistics are often conflicting and may be misleading in some instances. A recent *Rehab Brief* on "Disability Statistics" (1993, p.1) noted that " . . . the definition of the term, and therefore the statistics on the size of the population of individuals with disability, depend on various program statistics serving selected eligible people, on information collected in surveys addressing broad social purpose, or on interpretation of data designed to achieve particular programmatic purposes." Data collected from agencies of the federal government (the Census, Congress–most recently the Americans with Disabilities Act, the President's Committee on the Employment of Persons with Disabilities, or other agencies); from the Louis Harris and Associates Disability Survey and from state agencies may vary because the definitions used and/or the purposes of surveys or reports commissioned by these organizations vary. In other words, the number of persons with disabilities will vary dependent on the source.

As an example of such variances, the 1990 Census found the number of Virginians with disabilities to be 297,515 or 4.8 percent of the total state population. Congress, in the preamble to the Americans with Disabilities Act, found that approximately 43 million persons or 17 percent of all Americans have one or more physical or mental disabilities. While such a discrepancy may seem quite large, it merely reflects the methodology the surveys used. In this case, one data set considered all persons who have disabilities (ADA) while the other data set considered only persons 16 through 64 years of age (Census).

The definition of disability and the manner in which that definition is presented to respondents also determines the magnitude of disabilities reported. Without providing respondents with qualifying information or criteria to determine what is and what is not a disability, what one person considers to be a disability, another may not. Surveys which rely on self report or that define disability narrowly will affect the reported magnitude of disability.

Obviously, statistics must be viewed in the context in which they are presented.

The finding of the United States Congress that 43 million persons, or approximately 17 percent of the U. S. population, have disabilities may be considered to be an appropriate estimate of disability found throughout the life span. Further, the Harris Poll (1986) found that approximately 44 percent of all persons with disabilities have physical disabilities, 13 percent have sensory disabilities, 6 percent have mental disabilities, and 32 percent were classified as other serious health impairment (e.g., heart disease, respiratory disease, cancer, diabetes, etc).

In 1994, the Census Bureau's Survey of Income and Program Participation (SIPP) data noted that of the 29.4 million working age persons with disabilities, 14.2 million had severe disabilities. Over the time period, 1991 to 1994, the number of persons with disabilities employed increased from 14.26 million to 15.39 million or from 52 to 52.3 percent of all persons with disabilities employed. Employment for persons with severe disabilities increased from 2.92 million to 3.71 million, or from 23.3 to 26.1 percent. Overall, the number of persons employed in the general population was 82.1 percent. When viewed from this perspective, it is obvious that persons with disabilities have not achieve parity with Americans who are employed (President's Committee of Employment of Persons with Disabilities, 1997). Eight of every ten persons with a disability, according to the 1994 Harris Poll, want to work. The 1998 Harris Poll found that 29 percent of all persons with disabilities work either full or part-time. Compared to those persons without disabilities who work, a gap of 50 percent is revealed; that is, 79 percent of all Americans without disabilities engage in remunerative employment while 29 percent of Americans with disabilities work either full or part-time. This finding, when compared to the 1986 and 1994 Harris Polls, revealed a decline in employment for persons with disabilities from 34 to 31 to 29 percent. Moreover, the average earnings of persons with disabilities were 35 percent less than that for all others (President's Committee on Employment of Persons with Disabilities, 1995).

From the Census data, we know that rates of disability increase as persons age (age related disabilities) and may interfere with or completely handicap a person's ability to engage in employment. Note, for example, the percentages of persons reporting disabilities that handicap them in gaining or maintaining employment within the various age ranges from 16 through 64 (Disability Statistics Abstract, 1991):

Age Range	*Percent Reporting Disability*
16-24	3.7 percent
24-34	5.7 percent
45-54	7.8 percent
55-64	21.9 percent

These data do not consider those persons under age 16 or over age 64, nor do they indicate that males are more likely (slightly) to incur work-related disabilities and to experience a greater percentage of severe or total work limitation. Whites and blacks tend to have equal percentages of work disabilities, but African-Americans tend to experience a higher percentage of total work disability than do whites.

Children with disabilities, whether enrolled in special education or in regular education, face considerable barriers in gaining employment and/or postsecondary training and education. The issue of transitioning has been given national attention in the reauthorization of PL 94-142, the Individuals with Disabilities Education Act.

In sum, then, approximately 14.2 million persons (ages 16-64) of the American population has chronic medical impairments which has the capacity to prevent remunerative employment. Of that number, about one-half are receiving Social Security Disability benefits and the remainder have experienced significant impediments in securing or maintaining employment (Disability Statistics Abstract, 1992). Presumably all of these persons meet the eligibility criteria for vocational rehabilitation services. That is (1992 Amendments to the Rehabilitation Act):

- the individual has a physical or mental impairment which constitutes or results in a substantial impediment to employment,
- the individual can benefit in terms of an employment outcome from VR services, and
- the individual requires vocational rehabilitation services to prepare for, enter, engage in, or retain employment.

Philosophical Considerations

The impact of a disability may be slight or overwhelming, insignificant or devastating to the person who has a disability as well as to that person's parents, siblings, spouse, girlfriend, boyfriend and others who share in that person's life. Indeed, society in general is affected by the effects of disability through lost productivity–sometimes because of the resultant handicaps imposed by the disability but more often from attitudinal barriers imposed by society. Well meaning persons throughout the relatively short history of the federal-state program of rehabilitation have sought to reduce the effects of disability, particularly as related to employment. Much of the legislation related to the rehabilitation movement in America has been formulated on the basis that all persons as members of a free democratic society have an inherent right to work and to provide for themselves and their families (Bitter, 1979). While employment of persons with disabilities remains as a central focus of the state-federal program of rehabilitation, much of the recent legislation has been directed to the issues of architectural barriers, transportation and services for independent living. The independent living legislation created a co-equal goal for the state-federal program of rehabilitation; that is, co-equal with remunerative employment as a final outcome of the rehabilitation process. Independent living services are provided to persons with significant disabilities whose opportunity for remunerative employment is slight but whose quality of life may be enhanced through the acquisition of activities of daily living (ADL) skills. Access to rehabilitation services has been considered by many as a basic human right. Rubin and Roesler (1983) have noted that " . . . the assumed human rights to education, health, medical care, income, and a productive role (is) a powerful rationale for federal and state tax-based financial support for rehabilitation programs and environmental barriers removal" (p. 59). In a latter statement, Rubin and Roessler (1995) observed that "(c)ompatible with the right to normal opportunity would be to guarantee persons with disabilities the right to restoration services and to accessible environments in order to make the opportunity of persons with and without disabilities more equal" (p. 107).

In addition to the inherent right of people to work and provide for themselves and others, Bitter (1970) many years ago identified " . . . three principles which form a philosophical foundation for the practice of rehabilitation in America" (p. 4):

> 1. Equality of opportunity must be present for all United States Citizens (Garrett, 1969).
> 2. A person is holistic, that is, he [*sic*] cannot be divided into parts such as physical, mental, social, vocational and economic. Each person is a complete individual and in each, these dimensions interact with the others to form the whole (Jaques, 1970).
> 3. Every person is unique. The psychological and personal reactions to disability vary from individual to individual. No two people have exactly the same needs or potential; each has unique assets, ways of coping, and goals (p. 4).

These three principles–equality of opportunity, holistic nature of people, and individualism–have provided the foundation from which much of the philosophy of rehabilitation has emerged.

Equality of Opportunity

Perhaps one of the most significant legislative events of this century was the passage of the Rehabilitation Act of 1973 and passage of amendments to

PL 93-112 in 1978, the Rehabilitation Comprehensive Services and Developmental Disabilities Amendments. PL 101-336, the Americans with Disabilities Act, and the 1992 and 1998 amendments to the Rehabilitation Act, as well, were watershed events in the disability movement. There would not, however, have been an ADA or any amendments without passage of the 1973 Rehabilitation Act. The major focus of the 1973 Rehabilitation Act dealt with equality of opportunity through its provisions relating to consumer involvement, emphasis on persons with severe disabilities, creation of the National Institute of Handicapped Research (now, National Institute on Disability and Rehabilitation Research), emphasis on program evaluation, and the advancement of the civil rights of persons with disabilities. Most notably, sections 501, 502, 503, and 504 of Title V of the 1973 Rehabilitation Act addressed the following areas of concern respectively: nondiscriminatory federal hiring; accessibility (creation of the Architectural and Transportation Barriers Compliance Board); affirmative action and prohibition of discrimination against persons with disabilities in terms of programmatic and physical accessibility in schools, colleges, hospitals, and other institutions which receive federal financial assistance. Admission to schools and institutions of higher education, as well, was addressed by section 504 of Title V. This section noted:

> No otherwise qualified handicapped [*sic*] individual in the United States, as defined in section 7(7), shall solely by reason of his [*sic*] handicap, be excluded from the participation in, be denied the benefits of or be subjected to discrimination under any program or activity receiving Federal financial assistance or under any program or activity conducted by any Executive agency or by the United States Postal Service.

Vash (1981) has commented that these legislative changes occurred as a result of a heightened " . . . awareness among rehabilitation professionals that their efforts with disabled [sic] 'patients' or 'clients' would come to naught unless the social and physical world were altered to accommodate them." She further observed that "(it) was rehabilitation providers with political contacts who provided much of the early education and prodding of legislators to mandate changes now recognized as necessary" (p. 145). Consumer involvement–persons with disabilities, parents, siblings, spouses, rehabilitation professionals, and other advocates–provided the backdrop for this dramatic shift in public policy. These changes came about largely as a result of the daily attitudinal and environmental barriers faced by persons with disabilities. Vash had categorized these barriers and stated them in terms of "rights" that must be accorded to persons with disabilities (pp. 145-157):

- The Right to a Barrier-Free Environment
- The Right to Participate in Society
- The Right to Equal Opportunity for Jobs
- The Right to Economic Protection
- Confidentiality and the Right to Know (related to the provision of rehabilitation services)
- The Right to a Fair Trial (to be able to participate as a juror–to have interpreter service in court proceedings)
- The Right to Appropriate Treatment by Police (to provide educational experiences relating to disabilities and the effects of disabilities to sensitize police)
- The Right to Be a Parent (issue of involuntary sterilization, right of persons with disabilities to adopt, custody award, etc.)
- The Right to Redress (development of and provision of ombudsman services in federal-state programs)

The right to be equal is according to George Wright (1980) " . . . recognized in various societies as 'God given" meaning inherent in all humans" (p. 12). This concept when applied to persons with disabilities has definite implications for the public policies of a society's institutions and organizations. If this premise is accepted, the government has an obligation to provide rehabilitation services to citizens with disabilities so they, in turn, may contribute to their society on an equal footing with those individuals who do not have disabilities (Wright, 1980). This right to contribute to society begins with the right to self-support and extends outward, as stated by Wright, to ever increasing levels of responsibility to one's family, to one's community, and to one's nation.

People with disabilities, like all people, want to participate fully in the society in which they live. The desire to achieve and to be successful is not diminished by a disability, indeed, the opportunity to work and contribute to the support of self and family is considered a basic right in a free, democratic society, and as American citizens, people with disabilities have a right to equality of opportunity in education, employment, transportation, housing, health care, and leisure. A person's disability should not interfere with their full participation in any of these activities.

The attitudes of others about disabilities and their effects are often formed from beliefs and opinions that have no basis in reality. Generalizations that people who have disabilities are inferior, totally impaired, less intelligent, and need and desire the charity of others are not based on fact. Although these notions are not held by everyone, they are pervasive in our society and often are more devastating than the limitations imposed by disabilities. These mindsets are not abstract categorizations but very real and subtly held beliefs, and, as a result, people with disabilities have not enjoyed equal access in matters of education, employment, transportation, housing, or recreation.

Increased awareness of persons with disabilities and of the environmental and attitudinal barriers they encounter is generally credited as the major impetus for the passage of the 1973 Rehabilitation Act and its subsequent amendments, as well as the ADA. These legislative events signaled a change in public policy patterned largely after the Civil Rights Act. Employers were no longer asked to hire persons with disabilities on the basis of moral grounds, but asked to take affirmative action in hiring as well as to assume a posture of nondiscrimination. The involvement of those with disabilities, their families, rehabilitation professionals, and other advocates provided the backdrop for this dramatic shift in public policy.

While the last two decades plus have witnessed considerable progress toward the goal of equality of opportunity, much remains to be achieved. The subtle nature of discrimination and the pervasiveness of negative attitudes and stereotypes continue to exist. The services and resources of our governmental institutions, in particular, as well as in the private sector must be provided in a fair and equitable manner. With respect to persons with disabilities, we must assure that:

- Persons with disabilities are not lumped into one category of being "disabled", that is, not able. We must recognize that disabilities affect people in different ways, and we must accept each person with a disability as an individual.
- In planning for public services, the needs of persons with disabilities are incorporated with respect to accessibility and that all public buildings, housing, and transportation systems providing essential services are free from architectural barriers.
- Employment of persons with disabilities is continuously encouraged and based on merit and equality.
- Educational opportunities that take persons with disabilities to their maximum levels of potential are accessible.
- Health care services and recreational opportunities are accessible and provided in an atmosphere free of a "second class" attitude toward those with disabilities.

Persons with disabilities, like all citizens of a free, democratic society, must be afforded the same rights and privileges to participate fully in the work and play of our communities. This requires equality of opportunity--no more, no less.

Holistic Nature of People

The concept of holism refers to the idea, when applied to people, that the totality of an individual has a reality that is unique and a reality which is dependent upon the various attributes of that person. An individual's life, for example, can be artificially divided into physical, mental, psychological, educational, economic, and vocational aspects; each of these aspects of a persons's life, when taken separately, however, yields little information about the total person. These aspects, though, when collectively viewed, present a unique pespective of that person. Much like the uniqueness of a person's fingerprints, so too are the life patterns as revealed by the infinite combinations of a person's physical, mental, psychological, educational, economic, and vocational characteristics.

George Wright (1980) has observed that the holistic nature of people requires that a focus for persons with disabilities be present during the rehabilitation process. Because the individual with a disability will be exposed to a number of professions and professionals during the rehabilitation process, the potential for fragmentation of services is ever present. As such, the team approach to the provision of services and an approach which actively involves the person with a disability is mandatory. The rehabilitation worker provides this focus and, in turn, provides an environment that is conducive to the holistic nature of people and one which contributes to the success of the rehabilitation effort.

Individualism

Americans, in particular, value the person who strives and achieves; so much so the better if that person succeeds against hardship and adversity. This "rugged individualism," as noted by Rubin and Roessler (1983), has its philosophical roots embedded throughout the history of the United States. Most recently, this philosophy has been manifested in the blueprints of the administrations of Franklin D. Roosevelt (New Deal), John F. Kennedy (New Frontier), and Lyndon B. Johnson (Great Society). Persons with disabilities, like all people, value this notion of "rugged individualism" and seek to emulate behavior that fosters success and independence. Indeed, as we have seen, much of the recent legislative efforts have been directed toward the enhancement of the individual and toward the removal of barriers–both environmental and attitudinal–which would allow the individual with a disability the opportunity to compete and to succeed.

Beatrice Wright (1983) has identified twenty "value-laden beliefs and principles" which relate to the person with a disability. They are framed from a perspective of individualism tempered with a knowledge of the reality of the social, economic, and political circumstances that are present in contemporary American society. These guidelines offer a philosophical understanding of the circumstances of disability and are directed to those who work with or aspire to work with persons who have disabilities. They may be considered as the ultimate concern and regard for individualism:

1. Every individual needs respect and encouragement; the presence of a disability, no matter how severe, does not alter these fundamental rights.
2. The severity of a handicap can be increased or diminished by environmental conditions.
3. Issues of coping and adjusting to a disability cannot be validly considered without examining reality problems in the social and physical environment.
4. The assets of the person must receive considerable attention in the rehabilitation effort.
5. The significance of a disability is affected by the person's feelings about the self and his or her situation.
6. The active participation of the client in the planning and execution of the rehabilitation program is to be sought as fully as possible.
7. The client is seen not as an isolated individual but as part of a larger group that includes other people, often the family.
8. Because each person has unique characteristics and each situation its own properties, variability is required in rehabilitation plans.
9. Predictor variables, based on group outcomes in rehabilitation, should be applied with caution to the individual case.
10. All phases of rehabilitation have psychological aspects.
11. Interdisciplinary and interagency collaboration and coordination of services are essential.
12. Self-help organizations are important allies in the rehabilitation effort.
13. In addition to the special problems of particular groups, rehabilitation clients commonly share certain problems by virtue of their disadvantaged and devalued position.
14. It is essential that society as a whole continuously and persistently strives to provide the basic means toward the fulfillment of the lives of all its inhabitants, including those with disabilities.
15. Involvement of the client with the general life of the community is a fundamental principle guiding decisions concerning living arrangements and the use of resources.
16. People with disabilities, like all citizens, are entitled to participate in and contribute to the general life of the community.
17. Provision must be made for the effective dissemination of information concerning legislation and community offerings of potential benefit to persons with disabilities.
18. Basic research can profitably be guided by the question of usefulness in ameliorating problems, a vital consideration in rehabilitation fields, including psychology.
19. Persons with disabilities should be called upon to serve as co-planners, coevaluators and consultants to others, including professional persons.

20. Continuing review of the contributions of psychologists and others in rehabilitation within a framework of guiding principles that are themselves subject to review is an essential part of the self-correcting effort of science and the professions. (pp. xi -xvii)

In essence, Beatrice Wright has provided rehabilitation workers with a set of beliefs that, if accepted, creates a covenant between the rehabilitation worker and the person with a disability. This covenant assures that each person with a disability will be seen as an individual; that the effects of a particular disability upon a person may and often does differ significantly; and that the approach and course of the rehabilitation process will differ for each person recognizing the individualistic nature of the disability and its effects upon the person.

George Wright (1980) has similarly written much regarding the philosophical tenets of rehabilitation. He has observed that the belief systems of rehabilitation, particularly when subjected to reason and thought, provide a foundation upon which to guide the practice of rehabilitation. Wright listed the following philosophical tenets which relate to individualism:

Self-Determination
All people have a right to self-determination insofar as they are capable of reasonable judgments; people should make their own decisions, set their own goals and also decide how they achieve those goals. (p. 11)

Human Spirit
Belief in the spirit of human beings comes from witnessing miraculous recoveries accomplished by case after case in rehabilitation. (p. 12)

Focus on Assets
A tenet in rehabilitation is that the focus must be on the assets a person has left following disablement [*sic*]. This is not only philosophically wise but also operationally sound in practice. All physical tasks, activities and jobs demand abilities; consequently, rehabilitation requires the development and utilization of abilities–not disability. (p. 12)

Motivation for Good
People are motivated for good. In psychological terms this means that individuals are capable of changing: of changing for the better, in the instance of rehabilitation. A person can be rehabilitated no matter how ingrained the negative attitudes and behavior patterns have become because of the deprivations and insult of disablement [*sic*].(p. 13)

> *Intrinsic Value*
> There is intrinsic value in the human being. This principle is fundamental in rehabilitation. People have an inherent dignity and value simply because they are human beings. (p. 13)

The concept of viewing the person as a unique individual from the perspective of the above noted concepts adds much to the philosophical base of rehabilitation; that is, the individual with a disability is viewed as a person, like all persons, who seeks independence within a framework of interdependence.

REFERENCES

Allen, W. S. (1958). *Rehabilitation; A community challenge.* New York: Wiley.
American Psychological Association (1994). *Publication manual of the American Psychological Association* (4th ed.). Washington, D.C.: Author.
Americans with Disabilities Act of 1990, Public Law 101-336.
Bitter, J. A. (1970). *Introduction to rehabilitation.* St Louis: C. V. Mosby.
Burgdof, R. L. (1980). *The legal rights of handicapped persons.* Baltimore: Paul W. Brooks.
Education for All Handicapped Children Act of 1975, 20 U.S.C. Section 1400 et.seq.
Henderson, G. & Bryan, W. V. (1997). *Psychosocial aspects of disability* (2nd ed.). Springfield, IL: Charles C. Thomas.
Individuals with Disabilities Education Act of 1990, U.S.C. Section 1400 *et.seq.*
Jaques, M. E. (1970). *Rehabilitation counseling: Scope and services* (Guidance Monograph Series). Boston: Houghton Mifflin.
Lou Harris and Associates. (1994). *NOD/Harris survey on employment of Americans with disabilities.* New York: Author.
Lou Harris and Associates. (1986). *Harris survey on employment of persons with disabilities.* New York: Author.
Lou Harris and Associates. (1986). *ICD survey of Americans with disabilities.* New York: Author.
Lou Harris and Associates. (1995). *NOD/Harris survey on employment of persons with disabilities.* New York: Author.
Lou Harris and Associates. (1998). *1998 NOD/Harris survey of Americans with disabilities.* New York: Author.
Maki, D. R. & Riggar, T. F. (1997). *Rehabilitation counseling: Profession and practice.* New York: Springer.
McBride, E. D. (1963). *Disability evaluation.* Philadelphia: J. B. Lippincott.
National Institute on Disability and Rehabilitation Research (1993). *Rehab brief: Disability statistics, 14* (8).
Obermann, C. E. (1965). *A history of vocational rehabilitation in America.* Minneapolis: T. D. Denison.

Parker, R. M. & Szymanski, E. M. (1998). *Rehabilitation counseling: Basics and beyond* (2nd ed.). Austin, TX: PRO-ED.

President's Committee on Employment of People with Disabilities (1995). *Profit from our experience.* Washington, D.C.: Author.

President's Committee on Employment of People with Disabilities (1998). *Opening doors to ability.* Washington, D.C.: Author.

President's Committee on Employment of People with Disabilities (1997). *Ability: The bridge to the future.* Washington, D.C.: Author.

President's Committee on Employment of People with Disabilities (1996). *Ability for hire.* Washington, D.C.: Author.

Rehabilitation Act of 1973. Public Law 93-112.

Rehabilitation Act Amendments of 1974. Public Law 93-651.

Rehabilitation Act Amendments of 1978. Public Law 95-602.

Rehabilitation Act Amendments of 1984. Public Law 98-221.

Rehabilitation Act Amendments of 1986. Public Law 99-506.

Rehabilitation Act Amendments of 1992. Public Law 102-589.

Rehabilitation Act Amendments of 1993. Public Law 103-73.

Rehabilitation Act Amendments of 1998.

Rubin, S. E. & Roessler, R. T. (1995). *Foundations of the vocational rehabilitation process* (4th ed.). Austin, TX: PRO-ED, Inc.

Rubin, S. E. & Roessler, R. T. (1983). *Foundations of the vocational rehabilitation process* (2nd ed.). Baltimore: University Park Press.

U.S. Department of Health and Human Services (1997). *Social security handbook/ 1997.* Washington, D.C.: U. S. Government.

Vash, C. L. (1981). *The psychology of disability.* New York: Springer.

Wright, B. A. (1983). *Physical disability–A psychosocial approach* (2nd ed.). New York: Harper & Row.

Wright, G. N. (1980). *Total rehabilitation.* Boston: Little Brown.

Chapter 2

HISTORICAL ANTECEDENTS OF THE REHABILITATION ENTERPRISE IN AMERICA: A REHABILITATION MOVEMENT

ROBERT A. LASSITER AND MARTHA HUGHES LASSITER

As a profession and process, the rehabilitation movement has experienced an acceptance and recognition of its concept and philosophy in recent years unprecedented during its history and growth. Despite the retrenchment caused by political and economic factors during the 1970s and 1980s and the increasing consumer involvement and participation in the 1990s, the state-federal program remains strong, and nonprofit rehabilitation centers and facilities have continued to extend and expand service programs. The professional interest in private rehabilitation practice and organizations that are based on a profit motive have proved the old adage, "rehabilitation has become too important to leave with the traditional professionals–it has become too powerful to ignore and the cost far too big" (Lassiter, 1972, p. 106). Thus, the growth in the movement into a much broader and more comprehensive enterprise has resulted in a stronger support for the rehabilitation counselor and for other professional people engaged in this act of restoring individuals with disabilities to the fullest physical, mental, social, vocational, and economic usefulness of which the person is capable.

Throughout this period of growth, persons with disabilities, their families, and others were increasingly joining the leadership of professionals–not only in asking for a more "person centered" program but insisting on active participation in the planning and direction of these programs. This new partnership in program planning and evaluation is evident in the independent living area of rehabilitation: " . . . the movement is more than a grass roots effort on the part of the disabled [*sic*] to acquire new rights and entitlements; it is also reshaping the thinking of disability professionals and researchers . . . it is a social movement with a distinct constituency and history . . . the movement is heavily indebted to a variety of other contemporary social movements such as civil rights, consumerism, self-help demedicalization, self/care and deinstitutionalization" (DeJong, 1979, p. 7).

The increased use of this approach in meeting the needs of people with disabilities reflects the public's growing recognition of not only a social obligation to help people with disabilities move toward their independence and self-sufficiency but the increasing realization of the economic benefits that come as a result of the rehabilitation process. Also, there appears to be an emerging consciousness of the purely humanitarian aspects of rehabilitation. As early as 1964, Mary Switzer, former Administrator of the Social and Rehabilitation Service and an icon in the rehabilitation movement, noted that:

> Vocational rehabilitation, like many other aspects of human affairs, has evolved through three stages of public attitude–compassion without action, followed by willingness to act for economic reasons, following by willingness to act for social reasons. It seems to me that we are at a transitional stage between the last two, with almost universal acceptance of the economic soundness of returning disabled [*sic*] people to employment and a slowly growing philosophy that an advanced civilization like ours should so order its system that all disabled [*sic*] people will be restored as fully as possible regardless of economic benefits to anyone. (Switzer, 1964, p. 14)

It can be seen, then, that the concept of rehabilitation offers hope to many in politics and government for a solution to some major social problems. Problems come, however, from the fact that there are few charts or guidelines available to those who are responsible for the expansion of a program. Through a more comprehensive understanding of the past, the rehabilitation concept will be less likely to be misinterpreted and new decisions will result in an improved program of services for people with disabilities.

The vocational rehabilitation program in America began on June 2, 1920, with the passage of a minor act in the Sixty-sixth Congress, Public Law 236. The act opened with these words, " . . . that in order to provide the promotion of vocational rehabilitation of persons disabled [*sic*] in industry or in any legitimate occupation," and the fact provided a first attempt in defining the terms: " . . . the term 'disabled [*sic*] person' shall be construed to mean any person who, by reason of a physical defect or infirmity, whether congenital or acquired by accident, injury or disease, is, or may be expected to be, totally or partially incapacitated for remunerative occupation; the term 'rehabilitation' shall be construed to mean the rendering of a person disabled [*sic*] fit to engage in remunerative occupation" (Sixty-sixth Congress, 1920, p. 735). A twofold program of vocational guidance and vocational education for people with physical disabilities, as contained in this act, was evidence of the federal government's early concern for the welfare of individuals. It was also the result of a greater awareness in this country of the need to conserve human resources for economic benefit to society as a whole.

For an understanding of this new legislation, it must be viewed in the light of the historical forces and social movements of the late nineteenth and early twentieth centuries, during the period that has been described as the second phase of the Industrial Revolution (Blum, 1968). The concept of rehabilitation is much broader than the story of the state-federal partnership might reflect. Consequently, this chapter will focus on the historical antecedents of the modern rehabilitation enterprise in America and the following two chapters will elaborate on the history of that complex enterprise.

Industrialization and the Rehabilitation Movement

Within a thirty-year period (1890-1920), the demands made on society by industrialization, immigration, and urbanization created new individual and social needs which could be met only by a responsive federal government, a government based on the philosophy that every individual has the right to life, liberty, and the pursuit of happiness as guaranteed in the American Constitution. "The history of vocational rehabilitation is the history of a long struggle to establish dignity and opportunity as a right of disabled [*sic*] persons, just as history in general is the story of the long struggle to establish dignity and opportunity as a right of every human being" (Obermann, 1965, p. 131).

The origins of the rehabilitation movement can be found in an examination of some of the historical forces at the turn of the century. Historical perspective can be gained by an analysis of some of the social movements which were developing prior to (and parallel with) the program of vocational rehabilitation.

With an increasing industrialization of America, all social problems became more complex. The immigration movement contributed to the labor needs of a rapidly growing industrial nation, but a *laissez-faire* system of government in the nineteenth century created serious vocational and education problems for immigrants. "Immigration had transformed the entire economic world within which they (the immigrants) had formerly lived. From surface forms to inmost functions, the change was complete. A new setting, new activities, and new meanings forced the newcomers into radically new roles as producers and consumers of goods. In the process, they became, in their own eyes, less worthy as men [*sic*] (Handlin, 1951, p. 94).

Labor unions were organized as a protest to this feeling of alienation as well as revolt to the long hours, low pay, and poor working conditions which prevailed at the close of the nineteenth century. Samuel Gompers (an immigrant himself) provided leadership for the new American Federation of Labor which became a major force in raising the standards of American labor (Morrison, 1965). Prior to the activities of Gompers and other labor leaders in the early years of the twentieth century, many of the social ills caused by the Industrial Revolution were accepted as necessary evils by the government: "The accident toll taken by heedless negligence and the damage done to workers' health by poor ventilation and lighting, dust and fumes, were all charged off as the cost of progress" (Blum, 1968, p. 456). When the government intervened at all in the nineteenth century, it was to extend loans, grant subsidies, and provide public resources for industry. Gompers emphasized the need for the government to regulate working conditions through safety and insurance programs, and he saw labor's major responsibility as gaining higher wages. He, unlike more radical leaders, felt that labor should accept the capitalist system and win for itself a legitimate position within that economic world. Another group of workers who felt the anguish of this period of industrialization were the farmers who began to migrate to the cities. America had gradually become an urban nation. Even in 1890, there were as many industrial wage earners as farm laborers, tenants, and farm owners combined. New adjustments were required of these farmers as they took jobs in the factories and mills, just as with the immigrants from overseas (Blum, 1968).

Industrialization increased the division of labor which produced additional problems for workers:

> First, it resulted in the breakdown of craft skills into a series of mechanized operations. Each special-purpose machine created a new job . . . the development of interchangeable parts led to an increase in the number of narrowly specialized jobs in assembly operations . . . the size of the work force required by the rapidly growing factories . . . The growth of cities also increased the division of labor since a great many more service activities are required in urban than in rural areas. (Faunce, 1968, pp. 21-22)

This increasing and more complex division of labor and the break that came from a change in the traditional bases of status and power were a part of the basic conditions that would be necessary for the later development of an interest in vocational guidance matters:

> The job was regarded as a sacred calling, and success at work was evidence that one had been chosen for salvation . . . . With an increasingly differentiated occupational structure serving as the basis for status distinctions, instead of land hold or aristocratic birth, which had been more important earlier, the foundation was established for the elaborate occupational status structure characteristic of modern industrial societies. (Faunce, 1968, pp. 21-22)

In a thirty-year span (1890-1920), population in the United States increased over 100 percent, with more of the increase occurring in the cities. "The growth of the people of the United States is one of the remarkable phenomena in history . . . . Immigration increased from 50,262,000 in 1880 to 76,129,000 in 1900, to 107,180,000 in 1920" (Landis & Hatt, 1954, pp. 27 28). As technical invention and technology proceeded along with this growth, higher qualified workers in all fields were in demand, as well as a greater variety. Also, young women were able to become employed as wage earners.

Urbanization and the Rehabilitation Movement

"The city, with its immense need for new facilities in transportation, sanitation, policing, light, gas and public structures offered a magnificent internal market for American business. Business looked for the sure thing, for privileges, above all for profitable franchises and for opportunities to evade as much as possible the burden of taxation. The urban boss, a dealer in public privileges who could also command public support, became a more important and powerful figure" (Hofstader, 1956, pp. 173-174). One urban boss, George Washington Plunkett, who became a millionaire as a Tammany leader, enjoyed telling how he made his fortune through politics:

> Everybody is talking these days about Tammany men growin' rich on graft, but nobody thinks of drawing the distinction between honest graft and dishonest graft . . . . Yes, many of our men have grown rich in politics. I have myself. I've made a big fortune out of the game, and I'm gettin' richer every day, but I've not gone in for dishonest graft . . . . I might sum up the whole thing by sayin': I seen my opportunities and I took 'em. Just let me explain by examples. My party's in power in the city, and it's goin' to undertake a lot of public improvements. Well, I'm tipped off, say, that they're goin' to lay out a new park at a certain place. . . . I go to that place and buy up all the land I can in the neighborhood . . . and, there is a rush to get my land, which nobody cared particular for before. Ain't it perfectly honest to charge a good price and make a profit on my investment and foresight? Of course it is. Well, that's honest graft. (Riordon, 1905, p. 405)

Pressures for reform in politics and government mounted–not only to eliminate "honest" as well as "dishonest graft" from the city government but also to promote assistance from the federal government for the welfare of individuals who were victims of the system. These pressures were expressed in the Populist-Progressive political movement, which began in the 1890s and continued to the beginning of World War I. This effort in political reform is considered "the first modern political movement of practical importance in the United States to insist that the federal government has some responsibility for the commonwealth; indeed, it (populism) was the first such movement to attack seriously the problems created by industrialization" (Hofstadter, 1956, p. 61). This political movement gave support to the fight for women's suffrage, led by Susan B. Anthony and other women pioneers in the late nineteenth and early twentieth century. "In January of 1886, a bill to enfranchise women was presented to the Senate for the first time and suffered its first defeat. Through the years, the same measure was submitted to Congress regularly, until the number of Congressmen favoring women's suffrage grew to a majority. In June, 1919, with President Wilson as an ally, the Nineteenth Amendment was passed, and ratification of the amendment by thirty-six states occurred in August, 1920" (Burnett, 1953, p. 311-312). The employment of larger numbers of women in industry and business during this era already had provided women an increasing economic independence which helped in the preparation for this new political freedom. There were many women who had become prominent in literature and the arts who contributed to this new climate of acceptance. Also, the women involved in social reform who were concerned about the plight of women workers in industry were helping in the crusade for women's suffrage. The final passage of the Amendment, however, was due to the aggressive work of key leaders such as Miss Anthony (Burnett, 1953, p. 317), whose major concern was in the field of women's rights.

The progressive movement in politics was maintained by a new journalism being practiced in the United States during this period. Technical advances in the communication field (for example, rapid printing machines and the telegraph) and the emergence of newspapers and magazines provided the expression for reform, and the financial resources that were made available to the muckrakers helped to draw nationwide attention to the need for reform (Hofstadter, 1956). "Progressivism fed on indignation, and the turn of the century witnesses a revolution in journalism and literature which made it easy for conscientious people to stir up indignation" (Mayer and Forster, 1958, p. 51). *The Jungle* by Upton Sinclair and the writings of Jack London are examples of the literature of the period which contributed to the public's recognition of a need for reform.

Industrial Development in the South and West

In the South, industrialization began to influence the development of a "New South," as expressed by Henry W. Grady, editor of the *Atlanta Constitution* in 1886 in a speech in New York: "We have sowed towns and cities in the place of theories and put business above politics. We have challenged your spinners in Massachusetts and your ironmakers in Pennsylvania. . . . We have fallen in love with work" (Blum, 1968, p.404). For all the progress that was made in the increasing industrialization of the South during the latter part of the nineteenth century, this section of the country, even in 1900, had a smaller percentage of the factories and industrial wealth of the nation than it had in 1860, at the start of the Civil War. "A lost war, a late start and lack of capital were some of the reasons. These disadvantages might have been overcome more readily, however, had it not been for certain artificial barriers: a host of practices and rules adopted to suit the convenience of private interests in the North while the South was out of the union and later when the section was without significant influence in national decisions" (Blum, 1968, p. 409).

Industrialization and urbanization reached the West at a slower pace; however, the West as a region, held a greater percentage of the national wealth in agriculture and industry than did the South. The potential for development in the West was heightened by the railroad and its expansion. Transportation was the key in the migration of workers westward as well as industrial development of the rich natural resources. By 1900, there were more miles of railroad track in America than in all of Europe (Morrison, 1965, p. 743). Industrialization and the use of machinery in farming on a grand scale helped to raise the living standards of the people just as the industrial revolution in the East resulted in better living conditions generally; but, again this industrialization brought on many social problems that made life difficult for large numbers of people (Blum, 1968, p. 456).

Medical Science and Practice

The progress made in technical inventions and science in this era contributed to the development of modern medicine which is ascribed to the period 1870-1920. Medical science began to offer a means of preventing disease and disability and also offered hope for the cure and rehabilitation of people with disabilities. Excess wealth accumulated over the years prompted many millionaires to contribute large amounts of money to the support of medical research and education. "This era was the great turning point in the history of American medicine. After three centuries of dependence on European science, American medical research attained a status equal to that of the better European centers. After an equally long period of mediocre or inferior training, medical education attained a level similar to that reached in the old world. Last, but not least, the average practice of the younger, native physicians became at least as reliable as that of their counterparts in Western

Europe" (Shyrock, 1966, p. 32). This new medicine in America and its technical advances facilitated the establishment of large and improved hospitals, research institutes, medical schools, medical societies, and professional publications. It can be seen that the development of a vocational rehabilitation program would be dependent on a medical science which could provide an optimistic way of helping people with disabilities.

The establishment of the Public Health and Marine Hospital Service in 1902 provided a federal base for extending public health services to meet the health demands of an increasingly complex society. Progress in science and medical practice gave public health leaders the knowledge and skills needed in the development of programs in sanitation, immunization, and other preventive procedures and, in 1912, the United States Public Health Service was set up in the federal government (Hanlon, 1955, p. 49-50). The emphasis was placed on preventing disease and health problems for the masses rather than stressing a social medicine program that would be concerned with the individual. The public health leaders may have felt that the promise of sanitation and immunization would eliminate disease entirely, and there would be no need for direct care to individuals (Galston, 1949).

Development of Workers' Compensation

At the close of the nineteenth century, industry followed the common law which stated that the master or employer was responsible for the injury or death of employees, when the employer was negligent. With the expansion of production, the number of accidents increased and the law suits made against employers to prove "negligence" also increased. Many states, between 1900 and 1910, by judicial decision, adopted a rule that employees need not accept responsibility for disabilities resulting from work and, in 1910, the first complete workers' compensation law in the United States was passed in New York. By 1921, forty-five of the states and territories had passed legislation for workers' compensation. They were not all the same as they varied in scope, benefits, and administration (Obermann, 1965). State legislators attempted to enact laws that would cover the following points:

> 1. provide compensation to victims of work accidents and their dependents,
> 2. free the courts from delay, cost and work load,
> 3. relieve public and private charities of the financial drain,
> 4. eliminate economic waste in the payment of fees to lawyers and witnesses,
> 5. to supplant the practice of concealing the fault by a spirit of a frank study of the causes to provide a program of prevention. (U.S. Chamber of Commerce Pub., Jan, 1958, p. 3)

The initial laws of workers' compensation did not include services for vocational rehabilitation, but the people who supported legislation for workers' compensation also supported the concept of vocational rehabilitation. It was clear to them that help was needed for injured workers to return to employment, but specific legislation was to come later. Dr. R. M. Little, active in the workers' compensation movement and the first director of vocational rehabilitation in New York, felt that the leaders in workers' compensation programs and in organized labor were more influential than others in the early discussion of vocational rehabilitation and that neither education nor social work took the lead in the development of legislation (Obermann, 1965).

Efforts by industry to prevent accidents and preserve the health of employees were based on the profit motive–how to avoid loss in production resulting from the workers' temporary or permanent absence. Large industries were the first to introduce industrial medicine programs for employees. Public health measures and laws, such as those in workers' compensation, placed on the employer the responsibility for the elimination of hazards and for the medical care and compensation of injured workers. In 1909, Sears Roebuck and Company set up one of the first programs for periodic physical examinations of all employees and, in that same year, cooperation between voluntary health agencies and employers began when the Milwaukee Visiting Nurse Association placed the first nurse in an industrial plant. "By 1915, although most states had not as yet passed workers' compensation legislation, occupational health programs maintained on a voluntary basis by industry had so far developed that industrial doctors met to form the American Association of Industrial Physicians and Surgeons" (Maisel, 1960, p. 4).

Psychology and the Rehabilitation Movement

From the 1890s through 1915, there was a corresponding growth in the new field of psychology. American psychology was influenced by the European movement, but Americans also made their own unique contributions to this developing profession. For example, William James, America's first prominent psychologist, stressed the individual rather than the social goals of education. He helped to bring psychology into the classroom by stressing its application to everyday problems (Watson, 1968). G. Stanley Hall, the first president of Clark University and a professor in psychology, established the *American Journal of Psychology* and, in 1892, he helped found the American Psychological Association. Hall emphasized in his studies of children and adolescents the uniqueness of the individual. His studies brought about great public interest and led to the establishment of the child study movement (Watson, 1968). Also, in 1909, Hall invited Sigmund Freud to Clark University for a series of lectures which provided American psychologists an opportunity to examine Freud's use of psychoanalysis as therapy for individuals with mental problems. Many of the American pioneers in psychology were present, including William James, and Freud's lectures were published in American psychological journals (Watson, 1968). At about the same time, considerable interest was shown in America in the objective measurement studies by the French psychologist Alfred Binet. These studies of individual children's intelligence led to the development of the first intelligence scale–the Binet-Simon IQ Test. In 1916, Louis Terman adopted the intelligence quotient (IQ) in his work at Stanford University as he revised the Binet Scales; consequently, the well-known Stanford-Binet Test for intelligence was developed (Watson, 1968).

This national interest in psychology and its application to work with individuals contributed extensively to the developing concern for the lot of the individual in America. The principles of psychology and objective measurement techniques were to be utilized by industry in the new field of industrial psychology. In 1911, Professor Hugo Munsterberg of Harvard was employed by the Boston Elevated Railway to develop psychological tests for the selection of streetcar operators (Maisel, 1960). As Brewer states in his history of guidance, these developments and the growing complications of technology helped to set the stage for the need for vocational guidance, although they did not lead directly to the development of a vocational guidance movement. Frederick W. Taylor, the father of "scientific management," the forerunner of industrial psychology, represented the early concern for individual workers on the part of industry.

Other parallel events were taking place in the general field of psychology during this thirty year period, and the developing movement in mental health was significant. In the late nineteenth century, Dorothea Dix, in her concern for a more humane treatment of people with mental illness led the drive to build state hospitals for the mentally ill in this country. "From thirteen institutions for the mentally ill in 1843, the number had risen to one hundred and twenty-three in 1890 of which seventy-five were state owned . . . in the founding of thirty-two of the seventy-five state hospitals, Dorothea Dix had had an intimate part" (Marshall, 1937, p. 245). Clifford Beers, a former mental patient, wrote a book in 1908 describing his experiences in two state mental hospitals in Connecticut. This book, *A Mind That Found Itself,* facilitated the growth of the mental health movement, and Beers, with the help of psychologists, psychiatrists, and private citizens, established a national organization that became the National Association of Mental Health. William James, on reading the manuscript for *A Mind That Found Itself,* wrote the following in a letter to Beers:

> The book ought to go far toward helping along that terribly needed reform, the amelioration of the lot of the insane of our country, for the Auxiliary Society which you propose is feasible (as numerous examples in other fields show) and ought to work important effect on the whole situation. . . . You have handled a difficult theme with great skill and produced a narrative of absorbing interest to scientist as well as layman. (Beers, 1913, p. 244)

Religion and Rehabilitation

There were other movements, in addition to those in mental health, which provided a stimulant for an awakening of the American social conscience. Religion, at the height of industrialization in the late nineteenth century, with its chief concern for the spiritual needs of people, was dedicated to individualism and the doctrine of *laissez-faire*, in the main. Henry Ward Beecher, a prominent Protestant minister, preached the theory of Social Darwinism–survival of the fittest in the economic world (Blum, 1968). Later, a few Protestant clergymen, responding to the social crises, began to preach the need for social reform and the concept of good works which led to the movement known as the Social Gospel. One of the leaders of that period, F. Ernest Johnson, held this idea about the need for reform:

> The point is that the Christian ideal of life is definitely blocked, thwarted and travestied by the all-pervading influence of economic self-interest and of the competitive struggle. The social gospel program aims at clearing the way for a new advance by the spirit of man. (Johnson, 1935, p.64)

Since the new immigrants were predominantly Roman Catholic, the American Catholic Church of this period became the church of the city, the worker, and the immigrant. The papal encyclical *Rerum Novarum* of 1891 pointed out social ideals and responsibilities that supported the social views of many Americans. Earlier, James Gibbons, in Rome to be installed as a cardinal, defended the cause of American labor before the Holy See (Blum, 1968).

Roman Catholics and Jews, because of their smaller numbers in the total population, were not as influential in the social reform movement as were the Protestants in their total effort; however, in some way, they were more effective on specific issues because they were less restricted than the Protestants with their close alliance to the economic system. Reverend Johnson stated in his social gospel book:

> I have often envied my Catholic friends in their ability to cite unquestioned, authoritative doctrine of vast social import in support of their preachments.

> The Jewish tradition lends itself to a more active support of social idealism than has characterized Protestantism. (Johnson, 1935, p. 33)

Despite the problems, many of the new social programs emerged from the Protestant faith. The Salvation Army came to America from England in 1879 with a goal of reaching the city's poor people. Using evangelistic methods, they preached repentance to "rumdom, slumdom and bumdom" (Blum, 1968, p. 474). They also added a social program to bring welfare relief with the gospel. The growing concern in the Protestant church for the poor can be seen in the first program of Goodwill Industries, established in 1902 by Dr. Edgar James Helms, a Methodist minister in Boston. The idea of hiring unemployed persons to do the renovation and repair work on clothing and materials donated by the public and paying the workers from funds derived from the sale of these repaired products was developed. It was in 1918 that the Board of Missions of the Methodist Church took over Goodwill Industries, continuing the nondenominational approach and also emphasizing a sheltered workshop program for people with disabilities (Obermann, 1965).

In tracing the historical development of the influence of the Jewish community on social ethics, Sidney Goldstein describes the major Jewish religious philosophy on social welfare issues: "It is only when mysticism becomes a pseudo-communion between the individual and God, an experience to be sought for itself and a form of emotional indulgence, that it fails to move men to social action. The legitimate, the necessary, the inevitable expression of the religious spirit of Judaism is the social passion . . . a more powerful expression of communion than is either creed or ceremony or the Commandments" (Goldstein, 1955, p. 311). B'nai B'rith, a welfare and educational organization established by American Jews in 1843, developed rapidly during the late nineteenth and early twentieth centuries. Its present program in vocational guidance and its sponsorship of various nondenominational vocational training centers for people with disabilities grew from this experience of B'nai B'rith during the early years of this century (Baron, 1937).

In addition to these church-based or church-connected charitable programs, there were other eleemosynary organizations active during this period. For example, there was encouragement from the government: Rockefeller set up the Rockefeller Foundation; the Carnegie Corporation was established in 1911; and Woodrow Wilson, in 1913, pointed out the human cost of the industrial achievements of the country and suggested that industry should help to alleviate some of the misery created in its development. Many of the volunteer health, education, and welfare organizations were established to provide a variety of services for people in trouble: The

American Red Cross (1881), with its Red Cross Institute for Crippled and Disabled Men in New York City and its early sponsorship of Braille transcriptions for the blind (later to be administered by the Library of Congress); The National Tuberculosis Association in 1904; the National Easter Seal Society for Cripple Children and Adults, which began in Ohio in affiliation with local Rotary Clubs; and the National Association of Mental Health founded by Clifford Beers in 1909 (Obermann, 1965).

Social Reform and Rehabilitation

Jane Addams, the most famous of the early pioneers in social work, created the first organized secular program of social welfare in America in 1889, Hull House in Chicago, which was established to help educate immigrants and to protect them from exploitation. It was at Hull House that Miss Addams developed the casework approach in helping individuals adjust to their environments–family, school, neighborhood and country. "It was her method of approaching political and social questions that distinguished Jane Addams from other reformers. Like other progressives, she wanted to substitute explanation and analysis for moral exhortation. Therein lay her originality and the originality of her generation" (Lasch, 1965, p. 124). Some of the reforms with which she helped were the first 8-hour day laws for women, the first state child-labor laws, and the first juvenile court. She was a strong supporter of reform in education as well. "Jane Addams' ideas paralleled and supported the educational theories of John Dewey. It is difficult to say whether Dewey influenced Jane Addams or Jane Addams influenced Dewey. They influenced each other and generously acknowledged their mutual obligations" (Lasch, 1965, p. 176-177). Dewey served on the first board at Hull House, and one of his teachers was a resident of the settlement house. It was later that Miss Addams became the first president of the National Conference of Charities and Corrections (which was to become the National Conference on Social Welfare). Lillian Walk, founder of the Henry Street Settlement in New York, was the first person to propose that a children's bureau be set up in the Federal Government, and the first two heads of that agency came from Miss Addams' program at Hull House. The authors of *The National Experience* wrote:

> It was these middle class reformers rather than the trade unions that launched the movement for social legislation in America. They led the agitation that put through the first child-labor laws and they helped to focus the nation's attention on the evils of the slums (Blum, 1968, p. 472).

Public Education and Rehabilitation

A great system of free public education was developing in America during this period–1890 to 1920. "The cause of free public education was advanced as a practical necessity to fill the needs of a growing industrial America while serving as a fulfillment of a dream never before translated into action on a national scale" (Glanz, 1964, p. 26). That dream was to give every child a free education. By 1900, thirty-three states had passed statewide compulsory attendance laws and others were to follow, so that by 1920 all states had these laws (Beck, 1955, p. 89-90). Efforts made toward federal aid to education in these early years of the twentieth century were unsuccessful; however, certain legal precedents were set in such legislation as the Morrill Act of 1862, which offered states land grants to endow colleges of agriculture and mechanical arts (Blum, 1968).

In the period from 1890 through 1920, one person stands out in the public school movement–John Dewey–the famous American psychologist and philosopher who had been a pupil of G. Stanley Hall. Interested in a child-centered school (that is, progressive education), Dewey established a laboratory school in Chicago which was the first school based on a psychological theory and it became one of the most influential schools in the Western World. Dewey's experiment continued for eight years (1896-1904) and much of its theory was published; also, thousands of educators from all over the world visited the school. The emphasis was on the individual child and the conditions necessary for its growth.

Five basic conditions were sought:

1. Freedom for the child to investigate and experiment.
2. Choice of school experiences to fit the child's changing interests, attitudes and stages of growth.
3. The program built around the solving of problems–considered important beyond all the rest.
4. The use of scientific material and the scientific way of working.
5. Provision of cooperative activity, because the school is a miniature community. (Rugg & Withers, 1955, p. 502-503)

Occupational Therapy, Physical Therapy and Other Disciplines

During and following the First World War, with soldiers and sailors acquiring disabilities in large numbers and with medical practice based on science allowing larger and larger numbers of the military and veterans to survive, increasingly, the focus went beyond saving lives to providing assistance to accelerate treatment and to providing collateral services that were to make up the veterans rehabilitation program in America. The first professional organization to attempt to pioneer in this new field of rehabilitation was occupational therapy. A small group set up the American Occupational Therapy Association in 1917 with the primary objectives being to improve and advance the practice and to improve the professional education and to offer research that could be shared in the dissemination of knowledge in the field (Wright, 1980). Four years later, in 1921, the American Physical Therapy Association was founded with similar goals and objectives in the area of physical therapy and, in 1925, the American Speech and Hearing Association was founded with like purposes with professionals working in order to improve the practice, education, and research with patients with speech and hearing disabilities. All three of these groups became prominent and are now considered essential to the rehabilitation team approach, working closely with physicians, rehabilitation counselors, social workers, rehabilitation nurses, and others. With the exception of the basic requirements for medicine, there probably are no other specialists in the field of rehabilitation that adhere to such rigid standards and requirements in both academic preparation and practice.

The Vocational Education Movement

Many of the educational leaders (as well as industrial leaders) saw the unique opportunities presented by an industrial arts or a vocational education program in the public schools. Dewey's support is seen in this statement as he expressed the need for an integrated rather than an isolated approach in vocational education or manual arts training: "They (the manual arts) afford the most permanent and persistent occupations of the great majority of human kind. They present man [*sic*] with his most perplexing problems; they stimulate him [*sic*] to the most strenuous putting forth of effort" (Archambault, 1964, p. 420). There were, however, only isolated vocational educational programs in the public schools in the early years of the twentieth century. Vocational training, for the most part, was confined to industrial schools for poor and delinquent children and in correctional institutions:

> It took the need for skilled labor, made manifest by World War I, to win from Congress federal support of vocational education. The Smith-Hughes Act became law in February, 1917, inaugurating a succession of enactments that reimbursed states for the teaching of vocational agriculture, home economics and industrial arts. (Beck, 1955, p. 91)

Through federal support, vocational education became a part of most curricula in the public schools. The principles of vocational education, derived from this experience in the public schools, were fundamental to the development of vocational rehabilitation.

Special classes or special schools for children with disabilities developed in the public schools in the latter part of the nineteenth century, although most of the programs were located in large cities and they were few in number. Earlier in the nineteenth century, separate private schools for children with hearing and visual disabilities were established: Thomas Gallaudet, a pioneer in work with the deaf, opened the first school for the deaf in 1817 in Connecticut, and the Perkins Institution and Massachusetts School for the Blind were started in 1823 (Baker, 1959). These private schools and their special programs for children with disabilities led to the development of numerous state schools or institutions for children with disabilities in the late nineteenth and early twentieth centuries. These public institutions for indigent children who were blind, deaf, or mentally retarded placed an early emphasis on vocational training, but later this emphasis changed as the institutions, in the 1900s, became, for some years, "asylums" where stress was placed on custodial care (Obermann, 1965). Classes for children with disabilities in the public schools began during the latter part of the nineteenth century; special classes for the mentally retarded were instituted in Springfield, Massachusetts, in 1896; the first class for children with visual impairments was started in Chicago in 1900; and the Detroit Day School for the Deaf was organized in 1900 with two classes for children with hearing disabilities (Baker, 1959). Special Education, as a distinctive profession within public education, was slow to develop. Beck provides one answer for this: "Agitation for special provision for the education of the handicapped [*sic*] was noticeably minimal, at least in the United States. Voluntary groups of laymen, of parents, did not organize; perhaps parents of handicapped [*sic*] children were too ashamed to make their plight public" (Beck, 1955, p. 124).

Vocational education and vocational guidance were indicated in the original Vocational Rehabilitation Act of 1920 as the two services which would be provided to people with physical disabilities. Of greatest impact on the developing vocational rehabilitation program would be vocational guidance, a relatively new discipline. Only twelve years before, Frank Parsons, a social worker, organized and established the Vocational Bureau in Boston (1908), the first organized vocational guidance program in America. "It was his concern that the strengths and weaknesses of individuals be understood and brought into harmony with vocational opportunities" (Farwell & Peters, 1960, p. 2). In his book *Choosing a Vocation*, Parsons stated three broad factors in outlining a theory of vocational guidance: "1) a clear understanding of yourself. . . . 2) a knowledge of the requirements and conditions for success

. . . in different lines of work, and 3) true reasoning of the relation of these two groups of facts" (Brewer, 1942, p. 61). Parsons' intelligent spirit of reform and his farseeing vision are reflected in this passage from his book:

> Not till society wakes up to its responsibility and its privileges . . . shall we be able to harvest more than a fraction of our human resources, or develop and utilize the genius and ability that are latent in each new generation. When that time does come, education will become the leading industry, and a vocation bureau in effect will be a part of the public school system in every community–a bureau provided with every facility that science can devise for the testing of the senses and capabilities and the whole physical, intellectual and emotional makeup of the child and with experts trained as carefully for the work as men [*sic*] are trained today for medicine and law. (Parsons, 1909, p. 165)

The movement in vocational guidance grew out of the efforts of pioneers in the public schools as well. Eli W. Weaver, in 1904, set up a program in Brooklyn, New York, to help high school boys in job placement, work for the summer and part-time work after school. Jesse B. Davis, from 1898 to 1907, while principal of the Central High School in Detroit, provided counseling for students relative to their vocational and educational problems (Brewer, 1942). David S. Hill, an early leader in educational research in New Orleans, thought that the educational system should be based on scientific research. "Hill used more complete methods to study individuals than any of his contemporaries. He utilized the techniques of medical science to examine the physical fitness of boys and girls who were referred to his research bureau; he used the newest psychological tests including the Binet individual intelligence test, and he sent a trained social investigator into homes to learn about the environments of children. Society, according to Hill, was constantly evolving, and it was necessary for an individual to adapt himself to the changing conditions within the society in order to survive" (Smith & Mink, 1969, p. 12). Hill felt that the application of scientific principles would help education and industry move toward a greater cooperation that would result in progress for the whole society (Hill, 1920).

As these concepts in vocational guidance spread, educators, social workers, business and government leaders, and psychologists–those who were interested in applying its principles–joined together in founding the National Vocational Guidance Association in 1913, the forerunner of the American Personnel and Guidance Association which is now know as the American Counseling Association.

An observation by the authors of *Guidance: A Developmental Approach* indicates the direction that guidance would take in the public schools as it became a major concern of American education:

> The optimal development of the individual became a concern of the affluent society, still bridled by many severe problems but saddled more precariously with the vast majority of normally or adequately functioning individuals who could improve their level of living. Indeed, this was an area for prime consideration by school staff. It would be different from the secondary school guidance offered by Jesse B. Davis, in Detroit Central High School, at the turn of the century (Peters & Farwell, 1967, p. 28).

The First World War (1914-1918) provided an opportunity for increased emphasis on the need "to choose the right man [*sic*] for the right job" which Parsons stressed in his vocational guidance theory. Selective tests were devised to determine aptitude as well as intelligence. The first group of intelligence tests, the Army Alpha and the Army Beta, were used for literate and illiterate recruits respectively. Tests were constructed also to measure skills in the various trades: "These tests were of three kinds: questions on materials, tools and processes (what to do), questions based on pictures and performance assignments. Scores gave a four-fold classification in some eighty occupations: novices, apprentices, journeymen and experts" (Brewer, 1942, p. 203). Following World War I, these techniques and methods would be extended to all areas of vocational guidance, including the new program in vocational rehabilitation.

Summary

An attempt has been made in this chapter to provide significant facts about the historical antecedents of the complex rehabilitation enterprise which exists in America today. A concept of a total rehabilitation movement in our country has developed from the basic values of our system of government–the ideals, customs, and traditions of the American people–which found expression in the public support of rehabilitation services for people with disabilities. The next two chapters will elaborate on the development of the modern rehabilitation enterprise in America. It can appropriately be described as an early and recent history of the rehabilitation movement. These chapters are written with the hope that a review of the past can lead to understanding and wisdom on the part of all who attempt to help others through the broader concept of rehabilitation.

Time present and time past are both perhaps present in time
future, and time future contained in time past
T. S. Eliot
Four Quartets, Burnt Norton

REFERENCES

Archambault, R. B. (Ed.). (1964). *John Dewey on education: Selected writings.* New York: Random House.

Baker, H. J. (1959). *Introduction to exceptional children.* New York: Macmillan.

Baron, S. W. (1937). *A social and religious history of the Jews.* New York: Columbia University Press.

Beck, R. H. (1955). *A social history of education.* Englewood Cliffs, N J: Prentice-Hall.

Beers, C. (1913). *A mind that found itself* (3rd ed.). New York: Longmanns, Green.

Blum, J. M. (1968). *The national experience: A history of the United States* (2nd ed.). New York: Harcourt, Brace & World.

Brewer, J. M. (1942). *History of vocational guidance.* New York: Harper.

Burnett, C. B. (1953). *Five for freedom.* New York: Abingdom.

De Jong, G. (1979). *Report of the national conference on independent living service rehabilitations per P.L.95-602,* March 7-9, 1979. Boston: Medical Rehabilitation and Research Training Center, Tufts-New England Medical Center.

Farwell, G. F., & Peters, H. J. (1960). *Guidance readings for counselors.* Chicago: Rand, McNally.

Fraunce, W. A. (1968). *Problems of an industrial society.* New York: McGraw-Hill.

Galston, I. (1949). *Social medicine.* Cambridge, MA: Harvard University Press.

Glanz, E. C. (1964). *Foundations and principles of guidance.* Boston: Allyn & Bacon.

Goldstein, S. E. (1955). *The synagogue and social welfare: A unique experiment.* New York: Bloch.

Handlin, O. (1951). *The uprooted.* New York: Grosset & Dunlap.

Hanlon, J. J. (1955). *Principles of public health administration.* St. Louis, MO: C. V. Mosby.

Hill, D. S. (1920). *Introduction to vocational education.* New York: Macmillan.

Hofstadter, R. (1956). *The age of reform.* New York: Alfred A. Knopf.

Johnson, F. E. (1935). *The church and society.* New York: Abingdom.

Landis, P. H., & Hatt, P. K. (1954). *Population problems.* New York: American Book.

Lasch, C. (Ed.). (1965). *The social thought of Jane Addams.* New York: Bobbs-Merrill.

Lassiter, R. A. (1972). History of the rehabilitation movement in America. In J. G. Cull & R. E. Hardy (Eds.), *Vocational Rehabilitation: Profession and Process.* Springfield, IL: Charles C Thomas.

Maisel, A. Q. (1960). *The health of people who work.* New York: National Health Council.

Marshall, H. E. (1937). *Dorothea Dix: Forgotten semaritan.* Chapel Hill, NC: University of North Carolina Press.

Mayer, G. H., & Forster, W. O. (1958). *The United States and the twentieth century.* Boston: Houghton Mifflin.

Morrison, S. E. (1965). *The Oxford history of the American people.* New York: Oxford University Press.

Moser, L. E., & Moser, R. S. (1963). *Counseling and guidance, an exploration.* Englewood Cliffs, NJ: Prentice-Hall.

Obermann, C. E. (1965). *A history of vocational rehabilitation in America.* Minneapolis, MN: T. S. Denison & Company.

Parsons, F. (1969). *Choosing a vocation.* Cambridge, MA: Houghton Mifflin.
Peters, H. J., & Farwell, G. F. (1967). *Guidance: A developmental approach* (2nd ed.). Chicago: Rand, McNally.
Riordon, W. L. (1905). *Plunkett of Tammany Hall.* New York: McClure, Phillips.
Rugg, H., & Withers, W. (1955). *Social foundations of education.* New York: Prentice-Hall.
Shyrock, R. H. (1966). *Medicine in America: Historical essays.* Baltimore, MD: John Hopkins Press.
Sixty-sixth Congress. (1920). United States Statutes at Large, *41.*
Smith, C. E., & Mink, O. G. (Eds.). (1969). *Foundations of guidance and counseling.* New York: J. B. Lippincott.
Switzer, M. E. (1964). *Rehabilitation Record,* 1, 14.
U. S. Chamber of Commerce Publication (1958). *Analysis of workmen's compensation laws.* Washington, D.C.: United States Chamber of Commerce.
Watson, R. I. (1968). *The great psychologists, from Aristotle to Freud* (2nd ed.). New York: J. B. Lippincott.
Wright, G. N. (1980). *Total rehabilitation.* New York: Little, Brown.

Chapter 3

THE DEVELOPMENT OF THE REHABILITATION ENTERPRISE IN AMERICA: AN EARLY HISTORY OF THE REHABILITATION MOVEMENT

ROBERT A. LASSITER AND MARTHA HUGHES LASSITER

Legislation passed by the Congress during World War I led directly to the enactment of Public Law 236 which established the state-federal program in vocational rehabilitation. Thus, the development of the modern rehabilitation enterprise in America had begun. The National Defense Act of 1916 indicated the importance attached by Congress to the area of vocational training: "In addition to military training, soldiers while in active service shall hereafter be given the opportunity to study and receive instruction upon educational lines of such character as to increase their military efficiency and enable them to return to civilian life better equipped for industrial, commercial and general business occupations. Civilian teachers may be employed to aid the Army officers in giving such instruction, and part of this instruction may consist of vocational education either in agriculture or the mechanic arts" (Sixty-fourth Congress, 1916, p. 186). On February 23, 1917, the second session of the Sixty-fourth Congress passed the Smith-Hughes Act which set a precedent for federal funding of educational programs of all types and also established a pattern of vocational education in the United States. The act created the Federal Board of Vocational Education which later administered the vocational rehabilitation program for World War I veterans and the state-federal program in vocational rehabilitation (Sixty-fourth Congress, 1916, p. 929). The Soldier Rehabilitation Act of 1918 was passed by the Sixty-fifth Congress on June 27, 1918. The Federal Board for Vocational Education was authorized to operate a program of vocational rehabilitation for veterans: "an act to provide for the vocational rehabilitation and return to employment of disabled [sic] persons discharged from the military and naval forces of the United States and for other purposes" (Sixty-fifth Congress, 1916, p. 617). Eligibility for services was outlined and a veteran with a disability was defined as one who "is unable to carry on a gainful occupation, to resume his former occupation or to enter upon some other occupation, or having resumed and entered upon such occupation is unable to continue the same successfully, shall be furnished by the said board, where vocational rehabilitation is feasible, such course of vocational rehabilitation as the board shall prescribe and provide" (Sixty-fifth Congress, 1916, p. 617). This act which became known as the Smith-Sears Veterans' Rehabilitation Act was signed by President Wilson on June 27, 1918. The passage of this act, and the previous enactment of the Smith Hughes Act in 1917, helped gain support for vocational rehabilitation for civilians. Many of the same legislative and lay leaders who supported this earlier legislation for veterans were also committed to a program of vocational rehabilitation for civilians (Pattison, 1957). In order to avoid a delay in the passage of the veteran's bill in 1918, these leaders decided to wait for another time and this time came only three months later (September, 1918) when Senator Hoke Smith of Georgia and Representative William Bankhead of Alabama first introduced their bill to set up a program for the vocational rehabilitation of civilians. Before this bill would become law (1920) many hearings would be held, and the following men were among the key spokesmen: Dr. R. M. Little, of the United States Employment Compensation, whose interest was in extending the state worker's compensation programs; W. E. Faulkes, a supervisor of vocational education in Wisconsin, who represented the growing interest in vocational rehabilitation by state education departments (Faulkes would later become the first state director of vocational rehabilitation in Wisconsin, and as president of the National Rehabilitation Association (1924-1927), he would become a national leader for federal legislation in the field); Dr. Charles A. Prossner, Director of the Federal Board of Vocational Education, who was interested in following the same administrative pattern as had been established with the Smith-Hughes Act and the Smith-Sears Act–administration by the Federal Board of Vocational Education in partnership with the state vocational education department (Obermann, 1965); Lieutenant Colonel Harry E. Mock of Surgeon General's office and a distinguished orthopedic surgeon who argued for a more extensive bill which would have provided a program of prevention, medical care, compensation and insurance, vocational training and re-employment; and Douglas C. McMurtie, Director of the Red Cross Institute for Cripple and Disabled Men in New York, whose organization was active in research and demonstration projects in the rehabilitation field and also in promoting state legislation for vocational rehabilitation. (A few states had some form of vocational rehabilitation programs prior to the enactment of the federal act in 1920 [Patterson, 1960]).

Following the passage of the Vocational Rehabilitation Act of 1920, thirty-four states within an eighteen-month period had passed acceptance or enabling legislation and had taken steps to organize a program of services to accommodate the federal funds which were made available on a fifty-fifty matching ratio through the Federal Board of Vocational Education (Patterson, 1960).

Prior to the federal legislation in June, 1920, several states had enacted vocational rehabilitation laws to accept provisions of the anticipated federal act.

> The first legislative action occurred in Massachusetts in1918 with the passage of an act to provide for training and instruction of persons who capacities to earn a living had been destroyed or impaired through industrial accident. Other states soon followed and by June, 1920, twelve had enacted vocational rehabilitation laws. (Blauch, 1938, p. 4)

Usually the states' legislation consisted of a few brief statements amending a public law dealing with vocational education. This procedure represented only an acceptance act; no attempt was made to define the scope of the work or to advise the state boards of vocational education on procedures to follow; and all regulations and policies were left entirely with the federal legislation. Funds were appropriated to match the federal monies made available in the act on a fifty-fifty matching ratio.

The Federal Board for Vocational Education issued a statement of policies for use by states in the administration of the vocational rehabilitation act in September, 1920. This publication made it clear that the Federal Government was reluctant to establish a new federal program.

> Under this act the Federal Government does not propose to undertake the organization and immediate direction of vocational rehabilitation in the states, but does agree to make substantial financial contributions to its support. (Blauch, 1938, p. 12)

Congress, by passing only temporary legislation, probably held the opinion that the funds would stimulate the development of programs carried on entirely by state governments at some future time. This first policy statement reflects the philosophy of responsible officials in the federal vocational education agency who viewed vocational rehabilitation as being synonymous with vocational education, except that this new area would be concerned only with people with disabilities. The authors of the bulletin state:

> The industrial rehabilitation law provides practically the same administrative procedures as is required in the administration of the vocational education act. In so far as possible, the same methods of administration and relationships with state boards will be maintained. (Federal Board for Vocational Education, 1920, p. 9)

Requirements for the states' participation, which were based on the federal act, were provided in the bulletin:

> 1. the expenditure of funds in the state must be equal to the amount expended in federal funds (fifty-fifty matching formula established with all states);
> 2. the development of a state plan for approval by the federal agency (guides were provided but emphasis was placed on each state developing an individual plan which would meet its unique needs);
> 3. submission of an annual report to the federal board;
> 4. administration of the state program placed under the state vocational education board and a cooperative agreement established with the state's workmen's [sic] compensation commission or bureau;
> 5. a prohibition of expenditure of funds for buildings or equipment (setting the early policy of a "purchase of service plan"). (Federal Board for Vocational Education, 1920, p. 13)

Information was also provided on the forms to use in statistical and financial reporting. A question and answer section was included in this early bulletin to provide an interpretation of the law by the various state departments of vocational education:

> The board interprets the term "vocational rehabilitation" as used in this act not to include the work of physical rehabilitation, although such work may be necessary preliminary to or accompaniment of vocational rehabilitation. (Federal Board for Vocational Education, 1920, p. 31)

The question of purchasing artificial appliances was presented since the experience of worker's compensation programs showed the majority of serious industrial accidents resulted in amputations. This question was answered in a somewhat ambiguous way which may have helped to set a pattern for the future establishment of a comprehensive physical restoration and treatment program: "In such a case, it would be clear that this would be outside the purview of vocational rehabilitation, since like medical care and occupational therapy, it is physical restoration. . . ." (Federal Board for Vocational Education, 1920, p. 31).

In response to the question of providing "specialized" vocational prostheses, the authors of the bulletin replied, "If in these instances, they are real supplies of an instructional nature necessary for the individual in training, it is possible. . . ." The question regarding the provision of job placement only was answered in the negative, and this, for many years, resulted in the reluctance of rehabilitation workers to assist a person with a disability who needed only counseling and job placement services:

> A rehabilitation agency which contemplates placement only is not in harmony with the spirit of the Federal Act. The emphasis is laid by the act upon courses of study, supervision, etc. and it is made clear that the chief thing in mind was the vocational retraining of the disabled [*sic*]. (Federal Board for Vocational Education, 1920, p. 33)

In answer to the question of a minimum age, the Federal Board provided an answer that was accepted as a policy in all states: "The Federal Act does not specify a minimum age. It is evident, however, that the minimum age in any state would be the minimum age of legal employability in that state" (Federal Board for Vocational Education, 1920, p. 37). Rigid adherence to this interpretation (and not to the law) over the years hampered efforts to provide counseling and other service of a prevocational nature to people under age sixteen. The answer given to the following question was answered affirmatively, "What about homemaking as an occupation? Persons engaged in homemaking, whether working for a wage or not, will be considered as engaged in a legitimate occupation" (Federal Board for Vocational Education, 1920, p. 37). This interpretation, however, was based on the vocational education act which had included home economics as a major educational program and the implications for the future development of vocational rehabilitation services for housewives and other unpaid family workers were not foreseen. It is clear that an action and service-oriented program was envisioned from the beginning. In answer to a question about the use of funds for preliminary survey (research) prior to establishing a program, the federal official stated:

> The general principles on which the work should be constructed are fairly well recognized and are easily ascertainable. Further progress depends upon the contract with individual cases and actual work in vocational rehabilitation. A preliminary survey should include contacts looking toward an early beginning of training since the Federal Act has clearly in mind a definite undertaking of the work of vocational rehabilitation. Such a survey would be only incidental to the actual starting of the work. (Federal Board for Vocational Education, 1920, p. 33)

The last statement may have been needed in order to encourage a pioneering-type activity which was necessary in the development of a new program;

however, it may have been somewhat shortsighted in the exclusion of an early emphasis on research and study, which could have accompanied the developing service program, to provide the data needed for improvement of services and sound planning for the extension of services in future development and growth.

The Federal Board for Vocational Education issued its second bulletin on vocational rehabilitation during March, 1921, months before most of the states had established programs. Additional interpretive data for the states to follow in setting up new programs were provided in this second bulletin. The first clear statement on the techniques and methods to be used by rehabilitation agents (later called rehabilitation counselors) was included. This was a case method approach adopted from the social work field. The employment of federal supervisors to work specifically in vocational rehabilitation and the experiences of a few states in attempting to rehabilitate people helped to establish this method.

Even before the state agencies began to function, the methods for providing services moved from those of instruction, supervision and courses of studies to the case method technique. Vocational guidance and vocational testing are not mentioned in this second bulletin; however, early vocational guidance principles were implied by stating that the purpose of the person contacting people with disabilities was . . .

> To inspire the disabled man [*sic*] . . . with a feeling of receptivity and . . . of confidence. This may be accomplished by tact in giving encouragement, and proffering assistance, and by acquainting the injured . . . with the achievements and accomplishments of others who have suffered from similar or other disabilities. There should be induced, so far as possible, a mental state of hopefulness which will tend to counteract the almost inevitably discouraging effects of accidents or illnesses. (Federal Board for Vocational Education, 1921, p. 31)

A discussion of specific case procedures to be followed in the management of services was provided: (a) Determination of eligibility is made by the agent in three distinct areas–age, physical disability, and feasibility. (b) Determination of the job objective, "the whole interview should be so conducted that the disabled [*sic*] person rather than the agent is led to make a decision as to the selection of a job objective," and yet stress was placed on what the agent does for the person with a disability: "In order to determine what particular occupation or employment is best in the case of any disabled [*sic*] person, it is necessary that an intensive study be made of the case (no mention is made of an objective appraisal by tests) (Federal Board for Vocational Education, 1921, p. 33). (c) Formulation of a tentative plan of rehabilitation, "when a specific employment objective has been determined upon, the agency of the State Board will be face to face with the issue of making at least a tentative plan of vocational rehabilitation for the disabled [*sic*] person" (Federal Board for Vocational Education, 1921, p. 36). (d) Follow-up during training and the determination of employability: "This follow-up on the job must continue until, beyond a question of a doubt, the disabled [*sic*] person is independent, confident and happy, and all reports show that he [*sic*] is producing at his [*sic*] maximum efficiency" (Federal Board for Vocational Education, 1921, p. 36).

The Early Role of the Counselor in Rehabilitation

In these early bulletins, no information was provided on the qualifications of rehabilitation agents nor was any concern shown for their training other than the distribution of various policy statements. Perhaps the federal supervisors followed the tradition established in the Federal Board's work with states on the Smith-Hughes legislation which, for the most part, left selection and training of vocational education personnel to the state boards and department of education. The directors of these state programs were also in charge of planning and implementing a program in vocational rehabilitation and, in many states, the director of vocational education, for many years remained director of vocational rehabilitation, even though most authority was delegated to a supervisor of vocational rehabilitation.

In 1927, Homer L. Stanton, Supervisor of Vocational Rehabilitation in North Carolina (one of the early pioneers who served as the fifth national president of the National Rehabilitation Association [1922-1930]), in his history of the agency's work, refers to his experience in this area during the first six years of the program:

> In the early experience of rehabilitation, three divisions were made of the work: counsel and advisement, training and placement. However, experience soon taught that counsel and advisement is not a service that only needs to precede other steps in rehabilitation but must accompany all other processes to the conclusions of the rehabilitation program. Since the whole aim is fitting the handicapped [*sic*] individuals to the most suitable vocation, we may well call this service Vocational Guidance. (Stanton, 1927, p. 14)

Stanton continues later in this section of his study:

> . . . The report of the sub-committee on vocational guidance of the Commission on Reorganization of Secondary Education admirably described the process as applied to Rehabilitation. "Vocational guidance should be a con-

> tinuous process designed to help the individual to choose, to plan his preparation for, to enter upon, and to make progress in an occupation." (Stanton, 1927, p. 8)

This statement indicates the direction rehabilitation work was taking–moving from an educational emphasis to a social work approach, then to the field of vocational guidance, while retaining parts of all three areas in attempting to meet the needs of a neglected group in America, people with physical disabilities, the states were urged to find the means to get the necessary medical assistance they needed (Obermann, 1965, p. 231). Dr. Henry H. Kessler, a prominent physician in New Jersey and consultant to the New Jersey Workmen's Compensation program, which administered the vocational rehabilitation program in that state, helped to pioneer in the development of national legislation for these services to be included in the federal act. His views were representative of many orthopedic surgeons and other physicians who felt a mistake had been made in excluding medical services. New Jersey established a physical medicine program in its vocational rehabilitation act of 1919. Kessler commented on the federal act of 1920 in his book, *Rehabilitation of the Physically Handicapped* [*sic*]:

> The attendant newspaper publicity stressed the vocational benefits to be obtained but completely ignored the fact that in the case of the disabled [*sic*] World War I veterans, physical reconstruction had already been cared for in the veterans' hospitals. This oversight on the part of the publicists and the unwillingness of the educational group to broaden their vision and see rehabilitation in its true perspective, was to lead to a long, drawn-out controversy as to whether or not vocational rehabilitation should be preceded by physical rehabilitation in the case of the civilian handicapped [*sic*]. . . . (Kessler, 1947, p. 227)

However, many of the early leaders in the states gave support to physical medicine for adults with vocational handicapping conditions and sowed an early concern for preventive medical programs for children with disabilities which brought many benefits to the agency and to its clients. One significant result was the development of close ties with physicians which established a firm base for future development of physical restoration services in the states. Another important development originated with the rehabilitation affiliated clinics: a strong alliance with volunteer, nonprofit groups interested in helping children and adults with disabilities. From the beginning, sponsors for the clinic were found in the Kiwanis, Rotary, and Lion's Clubs. Involvement by volunteers in civic clubs set the stage for alliances with the newly developing private organizations for persons with physical disabilities.

Review of this period reflects the kinds of activities in which the state rehabilitation leaders participated:

> The years from 1921 to 1926 were filled with the spirit of development and growth of state-federal vocational rehabilitation programs. The national conferences in St. Louis, Washington, and Cleveland reflected this in their programs and proceedings. The philosophical base for the new movement was being formulated, the administrative machinery was being established, definitions were being agreed upon, the limitation of operations under the federal act were being explored, and the techniques of rehabilitation practice were discussed. (Obermann, 1965, p.246)

The first sectional meetings for the professional staff in vocational rehabilitation were held at the National Society for Vocational Education Annual Conference at Buffalo, New York, in 1923. At one of these sectional meetings, leaders from the state-federal vocational rehabilitation agencies established the National Civilian Rehabilitation Conference; and, in 1925, this organization began operation as a separate organization as it held its first annual meeting in Cleveland, Ohio. In Memphis, Tennessee, at its annual conference in 1927, the name of the organization was changed to the National Rehabilitation Association (Obermann, 1965, p. 354 358).

> The objectives of this new organization were listed as follows: (a) to provide through its meetings a forum in which all phases of vocational rehabilitation of disabled [sic] civilians and problems incidental thereto may be discussed, (b) to conduct a campaign of education to bring the general public to an adequate understanding of the importance of the civilian rehabilitation movement, (c) to further so far as possible and desirable agreement upon the principles and practices in the field of civilian rehabilitation and to promote comity between the various agencies, (d) to set up a medium through which expression may be given to the view of the membership upon pending legislation and public policies affecting the civilian rehabilitation movement. (Obermann, 1965, p. 357-358)

The other national forum for state supervisors and directors of vocational rehabilitation was provided by the Federal Board for Vocational Education as it sponsored national conferences on vocational rehabilitation.

At its second National Conference in Washington, D.C., in 1924, the first statements on qualifications for rehabilitation agents (counselors) were recorded: "There is no place in vocational rehabilitation for a routine worker or one who is contented with his present knowledge and methods of rehabilitation" (Federal Board for Vocational Education, 1924, p. 123). The report continued with the outlining of the duties of a rehabilitation professional worker:

1. interviewing applicants,
2. setting up feasible plans of rehabilitation,
3. supervision of training,
4. job placement,
5. soliciting funds for areas not covered,
6. securing cooperation of individuals and agencies. (Federal Board for Vocational Education, 1924, p. 123)

The report then described the kinds of personal qualities need to carry out these duties as:

> Tact, careful observation, patience and sympathy tempered by good judgment . . . a complete knowledge of the rehabilitation laws, policies and best practices, thoughtfulness, alertness, resourcefulness, ingenuity and common sense. . . . One must have a liberal education in order that he [*sic*] may meet all classes favorably and deal with them on their own level. One must be socially agreeable, that is, be able to get on well with people. This requires courtesy, tact, poise, cheerfulness and a good sense of humor. He [*sic*] should be a graduate of a standard college and should have some experience in rehabilitation, social services or other work that has given him [*sic*] experience. . . . (Federal Board for Vocational Education, 1924, p. 123).

Later one member spoke to this "necessary qualifications" list:

> Someone may say that we can't afford the type of men [*sic*] described. I want to say that you can't afford any other type of men [*sic*]. The success of the work depends upon the kind of men [*sic*] who are administering it, the largest item of expense in the rehabilitation work, is and rightly so, that of administration (salary). The poorest economy that can be practiced in rehabilitation work is the employment of cheap and incompetent officers. The effectiveness of the work in any state will depend on the ability of the staff that is in charge of the program. (Federal Board for Vocational Education, 1924, p. 127)

From 1926 to 1930, the vocational rehabilitation movement remained stable with little growth reflected either in the number of people rehabilitated or in the addition of staff members. Obermann provides, in his history of vocational rehabilitation in America, various reasons for this more static period of growth:

1. limited federal appropriations for federal staff and administrative activities,
2. vocational rehabilitation regarded by Federal Board for Vocational Education and the state boards as an extension of its programs in vocational training rather than as a unique program requiring new methods and techniques,

> 3. administrations of Harding, Coolidge and Hoover were conservative, and
> 4. federal agency supervisors were anxious to make the program appear very successful rather than to point out the problems resulting from a lack of funds. (Obermann, 1965, p. 247-248)

The development of a special vocational guidance discipline for people with physical disabilities can be seen in two documents published in 1928. One, the first national study made of rehabilitated people (1927), indicates that six years after the state-federal program began the emphasis continued to be placed upon serving people with orthopedic disabilities.

> It will be seen that a majority of the rehabilitated cases had disabilities affecting the lower limbs . . . 2,616 or 40.8 percent of the total number of cases had leg disabilities . . . 1,194 cases or 31.2 percent of the total number had disabled arms or hands . . . 688 persons were disabled [*sic*] by partial or total loss of vision . . . 108 by tuberculosis. It will be noted that the number of persons injured by heart disease and other disabling [*sic*] conditions was relatively small. (Federal Board for Vocational Education, 1928, p. 12)

The second publication, a report of the proceedings of the fifth national conference held in Milwaukee in 1929, indicates that vocational counseling and guidance had emerged as the dominant professional force. Dr. A.H. Egerton of the University of Wisconsin spoke to the conference in the "counsel and advisement" section. He commented on the changes he had observed in rehabilitation:

> Perhaps the most significant change which had taken place in counseling includes your specialized form of counseling. I refer to the change in attitude, namely, from counseling for individuals to counseling with them. (Federal Board for Education, 1928, p. 104-120)

Egerton also suggested ways that certain tests might be helpful in vocational guidance. In a discussion that followed this presentation, it was necessary for some to defend the use of tests in counseling since the majority of those rehabilitation agents present were opposed to using any of these new devices in helping people. Dr. Fairies, a psychologist representing the Institute for Crippled and Disabled Men in New York City, stated in this discussion:

> Having received my psychological training or training in psychology long before there was such a thing as a psychological test, I am not capable myself, having not kept up with psychology in the later years of its development, to give a test, but I do believe that every rehabilitationist should take advantage

> of the very best thought on the subject, because a great deal of attention is being paid to these tests. (Federal Board for Vocational Education, 1928, p. 104-120)

During these years, the state leaders who were acting as rehabilitation agents themselves (as well as supervisors) were establishing highly centralized state programs. The reasons for this highly centralized and authoritarian-type management provided by confident leaders are clearly seen:

1. A tight control of all activities prevented serious errors that could have harmed substantially the reputation of an unknown minor governmental agency attempting to grow and develop.
2. This type of management was encouraged by state government and was the approach used by industrial psychology and other personnel work in this period of time.
3. New staff, inexperienced in the field with no special college training, would benefit by acquiring skills needed to operate a limited program of services for a relatively large number of people.

Some of the disadvantages in administration are obvious, but perhaps the greatest disadvantage was the fact that a rigid pattern of administration was established early, which would, at a future time, become obsolete.

By 1930, there was a clear and strong design developing for the foundations of rehabilitation counseling, as a distinct professional area in the field of vocational guidance and counseling. Years later (1951), R. C. Thompson, an early leader and for many years director of the Maryland agency, wrote an article on the history of the National Rehabilitation Association and commented on the early concepts developing:

> . . . at Milwaukee in 1929, the efforts of some leaders such as Terry Foster to commit the Association to the scientific approach to rehabilitation through vocational guidance and aptitude testing had disclosed an alarming cleavage still existing in our ranks as to the basic concept of our profession. (Thompson, 1951, p. 15)

Despite the growing body of knowledge that contributed to professionalization of the work of the rehabilitation agent during this period, little growth, in terms of the number of people served, took place in the early 1930s. These early depression years created conditions that restricted growth and, on some occasions, threatened the very existence of this small state-federal program which was not well known by the general public, nor by many of the politicians. This more static and inactive period did provide an opportunity for consolidations of gains made in the development of the new concept. The framework for future growth was built as rehabilitation leaders were called on to participate in some of the federal government's attempts to improve the plight of America's middle class as well as its poor who were suffering from a major economic depression.

Vocational rehabilitation in 1933 became involved with the administration's total governmental effort to combat the Depression, President Franklin D. Roosevelt's New Deal. A monthly national allotment of $70,000 was made available through the Federal Emergency Relief Administration to the state vocational rehabilitation programs for the purpose of extending rehabilitation services to the unemployed people with disabilities who were on relief.

> These funds could be expended for appliances, tuition, supplies and equipment for trainees; their travel to attend training centers and their maintenance while in training. Administration of these funds for vocational rehabilitation was divided between the state's Emergency Relief Fund and the state supervisors of vocational rehabilitation. (Blauch, 1938, p. 8)

People on relief who received vocational rehabilitation services also were provided living expenses while they were in training. This inclusion of maintenance for a limited group led to legislation and regulations which came later when the total rehabilitation program was made more comprehensive.

When the functions of the Federal Board for Vocational Education were transferred by an executive order by President Roosevelt to the Department of the Interior in 1933, the Secretary of the Interior assigned the vocational rehabilitation division to the Office of Education (McDonald, 1944).

Terry Foster was the author of the first rehabilitation bulletin published by the Office of Education in the Department of the Interior. This bulletin, written in 1934, presented "a manual of instructions, policies and practices for the guidance of case workers in the field of vocational rehabilitation." Sample forms for record keeping and reporting were based on those developed by Foster and the director of the vocational rehabilitation program in Pennsylvania. For example, Foster wrote guidelines for counselors to use in making decisions about "re-opening" cases, stating that a case could be reopened, but "careful investigation should be made, however, before re-opening such cases" (U.S. Dept. of Interior, 1934, p. 47).

Broadening the Scope of Rehabilitation

Until 1935, emphasis was placed on the indigent "crippled"[*sic*] person, even though some services were available to people in all economic groups, for example, counseling and guidance and tuition for training; and limited services were also available to people with disabilities who did not have orthopedic disabilities. It is clear that this program in 1935 was a limited one and a priority of service was necessary; therefore, the needs of the indigent person with an obvious disability that could be corrected or minimized received the highest priority.

The Social Security Act of 1935 provided the first permanent base for the federal vocational rehabilitation program (Pattison, 1957, p. 845). "The Social Security Act, thus, accomplished three objectives of rehabilitation officials, namely, a permanent authorization, increased grants and increased support of federal administration" (McDonald, 1944, p. 80). This bill which was drafted by the House Ways and Means Committee in 1935 contained an authorization for a 75 percent increase in the grants to states ($1,938,000), and the federal administrative budget was increased from $80,000 per year to $102,000. "The report of the Ways and Means Committee declared that the provision for increased federal aid for vocational rehabilitation was made in recognition of the importance of such work in a permanent program for economic security" (McDonald, 1944, p. 79). Representatives of the National Rehabilitation Association appeared at the hearings to argue for this inclusion of vocational rehabilitation in the social security legislation, emphasizing to committee members that the bill already included services for children with disabilities.

In 1936, a new publication from the federal office provided additional information in the development of a vocational rehabilitation philosophy. John Kratz, chief of the federal division, wrote *Vocational Rehabilitation of the Physically Handicapped* [*sic*] and in one section stated:

> Of fundamental importance is the principle that from the inception of a rehabilitation case to its conclusion only one agent should deal with the disabled [*sic*] person. Functional handling of cases was tried in the soldier [*sic*] rehabilitation work, and it proved a failure. (U.S. Dept. of Interior, 1936, p. 44)

Kratz expressed his ideas on the importance of counseling:

> One of the most important services given by a rehabilitation agent is that of counsel and advisement. It is a continuous service designed to assist the disabled [*sic*] person in choosing, preparing for, entering upon and making progress in an occupation. . . . Such devices as psychological, individual, group, trade and intelligence tests have been used only to a limited extent, but it is not likely that they can ever be used in all cases as a general procedure in rehabilitation. A practical common sense trial and error process had been the procedure followed in most cases. . . . (U.S. Dept. of Interior, 1936, p. 49)

Kratz also provided a statement that reflected the growing recognition of the need to look at a client as a person of worth and dignity and, yet, as someone who still needed some manipulation and direction:

> It is far better procedure to have the person assume a measure of initiative and responsibility for the development of his [*sic*] own rehabilitation . . . the rehabilitation supervisor must be skillful in assisting the applicant to appraise his [*sic*] own abilities, capacities and deficiencies.

And, yet he goes on to say:

> If the agent is skillful, he [*sic*] leads the disabled [*sic*] person to follow his [*sic*] guidance and to enter into the rehabilitation plan which the agent suggests, as freely and as enthusiastically as if he [*sic*], himself [*sic*], had suggested and originated it. (U.S. Dept. of Interior, 1936, p. 50)

In this same bulletin, Kratz commented on the problems of administration and outlined the types of administration observed in the states without making a recommendation for the use of any particular kind. There were two basic types of organization: a central office, which handled all services in the smaller states, and a central office with district offices established throughout a larger state. In addition, Kratz mentioned two basic approaches used in administration–a centralized program with all or most decision-making taking place in the central office and a decentralized program which provided for some autonomy in the district offices (U.S. Dept. of Interior, 1936, p. 50).

Many chose the centralized approach for the delivery of services statewide, and, as Kratz outlined in his paper, most matters were cleared and handled in the central office with little autonomy found in district offices.

The Federal Security Agency was established in July, 1939, and all education, welfare, and health organizations were transferred to this new department. The Office of Education moved from the Interior Department to the new agency, and vocational rehabilitation was set up as a separate division within the Office of Education. "Thus, administrative reorganization, rather than legislative change . . . ended the subordination of vocational rehabilitation to vocational education . . . It remained within the Office of Education, however, an agency concerned with different problems" (McDonald, 1944, p. 100).

The first annual report of the Federal Security Administration was published in 1941 and, while very brief, it pointed out the new strength of this division: Congress last year (1940) increased the appropriation for the states from $1,938,000 to $3,500,000. Provision was made for the extension of services to people with physical disabilities who were not eligible before–services for people with severe disabilities who were either homebound or employed in a sheltered workshop. A new policy adopted during 1940 authorized the state agencies to provide services to people with disabilities who needed them to maintain a job; earlier, services were available only to people who were unemployed at the time of application. Moreover, for the first time, a limited program for paying living expenses for people with disabilities while participating in a rehabilitation plan was made available to the state agencies (Federal Security Agency, 1941, p. 26-27). These new policies combined with the legislation passed by Congress in 1940 had a liberalizing effect of vocational rehabilitation programs in the states.

World War II affected the vocational rehabilitation agency in many ways, as it influenced all activities in the nation and the world. The consequences of this war, for rehabilitation, however, were different from the effects that the war had on other peacetime programs supported by the government; federal legislation passed by Congress at the height of World War II resulted in the greatest period of expansion in the twenty-year history of vocational rehabilitation.

The 1941-1942 and 1942-1943 annual reports published by the Federal Security Agency provide information which indicates the expansion of services: "The number of people rehabilitated during the fiscal year 1942 showed a 48 percent increase over the preceding year and an 81 percent increase over the preceding year and an 81 percent increase over 1939-1940. . . ." (Federal Security Agency, 1941, p. 27-28). "On December 22, 1942, the Federal Security Agency, acting on instructions from the President, called a meeting of the administrators of all related federal agencies for a program for the rehabilitation of the war disabled [*sic*]. Recognizing that this problem would intertwine with that of supplying disabled [*sic*] civilian workers to war industries, steps were taken to plan a combined program for the rehabilitation of disabled [*sic*] civilians for employment in war industries and essential civilian industries both now and after the war" (Federal Security Agency, 1942, p. 28). In this same report, the agency announced that a new and completely separate administration known as the Office of Vocational Rehabilitation was established for the program on July 6, 1943 (Federal Security Agency, 1942, p. 28).

These events in the early years of the war, led to the development of a new federal act for vocational rehabilitation in 1943. Known as Public Law 113 (Seventy-eighth Congress, 1943, p. 374-376), this law was to have the greatest impact on the growth of the program since the original act was passed by Congress in 1920.

> It was a time when rehabilitation workers and their disabled [*sic*] clients were being given the opportunity to demonstrate to a broad and receptive audience

> that disability need not be an employment and productive handicap. . . . The tragedy of the war and the new approaches to personnel practices required by it (the need to seek out all workers who could be productive, e.g., "Rosie the Riveter") was advancing the cause of vocational rehabilitation far faster than would have been possible under conditions of peace and labor surpluses. (Obermann, 1965, p. 289)

During the war, the agency's services were in demand by industry and business because of the serious shortage of workers. Governmental agencies began to increase referrals to vocational rehabilitation by substantial numbers. The Selective Service Agency referred people who were rejected for the armed services because of disability, and the Employment Security Commission and the War Manpower [*sic*] Office referred people who were needed as productive workers despite their disabilities.

The major changes in the Barden-Lafollette Act of 1943 were:

> 1. all administration, guidance and placement costs, including salaries for professional and clerical staff, were paid by the federal government. This led to a rapid expansion of staff in the state program. (Services to clients remained on a fifty-fifty matching ratio.)
> 2. the use of federal funds for physical restoration services including hospitalization, surgery and therapeutic treatment.
> 3. maintenance for living expenses, occupational tools and equipment was authorized.
> 4. the mentally handicapped [*sic*] were included so that mentally retarded and mentally ill people for the first time were eligible for vocational rehabilitation services. (Pattison, 1957, p. 849)

The objectives of this new legislation were clear: "During the year (1943-1944), the two primary objectives defined by the Federal Security Agency on establishing the Office of Vocational Rehabilitation have been foremost: first, to channel disabled [*sic*] manpower [*sic*] into war production and essential business as rapidly as possible and, second, to provide a comprehensive service to enable the disabled [*sic*] to prepare for and secure employment in peacetime pursuits" (Federal Security Agency, 1945, p. 154). For the first time, the state vocational rehabilitation programs were given the opportunity to develop a comprehensive service program for civilians with disabilities.

It was during this period in the middle and late forties that a more sophisticated view of rehabilitation counseling emerged. For the first time in its publications, the Office of Vocational Rehabilitation in Washington provided a clear statement on the professional role of the counselor in the rehabilitation process and reported that an emphasis was placed on the training of staff beyond regional and national conferences. In the 1944-1945 Annual

Report of the Federal Security Agency, one section of the rehabilitation report showed the federal agency's growing concern for a trained professional staff:

> Counseling or advisement is an essential service extended throughout the rehabilitation process to all disabled [*sic*] clients. Furthermore, counseling is the one service extended to disabled [*sic*] people directly by the state rehabilitation agencies. As such, counseling becomes the very core of the rehabilitation process around which all other services revolve.... Because of the value of this service to disabled [*sic*] persons, effort has been directed toward improving the quality of this service through orientation institutes, preparation of staff development materials for use by the States and in-service training by State agencies; major emphasis was devoted to improving the quality of counseling (Federal Security Agency, 1945, p. 154).

In the states, opportunities were provided for orientation and in-service training through short-term institutes and workshops developed through the extension division of the colleges and universities. These training programs were provided for experienced staff members as well as for the new rehabilitation counselors.

In August 1945, Congress passed a joint resolution which established the President's Committee of Employment of the Handicapped (now the President's Committee on the Employment of Persons with Disabilities) and designated the first week of October as National Employ the Physically Handicapped Week (Seventy-ninth Congress, 1945, p. 530). Most of the states followed this action by establishing governors' committees on employment of persons with disabilities. The promotional materials emphasized the ability that people with disabilities have, rather than the disability, and these materials were distributed to employers and personnel managers throughout the nation.

The Development and Impact of Public Law 565

In the federal program of vocational rehabilitation in the early fifties, events were taking place which would lead to the enactment of the most significant legislation since the amendments of 1943. Miss Mary E. Switzer, a long-time government administrator in related programs, was named Director of the Office of Vocational Rehabilitation in the Federal Security Agency in 1951. In 1953, President Eisenhower appointed Mrs. Overta Culp Hobby as Secretary of the newly organized Department of Health, Education and Welfare, and Nelson Rockefeller as Undersecretary (Morrison, 1965, p. 1082). Eisenhower's philosophy of "dynamic conservation" (Morrison, 1965,

p. 1084) fitted in well with the vocational rehabilitation concept of helping people with disabilities help themselves to a productive life, thus bringing about economic benefits to the nation. Mary Switzer presented to Mrs. Hobby and Mr. Rockefeller a greatly enlarged program in vocational rehabilitation which had the potential of performing a humanitarian service for the welfare of citizens with disabilities and, at the same time, providing an opportunity for the government to "do something about what was considered by the administration as an increasing dependence of citizens on the welfare state" (Obermann, 1965, p. 311-312). Mrs. Hobby was impressed with possibilities presented by Miss Switzer; and Nelson Rockefeller was able to recommend this program to Mrs. Hobby as he had worked with Miss Switzer on committees previously and was a strong supporter of the vocational rehabilitation goals and objectives. When the Health, Education and Welfare proposals were presented to the President and the Cabinet in 1953, they were approved and plans were made to ask Congress for the greatest expansion of rehabilitation services in its history (Obermann, 1965).

Public Law 565, cited as the "Vocational Rehabilitation Amendments of 1954," became law on August 3, 1954 (Eighty-third Congress, 1954, p. 652). The purpose of this new act was stated in the Department of Health, Education and Welfare Annual Report of 1955:

> The law's avowed aim is to assist "the states in rehabilitating physically (and mentally) handicapped [*sic*] individuals, so that they may prepare for and engage in remunerative employment . . . thereby increasing not only their social and economic well being but also the productive capacity of the nation. . . . (U.S. Dept. of Health, Education & Welfare, 1955, p. 182).

Public Law 565 authorized $30 million for federal grants-in-aid for 1955; the use of federal funds for the training of doctors, nurses, rehabilitation counselors, physical therapists, occupational therapists, social workers, and other specialists to meet the personnel needs of the expanded rehabilitation program; extension and improvement grants and special project grants for research and demonstration (U.S. Dept. of Health, Education & Welfare, 1955, 182).

In addition to the greatly increased federal funds authorized for services to people with disabilities, this 1954 act established the foundation for the development of various rehabilitation facilities. The emphasis placed on in-service training of staff as well as the new graduate degrees available in rehabilitation counseling also helped the agency in its future growth and development. "In 1954, no plan for expanding rehabilitation services was realistic unless it took into account the serious shortages of professional personnel required to render these services. . . . Public Law 565 recognized this need and authorized a training program to provide funds for short-term specialized courses and long-term degree training" (McGowan & Porter, 1967, p. 31).

A stronger financial structure allowed for federal funding for case services and administration to be determined by a formula which gave consideration to the state's per capital income and population. This new formula eliminated the previous funding in full by the federal government for salaries and administrative costs; however, the new formula for allotment of federal funds to states helped the poorer states, particularly those in the Southeast. No major changes were made in the policies regarding "disability" and "handicapping condition" which might have extended services to new groups. The state agency was allowed for the first time to use its funds in expanding or remodeling buildings to make them suitable for the rehabilitation of persons with severe disabilities; for example, rehabilitation centers and sheltered workshops (Obermann, 1965, p. 316).

One organizational requirement in the new act was significant. The 1954 act permitted, for the first time, for state agencies to move from vocational education boards to other administrative units or to set up an independent agency of vocational rehabilitation. If they were to continue under the state boards for vocational education, however, the state directors of vocational rehabilitation were to have direct access to these boards (Obermann, 1965, p. 317).

An analysis of the 1956-1957 fiscal year for one state-federal program provided information which was characteristic of this period. Seventy-one and seven-tenths percent of the 2,930 people rehabilitated that year received surgery and/or treatment; 13 percent received training; 62 percent received hospitalization; 26.6 percent, artificial appliances; 12.9 percent received maintenance and 3.5 percent received tools and equipment (N.C. Dept. of Public Instruction, 1953). The positive effects of this greater emphasis on medical services during these years are obvious. Thousands of citizens were able to receive free medical care and attention from doctors, hospitals, and facilities meeting exceptionally high professional standards. Thus, these thousands of individuals were able to begin or return to employment, thus maintaining their independence. Arrangements were made for these services by a more experienced staff who were being trained in counseling and psychological techniques. The negative effects are also clear. Rehabilitation counselors became, in this period, coordinators who provided less and less vocational counseling and guidance services. These counseling skills were not entirely forsaken by the staff, but the emphasis placed on providing medical services to large numbers of people meant that people with disabilities who were in need of counseling services and job placement were many times referred to other agencies and professional individuals, and, as a result, persons with severe physical disabilities and people with mental disabilities were quite often excluded from services. It is possible that the tempo of the times combined with the lack of sufficient funds and training staff justified the shift to a service of coordination for those people with disabilities who could have their disabilities removed or minimized and return to productive work. Medical expenses became increasingly high and it was difficult to provide one person with a severe disability with a rehabilitation program when the same amount of funds would allow ten to twenty other people with lesser disabilities (who were also dependent) to become productive citizens. Whatever the opinion on the justification of this course of action, one significant result was the establishment of a coordinator's role for rehabilitation counselors generally. Perhaps the greatest problem for the emerging profession of rehabilitation counseling and for clients with more severe disabilities was the possibility of individual counselors losing a "counselor's attitude" as stated by McGowan in his book *An Introduction to the Vocational Rehabilitation Process*:

> The danger of holding to the Coordinator model is that the rehabilitation counselor could lose his [*sic*] perception of the client as a unique individual. That is, there seems to be a danger that the Coordinator would become too product oriented and begin to mechanically provide services without considering the personality dynamics involved in a client's problems. He [*sic*] then would be providing the services a client was entitled to by law without consideration of the client's individuality or needs. . . . Before the rehabilitation counselor can recognize the needs of his [*sic*] clients and adequately "coordinate" the indicated services, he [*sic*] needs to have all the skills associated with a professional counselor. (McGowan & Porter, 1967, p. 147)

The role of the rehabilitation counselor that emerges from this early history of the rehabilitation enterprise is first as a worker who is constrained by the inability to provide physical restoration services and one who must "counsel" and "guide" clients to a vocational goal in spite of their physical disabilities to that of a worker whose function is to coordinate medical services. Consequently, the professional education and training of this worker beginning in 1954 was at issue; that is, is the rehabilitation counselor to be a "counselor" or a "coordinator"? This issue, while not so pointed any longer, is a topic of importance that continues to occupy our attention.

REFERENCES

Blauch, L. E. (1938). *Vocational rehabilitation of the physically disabled.* The Advisory Committee on Education, Staff Study No.9. Washington, D.C.:Government Printing.

Eighty-third Congress. (1954). United States Statutes at Large, *68.*

Federal Board for Vocational Education. (1920). *Industrial revolution: A statement of policies to be observed in the administration of the Industrial Rehabilitation Act.* (Bulletin No. 57, Industrial Rehabilitation Series No. 1). Washington, D.C.: U.S. Government Printing.

Federal Board for Vocational Education. (1921). *Industrial Rehabilitation: General Administration and Case Proceedings.* (Bulletin No. 64. Industrial Rehabilitation Series No. 2). Washington, D.C.: U.S. Government Printing.

Federal Board for Vocational Education. (1924). *Proceedings of the National Conference on Vocational Rehabilitation of civilian disabled persons.* (Bulletin No. 8). Washington, D.C.: U.S. Government Printing.

Federal Board for Vocational Education. (1928). *A Statistical analysis of 6,391 disabled persons.* (Bulletin No. 132. Vocational Rehabilitation Series No. 17). Washington, D.C.: U.S. Government Printing.

Federal Board for Vocational Education. (1928). *Proceedings of the Fifth National Conference on Vocational Rehabilitation of Disabled Persons.* (Bulletin No. 136, Vocational Rehabilitation Series No. 18). Washington, D.C.: U.S. Government Printing.

Federal Security Agency. (1941). *First Annual Report.* Washington, D.C.: U.S. Government Printing.

Federal Security Agency. (1942-1943). *Annual Report.* Washington, D.C.: U.S. Government Printing.

Federal Security Agency. (1944-1945). *Annual Report.* Washington, D.C.: U.S. Government Printing.

Kessler, H. H. (1947). *Rehabilitation of the physically handicapped.* New York: Columbia University.

MacDonald, M. E. (1944). *Federal grants for vocational rehabilitation.* Chicago: University of Chicago.

McGowan, J. F., & Porter, T. L. (1967). *An introduction to the vocational rehabilitation process.* Washington, D.C.: Rehabilitation Services Administration, U.S. Department of Health, Education & Welfare.

North Carolina Division of Rehabilitation. (1953). *Reach 1*, 1-2.

Obermann, C. E. (1965). *A history of vocational rehabilitation in America.* Minneapolis, MN: T. S. Denison.

Pattison, H. A. (1957). *The handicapped and their rehabilitation.* Springfield, IL: Charles C Thomas.

Seventy-ninth Congress. (1945). *United States Statutes at Large, 59.*

Sixty-fifth Congress. (1918). *United States Statutes at Large, 40.*

Sixty-fourth Congress. (1916). *United States Statutes at Large, 39.*

Stanton, H. L. (1927). *The rehabilitation of disabled civilians in North Carolina.* Unpublished master's thesis, North Carolina State College of Agriculture and Engineering.

Thompson, R. C. (1951). Hotel Continental. *Journal of Rehabilitation, 18* (5), 15.

U. S. Department of Health, Education & Welfare (1954-55). *Annual Report.* Washington, D.C.: Office of Vocational Rehabilitation.

United States Department of Interior (1934). *Manual for caseworkers* (Bulletin No. 175, Vocational Rehabilitation Series, No. 23). Washington, D.C.: U.S. Government Printing.

Whitten, E. B. (1966). The challenge of PL 89-333. *Journal of Rehabilitation, 32* (1), 2.

Chapter 4

THE DEVELOPMENT OF THE REHABILITATION ENTERPRISE IN AMERICA: A RECENT HISTORY OF THE REHABILITATION MOVEMENT

E. DAVIS MARTIN, JR. AND GERALD L. GANDY

A remarkable period of growth in the vocational rehabilitation movement in the 1960s was due to increased state support, joint program agreements for persons with mental disabilities, and several other jointly administered units; for example, public school education programs and private and public rehabilitation facilities. Three key events which occurred in three of these years–1965, 1967 and 1968–influenced the course and the great potential of this extraordinary era of expansion.

First, the Vocational Rehabilitation Amendments of 1965 were passed unanimously by Congress (Eighty-ninth Congress, 1965, pp. 1282-1294). Obermann stated that these new expansive amendments "could almost have been written by an enthusiastic professional in the state-federal vocational rehabilitation program" (Obermann, 1965, p. 323). The new amendments provided for a substantial increase in federal spending and also provided a broader base for extending services to additional people with disabilities. An extended plan for evaluation was authorized in the new act, which, in effect, permitted the agency to waive the third item of eligibility in effect at that time: a reasonable expectation that vocational rehabilitation services may render the individual fit to engage in a gainful occupation. This 1965 act also provided special grants for construction and operation of sheltered workshops and other rehabilitation facilities to the state agencies or to private agencies which held joint program agreements with the official agency for vocational rehabilitation (National Rehabilitation Association, 1968, p. 2; Whitten, 1966).

The second of these events occurred in 1967 when the Department of Health, Education and Welfare reorganized and the Social and Rehabilitation Service was established to provide a rehabilitation emphasis to many of the welfare and health programs in the department (Gardner, 1968). John W. Gardner, who was Secretary of Health, Education and Welfare, asked Mary Switzer, Commissioner of Vocational Rehabilitation, to head up this new administrative unit.

> To better coordinate the programs, Health, Education and Welfare Secretary John Gardner has gathered five major welfare agencies under one office, named the Social and Rehabilitation Service (SRS). To Washington's surprise, Gardner went over the heads of HEW's brightest young men and selected as the first boss of SRS . . . 67-year-old . . . Mary Elizabeth Switzer [who] has spent forty-six years in government, the last seventeen as the highly successful head of the Vocational Rehabilitation Administration, which aids the handicapped [*sic*]. (Time Magazine, 1967, p. 14)

The Rehabilitation Services Administration, Children's Bureau, Administration on Aging, Medical Services Administration (Medicaid), and the Public Welfare Assistance Payments Administration were consolidated in the new SRS (Gardner, 1968). The reorganization, which favored a rehabilitation concept, provided greater visibility and a national recognition for the total state-federal program, and, occurring just two years after the 1965 federal legislation, it strengthened the federal base for future growth at the state level.

The third major event of this period occurred when Congress passed the 1968 Vocational Rehabilitation Amendments. Among the important changes and additions contained in this act were:

1. substantial increase in appropriations with the basic programs moving from a 75-25 matching ratio to a new formula for all states (80% federal-20% state, effective 1969);
2. approval for Vocational Rehabilitation to expend funds in new construction of rehabilitation facilities;
3. the definition of rehabilitation services was completely rewritten to include follow-up services in maintaining an individual in employment services to families when services can contribute substantially to the rehabilitation of a group of individuals; and
4. the state was permitted to amend the state plan to enable it to share funding and administration responsibility with another state agency to carry out a joint project (a policy already established in many states, informally).

In addition, the agency was recognized as having responsibility for assisting with the administration's efforts to combat poverty. For this specific purpose, Section 15 was added to the amendments. This authorized 90 percent of the costs for the establishment of vocational evaluation and work adjustment centers for "disadvantaged" individuals who were defined "to include the physically and mentally handicapped [*sic*] and other individuals disadvantaged by reason of age, youth, low educational attainments, ethnic or other factors such as prison and delinquency records" (National Rehabilitation Association, 1968, p. 3).

One other significant legislative event of this decade that merits attention was the passage of PL 90-480, The Architectural Barriers Act of 1968. This legislative event was the first effort to assure accessibility to public buildings for Americans with disabilities although its effectiveness would not be tested until the passage of the 1973 Rehabilitation Act and the subsequent creation of the Architectural and Transportation Barriers Compliance Board. Rubin and Roessler (1995) noted that even with the passage of PL 96-541 in 1976 'an amendment to the 1968 Architectural Barriers Act' which required federal agencies to develop accessibility standards 'moving from a posture of just recommending standards' " . . . the impact of the Architectural Barriers Act of 1968 and the establishment of the ATBCB in 1973 on the removal of architectural barriers still appeared to be minimal" (p. 63).

Civil Rights for Persons with Disabilities

The decade of the 1970s witnessed the emergence of several legislative events inspired by the growing consumer movement of persons with disabilities, parents and family members of persons with disabilities, and human services professionals. An account of the personal struggle of the civil rights movement for persons with disabilities is provided in *No Pity: People with Disabilities Forging a New Civil Rights Movement* (1993) by Joseph P. Shapiro. Within this book of vignettes is a very personal and awe inspiring view of this little noticed and often ignored movement (by government officials and the news media), a portrait of the issues which have impeded the lives of persons with disabilities emerges. The accounts of persons such as Ed Roberts, Judith Heumann, Justin Dart, Robert Burgdorf, Evan Kemp, Patrisha Wright, and others serve to illustrate the indomitable spirit of the human being. The optimism of the human being, particularly in a democratic society, serves to benefit all persons regardless of disability or attribute. As the decade of the 1970s begins, John Gardner at the close of the decade of the 1960s made the following observation with his usual insight:

> The capacity of our people to believe stubbornly and irrepressibly that this is a world worth saving and that intelligence and energy and good will might save it, is one of the most endearing and bracing of American traits. No sensible person relishes the immature aspects of our optimism, but if we lose that optimism, we will surely be less spirited people, a less magnanimous people and an immeasurably less venturesome people. Zest and generosity will disap-

pear from our national style. Our impact may well disappear along with them. (Gardner, 1969, p. 40)

The decade of the 1970s produced three of the most significant legislative accomplishments of the twentieth century: The Developmental Disabilities Services and Facilities Construction Act (PL 91-517), The Rehabilitation Act of 1973 (PL 93-112), and The Education for All Handicapped Children Act (PL 94-142). Each of these legislative events and subsequent amendments continuing to the present represented a paradigm shift that signaled an increased voice and influence for persons with disabilities regarding vocational, educational, and independent living choices.

With the passage of PL 91-517, the Developmental Disabilities Services and Construction Act of 1970, the term *developmental disability* first came into use (Kiernan and Schalock, 1995). The term *developmental disability* was defined to include the following specific disabilities: mental retardation, epilepsy, and cerebral palsy. Onset of the developmental disability was to have occurred at birth or prior to age 18 and have imposed severe limitation in the child's or person's ability to function. The Act established a formula grant program in which the states were encouraged to develop coordinated services for persons labeled as having a developmental disability. Braddock et al. (1998) noted that the " . . . states were required to establish interagency 'councils' representing numerous state government agencies relevant to the delivery of developmental disabilities services . . . (that would develop) . . . (e)very three years . . . formal state plans to set goals and improve the delivery of services" (p. 7).

In 1975, amendments to the Developmental Disabilities Services and Construction Act retitled the act as the Developmental Disabilities Assistance and Bill of Rights Act (PL 94-103). Categorical groupings of disabilities were maintained and the disabilities of autism and dyslexia (with some qualifications) were added. The 1975 amendments also specified essential services that should be available as basic rights to persons defined as having a developmental disability. Those services specified, among others, were residential services, employment services, treatment, transportation, and leisure services. These services were basic rights. These amendments were greatly influenced by " . . . a series of class-action law suits in which the courts ruled that the mentally retarded [*sic*] in institutions had constitutional rights to treatment, services, and habilitation that 'maximize the developmental potential of the person and are provided in the setting that is least restrictive of the person's personal liberty'" (Berkowitz, 1987, p. 207). Most notable of these class-action suits were Wyatt v. Stickney (344 F. Supp. 378, M.D., Alabama, 1972) and New York State ARC v. Rockefeller (357 F. Supp. 752, 1973) often referred to as the Willowbrook case.

The 1978 amendments now entitled as the Rehabilitation, Comprehensive Services, and Developmental Disabilities Act (PL 95-602) broadened the definition of developmental disability from the existing categorical basis to a functional basis, that is, a definition which no longer specifically denoted a particular mental or physical condition (e.g., mental retardation, epilepsy, etc.) but as a chronic and lifelong mental or physical condition that imposed substantial functional limitations in the performance of major life activities. Of the seven characterized major life activities, at least three must present substantial limitations to the person:

1. Self-care
2. Receptive and Expressive Language
3. Learning
4. Mobility
5. Self-Direction
6. Capacity for Independent Living
7. Economic Self-sufficiency

Braddock et al. (1998, p. 7), moreover, reported that the 1978 amendments established the Protection and Advocacy Program " . . . thus completing the triad of Developmental Disabilities Act funded organizations: university affiliated programs (UAPs), state planning councils, and advocacy agencies."

The 1973 Rehabilitation Act and Amendments

The passage of the 1973 Rehabilitation Act (PL 93-112) was, perhaps, one of the most significant events of the twentieth century, in particular, the effect and impact that Section 504 would have upon American society and for the rights of persons with disabilities. The major focus of the 1973 Rehabilitation Act dealt with equality of opportunity through provisions relating to emphasis on persons with severe disabilities, consumer involvement, creation of emphasis on persons with severe disabilities, creation of the now named National Institute on Disability and Rehabilitation Research (NIDRR), emphasis on program evaluation, and the advancement of the civil rights of persons with disabilities. The 1973 Rehabilitation Act represented a mandate to serve persons with severe disabilities.

Emphasis on Persons with Severe Disabilities

While the emphasis was to serve persons with severe disabilities, the creation of independent living rehabilitation options in the 1973 Rehabilitation Act were omitted, in large part, because President Nixon had vetoed two previous rehabilitation bills in 1972 that contained a provision related to independent living (Rubin and Roessler, 1995). The Nixon Administration, as noted by Rubin and Roessler (1995, p. 46), " . . . did, however, agree to a compromise–a Comprehensive Needs Study (CNS; Section 130 of the Act) to determine the rehabilitation needs of individuals who 'cannot reasonably be expected to be rehabilitated for employment but for whom a program of rehabilitation would improve their ability to live independently or function normally within their family and community'." It would not be until the 1978 amendments that the independent living rehabilitation program would be authorized.

Title VII of the 1978 amendments contained three parts which provided the basis for independent living rehabilitation options:

- Part A–authorized comprehensive services that would enhance the person's ability to function in employment or the home.
- Part B–authorized the state agency to make grants for the establishment of centers for independent living which would provide a wide range of services inclusive of peer counseling, independent living skills, assistance with housing and transportation, and personal assistance services.
- Part C–authorized independent living services to older blind persons.

Dejong stated that for the first time in fifty-three years, the professional rehabilitation leaders were joined in these efforts by an increasingly visible and effective leadership from people with disabilities. These people with severe disabilities were representing a growing and vigorous constituency: a most assertive and, at times, a more militant group who were insistent on change (Dejong, 1979).

Consumer Involvement

The essence of the rehabilitation process is the relationship between the counselor and the client or consumer. The 1973 Rehabilitation Act stressed the nature of this relationship as one of joint involvement and responsibility that should pervade the rehabilitation process from beginning to closure. Throughout the process, the consumer or client was to be informed of decisions that may have an impact (which may be perceived by the client as adverse) and given an opportunity to appeal those decisions. Eligibility, for example, was one area that may be subject to disagreement. Initially, no formal or organized programs were available to assist clients who questioned the decisions of counselors or supervisors. Client Assistance Projects were first authorized in the 1978 amendments and, ultimately, Client Assistance Projects would be required in each state in order to assure due process (the 1984 amendments).

The Individual Written Rehabilitation Program (IWRP) represented a real opportunity for the client and counselor to mutually plan a sequence of services that would enable the client to enter into employment. The basic nature of such a planning process had at its core the mutual involvement and joint formulation of a program that would have the capability to change the client's (and his or her family's) life. Such a momentous event requires nothing less than mutual respect and involvement in decision making.

Subsequent amendments to the 1973 Rehabilitation Act in 1978 and 1984 created the National Council on the Handicapped in 1978 and later renamed the National Council on Disability in 1984. This 15 person council appointed by the President of the United States and confirmed by the United States Senate is an independent federal agency whose overall purpose is " . . . to promote the policies, programs, practices, and procedures that guarantee equal opportunity for all individuals with disabilities, regardless of the nature of the severity of the disability; and to empower individuals with disabilities to achieve economic self-sufficiency, independent living, and inclusion and integration into all aspects of society" (National Council on Disability, 1996, p. 187). This Council represents, perhaps, the zenith in consumer involvement from a policy perspective.

Creation of the National Institute on Disability and Rehabilitation Research

The 1973 Rehabilitation Act provided for the continued funding of innovation and expansion grants, rehabilitation research and training centers, and other types of demonstration grants; however, the 1978 amendments established the, then named, National Institute of Handicapped Research (Rubin and Roessler, 1995). Rubin and Roessler (1995, p. 51) noted that the National Institute of Handicapped Research " . . . was established to direct the research thrust in rehabilitation, in particular, that of the Rehabilitation Research and Training Centers" . . . and to:

> (a) disseminate information on ways to increase the quality of life of individuals with disabilities;
> (b) educate the public about ways of providing for the rehabilitation of individuals with disabilities;
> (c) conduct conferences concerning research and engineering advances in rehabilitation; and
> (d) produce and disseminate statistical reports and studies on the employment, health, and income of individuals with disabilities. (pp. 51-52)

Emphasis on Program Evaluation

Meaningful consumer involvement in the rehabilitation process also required that the outcomes of that process be assessed as well. Program evaluation to be undertaken by state agencies, as noted by Rubin and Roessler (1995), " . . . meant that state rehabilitation agencies would be held accountable for providing information on

(a) the percentage of the existing target population being served,
(b) the timeliness and adequacy of their services,
(c) the suitability of the employment in which clients are placed and the sustention of that employment, and
(d) client satisfaction with rehabilitation services." (p. 51)

Needs assessments occurring on a three year cycle (CFR 361.29) and client/consumer satisfaction surveys are now a defined component of the state rehabilitation agency.

Advancement of the Civil Rights of Persons with Disabilities

Sections 501, 502, 503, and 504 of Title V of the 1973 Rehabilitation Act addressed the following areas of concern respectively: nondiscriminatory federal hiring, accessability (creation of the Architectural and Transportation Barriers Compliance Board), affirmative action and prohibition of discrimination against persons with disabilities in terms of programmatic and physical accessability in schools, institutions of higher education, hospitals, and other institutions which receive federal financial assistance.

Increased awareness of persons with disabilities and of the environmental and attitudinal barriers encountered by persons with disabilities is generally credited as a major impetus for the passage of the 1973 Rehabilitation Act and the subsequent 1978 amendments. These legislative events signaled a change in public policy patterned largely after the Civil Rights Act. No longer were employers or potential employers asked on the basis of moral grounds to hire persons with a disability but to take affirmative action in hiring and as well as assuming a posture of non discrimination. Admission to schools and institutions of higher education, as well, was addressed by Section 504 of Title V. This section noted:

> No otherwise qualified handicapped [*sic*] individual in the United States, as defined in section 7 (7), shall, solely by reason of his [*sic*] handicap, be excluded from the participation in, be denied the benefits of or be subjected to discrimination under any program or activity receiving Federal financial assis-

tance or under any program or activity conducted by any Executive agency or by the United States Postal Service.

Section 504 was originally envisioned as an antidiscrimination provision that would have more impact as a symbolic statement and not necessarily as a mandate (Percy, 1989). The origins of 504, as noted by Percy (1989, pp. 225-226) can be:

> . . . traced to Senator Hubert Humphrey and Representative Charles Vanik, who introduced bills in Congress to amend the Civil Rights Act to include protections for persons with disabilities. While this strategy produced little result, it set the groundwork for Section 504 to be included, quietly and without fanfare, in the Rehabilitation Act as the legislation was being marked up by staff members from the Senate Committee on Labor and Public Welfare and the House Committee on Education and Labor.

Senator Humphrey's advocacy for what ultimately became Section 504 stemmed, in part, from his experiences as a grandparent of a child with a disability.

Another powerful reason for inclusion of Section 504 in the 1973 Rehabilitation Act, as noted by Scotch (1984) and reported in Percy (1989, p. 53) was:

> Staff members were concerned that, when disabled [*sic*] individuals completed their training in the VR [vocational rehabilitation] system and were ready to enter the workplace, many employers appeared reluctant to hire them. Staff members felt the final goal of the VR program, getting disabled [*sic*] people into the mainstream of society, was being blocked by negative attitudes and discrimination on the part of employers and others.

The definition of disability and by extension who is protected by Section 504 was changed by the 1974 amendments to be much broader and inclusive than the original definition which was employment based (Percy, 1989). Broadening the definition allowed for inclusion of children with disabilities, older persons with disabilities, and persons with severe disabilities. A person with a disability according to this definition was defined as a person who:

> 1) has a physical or mental impairment that substantially limits one or more of such a person's major life activities;
> 2) has a record of such impairment;
> 3) or is regarded as having such an impairment.

One other concept that originated from Section 504 (and was applicable to Section 503 as well) was that of reasonable accommodation. Reasonable accommodation was defined ". . . with reference to examples that included making employee facilities readily accessible to and usable(,) . . . job restructuring, modifications in work schedules, changes in equipment, and provision of readers and interpreters. A limitation on mandated accommodations was included through the modifier "reasonable"" (Percy, 1989, p. 76). An employer did not have to make an accommodation if it was deemed to create an "undue economic hardship." Little guidance was provided in the interpretation of what was reasonable or unreasonable. Because of this lack of specificity and the nature of individualized accommodations, compliance became a case by case situation that sometimes was confusing and controversial. Perhaps most notable was *Davis v. Southeastern Community College* (442 U.S. 397, 1979) in which the Supreme Court reversed an earlier favorable decision by the 4th U. S. Circuit Court of Appeals. *Davis* was the first real test of Section 504. Davis, a licensed practical nurse, had applied for admission to the college's nursing program and had requested accommodations on the basis of her hearing impairment. The college denied her admission on the basis of safety (that Davis would not be able to lipread in clinical situations where masks are worn) and that to admit her would force the college to lower its standards. The Supreme Court found in favor of Southeastern Community College noting that this was a case about affirmative action, not an antidiscrimination case. Consequently, the issue of equality of opportunity and reasonable accommodation was sidestepped. Many regarded this decision as a continuing pattern of bias and prejudice against people with disabilities. In any event, it noted that the effectiveness and powerfulness of Section 504 may not be what was envisioned, particularly by persons with disabilities and other advocates.

Prior to the 1978 amendments, persons who pursued a legal course of action were not allowed to collect attorney's fees in litigation in which they prevailed. Section 505 was added to the 1978 amendments which corrected this situation as well as allowing for the same rights, procedures, and remedies as outlined in Title VII of the Civil Rights Act of 1964 (Percy, 1989).

Toward the end of the decade of the 1980s, the National Council on Disability observed that the current status of existing nondiscrimination laws, such as Section 504, were (Percy, 1989, p.224):

> . . . extremely important and have engendered much progress. (But) (i)n an overall context, however, our Nation's laws provide inadequate protection from discrimination for people with disabilities. Current statutes are not comparable in their scope of protection against discrimination afforded racial, ethnic, and religious minorities and women under civil rights laws.

As a result of this finding, the National Council on Disability championed the development and passage of new legislation in 1990, the Americans with Disabilities Act (ADA). The ADA, it was thought, would bring together and strengthen nondiscrimination policies for all persons with disabilities.

Individuals with Disabilities Education Act (IDEA)

Prior to the passage of PL 94-142, The Education for All Handicapped Children Act of 1975, children with disabilities–particularly those with significant disabilities–had few programs that were designed to accommodate instructional needs that differed from the mainstream. Parents and parent based groups, the National Association of Retarded Children, and the Council for Exceptional Children lobbied the federal government for programs to educate children with disabilities. A major, although small, gain was realized through this advocacy with the establishment of the Bureau for Education of the Handicapped within the Office of Education which took as its focus the development of training programs for special education teachers and initiated research programs on how to effectively teach children with disabilities (Percy, 1989). It would, however, ultimately be the courts to conclude that the state educational systems in America had failed to provide an education for children with disabilities (Tucker and Goldstein, 1992).

Two court cases, in particular, provided the foundation for the creation of PL 94-142: *Pennsylvania Association for Retarded Citizens v. Commonwealth of Pennsylvania* (343 F. Supp. 279, 1972) and *Mills v. Board of Education of the District of Columbia* (348 F. Supp. 866, 1972). In the PARC case, children who were labeled as mentally retarded ". . . sued the state claiming that they were denied the right to a public education . . . (on the basis of) . . . three claims: (1) a violation of due process because there was no notice or hearing provided before retarded [*sic*] children were excluded from public school or their educational assignments were changed; (2) a violation of equal protection due to the lack of a rational basis for assuming that mentally retarded [*sic*] children were uneducable and untrainable; and (3) a violation of due process because it was arbitrary and capricious to deny mentally retarded [*sic*] children a right to the education guaranteed by state law" (Tucker and Goldstein, 1992, p. 2:14). The *Mills* case, similarly, centered on the denial of a publicly supported education and involved not only children labeled as mentally retarded but children with other disabilities as well. Both the *PARC* and *Mills* cases demonstrated (*PARC* through a consent agreement and *Mills* through a summary judgment) that children with disabilities were entitled to a free and suitable public education based on the constitutional rights extended by the Due Process and Equal Protection clauses of the Fourteenth Amendment (Tucker and Goldstein, 1992).

The Education for All Handicapped Children Act was passed and signed into law by President Gerald Ford in 1975 and regulations were finalized in little less than two years later. PL 94-142 mandated that each child with a disability be provided with a "free, appropriate public education" (FAPE). The principles that FAPE rest upon, as noted by Taylor and Searl (1989, p. 40), were:

> • "Zero-reject." *All* disabled [*sic*] children are entitled to a public education under Public Law 94-142. The law specifically provides for the education of children ages five through eighteen, or the ages at which typical children are educated in a state.
> • Least restrictive environment. Public Law 94-142 endorses the principle of "least restrictive environment" as outlined in prior court cases. The federal regulations elaborate on the meaning of "least restrictive environment": "That to the maximum extent appropriate, handicapped [*sic*] children, including children in public or private institutions or other child care facilities, are educated with children who are not handicapped." The regulations further state that removal of a handicapped [*sic*] child from the regular educational environment occurs only when the child's handicap precludes education in regular classes with the use of supplementary services.
> • Individualized education program. Each handicapped [*sic*] child must have an individualized written educational program which must be reviewed at least annually.
> • Due process procedures. Children with disabilities and their parents are guaranteed "due process" in educational classification and placement. This includes notification prior to changes in a child's classification or placement and procedures whereby educational decisions can be challenged through an impartial hearing.
> • Protection in evaluation. The law and regulations contain provisions to ensure that educational tests and procedures used to evaluate children are free of racial and cultural bias and that educators do not rely on single procedure to determine the appropriate educational program for the child.

The concept of a "free appropriate public education" was welcomed, in particular, by parents of children with disabilities–who could deny the inherent worth and value of the above noted principles upon which this concept was formed? Free appropriate public education from a parental perspective means the best educational situation for any child to succeed. However, this was not exactly the meaning of free appropriate education as ultimately noted by the Supreme Court. Amy Rowley, a young girl who had minimal hearing, was an excellent speech reader. She was in the first grade and had been provided with a hearing aid and was receiving speech therapy and had a tutor for the deaf. Academically, Amy was doing well in her studies (upper half of her class) and passing from grade to grade. However, Amy's parents, who were deaf, felt that she was missing too much classroom instruction and requested that the school provide Amy with a sign language interpreter. The school refused and an administrative hearing officer and the state upheld the school's decision. The Rowley's filed suit in the federal courts and won at the district court level which was appealed by the school board. The Rowley's again won at the Court of Appeals for the Second Circuit and the school board appealed to the Supreme Court. The Supreme Court in its decision in *Board of Education of the Henrick Hudson Central School District v. Rowley* (458 U.S. 176, 102 S. Ct. 3034, 1982) found for the school board. The Supreme Court concluded that since Amy had access to and was benefitting from her educational program, this met the intent of free appropriate public education. In other words, it did not matter that she may achieve more with the provision of a sign language interpreter. Tucker and Goldstein (1992, pp. 16-5 and 6) noted that:

> Thus the Supreme Court in *Rowley* set forth a two prong test, one procedural and one somewhat substantive, for courts to apply in determining whether children with disabilities have been provided a FAPE. The Court indicated that the individual needs of the child, as determined by an IEP, are the appropriate focus. Furthermore, the Court held that children with disabilities do not have an enforceable right to achieve their maximum potential, but rather are entitled only to receive some educational benefit, the sufficiency of which is to be left to a case by case analysis.

Amendments in 1986 to the Education for All Handicapped Act (PL 99-457) authorized early intervention programs for preschool-age children with disabilities. In 1990, the Act was amended and retitled the Individuals with Disabilities Education Act (IDEA) of 1990. In addition to changing the title of the Act, IDEA represented a shift in thinking about children/youth with disabilities. IDEA abandoned the use of the terminology "handicap," "handicapped" to describe children and youth with disabilities and adopted person first language–a much sought after change which had the potential to reduce negative attitudes or stereotypes of what, mostly, children with disabilities cannot do. Children and youth with disabilities are, however, still labeled with such negative terms as educable mentally retarded, trainable mentally retarded, emotionally disturbed, severely and profoundly handicapped or disabled, among others (note discussion on language usage in Chapter 1). IDEA also required the development of an individual transition plan (ITP) for each student with a disability that would facilitate transition from school to postschool activities (e.g., work, training, further schooling, independent living, and so forth). Rehabilitation professionals have a significant role to play in this transition. Hayes, Bain, and Batshaw (1997) have noted that the provisions of the IEP should require:

1) the process to be outcome oriented,
2) students to be meaningfully involved in the process,
3) students' needs to be projected beyond one year,
4) schools to work with external agencies responsible for the provision of services or funding, and
5) schools to provide extensive community-based instruction. (pp. 761-762)

Moreover, Hayes et al. (1997, p. 762) observed that not all school systems are providing these services because " . . . educators believe that these requirements go well beyond the school's responsibilities or capabilities." The potential effect or reality is that some youth will not receive transition services and may likely "fall through the cracks" and end up at home watching television while awaiting services from unknown agencies.

Other Significant Legislation Passed in the 1980s

The 1986 amendments to the 1973 Rehabilitation Act emphasized the use of rehabilitation engineering services, supported employment services for persons with severe disabilities, and mandated a gradual reduction in federal financial assistance to the state programs from the, then, 80 percent to an anticipated 75 percent matching ratio in 1993 (Rubin & Roessler, 1995).

The Technology-Related Assistance for Individuals with Disabilities Act of 1988 (PL 100 407) had as its purpose to improve access to technology devices and services for individuals with disabilities. Kurtz and Harryman (1997, p. 719) noted that the Tech Act was to " . . . support not only the purchase or lease of equipment but also a range of services to ensure success with their use . . . . (Moreover) . . . (t)hese (services) include 1) evaluation of the child's technological needs, 2) maintenance and repair of equipment, 3) training in the use of the devices, and 4) coordination of technology with other therapy services." The Tech Act encouraged the states to engage in a competitive grant process that would allow the development of a consumer responsive system of technology services that would be accessible.

The importance of assistive technology cannot be understated. Assistive technology has the capacity to lessen or reduce the effects of disability which then allows for participation in education, employment and activities of daily living, that is, participation in the work and play of American society. It is the great equalizer for persons with disabilities. Technology is available but not always financially accessible. Wallace (1994, p. 79) noted that " . . . the funding of assistive technology continues to be the area of greatest need identified through consumer surveys across the country."

Americans with Disabilities Act

In 1986, the National Council on Disability issued its report *Toward Independence* which set the stage for the development of the Americans with Disabilities Act (ADA). Frank Bowe (1992, p. 3) credits the enactment of the ADA to the efforts of Justin W. Dart, Jr., and noted that

> . . . for three years . . . Dart chaired a private sector body created by Rep. Major R. Owens (D-NY), chairman of the Select Education Subcommittee in the House. Dart's U. S. House of Representatives' Task Force on the Human Rights and Empowerment of Americans with Disabilities brought several hundred thousand adults and children with disabilities from all 50 states into the ADA 'movement.' The Task Force was an entirely voluntary effort: no one was paid nor were any expenses covered by Congress. Dart himself traveled to every one of the states, at his own expense, holding hearings to solicit the input of people with disabilities, parents, employers, educators, and local government officials.

Section 2 of PL 101-336, the Americans with Disabilities Act, contained the findings and purpose of the Act which are quite instructive:

> Sec. 12101 Findings and purposes
> (a) Findings
> The Congress finds that–
> (1) some 43,000,000 Americans have one or more physical or mental disabilities, and this number is increasing as the population as a whole is growing older;
> (2) historically, society has tended to isolate and segregate individuals with disabilities and, despite some improvements, such forms of discrimination against individuals with disabilities continue to be a serious and pervasive social problem;
> (3) discrimination against individuals with disabilities persists in such critical areas as employment, housing, public accommodations, education, transportation, communication, recreation, institutionalization, health services, voting, and access to public services;
> (4) unlike individuals who have experienced discrimination on the basis of race, color, sex, national origin, religion, or age, individuals who have experienced discrimination on the basis of disability have often had no legal recourse to redress such discrimination;
> (5) individuals with disabilities continually encounter various forms of discrimination including outright intentional exclusion, the discriminatory effects of architectural, transportation, and communication barriers, overprotective rules and policies, failure to make modifications in existing facilities and practices, exclusionary qualification standards and criteria, segregation, and relegation to lesser services, programs, activities, benefits, jobs, or other opportunities.
> (6) census data, national polls, and other studies have documented that people with disabilities, as a group, occupy an inferior status in our society, and

are severely disadvantaged socially, vocationally, economically, and educationally;
(7) individuals with disabilities are a discrete and insular minority who have been faced with restrictions and limitations, subjected to a history of purposeful unequal treatment, and relegated to a position of political powerlessness in our society, based on characteristics that are beyond the control of such individuals and resulting from stereotypic assumptions not truly indicative of the individual ability of such individuals to participate in, and contribute to, society;
(8) the Nation's proper goals regarding individuals with disabilities are to assure equality of opportunity, full participation, independent living, and economic self sufficiency for such individuals; and
(9) the continuing existence of unfair and unnecessary discrimination and prejudice denies people with disabilities the opportunity to compete on an equal basis and to pursue those opportunities for which our free society is justifiably famous, and costs the United States billions of dollars in unnecessary expenses resulting from dependency and nonproductivity.
(b) Purpose
It is the purpose of this chapter–
(1) to provide a clear and comprehensive national mandate for the elimination of discrimination against individuals with disabilities;
(2) to provide clear, strong, consistent, enforceable standards addressing discrimination against individuals with disabilities;
(3) to ensure that the Federal Government plays a central role in enforcing the standard established in this Act on behalf of individuals with disabilities; and
(4) to invoke the sweep of congressional authority, including the power to enforce the fourteenth amendment and to regulate commerce, in order to address the major areas of discrimination faced day-to-day by people with disabilities.

For Senator Tom Harkins, an early legislative leader and supporter for the passage of the Americans with Disabilities Act, the potential impact of ADA meant:

> . . . inclusion, integration, and empowerment. For business, it means more customers, increased profits and additional qualified workers. For labor, it means greater protection from arbitrary action for members. And for government, it means more taxpayers and fewer persons on welfare, social security, and other social programs. (Harkins, 1994, p. 939)

Dart (1995) has noted that the substantive requirements of the ADA were based on Section 504 of the 1973 Rehabilitation Act and that the procedural requirements were based on Title VII of the 1964 Civil Rights Act. The ADA as envisioned by Dart (National Council on Disability and its staff and consultants) and observed that Sections 501, 503, and 504 of the 1973 Rehabilitation Act were useful but did not extend to the vast private sector of the American economy (Bowe, 1992). The creation of the ADA's five Titles were developed with this perspective:

Title I Employment	Prohibits discrimination on the basis of disability with regard to job application procedures, hiring, advancement, discharge, compensation, training, and other privileges of employment.
Title II Public Services	Prohibits discrimination on the basis of disability with regard to services and programs of local and state government including accessibility of such activities and programs. Public transient systems (operated by governmental agencies) accessibility are covered by this title.
Title III Public Accommodations	Prohibits discrimination on the basis of disability with regard to accessibility of public transportation services operated by the private sector. Covers restaurants, banks, hotels, and others regarding accessibility or exclusion. Sets standards for the accessibility in existing and new buildings.
Title IV Telecommunications	Prohibits discrimination on the basis of disability with regard to persons with speech and hearing impediments. Required the establishment of 24 hour relay services.
Title V Miscellaneous	Prohibits retaliation.

The effectiveness of the ADA has been the basis for many television news reports and has been studied by the various constituents who have been affected by its provisions. Professor Blanck (1994), in a comprehensive empirical study of the impact of the ADA, investigated 1100 persons with mental retardation in Oklahoma over a period of three years (1990-1993) vis-a-vis Title I of the Act. Blanck's findings revealed modest gains in integrated employment, wages, and independent living. Senator Bob Dole, an ardent supporter of the ADA, commented that Blanck's study focused on the correct issues for assessing progress; that is, employment and economic well-being but if employment was the major goal sought, then the results were not that encouraging. Dole (1994, p. 928), speaking from a national perspective, noted "(u)nfortunately, the news isn't so good. In 1986, 33% of disabled [*sic*] Americans worked; in 1994, this figure is 31%." The 1998 Lou Harris Poll revealed that this percentage had further declined to 29 percent.

West (1994) reported in The Milbank Memorial Fund's report, *Federal Implementation of the Americans with Disabilities Act, 1991-1994*, that no federal agency had plans to survey consumers regarding changes brought about as a result of the ADA, that only minimal funding for evaluation studies to determine effectiveness had been allocated, and that neither studies nor data collection activities to determine effectiveness of ADA-related tax code provisions had been planned. Nevertheless, this report did recommend that Congress:

> 1. Retain the current statute without amendment.
> 2. Establish minimal enforcement standards, including timeliness for complaint processing and closure. Adequate resources should be allocated to EEOC, DOJ, and DOT to enable them to comply with these standards.
> 3. Appropriate funds to the Civil Rights Division of DOJ for a comprehensive ADA public awareness/education campaign. This campaign should be developed and coordinated with EEOC, DOT, FCC, Access Board, NIDRR, NCD, PCEPD, and other relevant agencies.
> 4. Designate an internal ADA coordinator for each body and provide for an independent assessment of progress. (pp. x-xi)

McMahon, who has written extensively on this topic, has noted that the mixed effectiveness of ADA when viewed from the perspective of a currently robust economic climate is particularly distressing for persons with disabilities but may be explained by three parallel themes (1998, personal communication):

> *First*, the failure to secure universal health insurance coverage has meant that many persons with disabilities will not seek employment if they must forfeit healthcare coverage for themselves and their dependents.
> *Second*, financial disincentives in the form of long term disability insurance (including SSI and SSDI) continue to raise the threshold of interest for many Americans with disabilities. With 34% of Americans with disabilities now living below the poverty level ($15,000 annual income per household), many potential workers with disabilities earn more take home dollars by remaining on income maintenance programs.
> *Finally*, increased labor force participation is related to the success of special education programs in our country, and the high school drop-out rate has increased from 9% to 20% for special education students since 1986.

In assessing the public accessibility titles of the ADA, McMahon noted that " . . . implementation has been more successful." Moreover, "(a)rchitectural and especially communication barriers are being torn down on or ahead of schedule, access to goods and services through technology is greater, complaint and litigation levels are well below predicted levels, and compliance is high because competitive American businesses are eager to tap in to the purchasing power of 54 million Americans with disabilities."

It is obvious that more success has been achieved in the area of public accessibility than employment for persons with disabilities. From a historical perspective, the overall effectiveness of the ADA has been somewhat mixed; however, only a brief moment of time has elapsed since the enactment of this most significant and compelling legislation. McMahon, as well, has noted that this " . . . is a short period of time for such an ambitious statute . . . (and) . . . in the long term ADA will change the way we live and do business in America."

1992 Amendments to the 1973 Rehabilitation Act

The 1992 amendments to the 1973 Rehabilitation Act continued the strong emphasis toward provision of services to persons with severe disabilities, even introducing a new category of "most severe disability"; a continuing emphasis on employment outcomes introducing a career perspective; increased consumer choice and control in the rehabilitation process; broadened eligibility to denote that a consumer need only to "benefit" from provision of services; and increased consumer control through the establishment of Statewide Rehabilitation Advisory Councils and Statewide Independent Living Councils. The declaratory statement for vocational rehabilitation services contained in the 1992 amendments stressed the importance of work and of its centrality in American society and recounted the barriers to achievement of this goal. The language of this statement is quite instructive and reflective of the positive effects initiated by the disability movement and now incorporated into legislation:

Sec. 100. (a) (l) Congress find that -

(A) work -

(i) is a valued activity, both for individuals and society; and

(ii) fulfills the need of an individual to be productive, promotes independence, enhances self-esteem, and allow for participation in the mainstream of life in America;

(B) as a group, individuals with disabilities experience staggering levels of unemployment and poverty;

(C) individuals with disabilities, including individuals with the most severe disabilities, have demonstrated their ability to achieve gainful employment in integrated settings if appropriate services and supports are provided;

(D) reasons for the significant number of individuals with disabilities not working, or working at a level not commensurate with their abilities and capabilities, include -

(i) discrimination;
(ii) lack of accessible and available transportation;
(iii) fear of losing health coverage under the medicare and medicaid programs under titles XVIII and XIX of the Social Security Act (42 U.S.C. 1395 et seq. and 1396 et seq.) or fear of losing private health insurance; and
(iv) lack of education, training, and supports to meet job qualification standards necessary to enter or retain or advance in employment;
(E) enforcement of title V and of the Americans with Disabilities Act of 1990 (42 U.S.C. 1210 et seq.) holds the promise of ending discrimination for individuals with disabilities; and
(F) this provision of vocational rehabilitation services can enable individuals with disabilities, including individuals with the most severe disabilities, to pursue meaningful careers by securing gainful employment commensurate with their abilities and capabilities.

(2) The purpose of this title is to assist states in operating a comprehensive, coordinated, effective, efficient and accountable program of vocational rehabilitation that is designed to assess, plan, develop, and provide vocational rehabilitation services for individuals with disabilities, consistent with their strengths, resources, priorities, concerns, abilities, and capabilities, so that such individuals may prepare for and engage in gainful employment.

(3) It is the policy of the United States that such a program shall be carried out in a manner consistent with the following principles:

(A) Individuals with disabilities, including individuals with the most severe disabilities, are generally presumed to be capable of engaging in gainful employment and the provision of individualized vocational rehabilitation services can improve their ability to become gainfully employed.
(B) Individuals with disabilities must be provided the opportunities to obtain gainful employment in integrated settings.
C) Individuals with disabilities must be active participants in their own rehabilitation programs, including making meaningful and informed choices about the selection of their vocational goals and objectives and the vocational rehabilitation services they receive.
(D) Families and natural supports can play an important role in the success of a vocational rehabilitation program, if the individual with a disability requests, desires, or needs such supports.
(E) Qualified vocational rehabilitation counselors, other qualified rehabilitation personnel, and other qualified personnel facilitate the accomplishment of the employment goals and objectives of an individual.
(F) Individuals with disabilities and their advocates are full partners in the vocational rehabilitation program and must be involved on a regular basis and in a meaningful manner with respect to policy development and implementation.
(G) Accountability measures must facilitate and not impede the accomplishment of the goals and objectives of the program, including providing vocational rehabilitation services to, among other, individuals with the most severe disabilities.

Eligibility criteria for receipt of vocational services changed as noted below:

An individual is eligible for vocational rehabilitation services when:

1. He/she has a physical or mental impairment which constitutes or results in a substantial impediment to employment,

2. the individual can benefit in terms of an employment outcome from VR services, and

3. the individual requires vocational rehabilitation services to prepare for, enter, engage in, or retain employment.

This broadened definition of eligibility allowed for increased flexibility in working with consumers or customers with severe and most severe disabilities since it incorporated the qualifier "benefit" although the interpretation of this word often did not mean the same thing for a person with a disability as it did for the VR agency. This definition of eligibility also allowed counselors to work with persons in a preventive manner regarding retention of employment. Other provisions related to the establishment of time limits for the determination of eligibility (60-day limit); however, some consumers complained that they were put in a waiting status before being allowed to apply for rehabilitation services. Use of existing data, particularly from educational agencies as well as from the person with a disability and his or her family was encouraged. The VR agency was mandated to conduct an extended evaluation if a person's disability was considered too severe to serve. In this same vein, the agency was required to specify the reasons for a determination of ineligibility and concurrently advise the person of the availability of the services of the Client Assistance Program.

The Individual Written Rehabilitation Program (IWRP) continued to emphasize the importance of the planning process between the client and the counselor. The IWRP was to be jointly developed and reflect the unique strengths, resources, abilities and concerns of the person with a disability in terms of the vocational objective selected. The vocational objective was to have a career focus with job placement in an integrated setting. A statement of specific services to be provided and the data and duration of such services was to be specified. An assessment of the need for post employment services was, as well, to be included in the IWRP. Each client was to receive a copy of the IWRP and, in case of a disagreement regarding the plan or anticipated services, the person was to be informed of the availability of the Client Assistance Program (as well as how to access these services). The IWRP was to be reviewed at least annually allowing for changes and the development of revisions or amendments to the IWRP.

The 1992 amendments also provided that federal support of the VR program be increased from 75 to 78.7 percent beginning in 1993. An emphasis on minority recruitment to the field of rehabilitation was to be developed through supports to college and university programs that had minority enrollments of 50 percent or greater (Rubin and Roessler, 1995).

The 1998 Amendments to the 1973 Rehabilitation Act

The Rehabilitation Act amendments of 1998 were signed into law by President Bill Clinton on August 7, 1998 as a part of the Workforce Investment Act of 1998. The 1998 amendments continued and expands emphasis on consumer involvement and choice. Fredric K. Schroeder, Commissioner of the Rehabilitation Services Administration, released an information memorandum which detailed the following areas of emphasis contained in the 1998 amendments (1998, p. 2):

- expanding the exercise of informed choice by individuals with disabilities;
- streamlining administrative procedures to improve program efficiency and access to services;
- increasing opportunities for high quality employment outcomes; ensuring due process; and
- linking the VR program to a State's workforce investment system.

State VR agencies and the State Rehabilitation Councils (formally the Statewide Rehabilitation Advisory Councils) were to develop policies and procedures that will insure informed choice regarding eligibility determination, selection of vocational or employment goals, and the selection of services and service providers. The Individual Written Rehabilitation Plan (IWRP) was renamed the Individualized Plan for Employment (IPE) to emphasize the expanded role of the person with a disability vis-a-vis informed choice. The IPE continued the existent requirement for comparable benefits, postemployment services, and due process procedures.

Administratively, the amendments eliminated the strategic plan requirements and support the expansion of the VR services to persons with the most significant disabilities (a change in terminology from the qualifier "severe" to "significant"). Presumptively, persons receiving Social Security Disability Insurance (SSDI) and Supplemental Security Insurance (SSI) benefits who desire an employment outcome are eligible to receive VR services without going through an eligibility process. Employment outcomes characterized as "high quality," meaning the expansion of job opportunities in such areas as telecommuting and self-employment, including small business operation, are emphasized in the development of the IPE. The requirement for extended evaluation (when or if ineligibility is being assessed for persons with the most significant disabilities) was replaced with a requirement of trial work experience.

Due process requirements were enhanced for persons with disabilities who disagreed with decisions regarding eligibility, services, or case closure. Mediation is an option that is to be offered a client; the outcome, however, is not binding and cannot be used to delay or deny an impartial hearing. Decisions of the Impartial Hearing Officer, as a result of these new due process provisions, will no longer be reviewed by the state VR director.

Linkages to the state work force investment system (a consolidation of employment and training programs into a unified statewide system) were contemplated to lead to better coordination and cooperation among the various agencies regarding job opportunities for persons with disabilities.

Future Directions

The disability movement, as witnessed by the historic events of the preceding four decades, has come a long way toward the ideal of rehabilitation as expressed by the National Council on Rehabilitation in 1942 to the passage of the 1973 Rehabilitation Act to the passage of the Americans with Disabilities Act in 1990. But, in reality, we have only come a small distance when persons with disabilities are still being institutionalized because our society cannot or will not expend money for community options even in the light of economic gain. It costs less to provide services in the community than it does in an institutional setting. The legislative agenda for persons with disabilities has increasingly become more consumer or customer centered and directed and less process oriented. This is a most positive trend which holds great promise for the future not only for people with disabilities but for all people.

The National Council on Disability, in its recent report, *Achieving Independence: The Challenge for the 21st Century,* assessed disability policy of the recent past and concluded:

> Disability policy has made steady progress in the last decade in empowering people with disabilities; however, this progress is threatened, compromised, and often undermined by lack of understanding and support in the Congress and among particular segments of society.
>
> Most public policy affecting people with disabilities does not yet promote the goals of ADA–equality of opportunity, full participation, independent living, and economic self sufficiency.
>
> Most Americans with disabilities remain outside the economic and social mainstream of American life. (pp. 3-4)

The National Council on Disability also offered these recommendations as we approach the new millennium:

1. Existing laws should be more vigorously enforced.
2. People with disabilities should direct policy and decision making when they are affected by the outcome.
3. Outreach and awareness campaigns must be launched to educate the public about the human and societal benefits of achieving independence for people with disabilities and the important role that civil rights and community-based supports play in promoting independence.
4. Incentives for the inclusion of people with disabilities in all aspects of society must be further developed and implemented.
5. Principles of universal design should be universally applied.
6. Systems, services, and supports for people with disabilities must be further developed as a part of the mainstream of community life.
7. Accurate data about people with disabilities should be regularly collected, analyzed, and reported. (pp. 5-6)

Recent events and present-day trends in rehabilitation indicate that programs have become much larger and more complex. Because of the increasing size, its recognition by other professionals in the delivery of rehabilitation-related services and most significantly, the emerging importance of a strong partnership between the consumer or customer and the rehabilitation counselor or other professional personnel, the rehabilitation movement demonstrates a positive growth during the past four decades.

While the Independent Living program is in need of additional financial assistance from the federal government, this movement and its pioneering program development have the potential of becoming the comprehensive rehabilitation program for the future. Centers for Independent Living now provide services of increased scope ranging from assistance with housing to food preparation to vocational placement.

In spite of the phenomenal growth in the independent living field, thousands of people remain unnecessarily institutionalized and overprotected. Many of these individuals have not chosen the style of life they lead; they are awaiting the opportunity to acquire information and skills that they need in order to become independent; they are awaiting resources in their communities such as accessible housing, transportation, and attendant care; they are awaiting the continued growth of the independent living movement and new independent living programs that this growth will bring.

With this comparatively new awareness of persons with significant disabilities as being capable of living independently and with the recognition of accompanying advantages of increased quality of life, frequently with economic benefit, a thrust toward an emphasis on independent living in rehabilitation settings is on the increase. Professionals providing services focusing on skills for living independently are practicing from various disciplines: rehabilitation counseling, occupational therapy, therapeutic recreation, social work, psychology, rehabilitation nursing, special education, and others. With the firm establishment of the Independent Living movement and the new and increasing emphasis on support, encouragement and skill development for living independently, it is expected that the rehabilitation counselor of the future will have a heavy investment in the area of independent living.

A number of interrelated trends in the American society have emerged during this most recent period of legislative history that have influenced the disability movement and continue to exert influence regarding the development of policy which will shape the rehabilitation enterprise of the future:

1. ***The advance of medicine*** is reflected in the growing numbers of "at-risk" infants who are surviving. It is also reflected in the numbers of persons with significant disabilities who are able to survive for longer periods of time, as well as growing numbers of older Americans who are subject to age-related disabilities.

2. ***The advance of technology*** accompanied by the computer age has been a force in the field of medicine and in the allied field of rehabilitation engineering. It is also an important development for adaptation in the workplace for persons with disabilities and for the dissemination of information in the rehabilitation field. Assistive technology has, indeed, become the great equalizer for persons with disabilities especially for persons with significant disabilities. The ability to access that technology, however, continues to be problematic.

3. ***The advance of educational opportunities*** for children and youth with disabilities, largely the direct result of PL 94-142 and subsequent amendments (IDEA) which states that children and youth with disabilities must be educated in the least restrictive environment. This legislative event has introduced America's school students to children and youth who have cognitive, mental, physical, and sensory disabilities in increasingly greater numbers of inclusive educational settings. This movement has had a direct influence on the following trend.

4. ***The advance of attitudes of acceptance*** of the population of people with disabilities is reflected in the increase in opportunities in higher education; in employee assistance programs; in employment in general; in slowly crumbling barriers to housing, transportation, travel, and recreation. The advance in removing barriers has been uneven but inexorable. More must, however, be done.

5. ***The advance of attitudes toward increased responsibility for one's own wellness or fitness*** is reflected in a dramatic interest in exercise, good nutrition, and widespread information about maintenance of health that goes beyond the fad to look young and healthy. The general public is in possession of a much larger body of information than ever before about disease

processes and how some may be delayed or prevented and about the elements of good nutrition and physical activity and their possible relationship to physical and mental health. People are increasingly choosing physicians who will be concerned with the whole person, using the holistic approach to the practice of medicine. Private business, including insurance companies, and local, state, and federal government agencies have recognized the effects of this trend on their employees, their insurants (in the case of the insurance companies), and have begun to participate in support. Again, the interrelationships of the trends listed above are noted with an example: the rehabilitation consumer is able to take advantage of the advances of medicine, technology, educational opportunities, and attitudes for the opportunity for more control and more choices in every aspect of life–education, profession, the choice of physician and method of rehabilitation, the choice of marriage and raising a family, recreation, and others.

There are many obstacles, however, for rehabilitation to overcome in order to respond to the challenge of a new mission in the coming decades. Perhaps the greatest challenge the rehabilitation enterprise faces today and in the future is the problem associated with change. Carl Rogers, in an article on possibilities for the year 2000, stated:

> I am going to sketch possibilities, alternative routes which we may travel. One important reason for refusing to make predictions is that for the first time in history man [*sic*] is not only taking his [*sic*] future seriously, but he [*sic*] also had adequate technology and power to shape and form that future. He [*sic*] is endeavoring to choose his [*sic*] future rather than simply living out some inevitable trend. . . . Before I try to sketch some of these possibilities, I should like to point to the greatest problem which man [*sic*] faces in the years to come. It is not the hydrogen bomb, fearful as that may be. It is not the population explosion, though the consequences of that are awful to contemplate. It is instead a problem which is rarely mentioned or discussed. It is the question of how much change the human being can accept, absorb, and assimilate and the rate at which he [*sic*] can take it. Can he [*sic*] keep up with the ever-increasing rate of technological change, or is there some point at which the human organism goes to pieces? Can he [*sic*] leave the static ways and static guidelines which have dominated all of his [*sic*] history and adopt the process ways, the continual changingness which will be his [*sic*] if he [*sic*] is to survive? (Rogers, 1968, pp. 265-266)

We may ask the same questions of organizations as well as their individual members. Rehabilitation's major challenge is the adaptation to change that is required to provide new and additional services for new consumers or customers who can benefit from them. The growth of the rehabilitation program from 1921 until 1963 was an orderly process (except for those beginning years) with the first major expansion occurring twenty-two years after it started in 1943, prompted by war needs and then, in 1954, eleven years later, in answer to the government's search for an answer to the mounting welfare and dependency problems. There was time for consolidation of gains made and sufficient experience to make a case for new needs. In this most recent period, the situation has been much different. As C. Esco Obermann noted in the late 1980s ". . . the next big hero in the rehabilitation movement will be the one who can pull together the necessary thoughts and ideas and organize them into a working plan . . ." (Dietl, 1986, p. 15).

It is obvious that rehabilitation in the future will need to accommodate change if growth of services to people with disabilities is to continue. A whole new structure will be required to help rehabilitation counselors work with clients to maintain a quality of services needed by people with disabilities. Patience and tolerance of change and a clear understanding of the desperate need for change in rehabilitation will be required of all.

REFERENCES

Americans with Disabilities Act of 1990. Public Law 101-336.

Architectural Barriers Act of 1968. Public Law 90-480.

Batshaw, M. L. (Ed.). (1997). *Children with disabilities* (4th ed.). Baltimore: Paul Brooks.

Berkowitz, E. D. (1987). *Disabled policy: America's programs for the handicapped.* New York: Twentieth Century Fund Report.

Blanck, P. (1994). Employment integration, economic opportunity and the Americans with disabilities act: Empirical study from 1990-1993. *Iowa Law Review, 79* (4), 853-923.

Board of Education of the Henrick Hudson Central School District v. Rowley. 458 U.S. 176, S. Ct. 3034, 1982.

Bowe, F. G. (1992). Development of the ADA. In N. Hablutzel & B. T. McMahon (Eds.), *The Americans with disabilities act: Access and accommodations.* Orlando, FL: Paul M. Deutsch.

Braddock, D., Hemp, R., Parish, S., & Westrich, J. (1998). *The state of the states on developmental disabilities.* Washington, D.C.: American Association on Mental Retardation.

Dart, J. & West, J. (1995). Americans with disabilities act. In A. E. Dell Orto & R. P. Marinelli (Eds.), *Encyclopedia of disability and rehabilitation.* New York: Simon & Schuster Macmillan.

Davis v. Southeastern Community College. 442 U.S. 397, 1979.

Dejong, G. (1979). *Report of the National Conference on Independent Living Service Rehabilitation per P.L. 95-602, March 7-8, 1979.* Boston: Medical Rehabilitation and Research Training Center No. 7, Tufts–New England Medical Center.

Developmental Disabilities Services and Facilities Construction Act. Public Law 91-517.

Dietl, D. (1986). Two decades later–C. Esco Overmann: History is on his side. *Journal of Rehabilitation, 52*(1), 9-15.

Dole, R. (1994). Are we keeping America's promises to people with disabilities?–commentary on Blanck. *Iowa Law Review, 79* (4), 925-939.

Education for All Handicapped Children Act of 1975. Public Law 94-142.

Eighty-ninth Congress. (1965). United States Statutes at Large, Vol. 79.

Gardner, J. W. (1968). To extend the concept of rehabilitation. *Journal of Rehabilitation, 34* (1), 12-13.

Gardner, J. W. (1969, April 11). Toward a self-renewing society. *Time Magazine,* 40.

Hablutzel, N. & McMahon, B. T. (Eds.). (1992). *The Americans with disabilities act: Access and accommodations.* Orlando: Paul M. Deutsch.

Harkin, T. (1994). The Americans with disabilities act: Four years later–commentary on Blanck. *Iowa Law Review, 79* (4), 935-939.

Kurtz, L. A. & Harryman, S. E. (1997). Rehabilitation interventions: Physical therapy and occupational therapy. In M. L. Batshaw (Ed.), *Children with disabilities* (4th ed., p.). Baltimore: Paul Brooks.

Lou Harris and Associates. (1998). *NOD/Harris survey of Americans with disabilities.* New York: Author.

Lou Harris and Associates. (1995). *NOD/Harris survey on employment of people with disabilities.* New York: Author.

Lou Harris and Associates. (1986). *Harris survey on employment of people with disabilities.* New York: Author.

Lou Harris and Associates. (1986). *ICD survey of Americans with disabilities.* New York: Author.

Lou Harris and Associates. (1994). *NOD/Harris survey of Americans with disabilities.* New York: Author.

McMahon, B.T. *Personal Communication,* October 14, 1998.

Mills v Board of Education of the District of Columbia. 348 F. Supp. 866, 1972.

Morrison, S. E. (1965). *The Oxford history of the American people.* New York: Oxford University Press.

National Rehabilitation Association (1968, August). *Newletter 23.*

National Council on Disability. (1996). *Achieving independence: The challenge for the 21st century.* Washington: Author.

National Council on Disability. (1986). *Toward independence: An assessment of federal laws and programs affecting people with disabilities–with legislative recommendations.* Washington: Author.

New York State Association for Retarded Children v. Rockefeller. 357 F. Supp. 752, 1973.

Patterson, C. H. (Ed.). (1960). *Readings in rehabilitation counseling.* Champaign, IL: Stipes.

Pennsylvania Association of Retarded Children v. Commonwealth of Pennsylvania. 334 F. Supp. 1257, 1971.

Percy, S.L. (1989). *Disability, civil rights, and public policy.* Tuscaloosa, AL: The University of Alabama Press.

President's Committee on Employment of People with Disabilities (1990). "ADA: A special issue". *Worklife, 3*(3), pp 1-48.
Rehabilitation Act of 1973. Public Law 93-112.
Rehabilitation Act Amendments of 1974. Public Law 93-651.
Rehabilitation Act Amendments of 1978. Public Law 95-602.
Rehabilitation Act Amendments of 1984. Public Law 98-221.
Rehabilitation Act Amendments of 1986. Public Law 99-506.
Rehabilitation Act Amendments of 1992. Public Law 102-569.
Rehabilitation Act Amendments of 1993. Public Law 103-73.
Rogers, C. R. (1968). Interpersonal relationships: USA 2000. *Journal of Applied Behavioral Science, 4* (3), 265-266.
Rubin, S. E., & Roessler, R. T. (1995). *Foundations of the vocational rehabilitation process* (4th ed.). Austin, TX: PRO-ED.
Schroeder, F. K. (1998). The rehabilitation act amendments of 1998. *Information Memorandum, RSA-IM-98-20.* Washington, D.C.: Rehabilitation Services Administration, United Stated Department of Education.
Scotch, R. K. (1984). *From good will to civil rights: Transforming federal disability policy.* Philadelphia: Temple University Press.
Shapiro, J. P. (1993). *No pity: People with disabilities forging a new civil rights movement.* New York: Random House.
The Technology-Related Assistance Act for Individuals with Disabilities Act of 1988. Public Law 100-407.
Time Magazine. (1967, September 1). The administration, *90*(9), 14.
Tucker, B. P., & Goldstein, B. A. (1992). *Legal rights of persons with disabilities: An analysis of federal law* (Volumes I & II ed.). Horsham, PA: LRP Publications.
Wallace, J. F. (1994). *A policy analysis of national loan financing practices: Strategies for the development for the loan programs for the acquisition of assistive technology.* Unpublished doctoral dissertation, Virginia Commonwealth University.
West, J. (1994). *Federal implementation of the Americans with disability act, 1991-1994.* New York: The Milbank Memorial Fund.
Wyatt v. Stickney, 344 F. Supp. 752, 1973.

Chapter 5

EDUCATIONAL AND PROFESSIONAL ORGANIZATIONAL DEVELOPMENT OF THE DISCIPLINE OF REHABILITATION COUNSELING

GERALD L. GANDY AND E. DAVIS MARTIN, JR.

The first rehabilitation education program was established by Ronald Spaulding at New York University in 1941. Two other programs were established by Kenneth Hamilton at Ohio State University in 1944 and by John Lee in collaboration with Ralf A. Peckham at Wayne State University in 1947. They evolved from the disciplines of vocational education, social work and special education, respectively (Cantoni, 1985; Cobb, 1972; Jacques, 1970; Muthard, 1969). An estimated 12 rehabilitation counselors had graduated from American universities by 1949 (Woodrow Wilson Rehabilitation Center, 1973). However, in 1955, rehabilitation education would begin to expand in colleges and universities (Muthard, 1969). Public Law 565 of the 83rd Congress in 1954 provided for research foundations and university education programs. As a result 26 colleges and universities either had begun programs or had secured planning grants by the fall of 1955. There were 39 programs in 1965-66. A current membership directory of the National Council on Rehabilitation Education (1997-98) lists 85 colleges and universities.

Because of the effect of Public Law 565 on research and education, Wright (1980) observed that rehabilitation counseling had the unique distinction of being the only profession established by an Act of the United States Congress. The legislation helped to give rehabilitation counseling an identity extending beyond the public rehabilitation agency realm for services to individuals with all types of disabilities throughout the human services system.

Rehabilitation Counselor Education: Development of Masters Program

Rehabilitation counseling as a profession has pertained primarily to the master's degree (Wright, 1980). The master's degree has been considered the preferred level of training and terminal degree for the professional practice of rehabilitation counseling. However, the baccalaureate and doctoral degree in rehabilitation education have also served important needs in the rehabilitation field (Evenson, 1995; Gandy, 1983; Hylbert, 1963; Maki & Berven, 1994; Maki, Berven, & Allen, 1985). Baccalaureate degree programs provide generically-trained support personnel who can perform many counseling-related functions under the supervision of a master's degree rehabilitation counselor or an allied graduate trained rehabilitation professional. There has also been a need for doctoral level personnel to serve in a variety of academic, administrative, research, and clinical practice positions. All three levels of training, bachelors, master's, and doctoral, were incorporated in the development of the first rehabilitation education program at New York University in 1941 (Dvonch, 1985). More information regarding baccalaureate and doctoral level training will be provided later in this chapter.

The 1954 vocational rehabilitation legislation had its major impact on master's degree education (Jaques, 1970; Muthard, 1969; Wright, 1980). Rehabilitation counselor education during this period had its academic roots in counseling psychology (Wright, 1980). A major source of teaching personnel for these academic programs was individuals who had been counseling psychologists with the Veterans Administration's Vocational Rehabilitation and Education Program. A survey in 1963 indicated that three-fourths of the academic program directors were psychologists (Muthard, 1969). Consequently, the psychology profession had a major influence on the development of the profession of rehabilitation counseling in the United States. Wright (1980) has observed that the social work profession has probably had the most influence on rehabilitation counseling in most other countries around the world. With the later development of extensive research literature, special techniques and skills, professional associations and certification and accreditation standards, many now consider rehabilitation counseling in the United States to be a separate and independent profession. Moreover, very few rehabilitation counselor education programs are located in academic psychology departments (National Council on Rehabilitation, 1997-98). Although most programs are usually autonomous, they are often organizationally associated with counselor education, special education, educational psychology, allied health, community and public affairs, or other graduate programs.

Jacques (1970) notes that it is unknown when the term "rehabilitation counselor" was first used or who was responsible for its origin. She observes that it probably had its inception as a result of the first civilian Vocational Rehabilitation Act of 1920 but that this Act did not use the term. Finch (1937) was the first to use the term in the professional literature. Public Law 565 in 1954 was the first to mention rehabilitation counseling in the law. Oberman (1965, pp. 263-267) describes a federal bulletin which appeared in 1930 that laid some of the early foundations for the job description of the rehabilitation counselor. However, the person performing this function was referred to as a rehabilitation worker or agent.

McCauley (1972) reports that the administrators of divisions of vocational rehabilitation in the United States decided, at the 1946 Conference on the Rehabilitation of the Tuberculous in Washington, D.C., to adopt the title of "rehabilitation counselor" by a show of hands. This title was to be used by those employees who represented their agencies' services to people with disabilities. Prior to that time, there had been some fifteen job titles assigned to such personnel. Some examples were "rehabilitation representative," "rehabilitation coordinator," and "rehabilitation supervisor." Although the administrators agreed on the title of "rehabilitation counselor," they could not agree on the qualifications or training for this type of employee. Nevertheless, by 1949, nearly every state rehabilitation agency had adopted this title for the worker serving people with disabilities as agents of the program.

Rehabilitation counseling has generally been viewed as a process in which the counselor and the client work together to understand existing problems and potentials and to facilitate the client's effective use of personal and environmental resources for vocational, personal, and social adjustment (Jaques, 1970). However, since the 1954 vocational rehabilitation legislation, there has been considerable study and discussion of the specific details of the role and function of the rehabilitation counselor. Rubin and Roessler (1995, Chapter 8) provide a history of these discussions of the rehabilitation counselor role and function. Early attention advocated that there should be separate rehabilitation counselor and coordinator professionals. Later observations indicated that counselors must have both types of skills in order to be successful. A contemporary multifaceted viewpoint suggests that counselors must have counseling, coordinating, and consulting skills, as well as a variety of other competencies.

Jenkins, Patterson, and Szymanski (1992) indicate that, regardless of employment setting and client population, most rehabilitation counselors (a) assess client needs, (b) develop goals and individualized plans to meet identified needs, and (c) provide or arrange for the therapeutic services and interventions (e.g., psychological, medical, social, or behavioral) needed by the clients that may include job placement and follow-up services. Counseling skills are considered an essential component of all of these activities. Research conducted by Leahy, Szymanski, and Linkowski (1993) indicated that the following 10 knowledge domains represent the core competency requirements of rehabilitation counselors: (a) vocational counseling and consultation services; (b) medical and psychological aspects; (c) individual and group counseling; (d) program evaluation and research; (e) case management and service coordination; (f) family, gender, and multicultural issues; (g) foundations of rehabilitation; (h) workers' compensation; (i) environmental and attitudinal barriers; and (j) assessment.

Leahy and Szymanski (1995) note that a consistent trend in the historical development of rehabilitation practice over the years has been the ever expanding employment settings where practice takes place and the types of populations the counselor works with within the rehabilitation process. Public (e.g., state and federal programs), private nonprofit (e.g., rehabilitation centers), and private for-profit (e.g., workers' compensation, insurance rehabilitation, forensic rehabilitation) settings represent the primary employment settings for rehabilitation counselors. However, a number of nontraditional settings are emerging as a result of legislation and other social and economic influences. Such emerging settings include employee assistance programs, disability management programs within employer settings, school-based transition programs, university services for students with disabilities, and medical centers and clinics. Rehabilitation counselors continue to work with clients with physical disabilities but also now work with a variety of other populations, including those with developmental, cognitive, emotional, and addiction disabilities, depending on the employment setting in which they practice.

Baccalaureate and Doctoral Level Education

As mentioned earlier in this chapter, doctoral and baccalaureate studies as well as master's study were part of the first rehabilitation education program at New York University in 1941 (Dvonch, 1985). The master's degree is considered the terminal degree for the professional practice of rehabilitation counseling. However, doctoral training has generally been considered more appropriate for teaching and research positions in colleges and universities as well as marketable in a variety of nonacademic situations involving training, administration, research, and direct service. Maki and Berven (1994) recently conducted a comprehensive follow-up study of a comprehensive study by Maki, Berven, and Allen (1985) of doctoral programs in rehabilitation education in the United States. The follow-up study continued to reflect the employment settings indicated above. The number of programs identified had decreased from 38 to 30, with corresponding decreases in numbers of graduates. Nevertheless, citation of literature in the follow-up study indicated a recent documented need for an increase in doctoral-level professionals. The follow up study also supported the earlier study in suggesting substantial variability among programs. It was recommended that individuals wishing to pursue doctoral study in rehabilitation should select programs carefully, identifying the programs that will best meet their needs and facilitate their career goals.

Undergraduate rehabilitation education has historically served a broader purpose than doctoral or master's education (Evenson, 1995; Feinberg, Sunblad, & Glick, 1974; Gandy, 1983, 1987; Gandy & Martin; 1985; Hylbert, 1963; Witten, 1980\81). The National Council on Rehabilitation (NCRE) adopted a policy statement on undergraduate education in 1987 (Gandy, et al., 1987, 1989). Undergraduate education is viewed as providing a broad liberal arts education combined with an understanding of the nature of disability and rehabilitation. Individuals with the baccalaureate degree can perform many counseling-related functions under supervision. Although undergraduate educated persons more frequently work under the supervision of graduate trained rehabilitation counselors, they can perform similar rehabilitation activities under the supervision of graduate trained professionals in related rehabilitation areas such as social work, psychology, occupational therapy, recreational therapy, and others. They may choose to pursue graduate study not only in rehabilitation counseling but also in any of these related rehabilitation areas. Thirty three of the 85 colleges and universities listed in the current membership directory of the NCRE (1997-98) offer a baccalaureate degree in undergraduate rehabilitation education. Plans are currently under way for a Registry for Undergraduate Programs in Rehabilitation Education (NCRE, 1996).

Continuing Education and Research

In-service training and continuing development of rehabilitation personnel has been a strong component of the rehabilitation field since the 1954 vocational rehabilitation legislation (Wright, 1980). Regional Rehabilitation Continuing Education Programs (RRCEP) were established by state rehabilitation agencies through federal funding beginning in 1974. RRCEP projects focused on staff training to improve and renew professionally relevant rehabilitation knowledge and skills. The federal rehabilitation agency initiated an institute or workshop for state agency supervisors in 1947 which later became an annual activity known as the Institute on Rehabilitation Issues

(IRI). The proceedings of these institutes were initially published by the federal rehabilitation agency and later by several federally sponsored university Rehabilitation Research and Training Centers. Bolton and Parker (1992) note that almost all rehabilitation research in the United States is funded by the National Institute on Disability and Rehabilitation Research (NIDRR) in Washington, DC. The exceptions include the *Annual Review of Rehabilitation* and the various professional and academic journals published by nonprofit professional organizations .

Historical mention should be made of the contribution of Richard E. Hardy and John G. Cull of Virginia Commonwealth University (VCU) in Richmond (Thralls, 1980). They began work on the award-winning Social and Rehabilitation Psychology Series in 1969 which has included numerous textbooks and practitioner handbooks for counselors and university educators. Contributions to these textbooks have been made by many rehabilitation experts from throughout the world. Hardy was also responsible for the initiation of the first major alcohol and drug abuse rehabilitation counselor education specialization program in the United States at an already well established Department of Rehabilitation Counseling at VCU. He secured a grant from the Virginia Department of Health to train health care personnel including rehabilitation counselors in 1974. Mention should also be made of the contribution of George N. Wright (1980) of the University of Wisconsin-Madison. The working bibliography for his massive volume, *Total Rehabilitation*, consisted of 5,000 documents selected for relevant and practical information. His work indicates pioneering leadership in empirically grounded research in the discipline of rehabilitation counseling.

Professional Organization and Credentialing

As mentioned previously, psychologists had a major impact in the development of the profession of rehabilitation counseling (Jacques, 1970; Muthard, 1969; Wright; 1980). The Division of Counseling Psychology and the Division of the Psychological Aspects of Disability of the American Psychological Association (APA) were the major psychological organizations affiliated with the rehabilitation counseling field (Jacques, 1979; Wright, 1980). The Division of Counseling Psychology established an **ad hoc** committee in 1962-63 to study thc role of psychology in the preparation of rehabilitation counselors (Muthard, 1969). Their curricular recommendations presumed that rehabilitation counseling found its basic tenets and rationale in the discipline of psychology. However, rehabilitation counseling began developing an independent status from psychology with the formation of two professional associations, the American Rehabilitation Counseling

Association (ARCA) in 1957 and the National Rehabilitation Counseling Association (NRCA) in 1958 (Wright, 1980).

The ARCA developed as a division of the American Personnel and Guidance Association (APGA), now known as the American Counseling Association (ACA) (DiMichael & Thomas, 1985; Wright, 1980). The ARCA is affiliated with a parent association of counselors (school, metal health, employment, and others) and maintains a direct linkage to the generic field of professional counseling. The historical origin of the ARCA was influenced by the belief of some early leaders that rehabilitation counseling was a specialty of counseling rather than a separate discipline (Jenkins et al., 1992; Patterson, 1961). The NRCA developed as a division of the National Rehabilitation Association (NRA) (Wright, 1980). The NRA includes both professional and lay people involved in the general rehabilitation field. In addition to rehabilitation counselors and related personnel, members include physicians, nurses, psychologists, social workers, administrators, secretaries, and so forth. The historical origin of the NRCA was influenced by the belief of other early leaders that rehabilitation counseling should be a separate profession (Jenkins et al., 1992; Stone, 1966).

The presence of ARCA and NRCA, with similar missions and constituencies, has been the topic of much discussion and debate over the years (Leahy & Szymanski, 1995). The boards of both organizations created the Alliance of Rehabilitation Counseling in 1993 as a formal collaborative structure to marshal the strengths of both organizations into a unified professional policy and strategic planning voice for rehabilitation counseling, while at the same time respecting the autonomy, heritage, and value of each of the individual organizations.

The accreditation body for rehabilitation counselor education is the Council on Rehabilitation Education (CORE) and there were 84 accredited masters programs and one in candidate status for the 1996-97 academic year (Council on Rehabilitation Education, 1996). CORE was incorporated in 1972, and the CORE process is firmly grounded in research (Leahy & Szymanski, 1995). The knowledge standards against which program curricula are measured are constantly validated through an ongoing research process. Internal consistency reliability is examined annually for the questionnaires used in the multistakeholder review process, and interrater agreement is computed for review teams. Any areas of potential unreliability are remediated on a regular basis. The Council of Accreditation of Counseling and Related Educational Professions (CACREP), the accrediting body for the general counseling profession, has an ongoing collaborative relationship with CORE and there is a regular opportunity for joint review of departments that have both accredited programs (Linkowski & Syzmanski, 1993).

Another major development was the formation of the Commission on Rehabilitation Counselor Certification (CRCC) in 1973 (Hedgeman, 1985). The CRCC administers rehabilitation counselor certification examinations for the Certified Rehabilitation Counselor (CRC) credential. There are now over 13,500 CRCs in the United States and several foreign countries (Foundation for Rehabilitation Education and Research, 1997). Certification standards and content for the CRC have been empirically verified through ongoing research efforts and these standards represent the level of education, experience, and knowledge competencies required of individual practitioners to provide counseling services to individuals with disabilities. No formal mechanism exist for collaboration between the CRCC and the National Board for Certified Counselors (NBCC), a generic board, which awards certification for the National Certified Counselor (NCC) credential but some informal collaboration does occur (Leahy & Szymanski, 1995).

Although rehabilitation counseling has established and maintained a separate certification mechanism from that used by general counseling and other specialty areas, many believe that the profession should advocate strongly for general counselor licensure or the Licensed Professional Counselor (LPC) credential at the state level (Leahy & Szymanski, 1995; Sweeney, 1995). License for private practice is the province of respective states and is not the same as certification at the national level. Hardy, Luck, and Chandler (1982) conducted a national survey of the ARCA members a number of years ago that indicated that rehabilitation counselors should become a part of a national movement toward generic professional counseling laws in various states. Counselors in a variety of areas such as rehabilitation, mental health, and employment in various states have joined together to establish a generic counseling license. According to the American Association of State Counseling Boards (AASCB), there are counseling regulatory boards existing in 43 states, the District of Columbia, and the possession of Guam, for a grand total of 45 boards that govern the practice of professional counseling in the United States (AASCB, 1996).

An organization which is concerned not only with rehabilitation counselor education but all areas of rehabilitation education is the National Council on Rehabilitation Education (NCRE) (NCRE, 1997-98; Wright, 1980). The NCRE was formerly the Council on Rehabilitation Counselor Education (CRCE) but was reorganized to include other rehabilitation programs. Currently, it includes such typical areas as undergraduate, graduate, continuing education, research and training center, vocational evaluation and work adjustment, and facility administration. Doctoral candidates in rehabilitation education and research can also be recommended for membership. The NCRE is active in improving the quality and recognition of rehabilitation education and has had a significant impact on federal legislation.

Educational and Professional Summary and Conclusion

Rehabilitation education has become very well developed in regard to baccaculaureate, master's, and doctoral education. With the further development of professional associations, accreditation, national certification, and state licensure, the rehabilitation counseling profession has become clearly established. However, the view of the main authors/editors of this textbook is that rehabilitation counseling is part of a generic professional counseling discipline and that there should be more formal collaboration between the counselor accreditation, certification, and licensing entities mentioned in this chapter. Further discussion of this issue as well as additional ramifications of counseling credentialing are discussed in Chapter 15: Rehabilitation Counseling as a Professional Counseling Specialty.

REFERENCES

American Association of State Counseling Boards (AASCB). (1996). *The liaison, 3*, 1-9. Baltimore, MD: Author.

Bolton, B., & Parker, R. M. (1992). Research in rehabilitation counseling. In R. M. Parker & E. D. Szymanski (Eds.), *Rehabilitation counseling: Basics and beyond* (2nd ed.). Austin, TX: Pro-Ed.

Cantoni, L. J. (1985). Personal communications by correspondence dated November 25, 1985.

Cobb, B. (1972). The challenge of new dimensions in rehabilitation education in the seventies. In J. G. Cull & R. E. Hardy, (Eds.), *Vocational rehabilitation: Profession and process.* Springfield, IL: Charles C Thomas.

Council on Rehabilitation Education. (November, 1996). *Core news, 8*(1).

DiMichael, S. G., & Thomas, K. R. (1985). ARCA'S journey in professionalism: A commemorative review on the 25th anniversary. *Journal of Counseling and Development, 63*(7), 428-435.

Dvonch. P. (1985). Personal communication on April 2, 1985, at ARCA Symposium, American Association for Counseling and Development, New York.

Evenson, T. L. (April, 1995). *Update on development of standards for undergraduate rehabilitation programs.* April 21, 1995 Memorandum to Program Coordinators of Undergraduate and Graduate Programs in Rehabilitation. University of North Texas, Denton, TX.

Feinberg. L. B., Sundblad, L.M., & Glick. L. J. (1974). *Education for the rehabilitation services: Planning undergraduate curriculum.* Syracuse University.

Finch, F. H. (1937). Qualifications for rehabilitation counselors. *Occupations, 36*, 382-387.

Foundation for Rehabilitation Education and Research. (1997). *Rehabilitation counseling: The profession and standards of practice.* Rolling Meadows, IL: Author.

Gandy, G. L. (1983). Graduates of an undergraduate rehabilitation curriculum. *Rehabilitation Counseling Bulletin, 26*(5), 357-359.

Gandy, G. L. (1987). *Towards a clearer definition of undergraduate rehabilitation education.* Based on a paper presented at the 21st International Congress of Applied Psychology, Jerusalem, Israel, July, 1986. Richmond, VA: Center for Public Affairs Publication, Virginia Commonwealth University.

Gandy. G. L., & Martin, E. D., Jr. (1985). Undergraduate rehabilitation education: A humanistic approach. *Rehabilitation Literature, 46*, (11-12), 321-324, 327.

Gandy, G. L., Crawford, D., Dunlap, D. A., Evenson, T. L., Karst, R. H., Martin, E. D., Jr., Patterson, J. B., Thompson, J. K., & Witten, B. (1987). National Council on Rehabilitation Education position statement on undergraduate rehabilitation education. *Rehabilitation Education, 1*(1), 19-28.

Gandy, G. L., Crawford, D., Dunlap, D. A., Evenson, T. L., Karst, R. H., Martin, E. D., Jr., Patterson, J. B., Thompson, J. K., & Witten, B. (1989). National Council on Rehabilitation Education directory of undergraduate rehabilitation education programs. *Rehabilitation Education, 3*(1), 61-71.

Hardy, R. E., Luck, R. S. & Chandler, A. L. (1982). Licensure of rehabilitation counselors and related issues: Results of a national survey. *Rehabilitation Counseling Bulletin, 25*(30), 157-161.

Hedgeman, B. S. (1985). Rehabilitation counselor certification. *Journal of Counseling and Development, 63*(10), 609-610.

Hylbert, K. W. (1963). Experiment at Penn State: Bachelor of rehabilitation. *Journal of Rehabilitation, 29*(2), 23-24.

Jaques, M. E. (1970). *Rehabilitation counseling: Scope and services* (Guidance Monograph Series). Boston: Houghton Mifflin.

Jenkins, W. M., Patterson, J. B., & Szymanski, E. D. (1992). Philosophical, historical, and legislative aspects of the rehabilitation counseling profession. In R. M. Parker & E. M. Szymanski (Eds.), *Rehabilitation counseling: Basics and beyond.* Austin, TX: Pro-Ed.

Leahy, M. L., & Szymanski, E. D. (1995). Rehabilitation counseling: Evolution and current status. *Journal of Counseling and Development, 74*(2), 163-166.

Leahy, M. J., Szymanski, E. M., Linkowski, D. C. (1993). Knowledge importance in rehabilitation counseling, *Rehabilitation Counseling Bulletin, 37*, 130-145.

Linkowski, D. L., & Szymanski, E. M. (1993). Accreditation in rehabilitation counseling: Historical and current content and process. *Rehabilitation Counseling Bulletin, 37*, 81-91.

Maki, D. R., & Berven, N. L. (1994). Doctoral study in rehabilitation II: Status and trends. *Rehabilitation Counseling Bulletin, 37*(4), 264-276.

Maki, D. R., Berven, N. L., & Allen, H. A. (1985). Doctoral study in rehabilitation counseling: Current status. *Rehabilitation Counseling Bulletin, 28*(3), 146-154.

McCauley, W. A. (1972). The professional status of the rehabilitation counselor. In J. G. Cull & R. E. Hardy (Eds.), *Vocational rehabilitation: Profession and process.* Springfield, IL: Charles C Thomas.

Muthard, J. (1969). The status of the profession. In D. Malikin & H. Rusalem (Eds.), *Vocational rehabilitation of the disabled: An overview.* New York: New York University Press.

National Council on Rehabilitation Education. (1995-96). *1995-6 Membership Directory*. Logan, UT: author.
National Council on Rehabilitation Education. (Winter, 1996). Core commission on undergraduate education (CUE). *NCRE Newsletter, 21*(2), 9.
Oberman, C. E. (1965). *A history of vocational rehabilitation in America*. Minneapolis: T. S. Denison.
Patterson, C. H. (1961). Trends in vocational rehabilitation counseling, *Rehabilitation Counseling Bulletin, 5*, 59-67.
Rubin, S. E., & Roessler, R. T. (1995). *Foundations of the vocational rehabilitation process* (4th ed.). Baltimore: University Park Press.
Stone, J. B. (1966). Counseling and rehabilitation counseling. *Rehabilitation Counseling Bulletin, 10*, 127-133.
Sweeney, T. J. (1995). Accreditation, credentialing, professionalization: The role of specialties. *Journal of Counseling and Development, 74*(2), 117-125.
Thralls, L. A. (Ed.). (1980). *The Department of Rehabilitation Counseling: History and cope*. Richmond, VA: Virginia Commonwealth University.
Witten, B. J. (1980/81). Preparation and utilization of undergraduate workers in rehabilitation: Comparative perceptions of respondents (Doctoral dissertation, Syracuse University. 1980). *Dissertation Abstracts International, 42*, 754B.
Woodrow Wilson Rehabilitation Center. (1973). *Dedication of the Mary E. Switzer Building*. Fishersville, VA: Author.
Wright, G. N. (1980). *Total rehabilitation*. Boston: Little, Brown.

Part Two

THE REHABILITATION PROCESS

Chapter 6

THE REHABILITATION PROCESS: A PERSPECTIVE FOR THE REHABILITATION COUNSELOR

KEITH C. WRIGHT AND E. DAVIS MARTIN, JR.

Rehabilitation means many things to many people. It has been referred to in some circles as the third phase of medicine–a concept, as most of us realize, that is quite limited. We have heard rehabilitation alluded to as being basically a philosophy, a belief in people. In this context we recognize such concepts as the dignity and worth of the individual and the importance of attaining personal happiness through acceptance, healthy independence, and usefulness.

Rehabilitation has also been defined as an investment. From this perspective we view rehabilitation basically on economic factors. In this context we are concerned with the conservation of human resources–our country's most valuable resource. We are considering efficient utilization of human capital, earning power, tax savings, and reduction of disability costs.

Rehabilitation is often viewed merely as a series of services incorporated in a restorative or corrective context. To some persons it is looked upon as a privilege for a select few–perhaps because of eligibility criteria and because of the necessity to set priorities for service. Others view it as a right for all citizens. To some, it is equated with equality of opportunity.

Rehabilitation has also been viewed in relationship to the ecological movement–the relationship between persons with disabilities and their environment. This viewpoint includes the concept of recycling–the recycling of an unproductive person to one of productivity–the recycling of a person from a state of negative dependence to one of healthy independence–the recycling of a person from a status of dysfunction to one of function. This concept also relates to the conservation of resources. This **rehabecology** concept would define the role of a rehabilitation counselor as being a human ecologist. Maki and Riggar (1997, p. 19) expressed this relationship to the environment very well with the following observation:

> This . . . (concept) . . . highlights the importance of not only assessing traits and factors, but the transactions that dynamically describe the interactive nature of person(s) and environment(s). It is suggested that adaptation as a dynamic concept describing the extent to which a person accepts disability as one of his or her many characteristics is a preferred concept to adjustment, which infers a more enduring, static and categoric description when referring to a person's acceptance of their disability.

With such a variety of concepts of rehabilitation–and there are undoubtedly more–it is obvious that definitions will also vary. Thus, rehabilitation has been defined as:

> . . . to improve the value of the client's potential contribution to an employer's output . . . The change can be made either by improving the client's functioning, or by making job accommodations, or both. (Berkowitz, 1984)
>
> . . . a comprehensive, individualized process, prescriptive in nature, and directed toward the development or restoration of functional independence and a quality of life. (Maki, 1986; Maki and Riggar 1997, p. 19)
>
> . . . a comprehensive sequence of services, mutually planned by the consumer and rehabilitation counselor, to maximize employability, independence, integration, and participation of people with disabilities in the workplace and the community. (Parker and Szymanski, 1998, p. 2)

The purpose of this chapter is to discuss rehabilitation as a process. Therefore, to avoid a definition of process as some type of assembly line standardization, it is necessary that readers, in their definition of rehabilitation, define the process as being individualized, flexible, sequential, comprehensive, and goal-oriented toward effective function.

In discussing the rehabilitation process, perhaps the most effective method would be, first, to identify typical steps in the process. These steps would necessarily include those activities which are usually entered into with every rehabilitation client. Such steps in the process would be:

1. Case-finding (including application and referral)
2. Diagnostic and case study procedures
3. Development of the Individualized Plan for Employment
4. Provision and coordination of services
5. Placement and follow along

The rehabilitation process has some unique characteristics that help to distinguish the role and function of the rehabilitation counselor.

The continuity of client-counselor relationship throughout the process constitutes a unique professional role. In many professions, the professional worker is primarily involved with his or her client at a specific point in time in the process. The physician, for example, is often involved with referral, diagnosis, and certification of disability and treatment. The occupational and/or physical therapist and other members of a rehabilitation team often find their involvement at a specific point in the provision of physical restoration services. Rehabilitation team concepts and team practices have essentially modified the role of the rehabilitation counselor. Schumacher many years ago observed that the counselor . . ." becomes the interpreter of services, facilities and strategies necessary for rehabilitation (1977)." One of the counselor's most important professional concerns in present-day practice is to give meaning to the role and function of all other members of the team who will be actively involved in the client's rehabilitation program. It is the rehabilitation counselor who has the global picture of client impediments and a plan for eliminating or modifying them. It is to the counselor, therefore, to whom the client or consumer turns for interpretation of relationships in services and coordination of such services. The continuity of client-counselor relationship throughout the rehabilitation process is, indeed, one of the unique and essential aspects of the rehabilitation counselor's role as a case manager and coordinator in addition to counseling.

A second unique characteristic of the rehabilitation process is the comprehensiveness of the diagnostic and case study procedure. The "cluster principle" recognizes that a person with a missing limb is more than an amputee–"tis neither this nor that, but both and more." This person would probably have a cluster of handicaps or impediments because of the disability that would impact significantly on medical, psychological, social, educational, economic, and vocational concerns. Thus, the rehabilitation counselor becomes involved in these case study linkages that impact on client function.

A third unique characteristic of the process that impacts on counselor role is the functional emphasis in diagnostic and case study procedure. In each area of evaluation, the emphasis is on function. The counselor is interested in what the client can do–what experiences can be built upon–is there a family support system, etc. Certification or diagnosis of disability is only the first step in the diagnostic and case study procedure and is primarily used for eligibility determination.

A fourth characteristic of the process impacting on counselor role is the utilization and coordination of services outside the agency structure–putting the community together–utilizing the community and its resources as a comprehensive rehabilitation center without walls. The counselor coordinates and supplements these services. One of the most valuable functions of the rehabilitation counselor in providing this linkage is the coordination of services from multiple systems . . . (Sixth IRI, 1979, p. 2). Thus, management and coordination skills requirements have given special emphasis to the counseling function.

Today, the rehabilitation counselor represents a link between the experiences of the person with a disability and the world of personal, social, and vocational performance (Schumacher, 1977). Cassell, Mulkey, and Engen (1997, p. 214) have observed that the " . . . practice of rehabilitation counseling rests on the confluence of two professional resources: counseling and management." Moreover they noted " . . . (n)o single professional force can be said to predominate, as synergy is only established through concepts and practice surrounding a 'balance' principle." In other words, rehabilitation is, as noted by Rubin and Roessler (1995, p. 222), " . . . a multispecialty-oriented program requiring the coordination of many disciplines to meet the needs of people with severe disabilities."

The process is individualized, and is a coordinated, interagency, interdisciplinary method of service requiring knowledge of the community and its many resources–public, private, and voluntary. Obviously, the counselor is a diplomat.

Accountability in rehabilitation has been much too superficial–usually related to numbers of referrals, numbers of persons served and/or rehabilitated, referral sources, types of disabilities, agency costs and compliance with regulations. It has been primarily a budgetary and "in house" accountability. Annual reports often make reference to cooperative interagency agreements, but place little emphasis on rehabilitation's role of putting the community together for their clients. This coordinating and unifying role of rehabilitation, if well done, could very well provide for a qualitative and budgetary accountability not yet attained.

Case-Finding

Case-finding is a necessary and logical step with which to begin the rehabilitation process. It might be defined as the activity of locating persons who may be in need of and eligible for rehabilitation services. It includes interpretation of objectives and services of the agency to persons with disabilities, to interested agencies, and to the public–through personal contact and through public information media. It also includes the development and maintenance of regular channels of referral and early agency attention to those referred.

Case-finding as an initial step in the rehabilitation process is very important because there are several factors which indicate a real need for case-finding activities. We know, for instance, that the present rehabilitation program reaches only a fraction of the total number of prospects in need of rehabilitation services. We know that many persons do not know about rehabilitation services–or how to access them. Statistics confirm the fact that many persons apply for or are referred to rehabilitation programs many years after the onset of their disability. Since an application is necessary for almost all of the governmental helping services, it is very important that the helping agencies and the professionals serving them conduct an on-going case-finding program.

Eligibility criteria, as well as rehabilitation resources, continue to expand. Emphasis on serving persons with disabilities has made it possible to serve persons who were previously denied service because of the severity of their disability. Advances in medical knowledge and treatment and the utilization of rehabilitation engineering require continued emphasis on case-finding. The recognition of independent living as an appropriate rehabilitation goal has significantly expanded the eligibility criteria as has the concept of follow along and support after vocational placement (postemployment services).

There are several characteristics of an adequate case-finding program. Some of these are as follows:

1. Referrals should occur early.
2. Referrals should be representative of the population of persons with disabilities.
3. Referral should come from all potential sources.
4. There should be a close coordination and exchange of services by all agencies serving persons with disabilities.
5. There must be a mutual respect, courtesy, and reporting back to referral sources.
6. Good casework.

Some counselors have a tendency to work in those locations and with those types of problems in which they have experienced the most success. This situation usually results because of insufficient resources to serve the needs of all persons in need of assistance and, thus, forces adoption of a priority or selection system.

Diagnostic and Case Study Procedures

As mentioned earlier in this chapter, one of the unique characteristics of the rehabilitation process is the comprehensiveness of the diagnostic and case study procedures. In the rehabilitation counselor's efforts to be comprehensive, evaluation of clients from six major vantage points, as follows, are necessary:

1. Medical
2. Psychological
3. Social
4. Educational

5. Economic
6. Vocational

A medical evaluation is required of all applicants to rehabilitation for several reasons. The counselor wants to establish the nature and extent of the disability, as well as to appraise the total health of the applicant to determine capacities and limitations. These two reasons will allow the counselor to certify the existing disability and the functional handicaps or impediments that exist because of the disability. The counselor wants to ascertain if physical restoration services could remove, correct, or minimize the effects of the disability. The medical evaluation is also utilized to contribute a sound medical basis for selection of a rehabilitation objective, and it contributes significant information for use in counseling.

Medical reevaluation may also be provided. This might be indicated for some of the following reasons:

- periodically for health maintenance purposes in long-term training cases.
- when extensive or lengthy physical restoration services have been initiated.
- cases of chronic disease which may involve acute episodes such as rheumatic heart disease, epilepsy, diabetes, etc.
- instances of otherwise unexplained failure in vocational training or other rehabilitation activities.
- appraisal of the individual's medical status just prior to placement.

A rehabilitation counselor utilizes a psychological evaluation for a variety of reasons. Disability may cause psychological problems. This evaluation may be done by review of existing reports and observation. All clients should not necessarily be required to take psychological tests or test batteries. Psychological testing may be provided as an aid for counseling to help clients better understand themselves and for making reasonable plans and decisions. It will also aid clients in identifying problems and understanding their relative strengths and weaknesses. This evaluation is often necessary to provide information or confirmation of a client's abilities, aptitudes, achievements, interests, and personality. It is important when data on the client's capacities and abilities are lacking, or are ambiguous or contradictory. Psychological testing is mandated when the potential client is referred because of perceived mental retardation, mental disability, or behavioral disorder or learning disability, and a disability diagnosis for eligibility must be affirmed.

A social evaluation is another major area of concern in which more counselor expertise is needed. This fact has been reinforced in our attempts to work with people who are socially and culturally deprived. We have failed many times to understand the social values and the value systems often imposed on clients because of disability, environment, or family influence.

We must recognize the fact that, as rehabilitation counselors, we do not necessarily have the most influence on the client. Family relationships are very important. Rehabilitation is essentially a family concern and many rehabilitation programs fail because we have not evaluated and utilized the attitudes and support of family members and significant others. The attitudes and relationships of family and friends have often conditioned the motivation and behavior of the person with a disability and therefore must be considered when developing a rehabilitation program. Home visits can be very important, as well as counseling sessions with other persons directly involved with the client.

Economic evaluation is for the purpose of determining what investment clients can make toward their own rehabilitation. This evaluation is directly related to a long-standing rehabilitation concept that we as counselors should not do for clients those things that they can and should do for themselves. This concept also recognizes that most clients do better when they have an investment in their own program. Generally speaking, insofar as economic need is concerned, rehabilitation services are basically intended to supplement and complement the existing resources of the person.

The existing resources of clients are often in the form of entitlements. These are referred to as "similar benefits" or "comparable benefits" and should be incorporated into the rehabilitation program when appropriate. In certain cases the vocational rehabilitation agency is prohibited from spending its own funds for services prior to a maximum effort to seek alternative funding for the similar service. This prevents duplication, aids cooperative programming, and establishes appropriate linkages in the human services network. Rehabilitation, since its inception, has not operated in a vacuum, and its success has been dependent on the condition of public and private resources in the community (Hardy & Wright, 1973, p. 79).

Educational evaluation provides the counselor with important information for rehabilitation planning. It is important to know how the client or consumer functioned in the educational setting, i.e., in what subjects did he or she do best and in what subjects did he or she perform poorly. Here we can get an idea as to learning ability, ability to accept instruction and some social data such as ability to get along with others. Perhaps the counselor can build on these educational experiences and attainments. Contact with teachers, the principal, guidance counselor, or school nurse can often result in information that could be helpful. An educational evaluation becomes even more important when development of a training plan is being considered.

Vocational evaluation can be defined as the gathering, interpreting, and then synthesizing of all the vocationally significant data regarding the client, and relating this information to occupational requirements and opportunities. The concept of vocational evaluation is much more than the mere collection of a work history on an individual. In essence, the vocational evaluation is a process in itself, whereby all of the above-mentioned evaluations are synthesized toward a meaningful vocational choice for the client.

Following evaluations in the six above-mentioned categories, the rehabilitation counselor and his or her client can then proceed to step three in the rehabilitation process–the development of the Individualized Plan for Employment (IPE).

The Individualized Plan for Employment

The 1998 amendments to the Rehabilitation Act modified the former provision related to the Individualized Written Rehabilitation Program [101(a)(9)], by changing the name to the Individualized Plan for Employment (IPE) and adding a provision that the IPE is to be accomplished (developed and implemented) in a timely fashion. Significantly, the provisions related to the IPE also (Schroeder, 1998, p. 3):

> . . . expand the role of the eligible individual as a collaborating partner with a qualified rehabilitation counselor in the development, monitoring, implementation and evaluation of the IPE.
>
> . . . individuals (or their representative) now have the option to develop their own IPEs or request the technical assistance of a qualified rehabilitation counselor in developing their IPEs.
>
> . . . incorporate current regulatory language with respect to the exercise of informed choice in the selection of the IPE's employment goal, services, service providers and procurement methods.
>
> . . . requirement that assessment services and services under an IPE must be provided in the most integrated setting that is both appropriate to the service being provided and also reflects the informed choice of the individual.

The IPE, like the IWRP, remains a statement of the ways and means by which the client is to overcome the handicap(s) created by disability and regain or acquire the capacity for work and/or independent living. It is a comprehensive, businesslike, organized statement of the problem(s) and the resources and methods for solving them. The IPE may be jointly developed by the counselor and consumer, by the client or consumer with or without the assistance of the counselor (hopefully with the assistance of a qualified rehabilitation counselor) and is based on a sound rehabilitation diagnosis, and involves individualized, coordinated and discriminating use of varied resources. It is an integral aspect of consumerism.

The philosophy prominent in rehabilitation, and particularly supported by the mandates for the IPE, is the belief that the client should be an active participant in the rehabilitation process. As rehabilitation counselors we must keep in mind that we do not really rehabilitate anyone; we help persons to rehabilitate themselves. The IPE helps to insure that clients understand the agency's services and procedures as well as their own responsibility toward their rehabilitation.

Client rights and appeal procedures if dissatisfaction occurs are provided at this stage of the process for eligible clients. For applicants deemed ineligible, the rights and appeal procedure accompanies the statement of ineligibility. All applicants must receive a statement in writing of their eligibility or ineligibility. Clients must also receive a copy of their IPE.

Counseling pervades the entire rehabilitation process. It should be emphasized, however, that at this stage of the process, the counseling relationship is critical. It is at this point that several evaluative areas are synthesized in a meaningful manner. It is at the point that interpretation of the evaluations in order to effect planning becomes essential. It is at this point in the rehabilitation process that the counselor and the client reason together in a problem-solving effort to determine the ways and means by which the client will overcome his or her impediments. It is at this point in the process that the client will be counseled as to the services that will be received, by whom, and in what order. It is at this stage that the responsibilities of both client and counselor are determined.

Provision and Coordination of Services

"One of the most valuable functions we perform is coordinating services from multiple systems for our clients" (Sixth IRI, p. 2). The issue of counselor versus coordinator has been discussed in several sources–originally by C. H. Patterson in 1957. This recognition of managing and coordinating skills has expanded the professional's role rather than taken away from the counseling function (Parker, p. 297). Whitehouse (1975) noted that the rehabilitation counselor was more than just a counselor or coordinator; that the counselor, as noted in Rubin and Roessler (1995, p. 210), was

> a professional whose skills include those of therapist, guidance counselor, case manager, case coordinator, psychometrician, clinical life reviewer, vocational evaluator, educator, team member, social and family relator, placement counselor, community and client advocate, life engagement counselor, long-term conservator, and clinician. Whitehouse stressed that his global concept of the counselor does not warrant the label 'jack-of-all trades,' but rather the highly respected label of 'rehabilitation clinician,' a professional who can serve a person with a disability from a multifaceted but integrated service standpoint.

Hershenson (1990), and as well reported in Rubin and Roessler (1995, p. 211), stressed a mediation role for the rehabilitation counselor:

> Through their counseling function, rehabilitation counselors enable people with disabilities to reexamine and reconstitute their self-concepts and personal goals. Coordinator skills are needed by the rehabilitation counselor to select and monitor the wide variety of physical, social, and vocational services that clients require to achieve their rehabilitation goals. Finally, through their consulting function, rehabilitation counselors work with the client's family, friends, and employers to redesign the environment in order to maximize access and opportunity for people with disabilities.

The rehabilitation counselor should . . ." be certain that the client knows that he or she is coordinating the process through which the client is passing. The client must strongly feel that continuity of services exists and that the process is coordinated through the counselor" (Hardy & Wright, 1973, p. 80).

It should be noted that it is difficult to coordinate uncoordinated legislation and/or regulations. This is one of rehabilitation's handicaps. The rehabilitation counselor may provide and/or arrange for any goods and/or services necessary to render an eligible individual fit to engage in a gainful occupation. In addition to evaluation, counseling and guidance, and placement services, the counselor can, when indicated, arrange and provide for physical restoration services, training, books and training materials (including tools), maintenance during provision of other services, equipment, initial stocks and supplies, transportation, business and occupational licenses, services to family members, and other goods and services. This wide array of possibilities gives the rehabilitation counselor and the client the opportunity to effectively develop an Individualized Plan for Employment specifically suited to the client. It also requires that the rehabilitation counselor be community-oriented as well as client-oriented.

Physical restoration services can be defined as medical or medically-related services necessary to correct or substantially modify, within a reasonable period of time, a physical or mental condition which is stable (static) or slowly progressive. In this instance, we would include psychiatric treatment and psychotherapy under this definition. Physical restoration services would include medical and surgical treatment, dentistry, nursing, hospitalization, convalescent care, drugs and supplies, prosthetic devices, physical therapy, occupational therapy, and other medically-related rehabilitation services such as speech and hearing therapy.

Rehabilitation training services can be defined as any type of training that may be necessary in order to rehabilitate a person with a disability. This would include vocational, prevocational, personal adjustment, and other training which contributes to the individual's vocational adjustment. The rehabilitation counselor can provide or arrange for several types of training in various settings, for instance, institutional training such as at a college or university, business or trade school, or rehabilitation facility. The counselor may also utilize employment or on-the-job training, supported employment, as well as correspondence training and tutorial training.

Prevocational training would include any form of academic or basic training given for the acquisition of background knowledge or skills which are prerequisite or preparatory to vocational training or to employment where the primary occupational knowledge and skills are learned on the job. Personal adjustment training could be provided for a variety of reasons–to assist the individual to function more effectively, to assist in developing an increase in work tolerance, to assist in the development of good work habits, and to assist in the provision of compensatory skills or techniques.

The rehabilitation counselor must advise each person at the beginning of a training program what is expected. The counselor must require periodic progress reports and promptly call the client's attention to evidence of unsatisfactory progress or attendance before such conditions become serious. The counselor should provide encouragement to the client with due commendation for effective efforts. The counselor should also make certain that the client enrolls in the courses necessary to qualify for the job objective. During the training program, the counselor must continue a close counseling relationship with close supervision.

Placement and Follow Along

The final step in the rehabilitation process is placement and follow-up. This involves assisting a person to find suitable work in a remunerative occupation and following up entrance into employment so as to assure that vocational rehabilitation has been achieved. This activity depends on much more than referral to employers. It is at this stage in the process that the counselor reevaluates the client in relation to the vocational objective. The counselor must determine whether or not the client is ready for work. The counselor must also ascertain that all necessary services identified in the IPE have been provided and that the client has sufficient work tolerance. Clients must understand their performance, abilities, and limitations in terms of their disability while also knowing the job objective in terms of performance standards, usual wages and benefits, working conditions, and opportunities for advancement. The counselor must also be assured that the client has the skills and knowledge required for the vocational objective and the attitude of a desirable employee.

In arriving at an evaluation of job readiness, the counselor must consider such factors as physical readiness, psychological readiness, occupational readiness, and placement readiness. The counselor might prepare the client for employment interviews, arrange for training in job-seeking skills, refer the client to the state employment service, or accompany the client to the employer for direct placement.

Several purposes for follow along become evident. For instance, follow along can provide the occasion for the giving of emotional support to the client when needed. It also provides the opportunity to effect needed adjustments, and often forestalls the client's quitting without attempts at such adjustment. It indicates the counselor's continuing interest in the client and affords the counselor the opportunity to determine if further counseling or training is necessary or desirable. Follow along is necessary to determine if a revised plan is needed. It allows for ventilation of client feelings.

Not only is follow along concerned with the client, but it also provides evidence of interest in the employer's welfare. It provides the counselor an opportunity to determine the employer's satisfaction with the client and with information concerning the possibility of future placements. It will also help to acquaint the employer with rehabilitation services. It is at this point that the counselor determines if employment is suitable, whether or not the work might aggravate the client's disability, and if additional training or other rehabilitation services are needed.

Prior to closing the case record, the counselor must consider at least three basic criteria. If these are determined as satisfactory, closure is appropriate. These criteria are: (1) the program of rehabilitation services has been completed insofar as possible, (2) substantial rehabilitation services have been rendered by the counselor, and (3) the client is suitably employed, preferably in the primary labor market.

REFERENCES

Berkowitz, M. (1984). The economist and rehabilitation. *Rehabilitation Literature, 45*, 354-357.

Bitter, J. A. (1979). *Introduction to rehabilitation.* St. Louis, MO: C. V. Mosby.

Cassell, J. L., Mulkey, S. W., & Engen, C. (1997). Systematic practice: Case and caseload management. In D. R. Maki & T. F. Riggar (Eds.), *Rehabilitation counseling: Profession and Practice.* New York: Springer.

Fifth Institute on Rehabilitation Issues (1978). *Similar benefits.* Menomonie, WI: Stout Vocational Rehabilitation Institute.

Hardy, R. E., & Wright, K. C. (1973). Cooperative alternatives to duplication in social and rehabilitation services. In J. G. Cull & R. E. Hardy (Eds.), *The big welfare mess.* Springfield, IL: Charles C Thomas.

Hershenson, D. (1990). A theoretical model for rehabilitation counseling. *Rehabilitation Counseling Bulletin, 33*, 268-278.

Maki, D. R., & Riggar, T. F. (1997). *Rehabilitation counseling: Profession and Practice.* New York: Springer.

Maki, D. R. (1986). Foundations of applied rehabilitation counseling. In T. F. Riggar, D. R. Maki & A. Wolf (Eds.), *Applied rehabilitation counseling.* New York: Springer.

McGowan, J. F., & Porter, T. L. (1967). *An introduction to the vocational rehabilitation process.* Washington, D.C.: U.S. Department of Health, Education & Welfare.

Parker, R. M., & Hansen, C. E. (1981). *Rehabilitation counseling.* Boston: Allyn & Bacon.

Parker, R. M., & Szymanski, E. M. (1998). *Rehabilitation counseling: Basics and beyond* (3rd ed.). Austin, TX: PRO-ED.

Rubin, S. E., & Roessler, R. T. (1995). *Foundations of the vocational rehabilitation process* (4th ed.). Austin: PRO-ED.

Schroeder, F. K. (1998). The rehabilitation act amendments of 1998. *Information Memorandum, RSA-IM-98-20.* Washington, D.C.: Rehabilitation Services Administration, United States Department of Education.

Schumacher, B. (1977). Rehabilitation counseling. In P. J. Valletutti & F. Christoplos (Eds.), *Interdisciplinary approaches to human services.* Baltimore: University Park Press.

Sixth Institute on Rehabilitation Issues (1979). *VR and the community.* Dunbar, WV: West Virginia Research and Training Center.

Sixth Institute on Rehabilitation Services. (1968). *Principles for developing cooperative programs in vocational rehabilitation.* Washington, D.C.: U.S. Department of Health, Education & Welfare.

Chapter 7

OCCUPATIONAL ANALYSIS, JOB DEVELOPMENT, AND PLACEMENT CONSIDERATIONS FOR REHABILITATION COUNSELORS

E. DAVIS MARTIN, JR., LARRY L. SINSABAUGH, GEORGE R. JARRELL, AND RICHARD E. HARDY

The placement of individuals with disabilities into jobs through which they can maintain themselves is the concept which has allowed rehabilitation counseling to make a substantial contribution to individuals with disabilities and society in general. Because rehabilitation counseling accepts the responsibility of job placement, this emphasis on the final outcome or product is a variable that distinguishes rehabilitation counseling from all other forms of counseling and other applied disciplines in the social services.

Recent technological advances, new diagnostic techniques, and new modes of medical treatment have prolonged the lives of people with chronic disease, or disabilities as a result of injury. For a substantial number of these individuals, treatment has been life saving, but medical science alone has not been able to return them to a predisability level of functioning. Placement in a job suited to the individual's abilities and interests is one important contribution toward achievement of that goal.

Matching an individual with a disability to a job is a difficult and complicated process. A number of factors including age, education, prior work experience, as well as residual functional capacity must be integrated with vocational factors to determine a suitable occupational goal.

Residual Functional Capacity

Medical reports serve as a basis for planning medical treatment as well as defining a suitable vocational goal. Well-written medical reports serve (1) to provide medical opinion as to the presence or absence of disease or injury, (2) to delineate periods and modes of treatment and (3) to state a probable prognosis. These are important elements, although other aspects of the medical report, usually not as prominent, may be of greater utility in establishing a vocational plan. When the physician includes estimates of the effects of a diagnosed illness or injury upon the individual's ability to function in the occupational market place, these are of paramount importance. Frequently in the aftermath of illness or injury, an individual is unsure of restrictions and may be prudent from a medical standpoint. When this happens, an aura of uncertainty permeates the process of vocational planning, job development, and placement. To eliminate uncertainty and provide direction, statements concerning an individual's physical ability are central to occupational analysis and placement.

Disability denotes any diminished capacity to function resulting from chronic disease, accident, or congenital malfunction. Residual functional capacity (RFC) is the maximum degree to which the individual retains the capacity for sustained performance vis-a-vis the physical/mental requirements of a job. Diminished capacity may manifest itself in one or more of the following spheres and delineates areas of informed medical opinion needed to begin the process of career adjustment and job accommodation.

Physical, affecting ambulation, coordination, speech production, vision.

Mental, affecting ability to think, remember, comprehend or general learning ability.

Social, affecting ability to communicate and establish relationships with other people.

Emotional, affecting self-image, self-acceptance, mental health.

Occupational, affecting vocational, homemaking or self-care abilities.

In reporting findings, physicians frequently use negative statements to describe a patient's ability to function, "No heavy lifting, no prolonged standing, cannot bend repetitively," are commonly used. What do these statements mean? "Heavy" may mean a hundred pounds to one physician while another may think in terms of forty to fifty pounds. Prolonged may mean anything from one to six hours. The rehabilitation counselor needs a more precise estimate of the individual's ability to function, preferably stated in positive terms. Physicians should be asked to complete a physical activities form (See Figure 7-1). This requires the physician to be very precise in the estimation of physical function or RFC and should serve to eliminate the counselor's need to infer physical capacity. Definitions utilized in the *Dictionary of Occupational Titles* (U.S. Department of Labor, 1991) to describe strength requirements of jobs frequently serve as the basis for such a checklist. Factors other than residual physical ability, such as the effects of a psychiatric impairment on the individual's ability to perform physical activity in a work setting are equally as important. The functional overlay checklist serves to focus professional opinion upon the residuals of psychiatric or other nonexertional impairment (See Figure 7-2).

Figure 7-1. RESIDUAL FUNCTIONAL CAPACITY

Exertional Factors

Give your best estimate., Any item not answered should be marked N/A. Complete in terms of what your clients can do today. In terms of an 8 hour workday, "occasionally" equals 1% to 33%; "frequently," 34% to 66%, "continuously," 67% to 100%.

I. On an 8-hr. workday, client can (Circle full capacity for each activity)

Total at one time

A) Sit	0	1	2	3	4	5	6	7	8	(hrs.)
B) Stand	0	1	2	3	4	5	6	7	8	(hrs.)
C) Walk	0	1	2	3	4	5	6	7	8	(hrs.)

Total during entire 8 hour day (alternating positions)

A) Sit	0	1	2	3	4	5	6	7	8	(hrs.)
B) Stand	0	1	2	3	4	5	6	7	8	(hrs.)
C) Walk	0	1	2	3	4	5	6	7	8	(hrs.)

II. Client can lift:	NEVER	OCCASIONALLY	FREQUENTLY	CONTINUOUSLY
A) Up to 10 lbs.	( )	( )	( )	( )
B) 11 - 15 lbs.	( )	( )	( )	( )
C) 16 - 20 lbs.	( )	( )	( )	( )
D) 21 - 25 lbs.	( )	( )	( )	( )
E) 26 - 50 lbs.	( )	( )	( )	( )
F) 51 - 100 lbs.	( )	( )	( )	( )

III. Client can carry:	NEVER	OCCASIONALLY	FREQUENTLY	CONTINUOUSLY
A) Up to 10 lbs.	( )	( )	( )	( )
B) 11 - 15 lbs.	( )	( )	( )	( )
C) 16 - 20 lbs.	( )	( )	( )	( )
D) 21 - 25 lbs.	( )	( )	( )	( )
E) 26 - 50 lbs.	( )	( )	( )	( )
F) 51 - 100 lbs.	( )	( )	( )	( )

IV. Client can use hands for repetitive action such as: (circle yes or no)

	SIMPLE GRASPING		PUSHING & PULLING		FINE MANIPULATION	
A) Right	Yes	No	Yes	No	Yes	No
B) Left	Yes	No	Yes	No	Yes	No

V. Client can use feet for repetitive movement as in pushing & puling leg controls:

RIGHT		LEFT	
Yes	No	Yes	No

VI. Client is able to:	NOT AT ALL	OCCASIONALLY	FREQUENTLY	CONTINUOUSLY
A) Bend	( )	( )	( )	( )
B) Squat	( )	( )	( )	( )
C) Crawl	( )	( )	( )	( )
D) Climb	( )	( )	( )	( )
E) Reach	( )	( )	( )	( )

VII. Highest possible exertional level indicated:

SEDENTARY	LIGHT	MEDIUM	HEAVY
( )	( )	( )	( )

Figure 7-2. Residual Functional Capacity

Non-External Factors

None:	No impairment in this area
Mild:	Suspected impairment of slight importance which does not affect ability to function
Moderate:	An impairment which affects but does not preclude ability to function
Moderately Severe:	An impairment that seriously affects ability to function
Severe:	Extreme impairment of ability to function

1. Estimated degree of impairment of ability to relate to other people:
None Mild Moderate Moderately Severe Severe

2. Estimated degree of restriction of daily activities, e.g., ability to attend meetings (church, lodge, etc.), work around the house, socialize with friends and neighbors, etc.:
None Mild Moderate Moderately Severe Severe

3. Estimated degree of deterioration in personal habits:
None Mild Moderate Moderately Severe Severe

4. Estimated degree of constriction of interests:
None Mild Moderate Moderately Severe Severe

5. Estimated degree of limitation in ability to do the following on a sustained basis:

a) Comprehend and follow instructions:
None Mild Moderate Moderately Severe Severe

b) Perform work requiring frequent contact with others:
None Mild Moderate Moderately Severe Severe

c) Perform work where contact with others will be minimal:
None Mild Moderate Moderately Severe Severe

d) Perform simple tasks:
None Mild Moderate Moderately Severe Severe

e) Perform complex tasks:
None Mild Moderate Moderately Severe Severe

f) Perform repetitive tasks:
None Mild Moderate Moderately Severe Severe

g) Perform varied tasks:
None Mild Moderate Moderately Severe Severe

h) Perform work requiring rotating shifts:
None Mild Moderate Moderately Severe Severe

Environmental Factors

Check all those which will influence or modify the client's ability to function

_____ Inside	_____ Wet	_____ Mechanical Hazzards
_____ Outside	_____ Dusty	_____ Moving Objects
_____ Hot	_____ Dirty	_____ Cramped Quarters
_____ Cold	_____ Odors	_____ High Places
_____ Sudden Temperature Changes	_____ Noisy	_____ Electrical Hazzards
	_____ Adequate Lighting	_____ Explosives
_____ Humid	_____ Adequate Ventilation	_____ Radiant Energy
_____ Dry	_____ Vibration	_____ Toxic Conditions

Although Figures 7-1 and 7-2 represent generic information required by the rehabilitation counselor, the variety of formats and forms used to acquire information about a client's RFC are unlimited. Both represent two common ways of summarizing such information. Physicians often complain about the lack of standardization of reporting formats; sometimes it seems that there are as many different styles of forms as there are requesters. Many physicians will not complete the work capacities form without examining the person and/or without the benefit of a formalized work capacities evaluation (i.e., a standardized protocol of measuring exertional capacities: amounts and durations of lifting and carrying, sitting, standing, stooping, pulling and pushing, reaching, and dexterity–both gross and fine motor movement–performed by an interdisciplinary team composed of physical therapist, occupational therapist, and vocational evaluator).

This type of physical capacity evaluation, while very precise, can be time consuming and expensive. Its utility may be more applicable in the area of workers' compensation and forensic rehabilitation where precision is often demanded because of the legal issues involved.

The Functional Capacities Checklist or similar checklists may have greater utility for the rehabilitation counselor and physician to ascertain exertional and nonexertional capacities in less time and for less cost. The FCC is available in two formats: (1) as a paper and pencil instrument (Burke & Dillman, 1984) and (2) as a computer software program (Burke & Dillman, 1990). The value of this instrument to the rehabilitation practitioner and to the physician lies in the systematic methodology it employs to explore and understand the person's perception about the daily barriers encountered regarding exertional and nonexertional limitations (Burke & Dillman, 1990).

The physicians's estimate of RFC should be recent enough to provide an adequate basis for evaluating the person's present state of functional ability vis-a-vis occupational planning, training, and work activities. Rehabilitation counselors in public sector programs may be less constrained by this factor than private sector counselors who are often required to have an RFC determination within a specified time frame. For example, in some states, a determination of job suitability under Workers' Compensation rules may not be made if the physician's decision about RFC is more than 21 days postinjury. Generally stated, the physician determines impairment, residual functional capacity, and percentage of disability while the rehabilitation counselor determines eligibility, vocational handicap (vocational assets and barriers), and access to the labor market (McGowan & Porter, 1967; Klein, Swisher, Lynch, Krewson, 1982; Weed & Field, 1991).

Vocational Factors

Work Experience

The term "work experience" means skills and abilities acquired through employment previously performed by the individual and indicates an area of work which an individual may prefer. Work for which the individual has demonstrated a capability is the best indicator of the kind of work that the individual may be expected to do. Such experience has current vocational relevance where the recency of the work and the skills acquired demonstrate the individual's ability to perform work. In our economic system, a gradual transition occurs in the tasks of most jobs so that by the time fifteen years has elapsed, it is no longer realistic to assume acquired skills and abilities continue to be relevant. An individual who has no prior work experience or has worked only sporadically or for brief but sustained periods of time, may be considered to have relevant work experience. Skills acquired through work experience are not vocational assets unless they are transferable to other skilled or semiskilled work within the individual's current physical and mental capacities. An individual with no work experience may be able to perform only unskilled work which requires the performance of simple duties that can be learned in a short period of time.

Skill Requirement

For purposes of assessing the skills reflected by an individual's work experience and of determining the existence of work the individual is competent to do, occupations are classified as unskilled, semiskilled, and skilled.

Unskilled work denotes work which requires little or no judgment in performing of simple duties that can be learned on the job in a short period of time. Considerable strength may or may not be required. As an example, where the primary work function of occupations consists of handling, feeding, and offbearing (i.e., placing or removing materials from machines which are automatic and operated by others) or machine tending, an average successful job performance can ordinarily be achieved or mastered within thirty days; such occupations are considered unskilled. Other types of jobs requiring little specific vocational preparation and little judgment are likely unskilled. No acquired skills can be attributed to persons who have performed only unskilled work.

Semiskilled denotes work in which some skills are involved but the most complex work functions are not required. Semiskilled jobs may require alertness and close attention to watching machine processes; or inspecting, testing or otherwise detecting irregularities; or tending or guarding equipment, property, materials, or persons against loss, damage, or injury, or other types of activities involving work functions of similar complexity. A job may be classified as semiskilled where coordination and dexterity are necessary as in the use of the hands, feet for the rapid performance of a repetitive task.

Skilled work requires qualifications in which the independent judgment of the individual determines the machine and manual operations to be performed in obtaining the proper form, quality or quantity of material to be produced. The individual may be required to lay out work, to estimate quality, suitability, and needed quantities of materials, to make precise measurements, to read blueprints or other specifications or to make necessary computations or mechanical adjustment to control or regulate processes. Other skilled jobs may require dealing with personnel, data, or abstract ideas at a high level of complexity.

An individual may have transferable skills when the skilled or semiskilled work functions which they have demonstrated in the past work can be applied to meet the requirements of skilled or semiskilled work function of other jobs or kinds of work. Transferability depends largely on the similarity of occupationally significant work functions among jobs in which (1) the same or a lesser degree of skill is required; (2) the same or similar raw materials, products, processes, or services are involved. There are degrees of transferability ranging from a close approximation of work function involving both factors to only remote and incidental similarities among jobs. A complete similarity of both factors is not necessary to help identify other types of work which may be suitable for the individual who has performed semiskilled or skilled work. Where an individual's work skills are so specialized or have been acquired in such a limited vocational setting that they are not readily usable in other industries, jobs, and work environments, they are not readily transferable and the concept of transfer of skills has little utility in identifying other areas of work suitability for the individual with a disability.

Analyzing a person's transferable work skills is a moderately technical process (Salome, 1996) of systemic examination of an individual's work history, functional limitations, and residual capacities related to current occupational and labor market information (Szymanski, E. M., Hershenson, D. B., Ettinger, J. M., & Enright, 1996; Weed & Field, 1994). Considerable expertness is required in using the *Dictionary of Occupational Titles* (U.S. Department of Labor 1991a), *Revised Handbook for Job Analysis* (U.S. Department of Labor 1991b), *The Classification of Jobs* (Field & Field, 1992), the *Occupational Outlook Handbook* (U.S. Department of Labor 1998) as well as demonstrating competency with one or more of the available job matching computer software programs to enumerate technical skills that apply to specific jobs or occupations (Witt, 1992). In making a determination about transferability of skills, the practitioner must differentiate between aptitudes, worker traits, and skills. Aptitudes imply that a person has the potential to do or to perform some activity that may evolve into skills. Skills are specific proficiencies that are learned from working (Witt, 1992). In other words, transferable skills are specific competencies learned on a job that can be used in other jobs and that provide the individual with a competitive advantage in the labor market. Those inexperienced with the concept of transferability of work skills analysis often confuse worker traits (i.e., distinguishing qualities or characteristics), personality characteristics (being a "people person," or is "attentive," "reticent" or "flexible," and work interests (liking to fix things, working with numbers, or helping people) for transferable work skills.

Age

The term "age" refers to chronological age and the extent to which it affects the individual's capability to engage in competitive employment. The factor of age, however, in itself is not determinative of ability to work. The Age Discrimination in Employment Act of 1967 (as amended) prohibits discrimination against persons aged 40 or more unless a bona fide occupational qualification can be demonstrated between age and job performance (Meyers, 1992; Equal Employment Opportunity Commission, 1993). Residual functional capacity, education, and previously acquired work skills all serve to transmute the effects of age on a person's ability to work.

In the case of a younger individual (under age 50), age in itsself is ordinarily not considered to affect significantly ability to adapt to a new work situation. For a person who is closely approaching advanced age (50-54), the factor of age, in any combination with a severe impairment and limited vocational background may substantially affect adaptability to a significant number of jobs in a competitive work environment.

Advanced age (55 and over) represents the point where age significantly affects the ability to engage in substantial gainful work. Where an individual is of advanced age and has a significant disability, such ability may be adversely affected except where the person has skills that are readily transferable to other less physically demanding jobs. Vocational planning for these individuals will require additional time and a thorough evaluation of medical and motivational factors. The concept of retirement, traditionally, becomes very appealing beginning at age 55.

Education

The term "education" is primarily used in the sense of formal schooling or other training which contributes to the person's ability to meet vocational requirements: (1) reasoning ability, (2) communications skills, and (3) arithmetic ability. Lack of formal schooling is not necessarily proof that the individual is uneducated or lacks such capabilities. For individuals with past work experience, the kinds of responsibilities assumed when working may indicate the existence of such intellectual capacities although their formal education is limited. Other evidence of such capacities, for those without past work experience, may consist of daily activities of living and hobbies and/or the results of testing. The significance of an individual's educational background may be materially affected by the time lapse between the completion of the individual's formal education and the onset of a physical or mental impairment(s). Formal education that was completed many years prior to the onset of impairment or unused skills and knowledge that was a part of such formal education may no longer be useful or meaningful in terms of the individual's ability to work. Thus, the numerical grade level of educational attainment is not necessarily representative of an individual's present educational competence, which could be higher or lower.

Illiteracy refers to the inability to read and write. An individual who is able to sign his or her name but cannot read or write and simple communication (e.g., instructions, inventory lists) is considered to be functionally illiterate. Generally, a person who has been labeled as illiterate is an individual who has had little or no formal schooling.

A high school education implies competence in reasoning, arithmetical and language skills acquired through formal schooling. Educational capacities at this level may qualify an individual for work at the semiskilled level of job complexity depending upon the specific curriculum the person completed.

Exertional Considerations

For the purpose of determining exertional requirement of work in the national economy, jobs are classified as "sedentary," "light," "medium," "heavy," and "very heavy." Such terms have the same meaning as they have in the *Dictionary of Occupational Titles*, published by the U.S. Department of Labor (1991a) and are as follows:

Sedentary work entails lifting ten pounds maximum and occasionally lifting or carrying such articles as dockets (e.g., files, ledgers, and small tools). Although a sedentary job is defined as one which involves sitting, a certain amount of walking and standing (two to three hours per eight hour day) is often necessary in carrying out such duties. Jobs are sedentary if walking and standing are required occasionally and other sedentary criteria are met.

Light work entails occasionally lifting twenty pounds maximum with frequently lifting or carrying of objects weighing up to ten pounds. Even though the weight lifted may be only a negligible amount, a job requiring walking or standing to a significant degree, or sitting most the time with a degree of pushing or pulling of arm or leg controls is classified as light. The full range of light work requires standing or walking, off and on, for a total of approximately six hours of an eight hour workday. The functional capacity to perform light work includes the functional capacity to perform sedentary work.

Medium work entails occasionally lifting fifty pounds maximum with frequent lifting or carrying of objects weighing up to twenty-five pounds and the ability to stand and walk at least six hours during the day. The functional capacity to perform medium work includes the functional capacity to perform sedentary and light work as well.

Heavy work entails lifting one hundred pounds maximum with frequent lifting or carrying objects weighing up to fifty pounds and the ability to stand and walk at least six hours during the work day. The functional capacity to perform heavy work includes the functional capacity to perform work at all of the lesser functional levels.

Very heavy work entails lifting objects in excess of one hundred pounds with frequent lifting or carrying of objects weighing fifty pounds or more. The functional capacity to perform very heavy work includes the functional capacity to perform work at all the lesser exertional levels.

Nonexertional Considerations

The assessment of impairments due to mental disabilities includes a consideration of such factors as the capacity to understand, to carry out and remember instructions, to respond appropriately to supervision, coworkers, and to customary work pressure in a routine setting.

Any medically determinable impairment(s) resulting in nonexertional limitations (such as certain mental, sensory, or skin impairments) must be considered in terms of the resulting limitations. When an individual has a nonexertional impairment in addition to an exertional impairment(s), the degree to which additional narrowing of the individual's work-related capabilities must be identified during the evaluation phase of the rehabilitation process.

Environmental Considerations

An impairment may leave an individual with the capacity to meet the strength requirement of jobs; however, the physical surrounding may pose a hazard to the individual's health and therefore must be considered. Environmental restrictions are those which result in the inability to tolerate some physical features that exist in certain types of work, such as the inability to tolerate dust or fumes or sudden changes in temperature. For example, arthritis may prevent an individual from performing jobs which occur in an environment where there are extremes in temperature. An individual with asthma cannot tolerate dust and fumes. Some burn survivors experience difficulties when asked to wear certain types of constricting clothing, in addition to extremes in temperatures, and exposure to dust and fumes.

Vocational Adjustment

An individual who is suddenly prevented from work by virtue of injury or disability may have the residual functional capacity to perform some types of work; however, he or she may lack the capacity to adjust to new work requirements and therefore be incapable of performing work. This is extremely important in those instances where injury or disability prevents the individual from engaging in his or her usual occupation. One of the nonexertional factors to be considered is whether or not the individual can accommodate new physical surroundings, new fellow employees, new tasks. Vocational adjustment must be considered for individuals who have

- a long work history in skilled occupations
- exhibited poor adjustment on the job
- received psychiatric treatment
- experienced traumatic injury after age fifty-five

Consideration of all these factors in conjunction with the person's age, education, and prior work experience must be reviewed and assessed with the person in order to effectively plan for that person's future employment.

Readiness for Employment and Job Placement

Planning for placement begins when the counselor first reads the client's rehabilitation referral form. The rehabilitation counselor must constantly learn about the client in order to effectively help the person secure employment. This is a multi-factorial determination based upon the client's residual functional capacity, vocational considerations, and psychosocial factors. In determining readiness, the counselor is, in effect, diagnosing the assets and impediments faced by the client so appropriate interventions may be planned for and implemented. Figure 7-3 contains a useful checklist for the counselor to determine readiness that has been published by the Job Placement Division of the National Rehabilitation Association (1992, pp 7-8).

FIGURE 7-3. CLIENT READINESS CHECKLIST

Criteria for Determining Job Readiness

A. Physical readiness
   1. Is the client at the maximum level of physical capacity?
   2. Can client travel to and from a job?
   3. Can client work a full work day? A full work week?
   4. Can client meet the physical demands of the kind of work sought?
   5. Does the client understand the nature of the disability and limitations imposed by the disability?
   6. Is client aware of activities and situations that would tend to aggravate the disability or impair general health?
   7. Does client know danger signs like fatigue or coughing as warning that rest or treatment may be necessary?

B. Psychological readiness:
   1. Does the client and the client's family accept the client's limitations?
   2. Does the client and the client's family recognize the client's capacity?
   3. Is client sincerely motivated toward employment?
   4. Is the client able to adjust to the strains and pressures of a work environment?
   5. Does the client react well to supervision?
   6. Does the client react well to other people?
   7. Is the client's behavior appropriate for the job demands?
   8. Are the client's personality traits in keeping with the job tasks?
   9. Are there personal or social problems that might affect the client's performance on the job?

C. Occupational readiness:
   1. Are the client's aptitudes, skills, knowledge and experience commensurate with job requirements, current and future?
   2. Can the client meet the mental demands of the kind of work sought?
   3. Is the client really interested in job under consideration?
   4. Are the job's non-monetary, psychological rewards in keeping with client's needs, values and long-range goals?
   5. Is client aware of opportunities and requirement of the job?
   6. Is client aware of wages? Hours? Special requirements of the job?
   7. Is client aware of possibilities and requirements for advancement in this field?
   8. Has client's preparation been flexible enough for reassignment to other jobs or tasks?
   9. Are the client's work habits and attitudes suitable for successful job performance?

D. Placement readiness:
   1. To what extent can client participate in job-finding process?
   2. Does client know sources of job leads?
   3. Can the client develop a personal information packet?
   4. Can the client satisfactorily complete an application?
   5. Can the client present himself/herself adequately in a job interview?
   6. Is the client prepared for the possibility of taking employment tests?
   7. Would the client continue the job search if a number of turndowns were initially experienced?
   8. Could the client conduct himself/herself appropriately if work were to begin tomorrow?
   9. Has the client's need for job related clothing been assessed?
   10. If client has less than high school education, has there been an assessment of his/her ability to obtain a GED?
   11. Should be client be placed in regular, sheltered, self, or homebound employment?

SOURCE: Job Placement Division, National Rehabilitation Association (Job Placement Digest, April/June, 1992, pp 7-8), Adapted and reprinted with permission.

In assessing job readiness, the counselor completes a Vocational Diagnostic Interview (VDI). The VDI is a specific, structured clinical interview that is used for the express purpose of acquiring vocationally relevant background data to determine whether or not the person (1) has the ability to perform work; (2) can get along with others; (3) has a knowledge of the job; (4) will be dependable and fit a company/employers' work image if offered work; and (5) has personal, medical, or environmental limitations that may present impediments to employment (Strum, Otto, & Bakermann, 1972; Cormier & Cormier, 1985). Strum, Otto, and Bakermann suggested that counselors organize information obtained from the VDI around the following areas: (1) job goal; (2) functional capacities (i.e., physical, learning); (3) job-seeking and retention issues; (4) environmental concerns (e.g., health, impairment prognosis, medical release, medications, limitations); (5) transportation; and (6) special concerns (i.e., marital and family, financial, legal, housing, chemical dependency). These data are then organized into an assessment format such as that displayed in Figure 7-4, the Vocational Appraisal Form.

Overall, the VDI is designed to assess work assets and impediments by determining (1) if the person is appropriate for vocational rehabilitation (VR) services or direct return to work with or without accommodations; (2) what the person wants or expects to accomplish using VR services; (3) the person's vocational problems; (4) personal, educational, and vocational assets; and (5) what services are needed. During the VDI, issues concerning job goals, job-seeking skills, and problems affecting job retention and environment are explored. This information, along with other relevant medical and psychosocial information, is used as a basis for a vocational diagnosis (Strum, Otto & Bakerman, 1972, pp. 3-4). All further job development and placement interventions are then based upon the client's readiness.

Role playing is an excellent method to use in preparing a person for employment interviews. In role playing, it is helpful for the counselor as well as the client to play the role of the employer. Current practice is to expose clients to didactic and experiential preparation, which includes role playing in what is known as "Job Seeking Skills." This practice emerged out of research conducted by the Minneapolis Resource Center (MRC). The MRC Job Seeking Skills (JSS) approach emphasized that clients must do four things within the first few minutes of a job interview to successfully demonstrate that he or she is the "right" candidate for the job: (1) explain skills and abilities; (2) answer problem questions about disability with short positive statements; (3) dress appropriately for the job; and (4) show enthusiasm. Within Figure 7-5, the specific performance factors that must be mastered by clients are detailed.

FIGURE 7-4. VOCATIONAL APPRAISAL FORM

I. Job goal

1. What is job goal?__________ Alternative__________
   a. Experience __________
   b. Related Experience__________
   c. Training__________
   d. Education__________
   e. Skills__________
   f. Licenses__________
   g. Interest__________
   h. Expectations (salary)__________
      (job duties)__________

2. Physical Capacities
   a. Sit__________
   b. Stand__________
   c. Lift__________
   d. Bend__________
   e. Respiratory__________
   f. Verbal__________
   g. Sight__________
   h. Hearing__________

3. Learning Capacity
   (if not fully qualified)
   a. Reading Level__________
   b. Math Ability__________
   c. Memory__________

4. Availability of Jobs
   a. Labor Market__________
   b. Openings__________

II. Job Seeking

1. Work history__________
2. How long since last job?__________
3. Reason left last job__________
4. Frequency of search__________
1. Knowledge of sources__________
2. Explain skills__________
3. Problem questions__________
4. Appearance/grooming__________
5. Enthusiasm__________
6. Money for search__________
7. Job readiness__________

III. Job Retention

1. Absenteeism__________
2. Tardiness__________
3. Co-workers__________
4. Supervisors__________
5. Quality__________
6. Quantity__________
7. Future plans__________

IV. Environmental

1. Health
   a. Prognosis__________
   b. Medical release__________
   c. Medication__________
   d. Limitation__________
2. Transportation__________
3. Family/Marital__________
4. Financial
   a. Garnishments__________
   b. Budgeting__________
   c. Destitute__________
5. Legal
   a. Workmen's Compensation__________
   b. Record__________
   c. Pending__________
6. Housing
7. Leisure Time__________
   (hobbies, etc.)__________
8. Personal__________
9. Chemical Dependency__________
   (alcohol)__________
   (tranquilizers)__________
   (addiction)__________

V. Statement of Problems

____

____

____

Comments:

____

____

____

SOURCE: Strum, Otto, Blakeman (1972). Vocational diagnostic interviewing. Minneapolis, MN: Multi-Resource Center, Inc., p. 6, adapted and reprinted with permission.

FIGURE 7-5. JOB SEEKING SKILLS

Ability to explain skills

Did I use several different statements to support my job choice such as: past work experience, related work experience, training aptitude or intelligence, hobbies?
Did I describe work skills using names of machines or other terms appropriate to my job goal?
Did I answer the question, "Why should we hire you?" by explaining my skills?
Did I explain my skills within the first few minutes of the interview?
Did I respond to open ended questions such as "Tell me a little about yourself," by mentioning my work skills and abilities?

Ability to answer problem questions

Did I explain my answers to all questions on the application blank especially in the areas of physical, history, little education, age, no experience in job for which I am applying, et cetera?
Were my answers to questions in these areas short and did they end in a positive statement about my being able to do the job?
If the problem is visible to the interviewer (age, physical handicap, et cetera) did I mention it within the first few minutes of the interview?

Appropriate appearance and mannerisms

I was neat and clean, wearing clothes similar to those worn by people who do the kind of work for which I am applying.
I maintained good eye contact with the interviewer, and tried not to show my nervousness.

Enthusiasm for work

I stated sometime during the interview that I wanted to work or indicated a desire to work by asking, e.g., about overtime.
I walked in and out of the interview situation briskly.
I had a firm handshake.
I asked specific questions about the job.
I used a "call back" closing.

SOURCE: Multi-Resource Center (1972). Job Seeking Skills Manual, adapted and reprinted with permission.

Some of the first research regarding reasons clients were not getting jobs resulted from the work of the MRC. In a landmark study (1966), the MRC found that many VR clients had difficulty in adjusting to the world of work in three areas: (1) lack of an appropriate job goal; (2) problems with job retention; and (3) poor job seeking skills. Astoundingly, the MRC (p. 3) found:

- 80 percent of the clients did not look for work frequently enough;
- 85 percent of the clients could not explain their skills and abilities to employers;
- 40 percent of the clients demonstrated inappropriate mannerisms; and,
- 90 percent of the clients could not effectively answer problem questions that arise during a job interview.

Many of the job techniques used today may be traced to these findings (Zandy & James, 1976).

After going through mock interview(s) which include a variety of questions, the counselor can provide feedback concerning how the person might improve their performance during an actual job interview. There are a large variety of instructional and job development techniques, and JSS formats and videos available to counselors to employ in role playing activities. Videos such as the *Very Quick Job Search* teach the basic approach necessary to access jobs in both the traditional and nontraditional job markets (Farr, 1991a; 1991b).

Clients must realize that getting a job is not an easy task and, to be successful, a person must actively participate in job securing activities. Bose, Geist, Lam, Slaby, and Arens (1998), in a recent study, concluded compliance with job search strategies was a major predictive factor in obtaining employment. When the client is able to, in fact, secure a job without counselor assistance, this may serve to indicate effectiveness of rehabilitation services. The ability with which the client will be able to do this will vary with motivation and the severity of disability.

For many clients, vocational training may provide a partial answer to many of the problems experienced by workers with a disability. In each case, the counselor should take an individual approach to helping. For individuals who have educational, developmental, or social impediments, various remedial programs may be necessary before actual work training programs can begin. The counselor must exercise considerable judgment concerning what a client needs in order to be totally ready for employment.

On-the-job training can be an effective arrangement for client training. It may be necessary for the counselor to help the employer arrange an appropriate payment schedule for the client, since the person, during training, is not a skilled employee and would not receive an amount equal to the earnings of a regular employee. Some clients take longer than others to gain competitiveness in an on-the-job training situation. In special cases, exemptions to the minimum wage requirements of the Fair Labor Standards Act can be requested when lower productivity is expected as a result of significant impediment or handicap.

Regardless of the technique that is employed, the focus of job placement has centered on assisting the person to prepare for, find, and keep jobs (Vandergoot and Worrall, 1979). For years, rehabilitation counselors have traditionally followed two primary models of job placement, that is, selective placement or client-centered placement approaches. Both of these models focus on jobs identified as existing in significant numbers in the labor market. Counselors who follow the selective placement approach emphasize services such as appraisal of readiness, resume development, and job-seeking skills while assuming major responsibility for job development and placement. Counselors following the client-centered model acquire information for the client and place greater emphasis upon the client to take a leadership role in locating and securing employment. Although each model has its particular strengths and weaknesses, both are generally referred to as the traditional method of job development.

The Entrepreneurial Job Development model popularized by Denise Bissonnette (1994) has emerged as another viable approach to job placement. This model emphasizes creativity and marketing skills of both the counselor and the client. In many ways, this model builds upon traditional approaches but differs as the counselor attempts to develop jobs that do not exist within a particular segment of the labor market. The entrepreneurial model focuses upon the hidden job market and upon determining employer needs. In many ways, this is an employer-focused model. Figures 7-6, A Comparison of Traditional and Entrepreneurial Job Development, summarizes the differences between the two methods.

The entrepreneurial approach to job placement represents a very innovative approach which is consistent with the precepts identified in the 1998 amendments to the Rehabilitation Act regarding the Individualized Plan for Employment.

FIGURE 7-6. A COMPARISON OF TRADITIONAL AND ENTREPRENEURIAL JOB DEVELOPMENT

Traditional Job Development	Entrepreneurial Job Development
Sees a limited job market	Sees a world of possibility
Views the corporate world as impenetrable,inhuman	Views the corporate world as a frame for approachable human systems
Sees organizations as static institutions	Sees organizations as ever-changing processes
Expects organizations to make sense	Expects the unexpected from the people who make up the organization
Focuses on the decision to hire, wants to talk to the decision maker	Focuses on the need to hire, the screening and recruitment process, and the decision to hire; will talk to anybody
Recognizes employers as experts in hiring	Recognizes employers as experts in the business they are running but possible amateurs at hiring
Defines a job by the duties and minimum qualifications	Defines a job by the results produced or needs met
Works to give applicants the best edge against competing job seekers	Works to remove applicants from competition with other job seekers
Seeks openings in the open job market	Seeks opportunities in the hidden job market
Responds to job orders for existing positions	Proposes to create new employment
Utilizes resumes	Utilizes employment proposals and resumes
Sees scarcity of identified employment	Sees abundance of as yet unidentified employment opportunities
Hears, "We're not hiring."	Hears, "We're not hiring yet."
Reacts to the whims of employers	Proacts to the needs of the business community

Source: Bissonnette, D. (1994). Beyond traditional job development: The art of creating opportunity. Chatsworth, CA: Milt Wright & Associates, Inc., reprinted with permission.

Private Sector Job Placement

The National Directory of the Association of Rehabilitation Professionals in the Private Sector (NARPPS) *Standards and Ethics* (1991) document defines three necessary conditions for successful job placement: (1) the client's readiness to participate in selective placement on the basis of skills, attitudes, and appropriateness of prospective jobs; (2) clearly-defined expectations for the client and the provider; and (3) the communication and confirmation of job offers. The Bridges Criteria addresses this first condition. Bridges (1946) many years ago offered four major guiding factors which are involved in the successful employment of persons with disabilities (regardless if placement is facilitated by the private or public sector counselor). These continue to remain as important considerations for counselors today, so much so, that they have been incorporated into the Americans with Disabilities Act (1990):

1. The worker should have the ability to accomplish the task efficiently–that is, to be able to meet the physical demands of the job.
2. The worker should not be a hazard to himself [*sic.*].
3. The work must not jeopardize the safety of others.
4. The job should not aggravate the disability or handicap of the worker.

Job placement is a major function of rehabilitation counselors in both the public and private sectors of rehabilitation but more so in the private sector (Bose, Geist, Lam, Slaby & Arens, 1998). Sinsabaugh (1994), in a review of private sector literature regarding this issue, noted that employers (responsible for paying for rehabilitation services for injured workers) began voicing concerns about public sector VR policies which stressed long-term training as a primary rehabilitative strategy. From this major concern, a new set of priorities for VR services in the private sector emerged. Known as the Welch model, return-to-work (RTW) decisions were organized in six hierarchical steps (Deneen & Hessellund, 1986; Field & Sink, 1981; Field & Weed, 1988; Schwartz & Carbine, 1987; Weed & Field, 1990). According to this model, private rehabilitation providers structured rehabilitation efforts in the following hierarchy:

1. same job, the same employer
2. same employer, a modified job
3. new employer, the same job
4. new employer, a different job
5. short term training
6. self-employment

The primary criteria for placement interventions with clients receiving workers' compensation has been this hierarchical model. One continuing criticism of the private sector is not having set standards for delivery of job placement services and engagement of inappropriate practices like "job stuffing." This is the practice of placing a workers' compensation claimant into "any job" for which the person is physically qualified without first considering the claimant's past work experience, education, or skills (Sinsabaugh, 1994; Sinsabaugh & Martin, in press; Ayella & Crook, 1989; JLARC, 1990; The Maryland Rehabilitation Association and the Chesapeake Association of Rehabilitation Professionals in the Private Sector, 1988, Smolkin et al., 1987).

On the other hand, private sector rehabilitation specialists have enhanced the practice of job placement by developing standardized protocols that are commonly followed by all rehabilitation counselors. For instance, once a suitable job has been located, certain practices should be followed to ensure that all stakeholders (the client–client's attorney, the payor, the employer, and treating physician) will be appropriately notified regarding the job placement. The O'Connor (1988) Return-to-Work model, as noted in Figure 7-7, is a widely accepted protocol for determining job suitability and for notifying the client and other stakeholders about reporting to work. Another feature of the O'Connor model is in its emphasis on successful postemployment follow-up of newly employed workers.

Generally, the rehabilitation counselor should attempt to place clients on jobs which they can "handle" and which do not require modification. In some cases, however, minor modifications can be made with little or no reengineering effort. The counselor will have to be careful in suggesting reengineering of a job, since this can be a costly undertaking in many instances. The major objective should be that of helping workers with disabilities integrate effectively into the total work force without major modifications or change in the work situation. As with other areas involving job placement, rehabilitation counselors must continually update their base of knowledge. Blackwell, Conrad, and Week (1992) developed a guide, *Job Analysis and the ADA: A Step by Step Guide*, to aid counselors in meeting the new employment standards as required by the Americans With Disabilities Act. This guide provides useful information regarding accommodations and is commended to the reader.

FIGURE 7-7. O'CONNOR RETURN TO WORK MODEL

1. Identify the medical restrictions and limitations.

2. Conduct an assessment interview with the person with a disability to identify a) the medical, work and environmental needs and b) the return to work (RTW) work attitude.

3. Conduct a job analysis for the following purposes: a) determine the need for job accommodation; b) identify alternative, light duty or transitional employment compatible witlf the physical restrictions set by the treating or consulting physician; and or c) determine if a task analysis or training analysis is required

4. Obtain medical approval for the RTW alternative. The specialist will: a) explain the job described in the job analysis to the treating physician, and b) obtain the physicians's approval for the job description.[1]

5. Arrange & Communicate job offer:

   a) The written job offer will include the following:

   (1) type of work,
   (2) job starting date,
   (3) where and to whom to report for work,
   (4) that medical approval has occurred,
   (5) scheduled hours expected to be worked,
   (6) whom to call if problems develop,
   (7) expected salary and benefits if applicable.

   b) Notification - The best practice is to deliver a job offer "in-person". The next best method is to send the notification by certified mail so that a written acknowledgment can be obtained. The RTW notice should be provided to the client during a face-to-face consultation. Copies documenting notification should be sent to: (1) the employer, (2) the claims representative, (3) the physician, (4) any other interested party authorized by the principal and client.

6. Conduct a timely RTW follow-up in order to:
   a) determine the adequacy of the regular or accommodated work,
   b) deal with adjustment problems so as to minimize any loss of time,
   c) re-evaluate the job to determine if it continues to match the workers' medical condition,
   d) keep in mind the Bridges (1946) criteria

SOURCE: O'Connor, S. (1988). Management of individuals with disabilities in the workplace. Journal of Job Placement 4(2), 18-21. National Rehabilitation Association, Job Placement Division, adapted and reprinted with permission.

[1]Some employers will attempt to circumvent the medical approval by changing the job so that the job actually performed by the claimant is not the same job which has medical approval. Therefore, jobs which are allowed by the employer must be re-approved by the treating physician. To avoid any misunderstanding the consultant should always attempt to have the employer sign or acknowledge that he or she understands the claimant's medical restriction and approved work authorized by the treating physician.

Eight Common Misconceptions about Job Placement

1. Because placement occurs toward the end of the rehabilitation process, the counselor's responsibility to the client diminishes.

2. Placement is an activity which requires no counselor training and is a matter of matching an available client with an available job.

3. Client location of a job or "self-placement" cannot be effective rehabilitation work.

4. When a client is ready for vocational placement, the information in the case folder is no longer of value to the counselor since the client has been, in a sense, readied for employment.

5. Follow-along after placement always can be handled easily by phone or mail communications with the employer or client.

6. Labor market trends, job information, and analysis are the responsibilities of placement specialists and employment services counselors, not of general rehabilitation counselors.

7. An employer will notify the counselor and the rehabilitation agency when dissatisfied with a client placement.

8. An employer will automatically call upon the rehabilitation agency to furnish additional employees when needed.

Follow-Along After Placement

A rehabilitation counselor is often tempted to consider the job completed when the client is placed in employment which appears suitable; however, this phase of rehabilitation, which begins immediately after the person has been placed in employment, is one of the most complex. Follow along involves the counselor's ability to work between the employer and client in order to help the client solve problems related to the disability that may arise after being hired. The counselor must be diplomatic and resourceful in maintaining the employer's confidence in the client's ability to do the job. At the same time, the counselor must let the client know that he or she has the counselor's full faith. The counselor, as well, must evaluate how the client is performing on the job and be available to help if problems arise which the client cannot solve.

In addition to the rehabilitation counselor's service to the client during follow-along, this period can offer real public relations opportunities for the counselor especially when the employer notes the interest with which the counselor "follows" the client. The frequency of follow-along varies according to the counselor's judgment of the client's job ability and adjustment and/or need for postemployment services.

Summary

The counselor's responsibility in vocational placement must not be underrated. The decisions made at this stage in the rehabilitation process not only affect the client's immediate feelings of satisfaction and achievement but also, of course, long-term physical and mental health. The counselor has a real responsibility to prepare the client for employment by giving that person the type of information needed about the job and about holding employment once it is achieved. Placement should be "client-centered" with strong emphasis given to the client's opinion about work and how it will affect the person and his or her family. Counselors must be ready to answer the questions that employers will ask about hiring persons with disabilities and about the rehabilitation program. Vocational placement is, in essence, high level public relations work.

The counselor must be knowledgeable about job analysis and be able to interrelate all medical, psychological, and social data with job analysis information in order to be successful in client-centered placement. Once placement has been achieved, the counselor must "follow-along" the client in order to make certain that the person is doing well on the job. Effective placement requires good planning, and counselors must constantly evaluate and update their knowledge of the world of work to insure their ability to achieve success in the placement of individuals with disabilities.

REFERENCES

Bissonnette, D. (1994). *Beyond traditional job development: The art of creating opportunity.* Chatsworth, CA: Milt Wright & Associates.

Blackwell, T. L., & Conrad, A. D. (1990). *Job analysis for private sector rehabilitation.* Athens, GA: Elliott & Fitzpatrick.

Bose, J. L., Geist, G. O., Lam, C. S., Slaby, M., & Arens (1998). Factors affecting job placement success in proprietary rehabilitation. *Journal of Applied Rehabilitation Counseling, 29* (3), 19-24.

Bridges, C. C. (1946). *Job placement of the physically handicapped.* New York: McGraw Hill.

Burke, L. K., & Dillman, E. G. (1990). *Functional Capacity Checklist* [computer program]. Athens, GA: Elliott & Fitzpatrick.

Burke, L. K., & Dillman, E. G. (1984). *Functional Capacity Checklist* [vocational instrument]. Athens, GA: Elliott & Fitzpatrick.

Cormier, W. H., & Cormier, L. S. (1985). *Interviewing strategies for helpers: Fundamental skills and cognitive behavioral interventions* (2nd ed.). Monterey, CA: Brooks/Cole.

Farr, J. M. (1991a). *The very quick job search* [Video Tape]. Indianapolis, IN: JIST Works.

Farr, J. M. (1991b). *The very quick job search: Get a good job in less time.* Indianapolis, IN: JIST-Works.

Field, T. F., & Field, J. (1992). *The classification of jobs* (revised ed.). Athens, GA: Elliott & Fitzpatrick.

Habeck, R. V. (1991). Managing disability in industry. *NARPPS Journal & News, 6* (4), 141-146.

Job Placement Division National Rehabilitation Association (1992). Job Readiness Evaluation and Criteria. *Job Placement Digest, Volume XXVII*(2) April June, [Reprint the Placement Handbook of the State of Iowa Division of Vocational Rehabilitation Services]. pp. 7-8.

Klein, M., Swisher, J. D., Lynch, R. & Krewson, C. (1982). The rehabilitation counselor and the medical consultant. *Rehabilitation Counseling Bulletin, 25* (4), 239-242.

McGowan, J. G., & Porter, T. L. (1967). *An introduction to the rehabilitation counseling process.* Washington, D.C.: U.S. Government Printing Office.
Meyers, D. W. (1992). *Human resources management: Principles and practice* (2nd ed.). Chicago: Commerce Clearing House.
Multi-Resource Center (1972). *Job Seeking Skills Manual.* Minneapolis, MN: Author.
National Directory of the Association of Rehabilitation Professionals in the Private Sector (1991). *Standards and ethics.* Brookline, MA: Author.
National Institute on Disability and Rehabilitation Research (1989). Rehabilitation counselors: Qualifications, credentials, and confidence. *Rehab Brief, 11* (12), 1-4.
O'Connor, S. (1988). Management of individuals with disabilities in the workplace. *Journal of Job Placement, 4* (2), 18-21.
Salomone, P. R. (1996). Career counseling and job placement: Theory and practice. In E. M. Szymanski & R. R. Parker (Eds.), *Work and disability: Issues and strategies in career development and job placement* Austin, TX: PRO-ED.
Sinsabaugh, L. L. (1994). *A study of issues critical to the private rehabilitation industry.* Unpublished doctoral dissertation, Virginia Commonwealth University.
Sinsabaugh, L. L., & Martin E. D., Jr. (1998). *A preliminary study of private sector practitioners: Issues critical to the survival of the private rehabilitation industry.* Unpublished manuscript.
Strum, T. E., Otto, V. R., & Bakeman, M. (1972). *Vocational diagnostic interviewing.* Minneapolis, MN: Minneapolis Rehabilitation Center.
Szymanski, E. M., Hershenson, D. B., Ettinger, J. M., & Enright, M. S. (1966). Career development interventions for people with disabilities. In E. M. Szymanski & R. R. Parker (Eds.), *Work and disability: Issues and strategies in career development and job placement.* Austin, TX: PRO-ED.
U.S. Department of Labor (1990). *OWCP rehabilitation manual.* Washington, D.C.: U.S. Department of Labor, Employment Standards Administration, Office of Workers Compensation Programs.
U.S. Department of Labor (1991a). *Dictionary of occupational titles* (4th ed.). Washington, D.C.: Author.
U.S. Department of Labor (1991b). *Revised handbook for job analysis.* Washington, D.C.: Author.
U.S. Department of Labor (1998). *Occupational outlook handbook* (Bulletin 2500). Washington, D.C.: Author.
U.S. Equal Opportunity Commission (1993). *Laws enforced by the U.S. Equal Employment Opportunity Commission* [Publication # 355-218/90016]. Washington, D.C.: U.S. Government Printing Office.
Vandergoot, D., & Worrall, J. D. (1979). *Placement in rehabilitation: A career perspective.* Baltimore, MD: University Park Press.
Weed, R., & Field, T. (1991). *Rehabilitation consultant's handbook* (revised ed.). Athens, GA: Elliott & Fitzpatrick.
Witt, M. A. (1992). *Job strategies for people with disabilities.* Princeton, NJ: Peterson Guides.
Zandy, J. J., & James, L. F. (1976). *Another view on placement: State of the art 1976.* Portland, OR: Regional Rehabilitation Research Institute, Portland State University, School of Social Work.

CASE ABSTRACTS OCCUPATIONAL ANALYSIS, JOB DEVELOPMENT, AND PLACEMENT

E. DAVIS MARTIN, JR., GEORGE R. JARRELL, AND LARRY L. SINSABAUGH

The following case abstracts have been developed to provide the reader with an opportunity to analyze and evaluate the various vocational factors commonly found in persons whose disability poses a barrier or impediment to employment. Being abstracts and not fully developed presentations, an element of ambiguity is, thus, introduced. The point of these abstracts is to allow the reader, either individually or in a small group exercise, to examine and explore the concepts of occupational analysis and placement previously presented in the text. For each case abstract, you are to determine an alternative vocational goal for consideration by the person. Source documents such as the *Dictionary of Occupational Titles, Occupational Outlook Handbook,* and *Enhanced Guide to Occupational Exploration* and others, as appropriate, should be consulted during this exercise. Assumptions may be made as long as those assumptions conform, in general, to the data provided in the case abstract. For each case, assume that maximum medical improvement has resulted in the physical capacities stated in the abstract.

The below noted questions should serve to guide the reader in this process of exploration and examination:

- What further information/data would be helpful in determining an alternative vocational goal?
- Consider the person's residual functional capacity to engage in gainful activity (work). Based on this assessment, what level(s) of work activity (sedentary, light, medium, heavy) can the person do and what level of work is the person unable to do?
- Consider the person's nonexertional residual functional capacities, if any, that may present a barrier to employment (e.g., pain). What effect will this have on the selection of an alternative vocational goal?
- Did the person's previous work provide any transferable skills? If so, what are they?
- What resources would be needed to achieve the alternative vocational goal? How long would it take? How much would it cost?

George T.

Mr. T., 26, is currently recuperating from a back injury sustained last June. At that time he was working as a manager for a fast food restaurant. His treating physician has not released Mr. T. for full-time work as of this date (six months postinjury). As a result of this injury, he has constant but tolerable pain in his right leg. Prolonged walking (2-3 hours at a time) causes his back to hurt. Mr. T. must sit in order to gain relief from this pain.

He is not able to walk for prolonged periods of time and cannot lift more than 20 pounds. Mr. T. is not able to perform the wide range of tasks associated with his previous employment. His managerial duties included inventory control, purchasing, monitoring preparation and quality of food, preparation of financial forms, and training and supervising all the employees. Mr. T. was also required to fill in for employees who were absent and had on numerous occasions performed the duties of cashier/clerk, cleaner, and sandwich maker. This was a fast-paced job which required the manager to stand and/or walk for long periods.

Mr. T. received an academic diploma from high school with a high B average. After high school, he enrolled in the local community college with the intent to major in data processing and computer programming. He completed thirty-eight credits with a 3.2 average. During his last two semesters he was a dean's list student. His college board scores and his grades in mathematics, both in high school and college, demonstrated an ability and knowledge in this area.

Mr. T. appears highly motivated to complete his college education or return to, in his words, "a suitable job." With his present credits, completion of the Bachelor of Science degree should require about 2 years.

Tom R.

Mr. R., 36, is still receiving treatment for a tear in the rotator cuff of his left shoulder. That injury was the result of an accident while employed by Brand X Foods. As a result of that injury, Mr. R. cannot raise his left arm above shoulder level. Any attempt to do so or to lift heavy objects with this arm causes sharp pain, which must be relieved by steroid injection. Mr. R. can manipulate small objects with his arms below shoulder level and he can lift objects up to 20 pounds waist high without discomfort. He can no longer reach above his head with his arm; therefore, Mr. R. cannot perform the full range of activities required in his usual occupation of master fitter and mechanic.

While an employee of Brand X Foods, he completed the following courses:

1. Brand X Training Course–Master Craftsman
2. Training Systems Course–Maintenance Management for First-Line Supervisors
3. Training Systems Course–Air Conditioning and Refrigeration Maintenance
4. General Education Development–Successfully completed requirements.

The results of the Strong-Campbell Interest Inventory taken by Mr. R. indicated a very high interest in mechanical activities. Mr. R. enjoys creating things with his hands and would prefer to work with objects such as tools or large machines. This independent career assessment suggests that Mr. R. should pursue a career in the mechanical/fixing area. His stated interests are compatible with and support the results obtained by the Strong-Campbell. Mr. R. prefers to work on those tasks which provide closure. He likes to know when a task is completed. The Self Directed Search supported a preference for technical jobs.

Mr. R. worked for two years as a master mechanic and fitter. Prior to that he has four years experience as a heating equipment mechanic. The majority of his vocational experience has required activities utilizing hand tools. Regardless of other considerations, Mr. R. prefers activities using these skills. He does not want any job in which desk work plays a prominent part.

Joe J.

Mr. J., 58, injured his back while working as a general laborer. This job involved heavy physical activity requiring constant walking, standing, pulling, and lifting heavy objects. Mr. J.'s prior work experience has been in similar types of jobs.

Dr. C. stated in his latest report: "It is my opinion that he could be employed in a sedentary capacity and it is also my feeling that if he goes back to heavy laboring work he could anticipate a recurrence of his problems. If he had the suitable training and background, I think it would be preferable to employ him in a sedentary capacity."

From an educational perspective, Mr. J. has a good beginning in preparation for an occupational future compatible with his physical capabilities. He received a high school diploma in general business and has completed thirty semester hours of courses in business related subjects over the past few years at the local community college. Earlier in his life, Mr. J. spent two years preparing for a career in business. Logic would dictate that this is an extremely strong area of interest. His stated interests and motivation appear to be directed toward a career in business, and administration of psychological or education tests appears to be redundant and of little value.

Eliott E.

Mr. E. is a 29-year-old journeyman iron worker who has just reached maximum medical improvement. He sustained serious bilateral upper extremity injuries approximately one year earlier in a fall from the building on which he was working. His medical rehabilitation required multiple surgeries and extensive physical therapy and aggressive hand therapy. Mr. E.'s treating physician refused to approve his return to work as an iron worker. Mr. E. is in agreement with the exertional restrictions that the doctor established for specific physical activities, that is, working an eight-hour day, but lifting and carrying restricted to ten pounds. Other physical activities such as squatting, crawling, and climbing are permitted only occasionally, while bending is permitted on a frequent basis. Mr. E. can use his hands to perform such activities as simple grasping and fine manipulation. Pushing or pulling activities must be avoided because of bilateral upper arm weakness. Mr. E. briefly sought psychiatric treatment for intrusive dreams as a result of the fall; however, he has no continuing nonexertional limitations. Mr. E. described having pain routinely at a level one on a scale of 0-10.

Mr. E. is worried about the future. He frequently remarks, "How will I take care of my wife and child?" "Iron work is the only trade I know." He reports disliking school. He says that he does not learn well from books, although he easily grasps an idea when someone takes the time to show him. Results from a vocational interest test suggests that he is "pulled" towards occupations in which he can visualize the results of his work. He likes building and repair activities involving objects. His lowest results were associated with jobs involving work with others. Mr. E. stated he "hates inside or desk work." Temperament testing revealed Mr. E. as flexible, quiet, active, consistent, and reticent. In the past he has supervised up to five ironworkers and six apprentices, but he does not eagerly seek leadership positions. Mr. E. lost his driving privileges approximately nine years ago because of a reckless driving conviction. He is not eligible to regain his driver's license until he pays a court imposed fine and is reexamined by the State Bureau of Motor Vehicles. He has no other felony or misdemeanor convictions. Mr. E. wants to become a forklift, crane, or heavy equipment operator.

Dr. N.

At age 56, Dr. N. was diagnosed as having chronic fatigue syndrome. Memory, alertness, and the ability to focus were her major nonexertional limitations. She experienced daily headaches and fatigue to the point where she remained in bed for the majority of each day. She was granted permanent disability from a private long-term disability policy she held.

Recently, her stamina and alertness increased to about four hours per day for three days per week. Her headaches occur every other day and are no longer severe. She can use the computer for up to two hours per day. Forgetting no longer seems to be much of a problem. With this increased endurance, Dr. N. called her insurance company requesting a consultation with a qualified rehabilitation counselor for the purpose of determining what work she may be qualified to perform within her current limitations.

Chapter 8

ETHICAL CONSIDERATIONS IN REHABILITATION COUNSELING: A PERSPECTIVE FOR THE COUNSELOR AND AGENCY

E. DAVIS MARTIN, JR. AND KEITH C. WRIGHT

The ethical treatment of persons with disabilities is the responsibility of all professionals who participate in the rehabilitation process. Because of the continuity of the counselor-client relationship and the counselor's coordination of services responsibility, this professional is placed in a position to set standards for others. Ethical behavior for the rehabilitation counselor or for that matter any human service practitioner represents an ideal (in terms of personal traits and characteristics) that must be constantly pursued (Corey, Corey & Callanan, 1984). Corey, Corey and Callanan have stated " . . . that counselors who are willing to continually look within themselves and struggle toward becoming more effective human beings are the ones who are most likely to make a positive difference in the lives of their clients" (1984, p. 26). Corey (1996) further reflected on the meaning of a counselor and the characteristics that model such behavior. The identification and subsequent development of a listing of personal qualities or characteristics, according to Corey, was not to define a "fixed model of perfection" but rather to identify ways counselors may assess themselves relative to the growth and development of their clients. In other words, to identify those personal qualities or values and beliefs that the individual counselor would aspire to in making a "significant difference" in the lives of those persons they counsel. From an ethical perspective, the identification and aspiration to such values and beliefs would frame the counselor-client relationship from a posture of counselor effectiveness. Corey (1996, pp. 16-19) noted the following markers of counselor effectiveness:

- Effective counselors have an identity.
- They respect and appreciate themselves.

- They are able to recognize and accept their own power.
- They are open to change.
- They are expanding their awareness of self and others.
- They are willing and able to tolerate ambiguity.
- They are developing their own counseling style.
- They can experience and know the world of the client, yet their empathy is non-possessive
- They feel alive, and their choices are life-oriented.
- They are authentic, sincere, and honest.
- They make mistakes and are willing to admit them.
- They generally live in the present.
- They appreciate the influence of culture.
- They are able to reinvent themselves.
- They are making choices that shape their lives.
- They have a sincere interest in the welfare of others.
- They become deeply involved in their work and derive meaning from it.
- They are able to maintain healthy boundaries.

Personal effectiveness as revealed through these characteristics certainly represents an ideal for the counselor to strive toward. The rehabilitation client deserves no less.

The focus of this chapter will be a review of ethical precepts and the application of these precepts to the rehabilitation counselor from both an agency-counselor perspective and a counselor-client perspective. Issues arising in both of these contexts will be examined and explored.

A Study of Ethics

Ethics is concerned with value judgments upon human behavior. Ethics as a philosophical discipline is concerned with conduct that uses such moral predicates as "ought," "should," "right," "wrong," "good," as they apply to our behavior. Ethics concerns principles or norms that ought to govern conduct rather than those that do. Cottone and Tarvydas (1998, p. 6) noted that "(e)thics, as a philosophy, cannot be separated from morality." Moreover "(m)orality deals with human conduct where judgments are made as to whether a human act conforms to the accepted rules of righteousness or virtue."

Garrett (1966) many years ago defined ethics as "the science of judging specifically human ends and the relationship to means to those ends . . . and . . . the art of controlling means so that they will serve specifically human ends." He added that "ethics really is or should be involved in all human activities" (p. 4).

Noting that all professions have codes of ethics and noting, also, that many civic organizations and businesses have creeds and ethical standards, it becomes apparent that no single or simple guide or rule could suffice for everyone, especially if we support the concepts of flexibility and innovativeness as positive values. As stated by Alfred North Whitehead: "The simple minded use of the notions 'right or wrong' is one of the chief obstacles to the process of understanding." Acceptance of this statement thus leads to a rejection of the Golden Rule as the answer to our ethical problems: "Do unto others that which you wouldst have others do unto you." Judaism taught more than 613 commandments of the Torah, or laws of righteousness of the tribes of Israel. Rules and guides for effective and proper living have been handed down to us for centuries through commandments, maxims, proverbs, and fables. Books directed toward effective living and ethics abound–yet, so do ethical problems. Parents, schools, churches, movies, television and limitless other sources are blamed for our problems.

Wasn't it Leo Durocher who once said, "Nice guys finish last"? Is sportspersonship a myth? Is the intentional foul a proper ethic? Are the following quotations indicative of today's ethics?

All is well that ends well–John Heywood
The end justified the means–Publilius Syrus
Do you remember the poem?
For when the one great scorer comes
To check against your name,
It's not whether you won or lost
But how you played the game.

Do you believe this? Do most coaches or managers? Do most athletes? Do you trust car salespersons, politicians, mechanics, or lawyers? Is there a specific segment of our population you don't trust? Have you given thought to the image of rehabilitation counselors?

Recognizing that the study of ethics is related to rightness and wrongness (appropriateness), let us consider wrongness but emphasize rightness. We give similar emphases in rehabilitation all the time. We consider disability and handicap but emphasize ability. Our very philosophy is opposed to discrimination due to disability. We are concerned with the dignity of the individual. Ethics and rehabilitation have grown up together. Rousseau provides us with an analogy here: "Those who would treat politics and morality apart will never understand the one or the other."

Vash (1981) commenting on a conservative United States senator's pronouncement that "You can't legislate morality," states " . . . morality is just what we do legislate–or try to. The Constitution put forth a moral order, and statutory law attempts to maintain it. Ideally, the goals of the law are what's right, fair and moral to the best of the lawmaker's ability to foresee and implement" (p. 141).

Ethical principles are derived from the general understandings or fundamental assumptions of the larger society regarding what is considered to be right and wrong (Cottone and Tarvydas, 1998). Cotonne and Tarvydas (1998, p. 135) have noted that " . . . (p)rinciple ethics involves objectivity applying a system of ethical rules and principles to determine what is the right or moral decision when an ethical dilemma arises." Beauchamp and Childress (1983) identified these principle ethics as: beneficence, nonmaleficence, autonomy, justice and fidelity.

Rubin, Wilson, Fischer, and Vaughn (1992) further amplify these five principle ethics as related to rehabilitation counseling as follows:

> **Beneficence:** The principle of beneficence applies to acting in a manner that promotes the growth and well being of the client.
> For example, rehabilitation practitioner actions that would be compatible with the principle of beneficence might be:
> 1. Providing a client with vocational training compatible with the recommendations contained in the client's vocational evaluation report.
> 2. Advocating for the client in the job placement process.
> 3. Funding a service such as surgery to prolong a client's productive life.
> 4. Providing support services to the family that are necessary to facilitate the client's rehabilitation gain.
> 5. Providing a client with home modifications in order to make their residence accessible.
> 6. Assisting a client to obtain needed medical services. (p. 10)
> **Nonmaleficence:** The principle of nonmaleficence applies to acting in a manner that does no harm to clients or prevents harm to clients.
> For example, rehabilitation practitioner actions that would be compatible with the principle of nonmaleficence might be:
> 1. Confronting a client concerning his/her self-destructive life style,
> 2. Intervening to meet the specific health care and safety needs of a client,
> 3. Withholding distressing information from clients who are not prepared to handle it, and
> 4. Assisting a client to leave an abusive home situation. (p. 13)
> **Autonomy:** The principle of autonomy applies to acting in a manner that respects the freedom of clients to control their own lives (to make their own choices).
> For example, rehabilitation practitioner actions that would be compatible with the principle of autonomy might be:
> 1. Supporting a specific type of training requested by the client,
> 2. Supporting a client's selection of a particular vocational objective or independent living goal,
> 3. Providing a client with the requested information about job opportunities in the local community,

4. Providing clients with complete information to enable them to make informed choices,
5. Providing a client with requested case file information,
6. Supporting a client's choice to move from a group home to an apartment, and
7. Encouraging a client to take responsibility for obtaining needed services. (p. 15)

Justice: The principle of justice applies to treating clients fairly.

For example, for many rehabilitation counselors the principle of justice generally applied to the fair allocation of available caseload monies to clients, as well as the fair allocation of their limited time to provide direct client services and to complete other job tasks.

The fact that client needs and the time demands of the job role generally exceed available resources places rehabilitation counselors in the position of having to distribute limited money and professional work time among clients in a fair or just manner.

Rehabilitation practitioner actions that would be compatible with the principle of justice might be:

1. Refusing to provide an extremely expensive service requested by an individual client when limited funds are available,
2. Keeping individual case service costs down in order to provide services to a large number of clients in need,
3. Providing an individual with a severe disability with expensive adaptive equipment to enable him/her to have equal access to the community,
4. Being equally accessible to all clients on your caseload,
5. Refusing to continue to provide funds or spend limited available time assisting an unmotivated client who is not working toward his/her independent living or vocational goals,
6. Limiting the amount of time spent with any one client in order to provide services to a large number of clients in need, and
7. Spending a large portion of one's available service delivery time with an individual who has complex independent living service needs to enable him/her to have equal access to the community. (p. 18)

Fidelity: The principle of fidelity applies to keeping promises or commitments, both stated and implied.

For example, for rehabilitation counselors the principle of fidelity generally applies to counselor/client, counselor/colleague, and counselor/agency relationships.

Service delivery actions that would be compatible with the principle of fidelity might be:

1. Adhering with agency case movement guidelines,
2. Providing all services agreed to in the client's Individualized Written Rehabilitation Plan (now the individualized plan for employment),
3. Providing clients with case file information they request,
4. Carrying out a previous rehabilitation counselor's commitment to the client,
5. Completing required case file documentation,

6. Refusing to provide information on a client to other agencies without having the written permission of the client,
7. Abiding by a supervisor's recommendations, and
8. Adhering to organizational policy. (p. 20)

Joseph Fletcher (1966), in his classical treatment of ethics, **Situation Ethics: The New Morality**, permits us to look at ethics from three vantage points. By doing so, we are able to get a better perspective as to the enormity and complexity of the problem.

He describes *Legalism Ethics* as not too different from State Rehabilitation Agency standards and procedures with their rules and regulations, state plan, and manual. "With this approach," Fletcher stated "one enters into every decision-making situation encumbered with a whole apparatus of prefabricated rules and regulations. Not just the spirit but the letter of the law reigns. Its principles, codified by rules, are not merely guidelines or maxims to illuminate the situation; they are directives to be followed. Solutions are present, and you can 'look them up in a book'" (p. 18).

Legalism ethics makes it difficult to honor individual differences in both counselors and clients. It is suggested that the word uniqueness is unique in legalism thinking. Counselor flexibility, innovativeness, and imaginative planning can be seriously hampered. To be sure, we do need laws, rules, regulations, manuals, state plans, codes, and guidelines–yet these should not inhibit or eliminate necessary services to people. Perhaps many current legal requirements were initiated because of counselor malpractice or misinterpretation of program philosophies and principles.

Fletcher states that "Rules are like punt or fourth down or take a pitch when the count is three balls. These rules are part of the wise player's knowhow and distinguish him [sic] from the novice. They are not unbreakable. The best players are those who know when to ignore them" (p. 28).

Fletcher also discusses *Antinomianism Ethics*, a polar opposite of legalism ethics (literally, against the law). Here we can relate to counselors, for example, who have manipulated agency regulations illegally for client benefits. These counselors are certainly client-centered. In their own minds, they may have considered themselves as right and professional. It was the agency, with its regulations and pressures, that was wrong. These counselors were breaking the law. We have seen, not too long ago, situations whereby groups with vested interests, believing the law to be too slow or wrong, took the law into their own hands. They were ethical but against the law. Many revolutionaries practice antinomianism ethics.

Fletcher then discusses *Situation Ethics*. Here, " . . . situational factors are so primary that we may say 'circumstances alter rules and principles'" (p. 29). He qualifies this by stating, "It is necessary to insist that situation ethics is willing to make full and respectful use of principles, to be treated as maxims but not as laws or precepts. We might call it principled relativism" (p. 31).

The Agency and Ethics

The agency must be concerned with ethical practice in a variety of ways. True, it must detect and correct unethical practice either through dismissal of the offending counselor(s) or through rehabilitation measures. Detection and correction are not enough, however. It must set the tone and calibre of professional practice by example.

Accountability criteria for state rehabilitation agencies has been a topic of discussion for some time and may be of significance when discussing ethics. Rehabilitation counselors, educators and others had long ago challenged what has been referred to as the "quota system" or "numbers game" (Rule and Wright, 1974). Perhaps, as suggested by the National Citizen's Advisory Committee on Vocational Rehabilitation which predated Rule and Wright's observation that the "numbers game . . . resulted in a perversion of both program objectives and counselor satisfaction" (p. 30). Certainly, the consumerism movement starting with the passage of the landmark 1973 Rehabilitation Act (and its subsequent amendment and the provisions of the 1978 Rehabilitation, Comprehensive Services and Developmental Disabilities legislation) to the Americans with Disabilities Act (1990), to the 1992 amendments to the Rehabilitation Act and, most recently, the 1998 amendments to the Rehabilitation Act have had the effect of lessening the emphasis on "numbers." As a result of these very significant legislative acts, persons with significant disabilities are being afforded a greater opportunity to seek remunerative employment or to gain independent living skills through the provision of rehabilitation services.

Analyses of agency reports might reflect several ethical concerns expressing the values and the integrity of a program. Inference that rehabilitation is a one-time expense, in general–that it returns ten-fold in tax dollars, monies expended for services and other inferred values, might seriously affect a counselor's values and practice. If the agency does not publish the truth or promotes its program through inference, does it not then give license for the counselor to follow example. The annual report must not be merely a promotional report. It should identify problems and needs as well as success stories. It should be a hard-hitting, factual, informative progress report on the agency–a report that can be believed by administrators, counselors, legislators, and the public. Confidence in rehabilitation can be acquired through ethical reporting practice.

Employment of "qualified rehabilitation practitioners" has long been an issue for rehabilitation educators and has been emphasized within rehabilitation legislation beginning with the 1973 Rehabilitation Act and continuing to the present. The Rehabilitation Services Administration, along with its constituent programs, gave birth to and helped develop professional training programs for rehabilitation counselors in 1954. Millions of dollars have been invested over the years in support of this training–yet, incredibly, the standards and regulations for employment of rehabilitation counselors has only recently been given increased emphasis. A study by Froehlic, Garcia, and Linkowski (1998) regarding minimal hiring standards for rehabilitation counselors revealed that nationally no state required its rehabilitation counselors to hold the certification *Certified Rehabilitation Counselor* (CRC), although 30 states encouraged such certification; 13 states required a master's degree in Rehabilitation Counseling or a related area while 24 states encouraged such degrees; ten states required a bachelor's degree for its rehabilitation counselors; and four states did not even require this level of educational attainment. A study conducted by Lynch and McSweeney seventeen years earlier produced similar results. They noted that counselor education training programs and the certification program for rehabilitation counselors were often taken lightly by the employing organization. Froehlich et al. (1998, p. 201) noted that "(t)he goal of raising the minimum hiring standards for rehabilitation counselors is to provide better services and to improve the vocational outcomes for persons with disabilities." The often cited studies (Cook & Bolton, 1992; Szymanski & Danek, 1992; Szymanski & Parker, 1989) regarding client outcomes and level of education of the rehabilitation counselor are particularly relevant and point to the ethical need not only for the establishment of minimal standards of education but the adherence of those standards when hiring persons as rehabilitation counselors.

Finally, with respect to the agency, let us look at turnover as a possible clue to faulty agency ethics. The counselor who finds it necessary to question agency policies or pressure (he or she could be wrong), the counselor who is underpaid or who feels that he or she is locked in with no growth potential, or the counselor who is used to criticism–but is seldom praised for a job well done, may very well be the organization's problem employee and the one who resigns. When this happens, the agency would do well to examine its own practices as well as those of the counselor.

The Counselor and Ethics

Ethics is related to many things–to benefits, philosophies, and principles. It is measured by behavior. One aspect of counselor practice related to ethics is attitude. Many years ago, a very perceptive and still quite timely document (Rusalem & Baxt, 1969) referred to "attitudinal barriers" whereby the attitudes of a small minority of insecure, frightened, misdirected, and immature practitioners damage the image of the agency and the profession. They fail to realize that their attitudes (and actions) speak not only for themselves but for their coworkers, their employer, and their profession. One study cited revealed that "neither costs nor rehabilitation techniques, neither transportation nor severity of the disability, was found to be as critical as the attitudes of key professional workers" (p. 41). The attitudes and behaviors of counselors almost always reflect on the employer (and profession) wherever the counselor may be.

A few years ago, a true-false question on a case management exam read: "Referral is a good way of escaping responsibility." Some students responded True. Is there a good way of escaping responsibility? Does referral have a linkage with ethics and the counselor?

Although referral has become a rehabilitation staple, its effectiveness may be lessened by interagency rivalries, interpersonal tensions among or between workers for different organizations, and the disinclination of some professionals to "share" their clients with other workers." There are those who fail to use certain community resources because of personal antipathy to an agency's staff or program–those who deny some types of service to a client because they have personal feelings about this service–and those who would inhibit service because of a client's race, sex, religion, or personal characteristics . . . establish unilaterally their own personal service priorities" (Rusalem & Baxt, 1969, p. 40).

Rehabilitation practitioners involved in private sector rehabilitation are, likewise, confronted with ethical issues. Private sector rehabilitation, in general, is funded through third party arrangements–insurance carriers primarily. The issues involved for private and public sector rehabilitation practitioners are very similar–particularly regarding ethical conduct with one's clients–but, nevertheless, do differ on several major points–most notably issues dealing with ethical business practices. The National Association of Rehabilitation Professionals in the Private Sector (NARPPS) has, according to Rasch (1985), " . . . attempted to address a number of professional issues of critical importance to the private sector including practitioner standards, credentialing, ethics and research and training. (p. 11). As a result, NARPPS originally issued in 1981 a Standards and Ethics document (subsequently revised in 1991). This document, as noted by Rasch (1985), focused on minimum requirements for designation as a professional rehabilitation practitioner; confidentiality and client advocacy; ethics, business practices and issues related to compliance.

Perhaps the most direct and compelling statement of ethics is embodied in the Commission on Rehabilitation Counselor Certification's preamble to the Code of Professional Ethics for Certified Rehabilitation Counselors(CRC). In part, it reads:

> Rehabilitation counselors are committed to facilitating the personal, social and economic independence of individuals with disabilities. In fulfilling this commitment, rehabilitation counselors work with various people, programs, institutions, and service delivery systems. Rehabilitation counselors recognize that their actions (or inaction) can either aid or hinder clients in achieving their

> rehabilitation objectives, and they accept this responsibility as part of their professional obligations. Rehabilitation counselors may be called upon to provide various kinds of assistance including: counseling; vocational explorations; psychological and vocational assessments; evaluations of social, medical, vocational and psychiatric information; job placement and job development activities; and other types of rehabilitation services. They are required to do so in a manner that is consistent with their education and experience. Moreover, rehabilitation counselors must demonstrate the adherence to ethical standards and ensure that these standards are vigorously enforced. The Code of Professional Ethics (henceforth referred to as the Code) is designed to facilitate the achievement of these goals. The primary obligation of rehabilitation counselors is to their clients (defined in the Code as individuals with disabilities who are receiving services from rehabilitation counselors). The objective of the Code is to promote public welfare by specifying and enforcing ethical standards of behavior expected of rehabilitation counselors.

Corey (1996) has noted that professional codes of ethics serve a number of purposes: to inform the public about the profession and its responsibility (for the practitioner and the general public), as an accountability mechanism (to protect against unethical practice), and to improve practice (through reflection and self-monitoring). Because codes of ethics describe such a broad range of issues and expected behavior, only minimal standards are articulated for the practitioner to follow. Corey (1996, p. 55) has stated that "(t)here is a real difference between merely following the ethical codes and making a commitment to practicing with the highest ideals":

> *Mandatory ethics* entails a level of ethical functioning at which counselors simply act in compliance with minimal standards.
> *Aspirational ethics* pertain to striving for the optimum standards of conduct.

Tarvydas (1997) similarly has written that codes of ethics are an attempt by the professional organization " . . . to capture the profession's current consensus regarding what types of conduct are appropriate or inappropriate . . . ." Moreover, Tarvydas has observed " . . . they are normative statements rather than absolute dictates of situational guidance . . . ."

Specific issues that arise in rehabilitation counseling that must be addressed by the counselor or practitioner on a daily basis are:

Continuing maintenance of professional skills or competency–the need for the development of a pattern of lifelong learning. Change is a constant within our environment. In order to provide services that are timely and which meet the needs of clients, rehabilitation counselors must avail themselves of a variety of continuing education opportunities ranging from formal educational programs to professional organization meetings to home study to a regular schedule of journal reading and discussion with colleagues. A practitioner's *scope of practice* must constantly be examined by the practitioner regarding maintenance of existent skills and the acquisition of new skills that will benefit the client, consumer or customer.

The appropriate use of tests and test results. Notwithstanding the issue of who has the appropriate authority or competency to perform testing, the rehabilitation practitioner must assure that the testing protocol allows for appropriate accommodation(s) to reveal the true attributes of a client, consumer, or customer. Issues related to race, gender, religion, national origin, and disability are particularly relevant. Testing should be done to screen people, not to screen people out.

The acceptance of gifts (either from clients or from vendors). The giving of a gift, particularly for the client, consumer, or customer, may have great meaning. Obviously, only gifts of nominal monetary value may be accepted by the rehabilitation practitioner–to decline a gift may be interpreted as a very harsh statement or as rejection. Larger gifts, of course, may not be accepted by the practitioner but may, under certain circumstances, be accepted by the organization to fund or further notable client-related activities. Conflict of interest statues define acceptable monetary limits and organizational guidelines should, likewise, offer guidance. Situational ethics, as noted by Fletcher, should be the controlling guideline in these situations. Gifts from vendors, as well, should fall within professional and/or organizational guidelines. Publicly-funded agencies must be representative, for the most part, in the award of contracts for services. In the selection of a vendor, client outcome should be the guiding principle, not extraneous factors unrelated to the service.

Dual relationships. The essence of the rehabilitation process is the client-counselor relationship and it is always based on a professional plane. A personal relationship compromises the effectiveness of the counselor-client relationship and must be avoided. The rehabilitation counselor's role may, at times, be that of a mentor, employment coach or specialist, or other roles that occur within the community (recreation, independent living, social, or residential where life skills are being taught or acquired). Boundaries in these instances may become blurred. The rehabilitation counselor must maintain primary responsibility to assure healthy and appropriate relationship boundaries. Herlihy and Corey (1992) recommended five safeguards to assist counselors in the maintenance of healthy relationships as reported in Cottone and Tarvydas (1998, pp. 338-339):

> *Informed consent:* The counselor should fully inform the client of all possible risks involved, the limitations of the relationships, and the safeguards in place.
> *Ongoing discussions:* The counselor should have periodic discussions with all the parties involved in the relationships to identify and work through any conflicts or concerns that develop.
> *Consultation:* If the counselor does proceed with the dual relationship, an ongoing consultation with a colleague should be in place so that all aspects of the situation will be evaluated to guard against overlooking a problem.

Supervision: If the situation involves a high risk for harm, more continuous supervision may be warranted.
Documentation: Counselors should document all aspects of the dual relationships and issues that arise with the process, including the techniques used to manage the situation.

Relationships involving intimacy or a business partnership with other professionals when services for a mutual client are involved also fall under the category of a dual relationship (Cottone & Tarvydas, 1998). Relationships such as these may be potentially harmful to the client if one of the professionals exerts pressure (knowingly or unknowingly) on the other.

Confidentiality. Clients must be assured that all aspects of the counselor-client relationship are confidential and the counselor may not reveal the essence or any part of that relationship without the expressed consent of the client. The quality of the client-counselor relationship is based on trust. The basis for trust is established by the counselor's assurance of confidentiality. Issues that have the potential to pose ethical dilemmas for the rehabilitation counselor were identified by Patterson and Settles (1992) in a survey they conducted with Certified Rehabilitation Counselors and reported in Cottone and Tarvydas (1998, p. 334):

(a) maintaining confidentiality in institutional settings,
(b) knowing that a client is driving with poorly controlled seizures,
(c) recommending a client who is suspected of abusing substances to an employer.
(d) sharing information with family members about a client with chronic mental illness,
(e) conflicts between workers' compensation and state laws related to confidentiality,
(f) the requirement to report client information to an agency that results in disciplinary action against the client,
(g) learning that a client who has AIDS is not practicing safe sex, and
(h) discussing clients with others without signed written consent.

Confidentiality and privileged communication are not the same; they are, however, similar concepts yet very different. Privileged communication is granted by statute and extended to licensed professionals and not through professional certification. Privilege, as such, varies from state to state dependent on factors related to required qualifications to practice as a rehabilitation counselor either in the public or private domain.

Informed Consent. A central concept in rehabilitation counseling is the involvement of the client, consumer, or customer in the process of rehabilitation or habilitation. With the passage of the 1973 Rehabilitation Act and through its subsequent amendments, client involvement has been continuously encouraged and mandated. Beginning with the requirement that the

IWRP (Individual Written Rehabilitation Program) be jointly formulated by the client and counselor to the IPE (Individualized Plan for Employment) in which the client has the option to develop their own IPE (or request assistance from the rehabilitation counselor), the exercise of informed choice has matured into a consumer centered and directed process. Rehabilitation counselors must respect this major change, particularly for persons with significant disabilities, and assume a posture of assisting clients to successfully effectuate this responsibility. The intent of informed choice, as noted by Cottone and Tarvydas (1998, p. 336), " . . . is to be sure that clients have a sufficient understanding of the circumstances so they can exercise their autonomy and make informed choices."

These issues and others encountered in day-to-day practice require the counselor to develop a "responsibleness," as noted by Tennyson and Strom (1986), that goes beyond the mere application of professional standards. They have stated that " . . . counseling is a moral enterprise requiring responsibleness; that is, action should be based on careful, reflective thought about which response is professionally right in a particular situation" (p. 298). Tennyson and Strom further advise that counselor effectiveness may be enhanced when " . . . their beliefs, attitudes and actions are grounded in reasons that are openly examined through critical reflection. This self-reflection can be pursued independently but is enhanced through rational discourse with professional peers" (p. 302).

The resolution of ethical dilemmas poses a significant responsibility upon the rehabilitation counselor to consciously understand the principle ethics of beneficence, nonmaleficence, autonomy, justice, and fidelity. Several models of resolving ethical dilemmas are available to the counselor (Cottone & Tarvydas, 1998; Corey, 1996; Tarvydas, 1997; Rubin, Wilson, Fischer, & Vaughn, 1992; and Forester-Miller & Davis, nd) and the reader is advised to consult one or more of these citations for more detailed information. Corey (1996) has admonished counselors regarding the importance of continuously reviewing their professional and ethical responsibilities. Toward that end, Corey provides a listing of guidelines that counselors should periodically consider and reflect upon, which is quite instructive (pp. 79-80):

> 1. Counselors need to be aware of what their own needs are, what they are getting from their work and how their needs and behaviors influence their clients. It is essential that the therapist's own needs not be met at the client's expense.
> 2. Counselors should have the training and experience necessary for the assessments they make and the interventions they attempt.
> 3. Counselors need to become aware of the boundaries of their competence, and they should seek qualified supervision or refer clients to other professionals when they recognize that they have reached their limit with a given client. They should make themselves familiar with the resources in the community so that they can make appropriate referrals.

4. Although practitioners know the ethical standards of their professional organizations, they are also aware that they must exercise their own judgment in applying these principles to particular cases. They realize that many problems have no clear-cut answers, and they accept the responsibility of searching for appropriate solutions.
5. It is important for counselors to have some theoretical framework of behavior changed to guide them in their practice.
6. Counselors need to recognize the importance of finding ways to update their knowledge and skills through various forms of continuing education.
7. Counselors should avoid any relationships with clients that are clearly a threat to therapy.
8. It is the counselor's responsibility to inform clients of any circumstances that are likely to affect the confidentiality of their relationship and of any other matters that are likely to negatively influence the relationship.
9. It is important that counselors be aware of their own values and attitudes, recognize the role that their belief system plays in their relationships with their clients and avoid imposing these beliefs, either subtly or directly.
10. It is important for counselors to inform their clients about matters such as the goals of counseling, techniques and procedures that will be employed, possible risks associated with entering the relationship, and any other factors that are likely to affect the client's decision to begin therapy.
11. Counselors must realize that they teach their clients through a modeling process. Thus, they should attempt to practice in their own lives what they encourage in their clients.
12. Counseling takes place in the context of the interaction of cultural backgrounds. You bring your culture to the counseling relationship, and your client's cultural values also operate in the process.
13. Counselors need to learn a process for thinking about and dealing with ethical dilemmas, realizing that most ethical issues are complex and defy simple solutions. The willingness to seek consultation is a sign of professional maturity.

Summary

The ethical treatment of rehabilitation clients, as noted throughout this chapter, is dependent upon a multitude of factors–the most central of which is the good will and intent of the counselor. The employer of this professional, whether in the public or private sector of rehabilitation, is, likewise, an integral participant in the broader issues of ethics (e.g., employment standards for counselors) as they effect individual clients.

The increased awareness of ethical concerns by the consumer, as stated by Stadler (1986) has created an atmosphere where clients have been encouraged " . . . to demand that services be delivered ethically" (p. 291). This trend certainly must be recognized as good for those who receive services and those who deliver and administer such services.

Professional codes of ethics, while not always totally inclusive, have, nevertheless, provided a structure for counselor behavior and responsibility

(Mable & Rollin, 1986). The Commission on Rehabilitation Counselor Certification's Code of Ethics represents one such effort. This statement of ethical concern for the individual rehabilitation client and his or her family when coupled with the notion of "responsibleness" represents a most laudable ideal. Responsibleness in decision making will be of great importance as the ethical issues of the future become more apparent in our day-to-day existence. Preventive rehabilitation with its emphasis and concern on safety, for example, has led a number of legislators to champion mandatory seat belt laws–the desired effect being a decrease in the number of head and spinal cord injuries. The effect of such legislation may, however, further complicate the ethical issue and concern as to how much safety is necessary without unnecessarily invading individual freedom of choice. Ethical issues involving persons born with significant disabilities and the withholding of medical treatment (Section 504 of the 1973 Rehabilitation Act) as well as other similar issues will pose dilemmas requiring responsibleness in the decision-making process. Legislative solutions to many of these ethical issues may infringe on individual responsibility and may not always result in the best decision. Thomas Jefferson, perhaps, provided us with the most appropriate perspective when he noted that " . . . government is best which governs the least. . . ."

In sum, then, as we strive for excellence in the ethical treatment of persons with disabilities, we, as rehabilitation counselors, must continually examine the attitudes, beliefs, and values of our profession and, most importantly, our personal beliefs and values as they relate to persons with disabilities.

REFERENCES

Americans With Disabilities Act of 1990. Public Law 101-336.

Beauchamp, T. L., & Childress, J. F. (1983). *Principles of biomedical ethics.* Oxford: Oxford University Press.

Cook, D. W., & Bolton, B. (1992). Rehabilitation counselor education and case performance: An independent replication. *Rehabilitation Counseling Bulletin, 36* (1), 37-43.

Corey, G., Corey, M. S., & Callanan, P. (1993). *Issues and ethics in the helping professions* (4th ed.). Pacific Grove, CA: Brooks/Cole.

Corey, G. (1996). *Theory and practice of counseling and psychotherapy* (5th ed.). Pacific Grove, CA: Brooks/Cole.

Cottone, R. R., & Tarvydas, V. M. (1998). *Ethics and professional issues in counseling.* Upper Saddle River, NJ: Prentice-Hall.

Foehlich, R. J., Garcia, J., & Linkowski, D. (1998). Minimum hiring requirements for rehabilitation counselors in the states: A comparison across federal regions. *Rehabilitation Education, 12* (3), 193-203.

Forester-Miller, H., & Davis, T. E. (nd). *A practitioner's guide to ethical decision making.* Alexandria, VA: American Counseling Association.

Foundation for Rehabilitation Education and Research (1997). *Rehabilitation counseling: The profession and standards of practice.* Rolling Meadows, IL: Author.
Lynch, R., & McSweeney, K. (1981). The professional status of rehabilitation counseling in state/federal vocational rehabilitation agencies. *Journal of Applied Rehabilitation Counseling, 12* (4), Winter.
Mabe, A. R., & Rollin, S. A. (1986). The role of a code of ethical standards in counseling. *Journal of Counseling and Development, 64* (5), 294-297.
Maki, D. R., & Riggar, T. F. (1997). *Rehabilitation counseling: Profession and Process.* New York: Springer.
Oberman, C. E. (1972). *A code of ethics for rehabilitation counselors.* National Rehabilitation Counseling Association.
Patterson, J. B., & Settles, R. (1992). The ethics education of certified rehabilitation counselors. *Rehabilitation Education, 6,* 179-184.
Rasch, J. D. (1985). *Rehabilitation of workers' compensation and other insurance claimants.* Springfield, IL: Charles C Thomas.
Rehabilitation Act of 1973. Public Law 93-112.
Rehabilitation Act of 1978. Public Law 95-602
Rehabilitation Act Amendments of 1992. Public Law 102-569
Rehabilitation Act Amendments of 1993. Public Law 103-73
Rubin, S. E., & Roessler, R. T. (1995). *Foundations of the vocational rehabilitation process* (4th ed.). Austin, TX: PRO-ED.
Rubin, S. E., Wilson, C. A., Fischer, J., & Vaughn, B. (1992). *Ethical practice in rehabilitation: A series of instructional modules for rehabilitation education programs. Student's workbook.* Carbondale, IL: Rehabilitation Institute, Southern Illinois University.
Rubin, S. E., Wilson, C. A., Fischer, J., & Vaughn, B. (1992). *Ethical practices in rehabilitation: A series of instructional modules for rehabilitation education programs.* Instructor's manual. Carbondale, IL: Rehabilitation Institute, Southern Illinois University.
Rule, W. R., & Wright, K. C. (1974). A new slant to established values: Accountability and counselor reward. *Journal of Applied Rehabilitation Counseling, 5* (4), Winter.
Rusalen, H., & Baxt, R. (1969). *Delivering rehabilitation services.* Washington, D.C.: U.S. Department of Health, Education, & Welfare.
Schroeder, F. K. (1998). *The rehabilitation act amendments of 1998, Information Memorandum, RSA-IN-98-20.* Washington, D.C.: Rehabilitation Services Administration, United States Department of Education.
Stadler, H. (1986). Preface to special issue. *Journal of Counseling and Development, 64* (5), 291.
Tarvydas, V. M. (1997). Standards of practice: Ethical and legal. In D. R. Maki & T. F. Riggar (Eds.), *Rehabilitation Counseling: Profession and Practice.* New York: Springer.
Tennyson, W. W., & Strom, S. M. (1986). Beyond professional standards: Developing responsibilities. *Journal of Counseling and Development, 64* (5), 298-302.
Vash, C. L. (1981). *The psychology of disability.* New York: Springer.
Wright, K. C., & Rule, W. R. (1983). Rehabilitation: In need of its own service. *Journal of Rehabilitation,* January/February/March.

Part 3

COUNSELING AND PSYCHOSOCIAL ASPECTS OF REHABILITATION

Chapter 9

A PSYCHODYNAMIC APPROACH TO ACCEPTANCE AND ADJUSTMENT TO DISABILITY

RICHARD E. HARDY AND JOHN G. CULL

Introduction

In this chapter, material is offered that will be helpful in counseling persons with disabilities. The area of spinal cord injury has been chosen as an example of significant disability. The principles suggested here can be applied to various individuals who have severe or significant disabilities.

The fact that clients are much more similar to us than they are dissimilar is a truism, but they differ in one major respect. They have experienced the psychological impact of disability and have adjusted or are in the process of adjusting to this impact. In the case of the spinal cord injured individual, adjustment problems are severe in that emotional recovery or adjustment for the traumatically injured person is torturous. The counselor or therapist serving the spinal cord injured individual should recognize that the client will not necessarily show a severe disintegrative personality crisis that requires in-depth therapeutic involvement at an immediate period after injury, but the client may fall into an emotional depression over everyday problems of routine personal management and interpersonal relationships. Severe crisis can come about from so-called lower level problems (cues to client feelings are exaggerated demands, refusal to cooperate in medical treatment procedures in the development of psychosocial or psychoneurotic reactions). The point to be made here then is that treatment staff should be very much "tuned in" to various cues that may signal severe emotional distress. These cues are not

---

Adapted from R. E. Hardy & J. G. Cull, Chapter 28: Counseling with Severely Disabled Persons: A Basic Component in Independent Living Services in R. A. Lassiter, M. H. Lassiter, R. E. Hardy, J. W. Underwood, and J. G. Cull (Eds.), *Vocational Evaluation Work Adjustment and Independent Living for Severely Disabled People*, 1983. Courtesy of Charles C Thomas, Publisher, Springfield, IL.

necessarily indicative of severe personality disintegration but may be more indicative of an emotional adjustment crisis.

Characteristic Ingredients Necessary for Effective Counseling and Therapy

There are three central ingredients of a "helping relationship" which have been identified after extensive research and which are necessary interpersonal skills no matter what counseling or therapeutic approach is used by the counselor. These ingredients have been defined by Truax and Carkhuff (1967) and Truax and Mitchell (1971, p. 11) as follows:

1. An effective counselor or therapist is non-phony, non-defensive and authentic or genuine in his helping or therapeutic encounters;
2. An effective counselor is able to provide a nonthreatening, safe, trusting or secure atmosphere through his own acceptance, positive regard, love valuing or non-possessive warmth, for the client; and
3. An effective counselor is able to understand, "be with," "grasp the meaning of " or have a high degree of accurate empathic understanding of the client on a moment-by-moment basis.

These ingredients are required but not necessarily sufficient conditions in order for the therapist or counselor to bring about successful behavior change. In addition to accurate empathic understanding, warmth, genuineness, experiencing, and self-exploration, we must add the necessary and sufficient conditions for the successful intervention of a counselor or therapist in dealing with a particular client or helpee who has a special problem at this definite or particular time in his life (Mitchell et al., 1973).

Idiosyncratic Intervention Strategies

Knowledgeable researchers have experienced considerable difficulty in determining specific antecedents to psychotherapy and counseling outcome. Research has generally indicated that the ingredients listed earlier must be evident in order for any level of successful therapeutic outcome to be achieved. These ingredients must be offered by the therapist in all counseling situations with various clients in various idiosyncratic conditions. Even the length of time in psychotherapeutic treatment in terms of its relationship to outcome is now in dispute (Luborsky et al., 1971, & Mitchell et al., 1973).

The same two reports have shown differences in terms of the seriousness of diagnosis as this is associated with improvement as a result of counseling.

The Luborsky (1971) study showed less improvement with serious diagnosis and the Mitchell et al. (1973) study indicated that the more seriously diagnosed clients were associated with more improvement. The helping person will wish to explore various relationship elements with the client such as the quantity of verbal interaction (is the client doing more listening than talking or more talking then listening). The helping person will also wish to concern him or herself with the content of the verbal interaction of the helpee or client (is the person dealing mainly with external reality or inner feelings; is the helping person offering support mainly or doing selective interpretation).

Certainly the helping person must realize that immediately after the traumatic spinal cord injury is sustained, the client is almost helpless and few demands should be made on the person. The counselor must deal with the person in a direct manner and the helpee's questions must be answered realistically and objectively.

As the client begins to stabilize, the counselor or therapist may become more active. It is at this time that some elementary concepts in rehabilitation may be introduced. In terms of the client's idiosyncratic condition, time should be permitted to realize that no impending danger remains. After a short period, the counselor may increase the amount of challenging stimulation which the client experiences.

The client will actively attempt to deny injury and may withdraw into a passive dependent adjustment pattern. A helping person must constantly stay "on top of " these changing situational concerns. In other words as severe regression evolves, the counselor's perception of the client's situation must change as well.

The client must be helped in realizing that changes have occurred in physical capacity, and, while this change may be indicative of a lessened physical capability, it does not mean that the person as an individual has lessened in value. While the person may be different, he or she is not inherently useless or bad. After the clients's feelings of despair related to a changed body and sense of self have been accepted, the helping person may begin aiding the client in understanding feelings concerning helplessness. It is important for the counselor to offer support, encouragement, and acceptance as well as information which is useful in exploring emotional realities.

In a disability involving no damage to brain tissue, the physical limitation imposed by the disability may cause excessive frustration and, in turn, result in behavioral disorders. For example, an active "outdoorsperson" and nature lover may experience a greater psychological impact upon acquiring a significant disability than an individual who leads a more restricted and physically limited life.

It is obvious that the restrictions imposed by the disability demand a greater change in the basic lifestyle of the "outdoorsperson." Therefore, it is important to note in the predisability (premorbid) personality of the individual that factors directly associated with the actual limitations of the disability, as well as the individual's lifestyle, have an important bearing on the individual's reaction to the disability.

The helping person must explore the individual's attitude toward the spinal cord injury as a particular disability. The individual's adjustment to the injury is dependent upon, to some degree, the attitudes held prior to disability. If attitude toward other spinal cord-injured persons and persons with disabilities in general was quite negative and strong, the person will naturally have a greater adjustment problem than an individual with neutral or positive attitude toward disability and people with disabilities. A part of this attitude formulation prior to the onset of disability is dependent upon the experiences the client has had with other persons with disabilities and the stereotypes that were developed. If psychoanalytic theory is applied to stigma, we can hypothesize that a person without a disability who is prejudiced toward people with disabilities is a relatively immature individual with unexpressed hostilities and a need to feel psychologically superior (English, 1974). If one then wishes to take the psychoanalytic view, one can determine much about the individual's reaction to disability by the attitude held toward persons with disabilities prior to acquiring a disability.

The amount of fear a client expresses or emotion expended during the onset or duration of an illness or accident leading up to a disability also helps determine the psychological impact of the disability. Generally, the greater amount of emotion expended during onset, the better the psychological adjustment to the disability. If an individual is suddenly injured in a car accident, for instance, his psychological reaction to the disability is much greater than if a great deal of emotion has been expended during the process of becoming spinal cord injured.

In addition, the more information an individual has relating to spinal cord injury, the less impact the disability will have. If the individual is told about the disability in a simple and direct manner, the person will have an easier time accepting and adjusting to the disability than if it remained shrouded in a cloak of ignorance and mystery. Any strangeness or unpredictable aspect of our body associated with its function immediately creates anxiety. If not clarified, this anxiety can rapidly be totally debilitating; therefore, it is important for psychological adjustment to a disability that the individual have communicated, in terms that can be understood, the medical aspects of disability as soon as possible after onset.

When we are in strange or uncomfortable surroundings, our social perceptiveness becomes keener. Social cues that are below threshold or not noticed in comfortable surrounding become highly significant to all of us in a strange, new, or uncomfortable environment. Upon the onset of a spinal cord injury, the client will develop a heightened perceptiveness regarding relationships with family members, friends, and professional persons. If others start treating the person in a condescending manner and relegate that person to a position of less importance, reaction to the psychological impact of spinal cord injury will be poor. Professional helping persons can react to the client from an anatomical orientation (what is missing) or a functional orientation (what is left to use). The anatomical orientation is efficient for classification purposes but is completely dehumanizing. The functional orientation is completely individualistic and as such enhances a client's adjustment to disability.

Perhaps a key factor in the adjustment process is evaluation of the future and the individual's role in the future. In many physical medicine rehabilitation centers, a rehabilitation counselor is the first professional worker to see the patient after the medical crisis has passed. The purpose of this approach is to facilitate the patient's psychological adjustment. If the client feels there is potential for regaining independence and security, reaction to the cord injury will be improved. While the counselor cannot engage in specific vocational planning with the client at this time, the counselor can discuss in depth the available vocation rehabilitation programs, and through these preliminary informational sessions, the counselor can help the person evaluate his future.

The last factor that determines the adjustment process and helps the counselor understand the idiosyncratic situation of the client is based upon the individual's view of the purpose of his or her body and the relationship this view has with the type and extent of disability. Body image theory is a neopsychoanalytic system which has been used by many professional persons in explaining adjustment to disability. The concept of body image has been closely related to that of self-concept, although these are not equivalent concepts in the minds of those who advocate body image theory (Wapner & Werner, 1965). It is generally felt, however, that body perceptions accurately reflect generalized feelings of self.

The views individuals have of their bodies may be characterized as falling somewhere along a continuum. At one end of the continuum is the view that the body is a tool to accomplish work; it is a productive machine. At the other end is the view that the body is an esthetic stimulus to be enjoyed and provide pleasure for others. This later concept is much the same as that which we have for sculpture and harks back to the philosophy of the ancient Greeks. Everyone falls somewhere on this continuum. To adequately predict the impact of a spinal cord injury upon an individual, one has to locate the individual along this continuum; then evaluate the disability in light of the individual's view of the functions of his or her body.

The most obvious conclusion to be drawn from the information given is that the degree of psychological impact is not highly correlated with the degree of disability. This statement is contrary to popular opinion; however, disability and its psychological impact is a highly personalized event. Many helping persons fall into the trap of equating degree of disability with degree of psychological impact. It should be remembered that relatively superficial disabilities may have devastating psychological effects. The psychological impact of spinal cord injury is not necessarily greater than the psychological impact of disabilities which are less severe.

Special Roles of the Psychologist

One of the most important roles which the psychologist has in dealing with the spinal cord client is that of evaluation. Many clients are paraplegic or quadriplegic because of the dramatic traumatic injury such as falls, automobile and driving accidents. The psychologist must rule out the possibility of organic brain damage. Various tests are used for this purpose including the Bender-Gestalt, Graham-Kendall, and the Hooper.

The psychologist should be particularly aware of one characteristic that is associated with the sudden onset of disability–that of deep depression. When such a trauma occurs with resulting disability in terms of paraplegia or quadriplegia, the absence of the grief response indicates pathologic concerns. The meaning of the absence of grief is generally that the patient is denying the extent or permanence of the injury.

The psychologist works with the rehabilitation counselor and others and often is more concerned with organized group counseling and therapy than is the rehabilitation counselor, although functions overlap according to the level of training of individual team members. As the client progresses and time nears for leaving the rehabilitation setting, the client will become somewhat anxious about leaving a safe and protected environment. This reaction can be extreme and at times can reach panic proportions. Psychologists should work with other team members in order to expose the client gradually to the outside world. The family should be heavily involved in helping the patient make the transition from rehabilitation center or hospital to home. The psychologist often may wish to suggest weekend passes in order to aid the client in this adjustment.

Psychosexual Readjustment

We should like to preface our remarks with several statements of caution. A counselor or therapist should never exceed his or her professional competency in the name of providing services that one is not qualified to offer. In the area of sexual counseling, for instance, the counselor must be certain that he or she is the individual to do the job. This can be done only by evaluating one's credentials in comparison with those of other counselors who are specializing in the field of marital and sexual problems. In serving spinal cord injured individuals, rehabilitation counselors, psychologists, and others generally are doing the job which should be done in terms of providing useful information and meaningful relationships during so-called sexual counseling.

Many rehabilitation counselors and psychologists are not qualified to do in-depth therapy. The counselor and psychologist must evaluate whether or not the client is receiving the necessary services. If the client is not receiving such services because professional personnel are in short supply, then the rehabilitation counselor and/or psychologist must work to develop expertise under the guidance and supervision of highly trained persons in order to meet the needs of one's clients.

It is interesting that the psychosexual readjustment of the person with a spinal cord injury is a subject of such concern not only to clients but to professional staff members as well that films have been developed for the primary purpose of desensitization of staff members who are working with persons who have spinal cord disabilities (Coles, 1971a, 1971b). In other words, personal inhibitions are so strong among professional staff persons that desensitization is necessary in order for them to openly discuss sexual relations in counseling with clients. The foregoing statements are a good indication of the level of difficulty persons with spinal cord injuries themselves may have in dealing with their problems.

Generally speaking, persons with spinal cord injuries "cry out" for advice, information, and counseling related to altered sexual functioning. Rehabilitation centers and other staff persons may not have been thoroughly informing themselves concerning sexual functionability. Social role theory holds that related to successful role enactment is the concept of role reciprocity (Sarbin, 1954). In other words, every role is closely interwoven with one or more others. The person with a spinal cord injury is expected by others in terms of role set or attitudes or expectations to enact the "sick role." This expectation is constantly enforced by many persons including medical and therapeutic staff, family members, and others who should be supporting an attitude of exploration in order to determine an actual role rather than a sick role. In other words, is the individual exempt from certain routine duties of life? Is one not accountable for one's actions? Is one exempt from social responsibility? Must one always comply with medical advice and cooperate with medical experts? Must one always view health as necessary for optimal performance of the most important life tasks including sexual give and take? These ideas are applied to persons with spinal cord injuries by the authors using original concepts of Parsons (1951).

A factor which probably influences the effectiveness of staff persons in dealing with sexual problems is that of generation. Persons who are not members of the younger generation are quite accustomed to repressing sexuality as a part of their general mores or ways of life. Persons of the present younger generation appear to have many less inhibitions and fewer needs to repression of sexual thought and feelings. This fact in and of itself may lead to improved psychosexual readjustment of persons with spinal cord injuries..

Of course, the helping person must keep in mind that many factors influence sexual functioning. These include religious orientation and other psychological, social and emotional concerns. Hohmann (1972, pp. 108-109) has offered the following in reference to defining sexual relationships:

> Sexual relationship may be defined in many ways, only a few of which are mentioned here to point out that sexuality is indeed "a many splendored thing." It can be (1) a massive buildup of autonomic and striated activity culminating in orgasm; (2) a biological process serving the procreation of the race; (3) a means of bolstering the faltering ego and attendant self-esteem of the participants; (4) a means of manipulation and controlling another important individual involved in the patient's life and (5) a means of expression of two individual personalities and of merging them in symbolic and physical feelings of tenderness, respect and concern for each other and their pleasure.

We have already described some of the characteristics that counselors need in order for them to be effective. With great particularity, these concepts must be present in order for a sexual counselor dealing with clients to be successful. In other words, he or she must develop a relationship with the client that is conducive of good mental health. Inherent in an effective counseling relationship is the absence of threat. The counselor must remove threat if the client is to grow and be able to solve problems in an uninhibited manner. Counseling as a relationship is also typified by the types of feelings that many of us have for our closest friends. True close friendships are characterized by honest caring, genuine interest, and a high level of concern about helping a person in need. Real friendships often require that one person put aside his or her own selfish needs in order to listen long enough and with enough empathy so that a friend's problem may begin to work itself out in a natural and constructive manner.

The counselor should recognize that no matter what particular school of counseling he or she accepts as a practitioner, the most important factor determining outcome of counseling effectiveness is one's own personality. In other words, whether the counselor counts himself or herself as Rogerian, Ellisonian, or eclectic, one's personality will come through in the counseling sessions and affect the outcome to a degree that will determine whether or not the counseling session is effective. Just as teachers can bring about enormous growth and changes in students by modifying their attitudes toward various subject matters, the counselor can bring about substantial changes in clients for better or worse. The counselor who is helping the client deal with spinal cord injury must have accurate physiological, psychological, and neurological information at hand.

In working in the area of sexual concerns, the counselor must evaluate his or her own personality in terms of attitudes, "hang ups," religious feelings, moral values, etc., in order to ascertain whether or not he or she is free in the degree of openness that may be needed to help the client adjust to disability. Stories are legion concerning exploitation of clients by unknowing and knowing counselors as counselor needs are met instead of client needs. Examples include the frigid female counselor who may threaten a client by being seductive as she assumes that the client will be unable to even make a "pass" at her, and the male counselor who may use the client as he explores his own masculinity and psychosexual maturity.

In terms of a knowledge of the psychology of sexual relationships, it is most important for the counselor to be highly sophisticated. Counselors should have an in-depth understanding of the differences between typical males and females in terms of their needs, attitudes, desires, etc. Women for instance may be intensely more interested in love relationships and companionship than in orgasmic potency.

Generally speaking, the counselor working with persons with spinal cord injuries should assume that some sexuality may be possible until experience and careful neurological workups demonstrate that actual intercourse is not possible. Comarr (1970) has shown that in upper motor neuron complete lesions, between 8 and 43 percent of males with spinal cord injuries had been unsuccessful in attempting coitus. Of those with incomplete lesions who attempted coitus, there was one group (thoracic lesions between 7 and 12) in which unsuccessful attempts were at 20 percent. The counselor must always consider that the male client may be able to experience genital relationships through the use of reflexogenic or even psychogenic erections. According to Hohmann (1972), the range of functions is from those with incomplete lesions who may have normal genital sexual functions to those males with complete upper motor neuron lesions who are able to perform sexual genital acts with reliability and endurance in terms of reflexogenic behavior. In addition, many who are free of various sexual hang-ups and inhibitions may derive substantial pleasure for themselves and their spouses through various types of foreplay. This includes for both male and female various types of touching and caressing of both the primary and secondary erogenous zones, cunnilingus, fellatio, digital stimulations, and the use of prosthetic phallic devices. The counselor must be very certain that the client understands that such activities must be mutually pleasing to both parties and that attitudes in reference to sexual behavior will need to be explored gingerly by the counselor with either male or female clients or both and through mutual discussion between spouses.

The counselor may find a review of Individual Psychology as offered by Alfred Adler (1927) of help. The most important to Adler's theoretical constructs that may relate here deal with the stigmatization of persons with physical disabilities in terms of "striving for superiority," "inferiority," "compensation," and the general ideal of the "life-style." Adler has written that all people possess an innate drive to strive for superiority. This particular drive evolves into a pattern or life-style from early childhood. This striving for superiority seems to be motivated by an eagerness to compensate for certain innate feelings of inferiority. We can see from this pattern of reasoning then that the chances for unrealistic striving for superiority among cord individuals with spinal cord injuries are greatly increased over those without such disabilities. The point for the counselor to keep in mind is that there are substantial changes for occurrence of greater emotional difficulties among people with disabilities than among those without disabilities (this is especially true during adjustment phases), although the emotional stability of persons with disabilities has compared favorably overall with persons who do not have disabilities (Wright, 1960; English, 1968; McDaniel, 1969).

The importance of body image theory has been mentioned earlier (Schilder, 1950). In this particular theory, body attitudes are felt to be the result and reflection of interpersonal relationships. In 1960, Cleveland reported that body attitudes appear to change during psychotherapy, and, after later research, he observed that body feelings are often correlated with personality adjustment test results. There are other research studies that have been reported in the literature dealing with this subject, and it is not the purpose of this chapter to reflect all these studies. The point is simply that research has been done to indicate that attitudes toward the body are often the result of relationships among persons, and we know that these body attitudes can be particularly affected by sexual partners, and, especially, if one has an impediment in function.

We cannot overemphasize the importance of the establishment and maintenance of a successful meaningful relationship between the person with a spinal cord injury and spouse. This can do more for the improvement of self-concept than any other one factor.

The counselor should make every effort to encourage open willingness on the part of both partners to enter into mutual discussions among themselves concerning various problems related to sexual relationships. Central tenets should always be genuine concern and mutual respect as well as a gentleness in approaching conversations concerning new topics and problems. The client should realize that discussions on the topics of sexuality can take place along a continuum and that all problems will not be solved this year or the next. The topic of sexuality should be one that can be raised whenever the client wishes. The counselor should never force the client to talk about his or her sexual problems until the client is willing to do so. This will come about as the relationship between the client and counselor develops and as the client feels the need to discuss the subject.

The counselor should encourage group activity on the part of the person with a spinal cord injury. In other words, the client should, when possible, join groups of other persons with spinal cord injuries in order to gain information concerning sexual functionability, as well as other data helpful to adjustment. Spouses can also meet in groups. A great deal of very helpful information can be conveyed through such meetings, and these meetings should continue as long as individuals are receiving help from them.

It will be important for the counselor to meet with the spouse of the person with a spinal cord injury in order to discuss his or her attitudes in reference to sexuality and other care needs. Hohmann (1972) has stated there is a possibility of destroying the libidinous interest of the wife, especially when she is caring for a husband who is severely quadriplegic. Wives have reported that it has been nearly impossible for them to take care of routine bowel care, feeding, etc., for their husbands and still retain an interest in them as sexual beings. Hohmann has indicated that the wise counselor will quickly sense this problem and encourage outside resources such as personal care assistants for these chores.

Generally speaking, female spinal cord individuals are in better condition sexually than males in terms of sexual functionality. Regardless of the level of the cord injury, females, if they are in the childbearing period of their life, have the potential to give birth. Since females generally place a high value on the interpersonal relationship, they can often achieve a quite satisfactory sexual adjustment when a warm and genuine personal relationship exists with the spouse.

The Role of Defense Mechanisms And Psychoanalytic Concepts in Adjustment

The human mind has been described by Gunther (1969) as resembling an iceberg, eight-tenths being below surface (the unconscious). According to Gunther, all overt, objectively observable behavior, including that which appears inexplicable or irrational, has both unconscious as well as conscious origins and meanings to the individual. The counselor needs to understand the unconscious origin of any behavior if that behavior is to be fully understood and dealt with by both counselor and client.

Barker, Wright, and Gonick (1946) and Wright (1955) have offered information concerning adjustment to disability which relates to what has been called "the requirement of mourning." The mourning requirement, when interpreted through Social Role Theory by English (1974), has to do with the concept that there is an expectational demand made on any person with a disability that they act sick, whether they wish to be or not, for a time determined by society following acquisition of a disability. According to English's interpretation of Social Role Theory, the expectation to be depressed over the loss of functionality and to brood or mourn is universally imposed upon persons with disabilities. Mourning is almost always observed along with such related affective dimensions as self-devaluation and generalization of dysfunctional anxiety. Some have interpreted this as a period of body image death as well as a reintegration and a process of almost being reborn as a new individual. This has been particularly applied by Carroll (1961) in reference to blindness.

The person with a spinal cord injury goes through various stages in terms of reaction to this traumatic disability. The first stage is one of shock and may last for several hours or days. A person during this period is generally considerably slowed down in thought processes, feelings are rather flat, and the person appears confused and out of touch. At this period of time, the person has not fully realized what has happened.

After the shock period begins to subside, the client will enter a period of partial recognition of this problem and, as might be expected, the person becomes more responsive, less confused. The person will experience substantial anxiety. People will at this time attempt to protect themselves from their actual feelings concerning what has happened to them and they will give very little thought to the future. In a third stage, which has been called initial stabilization by Gunther (1969), the person becomes superficially reconciled to the disability. This stage may last for months or years. The client may become more cheerful and cooperative and appear more stable. At this time, outward behavior may be quite deceiving in that the person has not come to fully deal with feelings about the injury.

Denial

This state of regression may last for many months. It is an unconscious rejection of the obvious fact of injury that is too disruptive of the personality or too emotionally painful to accept; therefore, in order to soften reality, the obvious fact is denied. Immediately upon onset of disability, the individual denies it has happened. The disability is denied. Then, as the fact of the disability becomes so overwhelming that its existence can no longer be denied, there is a denial of permanency of the disability. While utilizing the defense of denial, the person with a spinal cord injury may adamantly maintain that he or she shall be whole again. There will be a miraculous cure or new surgical technique that emerges to rid oneself of the disability.

When the staff puts pressure on the person to be involved in a treatment program, the client may balk and fall back on primitive pathological attitudes. Projecting responsibility for illness and its cure and accusing personnel of various errors in treatments, etc., may occur. The client may later even become openly hostile and paranoid.

While there are few steadfast rules in human behavior, one is that rehabilitation, at best, can be only marginally successful at this point. Rehabilitation cannot proceed adequately until the client accepts the permanency of disability and is ready to cope with the condition. This is what is meant by many professional persons when they say a client must accept his or her cord injury. Denial is the front line of psychological defense, but it may outlast all other defenses. This is not to say, however, that one should not have hope for a cure, but one would better have a reality regarding the probability when such will occur.

Regression

Regression is the defense mechanism that reduces strain by avoiding it. The individual psychologically returns to an earlier chronological age period that was more pleasant. The person adopts the type of behavior that was attractive at that age but now has been outgrown.

As the individual withdraws, becomes egocentric and hypochondriacal, he or she may regress to an earlier age that was more satisfactory. This regression may be manifested in two manners. First, the person may, in regression, adopt the dress, mannerisms, speech, etc., of contemporaries at the age level to which he or she is regressing. Second, the person may adopt the outmoded dress, mannerisms, speech, etc., of an earlier time in his or her life. The second manifestation of regression is considerably more maladaptive since it holds the individual out to more ridicule, which at this point in adjustment to disability, quite possibly will result in more emphasis on the defense mechanism of withdrawal. This could be regressive as far as the adjustment process is concerned.

As the person becomes fully aware of altered bodily functions and begins to think about the future, the person may experience many agonizing feelings.

Repression

Repression is selective forgetting. It is contrasted with suppression which is conscious voluntary forgetting. Repression is unconscious. Events are repressed because they are psychologically traumatic. As mentioned earlier, the attitudes of clients relative to spinal cord injury and to others with similar disabilities has a major bearing upon adjustment. If these attitudes are highly negative, the client will have to repress them at this point if adjustment is to progress. Until the person represses the events, they will be unable to accept the required new body image.

Reaction Formation

When an individual has an attitude that creates a great deal of guilt, tension, or anxiety, and unconsciously adopts behavior typical of the opposite attitude, the person has developed a reaction formation. In order to inhibit a tendency to flee in terror, a boy will express his nonchalance by whistling in the dark. Some timid persons, who feel anxious in relating with others, hide behind a facade of gruffness and assume an attitude of hostility to protect themselves from fear. A third and last example is that of a mother who feels guilty about her rejection of a newborn child and may adopt an attitude of extreme overprotectiveness to reduce the anxiety produced by her feeling of guilt. This example is seen more often in cases of parents with children who have disabilities.

In this new and seemingly dependent role, the person will feel varying degrees of hostility and resentment toward those upon whom he or she is so dependent–wife, husband, children, relatives, and others. Since these feelings are unacceptable, the person may develop a reaction formation. The manifest behavior will be marked by concern, love, affection, closeness, etc.–all to an excessive degree.

Fantasy

Fantasy is daydreaming. It is the imaginary representative of satisfactions that are not attained in real experience. This defense mechanism quite often accompanies withdrawal. As the client starts to adjust to a new body image and a new role in life, the person will develop a rich, overactive fantasy life. In this dream world, the person will place himself or herself in many different situations to see how well he or she fits.

Rationalization

Rationalization is giving socially acceptable reasons for behavior and decisions. There are four types of rationalization that are generally accepted. The first is called blaming an incident cause–the child who stumbles blames the stool by kicking it; the poor or sloppy workperson blames his or her tools. "Sour grapes" rationalization is called into play when an individual is thwarted. A goal to which the individual aspires is blocked to him or her; therefore, he or she devalues the goal by saying he or she did not really want to reach his or her goal so much anyway. The opposite type of rationalization is called "sweet lemons." When something the individual does not want is forced upon him or her, he or she will modify his or her attitude by saying it was really a very desirable goal, and he or she feels quite positive about the new condition. The fourth and last type of rationalization is called the doctrine of balances. In this type of rationalization, we balance negative attributes with positive qualities. For example, beautiful women are assumed to be dumb; bright boys are assumed to be weak and asthenic; and the poor are happier than the rich.

The person with a spinal cord injury will have to rationalize disability to assist in accepting the permanence of the disability. One rationalization may be that the person had nothing to do with his or her current condition; something over which one had no control caused the disability. Another dynamic that might be observed is the adherence to the belief on the part of the client that as a result of the disability there will be compensating factors (for example, one might have more time to read and develop special competencies since one no longer has to work). We once worked with a client with paraplegia whose rationalization for his disability was somewhat as follows: All of the men in his family had been highly active outdoor types. They had all died prematurely with coronaries. The client was a highly active outdoor type: however, now that he had a severe disability, he would be considerably restricted in his activities. Therefore, he would not die prematurely. The logic resulted in the conclusion that the disability was positive and he was pleased to have become paraplegic. Granted, rationalization is seldom carried to this extreme in the adjustment process, but this case is illustrative of a type of thinking which must occur for good adjustment.

Projection

A person who perceives traits or qualities that are unacceptable may deny these traits and project them to others. In doing so, the defense mechanism of projection is used. A person who is quite stingy sees others as trying to steal. A person who feels inferior rejects this idea and instead projects it to others–that is, the person is capable but others will not give them a chance because they doubt their ability. These are examples of projection. With the spinal-cord injured person, many of the feelings that one has of oneself are unacceptable. Therefore, in order to adjust adequately the person projects these feeling to society in general. "They" feel he or she is inferior and to be devalued. This type of thinking, usually, leads directly into identification and compensation which are in reality the natural exits from the mental maze in which the person has been wandering.

Identification

The defense mechanism of identification is used to reduce an individual's conflicts through the achievements of another person or group of people. A person may derive feelings of social and psychological adequacy through clothes, a sports car, stereophonic paraphernalia, and so forth. People identify with larger groups in order to take on their power, prestige, and the respect attributed to that organization ("our team won"). The larger group may be a social club, lodge, garden club, college or professional group.

In adjusting to disability, the client will identify with a larger group. It may be a group of persons with their particular disability, an occupational group, a men's lodge, a veteran's group, etc. At this point in the adjustment process, the person will identify with some group in order to offset some of the feelings one has as a result of the projection in which they were engaging. If successful, the identification obviates the need to employ the mechanisms of denial, withdrawal, and regression.

Compensation

If an individual's path to a set of goals is blocked, and they find other routes to achieve that set of goals, the defense mechanism of compensation is being used. A teenager is seeking recognition and acceptance from one's peers. The person decided to gain this recognition through sports; however, after a spinal cord injury, the person is unable to make the team and decides to become a scholar. This is an example of compensation. Compensation brings success; therefore, it diverts attention from shortcomings and defects, thereby eliminating expressed or implied criticism. This defense mechanism is most often used to reduce self-criticism rather than external criticism. As the individual experiences successes, he or she will become less preoccupied with anxieties relating to disability and lack of productivity.

Identification and compensation usually go together in the adjustment process. When the person starts using these two defenses, it is at a point where the person may adequately adjust to the new body image and new role in life.

As will be noted from the above description of the adjustment process, there are four phases through which the individual passes in achieving adjustment. This is correlated with Siller's (1969) work with people with spinal cord disabilities. Siller discussed four behavior patterns in the adjustment to traumatization. These are passivity, dependency, aggression, and compensation.

In the above paradigm, the newly traumatized individual exhibits a strong element of passivity. At this point, the person begins employing the defense mechanisms of denial and withdrawal. By doing so, the person is escaping from the demands of the environment. According to Siller (1969), passivity has been defined as a mode of adaptation to one's environment that involves going back from it. This is exactly what we feel is occurring in the initial phases of adjustment.

Next, the individual enters a dependency period. When the person is employing the next series of defense mechanisms, as we have outlined above, the person is adjusting by adopting a dependent status. This allows the person to evaluate the extent and ramifications of disability in relation to life in the future. When this evaluation is complete and has been internalized or accepted, the person enters the next broad phase of adjustment–aggression. At this point in the adjustment process, the individual starts fighting back at the environment. The person aggressively reaches out and interacts with others. The person becomes action-oriented in their adjustment to the disability.

As one enters this period of aggressively dealing with the environment, one is becoming prepared for the next and final phase of adjustment–compensation. It is compensation that allows the person to compete on somewhat of an equal footing with others on one's social and vocational environments.

Postadjustment Life Styles of Persons with Disabilities

Allport (1954) outlined several traits that are defenses due to victimization. These traits include obsessive concern, denial of membership, withdrawal and passivity, clowning , strengthening in group ties, slyness and cunning, self-hate through identification with the dominant group, aggression against one's own group, prejudice against outgroups, sympathy, militantly fighting back, enhanced striving, symbolic status striving, neuroticism, and the self-fulfilling prophecy. While he applied these specifically to conditions that were highly ladened with prejudicial evaluations of other people, his description of many of these traits held especially true for the reactions of persons with disabilities and most especially for disability groups that have a high degree of visibility, such as persons with spinal cord injuries, blind, or those persons who have neuromuscularly impairments.

The first of these which Allport discusses is obsessive concern. In this type of reaction, the individual who is the object of the prejudice or stigmatization, the individual with a disability expresses an obsessive concern for this condition. The person is excessively sensitive about his or her condition. It is almost as if one is waiting for expressions of hostility or denigration from others. Each time a person with a disability is looked down upon or is rejected or relegated to a second class status, feelings of inferiority and inadequacy will be increased, which additionally will increase and support the rationale and validity of obsessive concern for rejection by others. As an example of the overconcern, Allport relates the following:

> One day in the late thirties a recently arrived refugee couple went shopping in a village grocery store in New England. The husband ordered some oranges.
> "For juice?" inquired the clerk.
> "Did you hear that," the woman whispered to her husband. "For Jews?"
> "You see, it's beginning here too."

This type of hypersensitivity is often observed in individuals with disabilities as a result of their disability. Many individuals are so sensitive to prejudice or the stigmatization they encounter, they often will reject any outward sign of the disability. For example, often blind people, as a result of this obsessive concern, refuse to use the guides and rehabilitative aids that are available to them. As such, many blind people refuse the use of the white cane, since they feel it symbolizes blindness and they do not want to be identified as being blind. Many persons with amputations will reject the use of artificial limbs and would rather have an empty sleeve than an artificial limb, since they feel this obsessive concern for the disability.

A particularly interesting reaction on the part of people with disabilities is the denial of membership in a group. As we mentioned earlier, one of the first ego defense reactions to disability is the denial of the permanence of the effects of the disability. Then, as the adjustment process proceeds, the need for employing this ego defense mechanism will fade. Related to this denial of the disability is denial of membership in various groups (that is, the individual not only will deny the disability, but will deny there is any similarity between oneself and others with this disability). Eventually, after the person adjusts to the disability to the extent that one can admit one has a disability, one may continue to deny membership in this group because denial of membership is maintaining perhaps the last vestige of resistance of the disability. In an individual who is expressing this denial of membership, there is an underlying theme of rejection of persons with disabilities; however, in denial of membership in a group, the individual will suffer a neurotic-like guilt, for unconsciously the person is aware of the fact that he or she belongs to this group, and by denying membership in the group, he or she is, to an extent, denying the reality of his or her own circumstances. As Allport quoted: "A Jewish student confessed with remorse that in order not to be known as Jewish, he would sometimes insert in my conversations delicate witticisms pertaining to Jewishness which, while not actually vicious, conveyed a total impression of gentile malice."

As you will note in the above quotation, the individual felt remorse and guilt at rejecting his heritage but still was compelled to deny his membership in the Jewish population. This reaction is most obvious with the person with a severe disability.

Withdrawal and passivity are very powerful tools that the individual with a severe disability has at his or her disposal. The person uses them to mask true feelings and prevent much of the hostility and strong emotionality from rising to the surface and being directed toward those upon whom the person is dependent and toward those who are critical and prejudicial. Many individuals with severe disabilities feel that this degree of passivity is the only way in which they can survive prejudice of those without disabilities directed toward those with disabilities. Often this feeling of severe prejudicial judgment on the part of those without disabilities is a misconception. Whether it is a misconception or an accurate evaluation of the situation, the reality for individuals with severe disabilities still is that they need to react as if prejudice were present within their environment. This withdrawal and passivity allows one to recognize the stigmatization which is occurring and, at the same time, gives one a safe secure approach to dealing with the stigmatization. Again, as we mentioned above, withdrawal occurs at the beginning of the adjustment process as a mechanism that allows the individual to retreat from the environment during an initial phase that will allow one to gain a new perspective of disability before the person begins to aggressively meet the environment and adjust to the disability. The withdrawal and passivity, which Allport is mentioning at this point, is not the more healthy withdrawal we mentioned above in the adjustment process. The withdrawal and passivity mentioned at this point is a persistent life style that is developed in order to combat perceived or implied criticism, prejudice, and stigmatization based upon the presence of a disability.

While Allport feels clowning is an ego defense mechanism, which alleviates the pressure of prejudice by accentuating the particular traits that are most susceptible to prejudice, we have seen clowning used so infrequently that we do not feel this is a true life-style of persons with disabilities. We are not saying this is not evident as a life-style, but we do not feel it is of sufficient prevalence to be singled out as being usual. However, there are examples of this approach to alleviating the internal feeling of prejudice on the part of the person with a disability. For example, we are aware of a well known entertainer, a comedian who is active on the night club circuit, as well as on TV. The comedian has a severe hearing loss. His particular and unique brand of comedy is centered around the misperception by a deaf person of words used in a conversation. For example, he converts the word "elocution" into the word "electrocution." He converts the word "diaphragm" to the word "diagram." By making slight changes in the phonemes and consequently in the meaning of responses in a dialogue between this individual and a hearing individual, therein lies the humor. There are other examples of this type of clowning. However, again we stress there are so few using clowning, we do not feel it is a major life-style of persons with disabilities. Both of us have had experience in working with blind persons, and we have noticed that in any particular geographic locale, blind persons form very strong intergroup ties. They have an accurate and active grapevine system in which they exchange information significant to the blind population as a whole. Their ties are so very strong that within hours the group can be mobilized for political action, etc. This is an example of a life-style characterized by Allport as strengthening in group ties. This example holds true for many of the disability groups. With persons with spinal cord injuries, there are very strong groups and very active groups involved in an effort to provide cohesiveness for this disability group. For example, there are the paraolympics; there are wheelchair basketball conferences; and there are groups, clubs, and associations that have one underlying theme and that is the association of individuals with spinal cord disabilities. In fact, the Paraplegia Foundation of America is predicated upon the development of cohesiveness in persons with spinal cord injuries and for their betterment. This cohesiveness has not been sufficient to the extent or exclusiveness to produce prejudice against this group. Perhaps this is because of the extreme minority status of this group of individuals. We feel that prejudice is demonstrated toward a minority group only when it becomes a substantial minority. In the case of disability groups, no one disability group is a viable minority.

While slyness and cunning is felt to be a logical life-style according to Allport, it is not encountered to any great extent among traditional victims of prejudice. This lack of prevalence is underscored when applied to persons with disabilities. Rarely does one encounter slyness and cunning as a life-style in persons with disabilities. One occasionally will see a person with a disability who exaggerates the disability in order to excite the urges of generosity in the passersby. Many of us who have worked in rehabilitation for a period of time have seen the street beggar who appears in dire financial straits. Upon offering him a chance for vocational rehabilitation with ultimate vocational adjustment in an occupation of his choosing, we have seen the individual demur and, when pushed toward vocational rehabilitation, flatly refuse any type of services. We feel this is an example of an individual using slyness and cunning as a life-style to better one's financial lot in life.

Identification with the dominant group that is expressed by self-hate is seen quite often with individuals with disabilities. In this situation, the individual attempts to see other individuals with disabilities through the eyes of persons without disabilities. In doing so, this person perceives people with disabilities in a negative light and, in turn, views himself or herself in this self-deprecating manner. The individual who adopts this life-style generally is a very unhappy person whose adjustment process is rarely, if ever, complete. This person is unable to identify with other persons with disabilities and becomes quite rejecting of them. This individual will try to please those without disabilities in order to be accepted but yet feels that he or she will not be accepted by them because of his or her disability. This is a never-ending circle, the key to which is one's own dissatisfaction with oneself and self-deprecating attitude.

This self-hate, which is a symptom of the identification with a dominant group, often is paired with the life-style of aggression against one's own group. Many times we have seen rehabilitation professionals and paraprofessionals with disabilities act quite punitively toward other individuals with disabilities and specifically other individuals whose disability parallels their own. The level of expectation expressed for a person with a disability by a professional or paraprofessional practitioner with a disability is often extremely high and almost impossible to meet. When the client fails to meet this level of expectation, the punitiveness is accelerated both in counseling sessions and in the quality of services being offered the client. Underlying many of the punitive expressions is the philosophy, "I'm disabled [*sic*]. I made it to this level in life–why can't you?" This question ignores social level, intellect, level of prior training and education, etc. It is a punitive aggression against an individual's own group.

While we feel the life-styles of prejudice against out-groups, sympathy, and militant fighting back are not particularly prevalent in those with disabilities, we do feel that enhanced striving is quite obvious and is a healthy productive life-style in those with disabilities. Not only does this enhanced striving result in improving the individual's lot in life, one also received a great deal of positive reinforcement from those without disabilities and others with disabilities. Compensation or enhanced striving is probably the most socially approved approach to real or perceived disabilities, physical, vocational, social, etc., in our culture. We are part of an aggressive culture. When an individual expresses frustration at his or her lot in life by compensation or, as Allport puts it, "enhanced striving," he or she will achieve in all spheres of life. This is a very prevalent life-style of people with disabilities. It is seen in most successful individuals with disabilities. In fact, this is one of the factors placement counselors use when approaching industry regarding the employment of persons with disabilities.

The last life-style that we feel is of significance in understanding the personality of people with disabilities is that of the self-fulfilling prophecy. What people think of us, we tend to become. This, we feel is particularly evident in individuals with disabilities. Self-fulfilling prophecy begins during the immediate medical crisis after disability, or in terms of congenital disabilities, rather than adventitious disabilities, it begins immediately after birth. There may exist many types of subtle influences that set out goals to be reached or standards that preclude an individual achieving certain goals. For example, it has been routinely accepted that persons with paraplegia and quadriplega could have no viable function in sexual relations. Some of the work being done by Coles (1971a, 1971b) refutes this thesis. However, many persons with spinal cord injuries are still told they will have no viable sexual functioning, and, therefore, they should sublimate the sexual drive through other types of creative activity. We feel the self-fulfilling prophecy exerts many pressures upon the individual with a disability at all points in his or her life, not only by family and friends but also by well-meaning medical and paramedical practitioners. When the individual is in a medical facility or rehabilitation center, this self-fulfilling prophecy type of activity continues on throughout the rehabilitation process, and it is not always a positive pressure. Often, it may be a negative pressure that precludes the individual from engaging in the enhanced striving we mentioned above.

General Implications for Professionals

Almost everyone in our society views disability from an anatomical point of view, rather than from a functional point of view. It is imperative that the counselor who is attempting to help, help the person view the disability functionally rather than anatomically. The client should gain an appreciation for the abilities left, rather than classifying oneself with a group based solely on an anatomical loss. The counselor should make sure that the information given the clients on sexual concerns, adjustment matters, etc., is factual, practical, concise and clear. The counselor should be certain that the individual's perception of the disability is correct, and the cause of the disability is completely understood. This understanding greatly enhances the adjustment of the client to the spinal cord injury.

Clients should be helped in exploring feelings regarding the manner in which they are currently being treated by one's spouse, other family members, friends, and the treatment team. The clients should be helped to understand the natural emotional reactions resulting from this newly acquired disability and should be aided in understanding that the feeling of family and friends are going to be different for a period of time while they themselves adjust to the disability. The client also should be helped to understand that negative feelings, which result from being place in a dependent role, are quite natural. As such, the client should not repress them but should try to deal with them and look at them very objectively.

The counselor or helping person should not fall into the trap of thinking that degree of disability is correlated with degree of psychological impact. Professional helping persons must realize that each individual's disability will be particular to him or her (Crew, 1997).

If the counselor is able to observe that the client is employing the defense mechanisms of denial and withdrawal, the counselor should be sure to make efforts to keep the client in complete touch with his environment. Allow the environment to be present for the client to call upon as much as possible without it becoming stifling and demanding in areas where the client cannot meet the demands. As the client becomes ego-oriented, the helping person can bring in outside stimulation in the form of news from the world at large, the family, friends, etc., so that the client can be reminded that he should function interdependently with the environment rather than independently of the environment.

If aberrant behavior is observed that will hold the person up to ridicule as a result of regression, the counselor should point out the manner in which the client is regressing. Help the person understand their actions, help them understand some of the mechanics that are taking place in their adjustment; however, counseling should be done in a manner that will preserve the integrity of the defense mechanism.

The counselor should assist in the client's fantasy world. If the counselor is fortunate enough to be called in to become a part of the fantasy life, the counselor should be aware of the fact that the client is trying on new roles to see how well they fit in these new roles as such, and the person will be asking the counselor to function as a mirror to see how they are adjusting to the various new roles in life.

When the defense mechanism of projection is being aired, the client may have difficulty realizing that one is projecting even though it may be patently clear to others. Perhaps the only real role the counselor can play here is one that is highly supportive of the client or of the client's abilities, but, at the same time, the client should be required to identify the people to whom he or she is projecting their feeling of inadequacy and inferiority. In other words, the client should be encouraged to identify the "they" to whom the client refers to so negatively.

Lastly, the counselor should remember that the most important aspect of the helping process is that of the personality of the counselor. The counselor must be a warm, empathic, accepting individual who has positive regard toward the client and one who is pragmatic in counseling and planning efforts with the client.

REFERENCES

Adler, A. (1927). *The practice and theory of individual psychology.* New York: Harcourt Brace.

Allport, G. (1954). *The nature of prejudice.* New York: Addison-Wesley.

Barker, R., Wright, B., & Gonick, M. (1947). *Adjustment to physical handicaps and illness: A survey of social–psychology of physique and disability.* New York: Social Science Research Council.

Bauman, M.; & Yoder, N. N. (1966). *Adjustment to blindness reviewed.* Springfield, IL: Charles C Thomas.

Bors, E., & Comarr, A. E. (1960). Neurological disturbances of sexual function with special reference to 529 patients with spinal cord injury. *Urology Survey, 10,* 191-222.

Bors, E. (1963). Sexual functions in patients with spinal cord injury. *Proceeding Symposium Royal College of Surgeons of Edinburgh, Scotland.*

Carroll, T. J. (1961). *Blindness.* Boston: Little, Brown.

Cleveland, S. E. (1960). Body image changes associated with personality reorganization. *Journal of Consulting Psychology, 24,* 256-261.

Coles, T. (1971a). *Just what can you do?*(Film). San Francisco, CA: Multimedia Resource Center.

Coles, T. (1971b). *Touching*(Film). San Francisco, CA: Multimedia Resource Center.

Comarr, A. E. (1962-63). Marriage and divorce among patients with spinal cord injury. *International Journal of the Indian Medical Profession, 9* (1-5), 4162-4430.

Comarr, A. E. (1970). Sexual function among patients with spinal cord injury. *Urology International, 25,* 134-168.

Coyle, C. P., Lesnik-Emas, S., & Kinney, W. B. (1994). Predicting life satisfaction among adults with spinal cord injuries. *Rehabilitation Psychology, 39* (2), 95-112.

Crew, N. M. (1997). Life stories of people with long-term spinal cord injury. *Rehabilitation Counseling Bulletin, 41* (1), 26-42.

English, R. W. (1968). *Assessment of change in the personal-social self-perceptions of vocational rehabilitation clients.* Unpublished doctoral dissertation, University of Wisconsin, Madison.

English, R. W. (1974). The application of personality theory to explain psychological reactions to physical disability. In J. G. Cull & R. E. Hardy (Eds.), *Rehabilitation techniques in severe disability.* Springfield, IL: Charles C Thomas.

Fisher, S., & Cleveland, S. E. (1968). *Body image and personality.* New York: Dover Publications.

Gunther, M. S. (1969). Emotional aspects . In D. Ruge (Ed.), *Spinal cord injuries* (p. 96). Springfield, IL: Charles C Thomas.

Hanson, S., Buckelew, S., Hewett, J., & O'Neal, G. (1993). The relationship between coping and adjustment after spinal cord injury: A five-year follow-up study. *Rehabilitation Psychology, 38* (1), 41-52.

Hohman, G. (1972). Considerations in the management of the psychosexual readjustment in the cord injured male. In W. R. Phelps (Ed.), *Proceeding of a seminar on serving the spinal cord injured patient* (pp. 105-118). Institute, W. V.: West Virginia Rehabilitation Center.

Hohman, G. (1966). Some effects of spinal cord lesions on experienced emotional feelings. *Psychotherapy, 3* (2), 143-156.

Luborsky, L., Chandler, M., Auerbach, A. H., Cohen, J., & Bachrach, H. (1971). Factors influencing the outcome of psychotherapy: A review of quantitative research. *Psychological Bulletin*, .

McDaniel, J. W. (1969). *Physical disability and human behavior.* New York: Pergamon.

McShane, S., & Karp, J. (1993). Employment following spinal cord injury: A covariance structure analysis. *Rehabilitation Psychology, 38* (1), 27-40.

Mitchell, K. M., et al. (1973). *Antecedents to psychotherapeutic outcome* (NIMH Final Report, MH 12306). University of Arkansas: Arkansas Rehabilitation Research and Training Center.

Parsons, T. (1951). *The social system.* Glencoe, IL: Free.

Poor, C. (1974). Groupwork with the severely disabled. In R. E. Hardy & J. G. Cull (Eds.), *Group counseling and therapy techniques in special settings* (p.). Springfield, IL: Charles C Thomas.

Sarbin, T. R. (1954). Role therapy. In G. Lindzey (Ed.), *Handbook of social psychology* (p. 223). Cambridge, MA: Addison-Wesley.

Schilder, P. (1950). *The image and appearance of the human body.* New York: Wiley.

Talbot, H. S. (1941). A report on sexual functions in paraplegics. *Journal of Urology, 61*, 265-270.

Talbot, H. S. (1955). The sexual function in paraplegics. *Journal of Urology, 73*, 91-100.

Talbot, H. S. (1970). Psychosocial aspects of sexuality in spinal cord injury patients. *Proceedings of the 17th spinal cord injury conference.* Washington, D.C.: Veterans Administration.

Tate, D., Davidoff, G., & Dijkers, M. (1993). Comparing two measures of depression in spinal cord injury. *Rehabilitation Psychology, 38* (1), 53-61.

Truax, C. B., & Carkhuff, R. R. (1967). *Toward effective counseling in psychotherapy.* Chicago: Aldine.

Truax, C. B., & Mitchell, K. M. (1971). Research on certain therapist interpersonal skills in relation to process and outcome. In A. E. Bergin & S. E. Garfield (Eds.), *Handbook of psychotherapy and behavior change: An empirical analysis.* New York: Wiley.

Wapner, S., & Werner, H. (1965). *The body perception.* New York: Wiley.

Wright, B. (1960). *Physical disability: A psychological approach.* New York: Harper Row.

Wright, B. (1955). The period of mourning in chronic illness. In R. Harrow (Ed.), *Medical and psychological teamwork in the care of the chronically ill.* Springfield, IL: Charles C Thomas.

Other Suggested Readings

Athelstan, G. T., & Crewe, N. M. (1979). Psychological adjustment to spinal cord injury as related to manner on onset of disability. *Rehabilitation Counseling Bulletin, 22,* 311-319.

Cook, D. W. (1976). Psychological aspects of spinal cord injury. *Rehabilitation Counseling Bulletin, 19,* 535-543.

Coven, A. B., & Glazeroff, H. (1978). The rehabilitation of the spinal cord street person. *Rehabilitation Counseling Bulletin, 22* (1), 22-28.

Cull, J. G., & Hardy, R. E. (1976). *Counseling strategies with special population.* Springfield, IL: Charles C Thomas.

Cull, J. G., & Hardy, R. E. (1974). *Rehabilitation techniques in severe disability: Case studies.* Springfield, IL: Charles C Thomas.

Goldenson, R. M., Dunham, J. R., & Dunham, C. S. (Eds.). (1978). *Disability and rehabilitation handbook.* New York: McGraw-Hill.

Hardy, R. E., & Cull, J. G. (1974). *Severe disabilities: social and rehabilitation approaches.* Springfield, IL: Charles C Thomas.

Kelman, H. R. (1964). Evaluation of rehabilitation for the long term ill and disabled patient: Some persistent research problems. *Journal of Chronic Disabilities, 17,* 631-639.

Krause, E. A. (1966). After the rehabilitation center. *Social Problems, 14* (2), 199-200.

Krause, J. S., & Anson, C. A. (1997). Adjustment after spinal cord injury: relationship to participation in employment or educational activities. *Rehabilitation Counseling Bulletin, 40* (3), 202-214.

Krause, J. S., Stanwyck, C. A., & Maide, J. (1998). Locus of control and life adjustment among people with spinal cord injury. *Rehabilitation Counseling Bulletin, 41* (3), 162-172.

Litman, T. J. (1970). *Biography of the sociology of medicine and medical care–The first fifty years.* Berkeley, CA: Glendessary.

Litman, T. J. (1968). Physical rehabilitation: A social psychological approach. In E. G. Jaco (Ed.), *Patients, physicians, and illness* (2nd ed.). New York: Free.

Litman, T. J. (1962). Self-concept and physical rehabilitation. In A. M. Rose (Ed.), *Human behavior and social process.* Boston: Houghton Mifflin.

Litman, T. J. (1966). The family and physical rehabilitation. *Journal of Chronic Disabilities, 19,* 211-217.

Litman, T. J. (1962). The influence of self-concept and life orientation: Factors in the rehabilitation of the orthopedically disabled. *Journal of Health and Human Behavior, 3,* 249-257.

Martin, E. D., Jr., & Gandy, G. L. (1990). *Rehabilitation and disability: Psychosocial case studies.* Springfield, IL: Charles C Thomas.

Nagi, S. Z., et al. (1965). Back disorders and rehabilitation achievement. *Journal of Chronic Disabilities, 18*, 181-197.

Roth, J. A., & Eddy, E. M. (1967). *Rehabilitation for the unwanted.* New York: Atherton.

Safilios-Rothschild, C. (1970). *The sociology and social psychology of disability and rehabilitation.* New York: Random House.

Sussman, M. B. (Ed.). (1965). *Sociology and rehabilitation.* Washington, D.C.: American Sociological Association.

Sussman, M. B., & Slator, R. Chronic illness study. *Institute on the family and bureaucratic society: Chronic disease and the family.* Cleveland, OH: Case Western Reserve University.

Taylor, G. P., Jr. (1967). *Predicted versus actual response to spinal cord injury: A psychological study.* Unpublished doctoral dissertation, University of Minnesota.

Chapter 10

A PERSONAL EXPERIENCE OF ACCEPTANCE AND ADJUSTMENT TO DISABILITY

James A. Rothrock

It was a cold, dark, snowy evening--perfect for sledding. After a dinner of warm vegetable soup, my brother and I left to go meet our friends and spend the evening enjoying the thrills of flying down icy streets on our sleds.

My evening was abruptly ended when during my first trip down the street I had a collision with a small Volkswagen coming out of a driveway which I never saw–or at least do not remember seeing.

After two weeks in intensive care and a series of surgeries, I finally became conscious enough to realize my new surroundings. My head was covered with bandages and approximately 100 stitches had been used to correct the damage resulting from numerous lacerations and contusions. A scar about 15 inches long formed a crescent shape on the left side of my stomach as a reminder of exploratory surgery to look for the cause of the massive internal bleeding. The constant noise from the suction tubing in my nose to my lungs, fighting the possibility of pneumonia, caused great discomfort. There was an annoying itching in my mid back where the incision was healing which resulted from the operation to relieve the pressure on my spinal column. Finally, there was the "nothingness" that I was aware of from my belly down, which not yet to be explained to me and about which I was much too terrified to ask. I was paraplegic, but I did not know what that would involve in the days and years that were ahead of me.

Hopefully, I have by now captured your attention. Obviously, this is not a typical chapter like the others in this text; however, my task is a bit different. My chapter is to provide a perspective on the acceptance and adjustment process based on my own experiences. I hope that this "story" will allow rehabilitation professionals to become more aware of the various coping mechanisms and improve their skills in becoming a positive influence on individuals who are in the process of recovering from a trauma and beginning their rehabilitation process.

I also wish to recognize the substantial impact that Dr. John Cull, one of my rehabilitation counseling professors in graduate school, had on me in explaining the process and allowing me to become a more effective professional in dealing with individuals who have shared experiences similar to mine (occasional references in my personal account will be made to the preceding Hardy and Cull chapter on a psychodynamic adjustment to acceptance and adjustment to disability).

Role of Body Image in Adjustment to Disability

Prior to my injury, I had a high level of congruence between my desired and actual body image. My desired body image called for the body of an "NFL bound" person. As a halfback and captain of my junior varsity football team, my actual body image was on the proper track for the desired image. At 5'10" and 155 pounds with little flab and a decent amount of muscle, I was not faced with a large difference between my desired and actual body image.

After the accident, my actual body image deteriorated dramatically with a weight loss to just a little above one hundred pounds and my strength evaporated into widespread atrophy. It was obvious, even to me, that I was no longer "NFL bound."

One of the more positive measures taken, as soon as my condition had stabilized, was the introduction of weight lifting. After I accepted that the most I could handle in one hand was a weight of three pounds, the idea of rebuilding my body appealed to my "semi-jock" mentality. Throughout my therapy sessions, I was always willing to lift weights to get my actual body image closer to my desired body image.

I should note at this time that one of the major contributing factors to my successful rehabilitation was that six months after my accident, my body looked similar to the body I had prior to my accident. Parts of my body did not function, but it looked basically the same. I feel that had my actual body image been more drastically changed– due to amputation, quadriplegia or disfigurement– my adjustment process would have been more difficult. It should also be mentioned that upon my return to school, nine months after my injury, my fellow classmates were much more capable of accepting me because, although I was using a wheelchair for mobility, my basic outward appearance–the actual body image–was not drastically altered. This facet could be one of the major factors in the adjustment process and, without careful evaluation, all other efforts might be wasted. As such, the rehabilitation professional must recognize the importance of body image in the adjustment process.

Factors Associated with Adjustment

When a rehabilitation professional is working with an individual who has experienced trauma resulting in disability, there are three major factors that need to be considered. Hardy and Cull stated that these three factors are those that: (1) associate directly with the disability; (2) arise from the individual's attitude toward disability, and (3) related to the individual's perception of the purpose of the body to the extent that the disability may impact on the perception of body use. In assessing my own adjustment process, I can look back and clearly evaluate those factors. My own adjustment process was influenced by these factors; it is of interest to see how these factors were at times quite positive, but in other instances they created problems, ofttimes greater than even my disability.

The first factor, as noted, is the direct effect of the disability. Prior to my disability, I was quite active; participation in sports, outdoor activities, and social events was a significant portion of my life. Paraplegia negatively impacted my ability to pursue these activities as I once had. In assessing the effect of this factor, I will devote thought to both the positive and negative aspects.

Based on my high level of social interaction and activity, I was able to channel much of my energy into those activities to sustain a level of activity, albeit decreased. My therapies were an outlet that allowed me to modify athletic ability and, at the same time, meet my therapeutic goals. Throwing a football was an activity I still enjoyed, but during therapy it also was an exercise in improving my body balance and control. Although I did use a wheelchair for mobility, my upper body function and strength allowed me to have some level of independent mobility. Had I not been able to move from place to place without assistance, I feel my frustration and negative behaviors would have been much greater. Upon my return to school after rehabilitation, I assumed a high level of social activities; no longer was I playing football, but at least I could go to the games with my friends.

Although I could attend functions and participate in some fashion, this was also a reminder of those things I could not do and this resulted in a large degree of frustration. Rather than playing, I was watching; rather than dancing, I was sitting; the list could go on and on. In order to maintain my high masculine self-image, I directed my energies from the positive pursuit of athletics into what I feel was the negative pursuit of excessive "partying." This included immature drinking and tobacco smoking habits that I then felt would equate those areas of achievement I could no longer realize through athletics. The more frustrated I became as a spectator on the sidelines, the more active I became as a participant in the postgame revelry. Fortunately (and I realize this is a value judgement), drugs had not come into vogue in my town in 1966, or I probably would have expanded my drug abuse. In summary, my high level of activity acted as a "double edged" sword; on one hand facilitating my recovery and entrance back into my peer group but on the other hand, causing a high level of frustration resulting in definite anti-social behaviors.

In assessing the second factor, my attitude toward disability, I offer several interesting illustrations of how it could impact on adjustment. My own perception of disabilities similar to mine was positive. As a Cub Scout, I had a very positive relationship with our Boy Scout pack leader; in fact, he could have been considered somewhat of a boyhood hero. Prior to my injury, he broke his neck in a diving accident and became quadriplegic. Although we did not remain close, I was aware that he had gone on to a technical school and became employed as a draftsman. Although he lived with his family, he was quite independent and had, indeed, completed successfully a rehabilitation program similar to mine. Another classmate of mine with a disability from polio had successfully passed through elementary school and had accomplished this with the use of crutches and braces. As a result of these relationships, I had a positive perception of individuals with physical disabilities.

I must admit that other disabilities were not as positively perceived. One of my most vivid memories of my sixth grade year was going to a football game and seeing one of the cheerleaders experience a grand mal seizure which terrified me. In the small town in which I grew up, there was also a man who was mentally retarded and who was the"mascot" of the local fire department. Although he was allowed to be part of the department, he was often the brunt of, what the firemen perceived to be, harmless jokes. These two experiences did not engender in me a positive attitude towards those individuals with disabilities other than physical. This negative stereotype became a real factor when I was in close contact with individuals having epilepsy, mental retardation, and other mental disabilities. During my stay in the "Rehab" Center, many of the persons with physical disabilities, including myself, exploited those clients with mental disabilities. After I became a rehabilitation counselor in the same center at which I had once been a client, I witnessed this same separation and gross stereotyping between those individuals with physical and mental disabilities. A commentary on the "human condition" can be offered since it appears that, based on my own experiences and observations, one group will take advantage of another group based on a perceived superiority; this is certainly one maladaptive behavior which I experienced and I felt is often found in the adjustment to disability in comprehensive rehabilitation centers. I offer this to encourage the rehabilitation professional to take whatever steps need to be taken to decrease the likelihood of this situation occurring.

In assessing this second factor, regarding attitude, I should offer a brief discussion of my own attitude to my disability immediately after my accident. Hardy and Cull mention the need for education and emotive expenditure. My adjustment process was retarded due to a lack of both. Perhaps my family and doctors felt that as a sixteen year old I would not be able to handle the multitude of implications paraplegia has on an individual; nonetheless, I received little information beyond the functional impact and was not allowed an opportunity to experience a healthy emotive expenditure. By retarding this process, I prolonged this experience and finally dealt with it about seven years after my initial injury.

In retrospect, my rehabilitation counselor was of little benefit. The occupational and physical therapists explained the functional implications of paraplegia. I learned more substantive information from other individuals at the center; picking it up "off the streets" is not the most advantageous learning situation. I must have been a real rookie to those who had been injured for a year or more and had "learned the ropes" the hard way. What a laugh they had when they asked me if I were a paraplegic, and I responded that I was not, but that I was a Southern Baptist. Bowel movements, catheterizations, sexual activity, etc. were all explained to me by the other clients in ways that did not always provide the best education. I was so overwhelmed with this that I was lost; but, in looking around me, I realized that I was in relatively good shape and this allowed me to maintain a grip on sanity, albeit uncertain at times. Gradually, I experienced the "rites of passage" and became an expert capable of sending a newly injured individual down to the post office to pick up the new shipment of spinal cords.

Hardy and Cull state that the greater the level of emotion expended during the onset of injury, the easier the adjustment to disability will be. I would agree with them to a degree. My activities, upon regaining consciousness, were so goal-directed that there was little time to become emotional. My schedule included release from primary care hospital, transfer to rehabilitation center, enter school with my junior class, take a summer break for some more therapy, complete high school, attend summer school prior to freshman year in college, complete four years of college, and become employed. Externally, I was quite happy and too busy to grieve, but actually I had little to grieve over since all my activities had been completed in a friendly, accessible environment that I could manipulate. Not until I became employed and entered the "real world" did I realize the real impact of paraplegia. Although I perhaps appeared to be quite the "super crip," I had many bouts with loneliness, depression, and inadequacy. Having become so independent, it was difficult to request help even though I desperately needed it. An experience in the haven of graduate school gave me the opportunity to put the pieces of my life together and, in fact, after my act was together, take it on the road. It was rough on my family, my friends, and myself; I wonder if things had not gone so well for me initially, would I have experienced these problems at the same magnitude six and seven years after my injury.

The last factor determining the adjustment process relates to how the person with a disability perceives the use of the body and how this interacts with the disability. Hardy and Cull cite an excellent example in mentioning the vast difference that a disability involving facial disfiguration would have on a laborer and an actor. Theoretically, this same disability could be managed well by the laborer; however, the actor could possibly be devastated.

Prior to my injury, I was incredibly achievement-oriented. My body was of use in meeting my goals in relation to athletic pursuits and fulfilling my image of an acceptable, good looking fellow interested in many kinds of social exchange. After becoming paraplegic, my body could not be depended on to meet my athletic goals; however, I changed my agenda to include student government activities, civic organization, involvement and academic pursuits. My level of social interaction remained the same based on my high level of mobility and a strong peer support group. To summarize, my achievement orientation was stronger than my body utilization, so with some redirection, I could continue to achieve without a significant dependence on my total body use. So far, I have only mentioned the positive side; as alluded to earlier, there was a "downside" too.

In graduate school, I was able to take an "Adlerian Lifestyle" course which was not only an exceptional learning experience, but it also gave me a deeper insight. Prior to my injury, I was totally involved in being the best possible fellow I could be; this made my family and friends quite proud of me and definitely enhanced my positive self-image. After my injury, when it became increasingly hard to be the "best of the best," I chose to be the "best of the worst." My college years were full of attempts to cut the most classes, to do the least amount of work, to play to the maximum, and to insure that I at least got by in my classes. I was probably the only "suite leader" expelled from the dormitory. I was a leader but not in the same direction that was evidenced prior to my injury. I continued to achieve and receive an amount of distinction, but the arena in which I operated had changed dramatically.

In summary, I would like to repeat the conclusions of Hardy and Cull and offer a few comments. The degree of disability is not a good indicator of adjustment to disability. One individual's minor inconvenience is another's total devastation. The factors mentioned earlier should be thoroughly evaluated in relation to each new client to develop an effective counseling strategy. If an individual was negatively impacted to a high degree by the inability to pass sophomore math, it could be predicted that the onset of a visual impairment would be a major problem. The ability of individuals to cope with life situations can be evaluated based on past coping experiences, and in this way, the rehabilitation professional can help the individual with a disability address the adjustment process in a positive fashion.

Role of Defense Mechanisms in Adjustments

Human beings are truly wondrous in their complexities that allow them to deal with different situations. Every person who has ever breathed uses defense mechanisms. In an initial effort to understand the adjustment process, I was naive enough to believe that only people with disabilities use the mechanisms. Fortunately, I developed an understanding of human nature that includes for all of us–with or without disabilities–the ability to cope. The same skills that one used to deal with the death of a loved one, the loss of a possession, the failure to achieve a goal, etc., are used to adjust to a disability. These defense mechanisms, as abnormal as they may appear to be, are the individual with a disability's link with sanity. Without these mechanisms, reality could overwhelm the individual and the situation could be perceived as being impossible to address. The rehabilitation professional can increase effectiveness by being aware of how the individual is using these defense mechanisms; however, it is imperative that the individual be allowed to continue to use them as they are the factors which allow the individual to continue coping. As noted by Hardy and Cull, these mechanisms are unconscious and not deliberate, but they do fulfill a need that the individual with a disability has. My interest in this entire subject began, when in a conversation with Dr. Cull, I expressed my disbelief in any kind of systematic use of defense mechanisms.

One afternoon in 1972, after a lecture by Dr. Cull on this topic, he was able to tell me specific behaviors that I had utilized to cope with my disability. Prior to this, I had refused to include myself in the population of normal, predictable people; I knew I was unique. My acceptance of my commonality with the rest of humankind was a positive step in my own adjustment process. Individuals do not employ defense mechanisms in the same manner or sequence; they cannot be predicted. The reality of the individual's coping mechanism must be accepted by the rehabilitation professional and with this mindset by the professional, the adjustment process can be facilitated. The remainder of this chapter will be devoted to addressing the mechanisms identified by Hardy and Cull and offering illustrations as to how I used them to "keep a grip" on my own humanity.

Denial

The denial mechanism is utilized to reject a reality that is too disruptive or painful to deal with in any positive manner. By denying the reality of a disability, the individual can temporarily deal with the situation until the reality is accepted, at which time another mechanism may be activated.

Denial was certainly a mechanism–the first–that I used and in fact was nurtured by my support surroundings–family, nurses, friends, doctors, and others. I agreed with those around me who insured that all would be ok in the future. As time passed, I accepted the reality that there would be at least some temporary loss, and in fact, began looking at different types of canes that I would use to make a triumphant return. I managed to retain a high level of denial to the permanence of paraplegia until the night prior to my transfer from the hospital to the rehabilitation center; during the late evening, one of my nurses told me she still believed in miracles. I certainly did not need a miracle–did I? Upon entering the rehabilitation center and seeing so many people with injuries similar to mine, I could no longer deny accepting the reality that my paraplegia would require more than a couple of smart-looking canes to help in returning to my pretrauma life-style.

In summary, my denial made the initial phase of my disability acceptable. I was treated specially and actually enjoyed some of the time I had in the hospital. It was such a "slap in the face" to see the reality of my situation by just looking around my new "rehab" center room. Very quickly I needed something to help me adjust to this new condition and environment.

Withdrawal

Withdrawal is defined as the act of reducing tension and anxiety by reducing the need for interaction with others. I was allowed to withdraw, which enabled me to prepare for a time when I would be ready to interact. After reaching the "rehab" center, my medical condition did not allow for any physical activity other than lifting weights in bed for about three weeks. By being "bedridden" and geographically removed from my hometown, I had lots of time to avoid the social interactions in which I once thrived. My world consisted of the small, four bed hospital room with a door that allowed me to begin to gain a flavor of what disability was all about. During this time, I began to get to know my body and its new method of functioning for the first time. My irrigations, bowel movements, turnings to prevent "pressure sores" and the placement of the pillows all around me to insure my stability became my main concerns. I was able to put together some pieces to my puzzle and figure out what new abilities I would have to develop in order to reenter the world–the one outside my small room. My roommates, two of whom were only a few years older than I with similar levels of paraplegia, became my models. By observing them in their activities, I became challenged. If they could get out and about, so could I.

Regression

In assessing my own adjustment, I cannot identify many of my behaviors that would support the use of this defense mechanism. Briefly stated, regression is another method of avoiding stress through avoidance. Often this mechanism is manifested in the individual regressing to mannerisms of an earlier, more comfortable stage in their life; it can even include outward manifestations such as significant changes in life-style, dress, behavior, and vocabulary. Several reasons that I cannot readily identify my use of regression–striving to be the "best," needing to be socially acceptable and active, and being young–I could not go too far back since I was only sixteen. Although I cannot give much personal comment to this, I can offer some observations from my work as a counselor in a "rehab" center relative to regression.

One of the most common behaviors I saw in an individual with new spinal cord injuries was regression. It was not uncommon to see a person in their thirties or forties regress back to a "teenage state." During my tenure in a counseling position in the mid-1970s, this was of great significance since these newly injured individuals would be dressing and acting as any twenty-year-old individual. At this time period, the "hippy" life-style was flourishing and these newly injured individuals fit nicely. This life-style allowed rebellion, contradictory attitudes and, of equal but certainly not as cerebral importance, an easy manner of personal care and dress. These changes were so interesting to witness and, although quite different from the preinjury personality, they were so valid.

Fantasy

Fantasy has been equated with daydreaming. My spare moments were filled with thoughts of how I would be received upon returning to school; I should note that these fantasies were, for the greatest part, quite positive. A great deal of thought is being spent by current theorists which promotes the positive visualization of an upcoming event; a basketball player will fantasize or mentally experience a successful foul shot prior to the actual shot. I wonder if a rehabilitation professional could positively impact on the adjustment process of a newly injured person by facilitating their fantasies. It would seem that positive fantasies would be more desired than fantasies in which a disaster is encountered; it happened for me so I feel it might work for others.

Rationalization

As an adjustment process evolves and supports the individual's eventual acceptance of the permanence of the disability, rationalization can become a key defense mechanism. Basically, rationalization can be defined as giving acceptable reasons for one's behavior. Being from a Southern Baptist background, others around me–not me–rationalized that my accident was an act of God and that my circumstances and eventual success would serve as an inspiration to others. As stated, I really never bought into this explanation. I did rationalize that I would be able to compensate for my limitation with talents that prior to my injury had not been exercised to the maximum degree.

In retrospect, I cannot realize how much rationalization I did during my initial adjustment process; however, I do know I use it a great deal now, and I have this in common with most of the people I encounter. Rationalization is wonderful in everyday use for everyone–we would all be much worse off if it were not for rationalization.

Identification

This defense mechanism is one that I can remember using most vividly and can offer some interesting observations explaining how it can work. Identification allows for an individual not readily capable of achieving to realize success through another person's or group's attainment of achievement. I could say that this was the most important mechanism that I used, and its manifestations were both positive and negative.

Upon my return to high school after completion of physical rehabilitation, I became immersed in trying to ensure that I would still be identified with those groups and individuals who would be perceived as the "movers and shakers" in my school. The football coaches allowed me to sit on the sidelines with the team, and this was the highpoint of my week–sharing those victories and experiences. At a time (1966-67) when clothes were becoming a bit more creative, I chose to stay quite close to my peers' conservative dress so as not to disassociate myself from them in any way. I also found myself quite easily led into some activities I might not have pursued prior to my injury to ensure my identification with the group who had become jokingly called the "Unholy Six." Fortunately, the people with whom I wanted to be identified were willing to continue and expand our friendships. Without this incredibly strong group of boys and girls who unwittingly became involved in my adjustment process, I would have never been able to cope with my situation.

After entering college, I also had a strong need to identify with a group based on my uncertainty as to my own level of ability. The group that was most attractive to me were not those scholarly fellows, but were the guys in danger of expulsion, at any time, from college. I posture that much of this desire was based on the incredible independence that these guys exhibited. I, too, wanted to be as independent as possible. After three years in hospitals, rehabilitation centers and home, I was ready to break loose. College also offered me a stiffer challenge at being the "best of the best"; thus, my decision to be the "best of the worst" was made easier.

After becoming a rehabilitation professional and working in a rehabilitation center, I witnessed this continued use of identification by newly injured persons. Many of these individuals would experience significant changes in their appearance and behavior to identify with those other "veterans" who were already there and had melded into a group personality. Another manifestation of this use of identification was in the linkage to athletic teams. Individuals who once may have been passingly aware of a team's progress became obsessed with the team. This could include the wearing of shirts and caps with team logos, the memorization of statistics of team members and the continued reference to their team's progress in conversation at any opportunity. This same process could be utilized to identify with a band or certain social groups. There would be little individual expression by any of these newly injured individuals.

Identification is of great importance to a newly injured person. It was of such great importance to me that it precluded the excessive use of many of the other defense mechanisms and I feel that my experiences were similar to many newly injured individuals.

Compensation

After my accident, I knew I would become smarter, due to my changed life-style which, for a while at least, would not allow for active athletics. I firmly believed this until my first report cards came in, which were pretty much the same as they had always been. Compensation can be explained by the individual having the way of achieving one set of goals blocked and then selecting another set of goals. As soon as I realized that I could be successful with my abilities, I realized that I did not have to develop an entirely new set of goals and methods to achieve them.

Implications for Professionals Working with Individuals with Disabilities

Rehabilitation professionals are thrown into situations that offer challenges unlike most other vocations. The individuals a rehabilitation professional works with have either been born with or had some experience which limits, for a time, their abilities. Ofttimes, these individuals will be absolutely lost, perhaps terrified, and certainly confused as to what the future holds. It is the rehabilitation professional's charge to allow this individual to realize the ability to cope with this situation and eventually to become able to live with it.

One of the first cautions I would offer, realizing it has been known for decades, is that you and your client are both human beings with many abilities. There is still an "ugly" feeling of superiority fostered by rehabilitation professionals; the situation is improving but is still present. Just because the rehabilitation professional is an "authority" makes that person no better or no worse than the client. The rehabilitation professional could improve efficiency by adopting a facilitative posture. In looking at a positive rehabilitation professional/client relationship, one will see a higher level of commonality than diversity. If this relationship can be engendered, a positive result can be expected in most situations. The rehabilitation professional should always respect the individual with a disability as an "equal" who has encountered some experience which has negatively impacted his or her level of participation in activities of daily living.

One major aid for any rehabilitation professional is to obtain a good idea of how the individual with a disability coped with life prior to the event resulting in the disability. The same behaviors used to cope prior to the injury will be used with slight modifications to deal with the posttrauma lifestyle. An exposure to "Adlerian Life-styles" is a major aid in accomplishing this view of coping mechanisms prior to injury.

In reflecting on my years as a rehabilitation professional in direct service delivery, I can quickly identify two areas in which I negated my overall effectiveness. My clients' rehabilitation was not their responsibility–it was mine. I accepted the responsibility for the success or failure; this was not healthy for me or the individual with the disability. What a fool I was! One of the major responsibilities of a rehab professional is to clearly identify the client's role and ultimate responsibility in the rehab process. The rehabilitation professional is clearly the facilitator in the process. To avoid this basic principle is to foster the dependency of the individual with a disability; this is obviously not a desired outcome. The other mistake I made was aligned with that of responsibility, in that I tried to make everything easy and not allow for failure. An individual with a disability can learn from mistakes; if the rehabilitation professional negates the opportunity for mistakes, then the opportunity for learning is limited. In summary, the individual with the disability should be given the independence and opportunity to adjust to his or her disability; at times, it is "easier" for the professional to make things happen, but in the long run, that is counterproductive.

The rehabilitation professional should be aware of the adjustment process and work with it rather than against it. At times, behaviors will be exhibited which the rehabilitation professional may consider bizarre or different; however, without these manifestations of the defense mechanisms, the individual with the disability would not realize any progress. By being aware of the adjustment process, the rehabilitation professional can facilitate the increased independence and overall adjustment of the individual. Not to acknowledge the reality and validity of these defense mechanisms is to virtually doom the possible progress that could be realized.

In summary, please remember that no one has ever been rehabilitated. Innumerable individuals have had their rehabilitation facilitated by rehabilitation professionals. There is a difference! Evaluate your attitudes and methods. Listen to those individuals with disabilities with whom you are working and make sure they realize their ownership in the rehabilitation process. Encourage independence rather than nurturing dependence. Ensure that any "failures" are turned into learning experiences. Respect at all times those individuals as fellow human beings rather than just "clients." Provide a facilitative environment for those individuals to "learn to live again" in the truest sense of what rehabilitation means. If these objectives can be achieved, you will become more effective and the services that you offer to individuals with disabilities will have a greater impact. This is a charge that requires a strong commitment but in the scope of life's activities can have such immense value.

Postscript

In the field of rehabilitation, there is an immense wave of change. As a profession, we continually see the impact of the Americans with Disabilities Act, supported employment, independent living, and assistive technology and realize that new paradigms need to be welcomed and not challenged. As a society, we track the rehab process of Christopher Reeve almost on a weekly basis and see other persons with severe disabilities achieving heretofore unexpected heights in the paralympics–moreover, the world is seeing this, not just we folks in the field. But, with these improvements, we need to again check ourselves and be sure that "we" are up to the task.

If "we" remember...

to acknowledge that our clients/consumers/participants ("they") own the rehab process...

to empower persons with disabilities and not foster dependence...

to be open to new ideas and not become captured by the way "we" do things because "that is the way "we've" always done them"...

to respect the inherent dignity of working and independence on all levels...

to offer choices to those who have not had them before and recognize the value of "choice making" regardless of the out come...

and

that there are few differences between our clients/consumers/ participants (them) and us and, in fact, there really is no "they", just "us"...

Then "we" will be up to the task, "we" will continue to change for the better, and "we" will realize the real value of the profession "we" chose.

Chapter 11

AN ADLERIAN APPROACH TO ACCEPTANCE AND ADJUSTMENT TO DISABILITY

WARREN R. RULE

The concepts of Alfred Adler have been receiving considerable attention in recent years. This renewed interest has been shown in rehabilitation settings as well as in the broad field of counseling. Adler's approach, which he termed "Individual Psychology" in order to stress the indivisible nature of the individual, has over the years influenced many eminent pioneers in the helping professions (e.g., Albert Ellis, Eric Berne, Rollo May, Victor Frankl) (Corey, 1996). In fact, Ellenberger (1970), in his comprehensive review of the history of psychiatry, observed that "It would not be easy to find another author from which so much has been borrowed from all sides without acknowledgment than Alfred Adler" (p. 645).

Adler was born in Vienna in 1870. After practicing general medicine for several years, he became associated with Sigmund Freud. However, Adler's developing concepts were in contrast with Freud's (particularly with Freud's view that the sexual instinct was omnipotent) and they parted ways. In Europe and later in the United States, Adler continued to refine ideas and establish practitioner-oriented clinics for people of all ages. He was active as a teacher, lecturer, and writer until his death in 1937. His influence has been receiving justified recognition; however, his contributions have often been oversimplified or misrepresented, even in the field of rehabilitation. Adler's earlier concepts (e.g., organ inferiority, compensation) tend to be exclusively focused upon contemporary rehabilitation, probably because these terms seem to sound like they are directly related to rehabilitation. However, his early emphasis on this limited organic perspective evolved over the subsequent quarter century into a sociopsychological explanation of behavior. This shift reflected an increased emphasis on the creativity of the individual and provided an even sharper emphasis of the personal attitude toward the acceptance and adjustment to disability. Adler believed that the attitude the individual adopted towards a disability was a function of the person's fundamental and unique mental pattern–one's life-style.

Life-Style

The term "life-style," coined by Adler (and as it used in this chapter), means something considerably more basic to the person than many contemporary uses of the word would suggest. A broad definition is "that unity in each individual, in his thinking, feeling, acting, in his so-called conscious and unconscious, in every expression of his personality" (Ansbacher & Ansbacher, 1956, p. 175). Expressed another way, life-style is seen as the individual's holistic pattern of beliefs and goals that the person uses for interacting with others and for measuring self-worth.

This concept, which is central to the Adlerian approach to individuals with or without disabilities, is pervasively at work in everyone's daily life. The life-style expresses itself (often dimly consciously) in our selection of friends, in our work, in our love relationships, in what we regard as our successes and failures, in the automobiles we buy, and in the viewpoint we take towards the limitations of a disability.

This overriding mental pattern is regarded by Adlerians as the unity which reflects those key cognitive dimensions on which a person takes a sensitive position. This mental pattern is useful to the individual because it works in terms of the person's subjective perspective (just as blinders on a horse serve to focus–and to limit–perspective and to get the horse through heavy traffic, so do our selective perceptions and goals get us through life). The overriding mental pattern, in turn, influences the individual's feelings and behaviors in reaction to life's challenges. Thus, this unique pattern of thinking, the lifestyle, with its built-in blinders and tunnel vision, leads us to both our successes and our failures.

Because of the consistency of the cognitive nature of the life-style, it is often helpful to the individual to have an awareness of this unique life-style pattern when facing decisions or facing problems. This is especially worthwhile, due to the fact that the life-style–the time-tested pattern of basic attitudes and expectations–becomes most obvious when the person is experiencing stress. The life-style concept, as well as the apparency-under-stress phenomenon, has many helpful implications for rehabilitation practitioners. However, before exploring specifically how this approach can be useful in facilitating acceptance and adjustment to disability, further discussion needs to be given to characteristics of the life-style concept.

Significant Life-Style Characteristics

Adler believed that early childhood has a large bearing on how each individual develops in later life. These early years certainly do not totally determine a person's life-style; rather, Adler believed in "soft" determinism as opposed to "hard" determinism. He felt that each person uses heredity and environment creatively to mold a unique life-style.

The emphasis in Adler's perspective is on social living. He believed that personal problems are basically social problems, i.e., an individual's personal difficulties occur in an interpersonal context. In each of us, there exists the desire to belong and to have a place of significance in the eyes of others. We each strive for a place of "somebodyness" differently. This "somebodyness" is largely–not totally–related to the conclusions drawn in early childhood about self, others, and life. Understandably, then, a congenital or acquired disability would be handled differently by different life-styles because both the perceived "place of somebodyness" and the social context would vary from person to person.

Adler believed that everything we do is goal-directed. Stated another way, all behavior, including emotions, is a function of our ideas–both unconscious and dimly conscious–about consequences to be obtained in the future. Behaviors that seemingly cannot be explained become more understood as the goal or purpose comes to light. Most of the time, we are not aware to our unique self-concerned goals that are indirectly related to our innate desire to enhance ourselves within a social context. In attempting to understand another person, a handy goal-oriented framework for the practitioner is "How is this person seeking to be known by others?" Thus, the individual operates from a subjective mental framework and is not always fully conscious of his or her own goals. It is necessary, therefore, to focus on the person's subjective or internal frame of reference. This appears necessary because the individual's perceptions, including the inner biases influencing perceptions, determine one's behavior more than "reality" does.

A wide range of behavioral patterns is sometimes available to the individual for any given life-style conclusion. The life-style approach claims that people can indeed change in major ways (in fundamental thinking as well as behaving); however, sometimes the person's sensitive position on a life-style conclusion or notion may actually be the common thread that continues to run through the "changes"–usually behavioral–that a person regards himself or herself as having made. Expressed another way, these changes, even major ones, may really be variations of the same theme. These changes could actually be different creative behavioral implementations–in response to changing circumstances in the social environment–of the same life-style conclusions that the person continues to take a sensitive position on. For example, Mosak (1958) discusses some of the different behavioral implementation an individual could choose who has taken a sensitive position on the life-style conclusion that "Life is dangerous."

> Such a person, behaviorally, may see danger where none exists. He may exaggerate the dangers of life. He may retreat from these perceived dangers with anxious or phobic behavior, or he may call upon certain defense mechanisms to cope with the omnipotent threat. In the compulsive individual, for example, one observes reliance upon ritual and feelings of omnipotence and the necessity to control as response to danger. Many compulsives are preoccupied with death because this is the greatest threat–the one force which cannot be controlled. Hypochondriacs may exaggerate each body symptom as expressing their conviction that life is fraught with danger. Other individuals may develop into towers of strength or become dependent upon or identify with "strong" people or groups in order to minimize the dangers of life. Still others may actually court or provoke personal disaster in order to confirm their basic attitude. Some flirt with danger in order to prove that they possess a charmed life. While these reactions do not exhaust the repertoire available to people who feel that life is dangerous, they do serve to exemplify the variety of reactions which are possible within a single dimension of an individual's perceptual frame of reference. (p. 306)

As illustrated above, the creativity of the individual is ever present as the person moves through life. Persons learn at an early age, through trial and error, not only what goals will be most likely to help them move toward a place of significance, but they also begin to experiment with which kinds of behavior–and emotions which energize behavior–are most useful in implementing the goals. Not surprisingly, people also learn behaviors and emotions, in keeping with life-style goals, that safeguard their vulnerabilities and sense of self-esteem. This pattern of life-style goals is organized around the subjectively determined concept of the ideal self. Thus, it is the network of life-style goals, patterned after the ideal concept of self, that provides the main thrust for the life-style that enables each of us to move, on a daily basis and throughout our lives, from a position of dimly felt inferiority or non-coping to a position of overcoming or coping. In the striving to measure up to the life-style self-ideal, the person hopes to move from the felt minus state of not enoughness to the felt plus state of enoughness. This subjective and ideal state of enoughness has obvious implications for individuals with developmental and acquired disabilities.

Acceptance and Adjustment to Disability

Individual Meaning of Disability

As Wright (1980) has observed, "It is the personal meaning of the disability to the individual that is critical in rehabilitation counseling practice" (p.

73). Similarly, Shontz (1977) concluded, after reviewing numerous studies related to the treatment of various disabilities, that:

> What has been uniformly regarded as crucial is the personal meaning of his [*sic*] disability to each individual client . . . . Virtually all of these authors have cautioned that psychological treatment must be directed toward individual situations and reactions rather than toward psychological processes that can be assumed to be constant from patient to patient. (p. 324)

The Adlerian belief is that the life-style approach offers a holistic perspective on this personal meaning, because a heightened awareness of a person's life-style goals and notions illuminates the psychosocial filter that is used for understanding self, others, and life as well as one's disability as it fits within this outlook.

Concepts and Misconceptions

From a broad rehabilitation perspective, the concept of disability means a variety of things to a variety of people both in the general public and the helping professions. Some of these thoughts are based on stereotypes, fallacies, and–occasionally–reality. Some general misconceptions related to personality and disability (primarily physical) are worth nothing.

The first commonly-held belief is that specific disabilities are associated with specific types of personality. Another widely held assumption is that different types of disability cause specific personality reactions. A third frequently held viewpoint is that severity of disability is directly related to degree of psychological impairment. Extensive review of the rehabilitation-related literature by Shontz (1977) and Roessler and Bolton (1978) indicated that all of these foregoing beliefs are misconceptions that have virtually no solid research support.

Regarding persons with a disability, Adler believed that the creativity of the individual is foremost and that general concepts and stereotypes–such as those stated above–which predict rigid, deterministic reactions to disability were useless. He was interested in what the person contributed subjectively to the situation, not in simplistic cause-and-effect relationships. For example, Adler felt that a number of possible responses exist, depending on life-style variables of the individual, e.g., courageous compensation, despair leading to retreat, a protective, hesitating attitude. As stated by one of Adler's advocates, Dreikurs (1967), the courageous response converts the difficulty into a blessing, the despairing response may mean retreat into disability, and the somewhat neurotic responses can mean, "How much better would I do if I had not had this disability!" (p. 174).

Dreikurs (1967) further attempted to clarify rehabilitation-related concepts that have a bearing on psychosocial adjustment and life-style: "Inferiority," "inferiority feelings," and "inferiority complex":

> Inferiority can refer to any objective inadequacy in function or in status. It does not necessarily produce an inferiority feeling. A person may be weak, deficient or of low status without any realization of inferiority. On the other hand, an inferiority feeling may exist without any real inferiority. The decisive factor in the dynamics of inferiority feelings in the person's assumption of being inferior, either physically, socially or in comparison to his own goals and standards. This assumption may not always be expressed on a conscious or verbal level as the individual may not be fully aware of it . . . . Only the inferiority feeling can stimulate a compensation of the part of the individual. The situation is different in regard to biological inferiorities and organ deficiencies because the whole organism takes them into consideration and may, therefore, prompt biological compensations and over compensations, without any necessary awareness by the individual. The term "Inferiority Complex" applied to an entirely different psychological mechanism. A discouraged individual may use a real or assumed deficiency for the purpose of special benefit, generally as an excuse or an alibi for nonparticipation and withdrawal or as a means to get special services or consideration. This is the only type of inferiority of which the individual is fully aware, as he [*sic*] tries to impress others and his [*sic*] own conscience with the magnitude of his [*sic*] defects. The "Inferiority Complex" does not lead to any compensation. It is a deadlock for any further development. (pp. 175-176)

In terms of purposes served with different life-styles, "inferiority" tends to be somewhat of an objective comparison or assessment; "inferiority feelings" have been existing in everyone at various times and influence future development, and "inferiority complex" appears to be a fatalistic reaction to a very difficult situation without attempting to improve it.

Relevant Issues

Wright (1980) concluded that the words "disability," "limitation" and "handicap" produce more semantic confusion than any others in rehabilitation terminology. The use of the term "disability," as used in this chapter, is intended to incorporate individually determined implications of the term "handicap" (i.e., lowered self-assessment, reduced function, or limited opportunities) because, as noted previously, the personal meaning of the disability to the individual is the important issue in the life-style approach.

According to Sechrest and Wallace (1967), the concept of general adjustment can be viewed from many perspectives: the survival model emphasizes adjustment to the basic disability, e.g., maintaining health, keeping alive, reproductiveness; the medical model highlights treatment of underlying causes, sometimes to the neglect of environmental influences; the positive-striving model focuses on the process of fulfilling one's self-potential, yet, may involve conflicts with pragmatism and idealism and other less recognized models, such as the engineering, drive reduction, and social conformity models. However, most of the above models, with the possible exception of the positive-striving model, do not holistically approach the significance of the disability to a person's life.

At least two basic issues are involved in defining adjustment: achievement versus process (Lazarus, 1969) and frame of reference (Sechrest & Wallace, 1967). In discussing these important concepts, Roessler and Bolton (1978) observed that the achievement or final state conception of adjustment implies a final, trouble-free state, which may create unrealistically high expectations and implies that all problems are solvable; conversely, the process orientation to adjustment emphasizes adaptation to a succession of situations and the overall expectation that life will not be trouble free. The second concept, frame of reference, is also very important to adjustment. Fundamentally, two frames of reference exist: (1) the person with the disability and (2) an external person, such as a rehabilitation practitioner. The consequences of both frames of reference are extremely important to the individual's process of acceptance and adjustment.

The life-style approach, with its emphasis on the personalized meaning of the disability to the individual, incorporates the key factors discussed in the preceding paragraph. Regarding the achievement versus process issue, life-style understandably focuses on goal-directedness or fixed consequences to be achieved within the context of a person's overall pattern of movement through life; thus, short-term goals are viewed within the perspective of dimly conscious overriding long-term goals. In regard to the second issue, internal versus external frame of reference, there is a shift within the life-style approach. The practitioner assists the client in getting, psychologically speaking (Carkhuff, 1980), from where he or she is to where he or she wants to be. This entails focusing primarily on the client's internal frame of reference in the earlier phases of helping with an increased blending of the practitioner's frame of reference (including gentle nudging) in the later stages.

The Life-Style Counseling Process

The life-style counseling process for acceptance and adjustment to disability can be viewed as having four phases: Relationship, Life-style Investigation, Life-style Interpretation, and Reorientation.

Relationship

This initial phase is not actually a "phase" in the sense that it has a distinct ending. Relationship variables continue throughout the complete counseling process; however, the rehabilitation practitioner begins the helping process by building a relationship of trust, respect and genuineness.

The relationship phase serves other purposes: (1) the practitioner learns more about the client's internal frame of reference; (2) the client has the opportunity to explore self in relationship to the disability; and (3) the opportunity exists for an exchange of specific rehabilitation-related information, such as procedural, work history, medical. The Carkhuff model (1980) offers helpful guidelines for attending, responding, and personalizing.

Shontz (1975) offers some broad considerations that may be helpful for the rehabilitation practitioner to keep in mind, particularly during this phase:

1. There are often multiple causes in life, rather than simple cause and effect relationships.
2. The person functions or attempts to function as an integrated unit.
3. The person responds to reality as he [*sic*] interprets it.
4. Behavior is determined by the context of the situation at the current moment.
5. Behavior maximizes construed consistency between past, present, and anticipated future experience.
6. Behavior is a function of relationships within an integrated organism-environment totality. (pp. 191-198)

Life-Style Investigation

Before actually gathering the client's childhood life-style information (to be discussed in later paragraphs), the practitioner often obtains specific information regarding how the client's life-style is functioning in the present. The helper is likely to explore with the client how he or she is functioning in the three tasks of life, sometimes also referred to as the three areas of social living. Adler believed that everyone takes a position–probably with differing degrees of failure or success–on each of the three tasks of life: friendship, work (or school), and love. The individual life-style, including its unique blind spots, strengths, and weaknesses, functions as a coping device in all areas of life. An increased awareness of how the client is functioning in the three tasks of life may yield a fuller picture on how the client's chosen life-style is contributing holistically to whatever problems the client is presenting.

Another technique that some Adlerians find useful at this point is that of asking "The Question." This simply entails asking the client what would be different if he or she did not have a disability. The answer to this question sometimes can indicate for what purpose the person is experiencing unusual difficulties, against whom or what the symptoms are directed, or against what threat or demand one is defending by having such difficulty accepting or adjusting to disability.

There are a number of ways in which the practitioner can conduct a formal life-style investigation of the client's remembered early childhood. One of the more frequent procedures is to use a life-style assessment form. Several versions exist; one of the more popular is a form, or its variations, developed by Dreikurs (1967). These forms pinpoint specific areas of questioning concept of self, family constellation, including siblings' development, age differences, ordering of sexes, alliance groups, etc. Moreover, questions are asked about parental influences and expectations, family values and atmosphere, peers, specific early memories; in short, whatever remembered significant information related to the first social group, the family, that contributed to the biased slice of life that was the only slice of life that the child had available to generalize from.

Very importantly, Adlerians believe that memory–especially early memory–is selective. Dreikurs (1967) asserted that people operate on an economy principle by selectively using their memories in accordance with this individual purposes. Accordingly, our memories from early childhood seem to serve as anchoring orientation points, reflecting the most significant conclusions, expectations, and goals that crystalized during this formative period. So, by asking relevant questions, the rehabilitation practitioner is able tentatively to reconstruct important aspects of the client's environment. Once this is accomplished, the helper can look at themes in the remembered early environment, which, because of the selectivity of memory phenomenon, reflect the dimly conscious notions and goals that the individual is presently using.

Particular emphasis is given in the Adlerian framework to family constellation from a socio-psychological perspective. Shulman (1973) listed five basic positions: only, eldest, second, middle, and youngest child. Each position has several modest probabilities of stereotyped characteristics attached to it. The rehabilitation practitioner considers and refines these tentative hypotheses in line with the direction of movement reflected by other life-style variables. For example, sometimes only-borns are very sensitive to what authorities, or "big," or accomplished people think and may be capable of viewing other people as curiosities; first borns may strive to be on top, might be sensitive to being "dethroned," and may attempt to be high achievers; youngest borns sometimes try to be charmers, might put others into their service by being the baby, the incompetent one, or the boss, etc.

In addition to family constellation considerations and other family-related variables, a client's specific early recollections and dreams round out life-style analysis. From the thousands and thousands of experiences to which a person has been exposed in early childhood, only those specific recollections are remembered that coincide with one's present outlook (here, as in other recollections of life-style information, the selectivity of memory phenomenon is in operation). In general, individuals can remember at least six specific incidents that occurred in early childhood. Each early memory reflects a current expectation. The Adlerian approach is to focus on the interpersonal movement of each early memory, not on hidden, symbolic meanings. Furthermore, each early recollection supplements and rounds out the outlook reflected by the other early recollections.

The rehabilitation practitioner subsequently studies the client's responses to the life-style interview. In searching for life-style "threads," or patterns (i.e., notions or overriding goals), the helper keeps an eye on general (nomothetic) laws and individually created (ideographic) laws. The helper is, in a sense, putting together a jigsaw puzzle or cognitive map. In essence, the rehabilitation practitioner is wondering "if this individual has drawn these conclusions about himself or herself, others and life, then what kind of overriding goals would he or she have chosen to guide himself or herself in striving to be a coping, significant person?"

Examples of different life-style themes are given by Mosak (1971), who emphasized that predictions cannot be made as to what behavior will coincide with a particular goal. Furthermore, he later (1979b) cautioned that the uniqueness of the person is violated by any typologies, which should be limited to didactic purposes. Examples of these themes are driving, getting, controlling, always being right, being the central or the best, pleasing, being admired for moral superiority, being against, being a martyr, being an excitement seeker, being victimized, etc. It is important for the rehabilitation practitioner to keep in mind that each of these terms is designed to reflect the powerful determination to enhance the self as well as that each theme works to both one's advantage and disadvantage, depending particularly on the behavior and the context.

An example of an extremely abbreviated life-style analysis is that of G. K. He was the second of two boys, having dethroned his older brother who experienced severe childhood emotional problems. G. K. especially pleased both parents by achievement as well as by goodness and charm. In many ways, he had the best of all worlds; his striving, not unusual for second borns, enabled him to surpass his older brother; his socio-psychological place as a functional youngest born enabled him to choose to develop skills, not unusual for youngest borns, of social seductiveness. His earliest specific recollection was of feeling special in kindergarten by sneaking under the teacher's desk and pleasantly surprising her. From a life-style analysis perspective, this information–although extremely limited–is typically consistent in its themes. The guess could be made that G. K., upon acquiring a severe disability, would probably dutifully strive to overcome its limitations–as long as he was able to achieve a very special place in the eyes of the "big people"–the rehabilitation professionals. The astute rehabilitation practitioner would remember these life-style threads as he or she worked with this client.

Life-Style Interpretation

Once the rehabilitation practitioner has tentatively identified the person's life-style patterns or threads (notions or goals), he or she usually shares these interpretations in a spirit of exploration and respect (e.g., "A guess that I have is . . ." Could it be that . . ."). Actually, a number of frameworks exist for presenting life-style information (Mosak, 1954, 1979a; Rule, 1982).

If possible, the rehabilitation practitioner should encourage the client to take responsibility for identifying relationships between daily living, especially the present and life-style notions or goals. Particular discussion could be given here, if timing is appropriate, to life-style blinders to acceptance and adjustment to disability. It is important to foster a positive attitude in the client toward understanding of his or her life-style, particularly as the practitioner and client move into the next and final phase.

Reorientation

In this phase, the emphasis is, as the term connotes, on change. Upon achieving insight into the daily implementation of the client's life-style, the client and counselor can now use this as a springboard for agreed-upon change.

The practitioner is well-served at this phase if the goal-directedness of behavior is especially kept in mind. "Whys" or "causes" imply past unchangeable reasons; "goals" indicate future-oriented, changeable targets. Sometimes, the client may want to learn new behavior to implement the same goals. Perhaps homework strategies may need to be devised that will assist the client in modifying the frequency or felt intensity of a life-style goal. Overall, the guiding emphasis is on removing agreed-upon barriers to acceptance and adjustment to the client's disability. This focus often involves initially clarifying when the client's life-style is working to his or her ultimate disadvantage and how to build on its strengths when it is working to his or her advantage. Suitable strategies from other approaches (e.g., Rational-Emotive, Behavioral, Gestalt, family therapy, stress management, etc.) may be useful here. The Rational Emotive Behavior Therapy (REBT) use of cognitive-behavioral homework strategies which incorporates techniques from other theoretical approaches would be very helpful (Ellis & Dryden, 1997).

The rehabilitation worker may want to use life-style awareness to suggest changes in facets of the client's environment, e.g., family members, job supervisors, medical staff, other rehabilitation professionals, etc. Sometimes, life-style awareness can provide insight into the client's unproductive use of chemical abuse, i.e., the goal(s) being met in an altered or euphoric state of mind.

The use of humor in conveying awareness and reminding the individual of life-style goals cannot be underestimated. This may be done by fables, metaphors, parables, cartoons, photographs, recordings, etc. This technique, as well as all Adlerian strategies, is handled in the spirit of encouragement, which conveys worth, uniqueness, and acceptance–not necessarily praise–to the client.

As noted previously, the life-style approach views people as basically social beings who are inclined to establish self-identity by relating to–and comparing self with–others. These comparisons, at varying levels of awareness, have particular implications for acceptance and adjustment to disability. The rehabilitation practitioner would be well-served to keep in mind the relationship between a client's unique life-style goals and comparison-related vulnerabilities for many individuals with disabilities, e.g., inferiority feelings, "near-normalcy," social consequences of loss of liberty, dependency, etc. Further readings on life-style and adjustment to various disabilities may be found in Rule (1984).

The term "resistance" has a somewhat different meaning in Adlerian life-style counseling as compared to many other approaches. As Dreikurs (1967) asserted, "resistance" is essentially a discrepancy between the goals of the client and the practitioner. Thus, "acceptance of the client as he[*sic*] is" (Mosak, 1977, p. 54) has special meaning when the client does not measure up to the practitioner's expectations. Ideas for confrontation and dealing with negativism, yet respecting the client's goals, may be found in Shulman (1972, 1977) and Rule (1977).

Behind what may be labeled as "resistance" by the helper may be client goals that are self protective devices against perceived dangers, such as (Shulman, 1973) being ridiculed, not getting necessary help, submitting to order, having to face unpleasant consequences, incurring disapproval, having to face responsibility, being taken advantage of, etc.

The creativity of the individual life-style is ever present, and the various methods for struggling against symptoms in order to maintain face (Shulman, 1973; Mosak, 1977) varies from life-style to life-style. Just as symptoms can serve as safeguards for self-esteem, so can related forms of behavior be in service of the individual life-style. For example, Shulman cited possible purposes for suffering: as manipulation ("If you don't do what I want, I'll die and then you'll be sorry"); as justification ("I have a right to my own way. Look how much I suffer when I don't get it"); as self-glorification ("The amount of my suffering proves my nobility").

It is important for the rehabilitation practitioner to remember that the client is doing the best and most useful thing–within the blinders of his or her life-style–that he or she can do at the time. Accordingly, the client deserves respect and acceptance, regardless of his or her dimly conscious goals, notions, feelings, behavior, dreams, or safeguards for self-esteem.

Creative New Directions

Adlerian practitioners continue to explore creative ways to implement Adler's ideas. In keeping with the basic spirit of the Adlerian approach as a "psychology of use," most clinicians experiment, on an ongoing basis, with whatever works. Often, these innovative approaches take the direction of combining traditional Adlerian thinking with concepts and practices from other schools of thought, both long-standing and new. Furthermore, Adlerians continually apply their time-tested ideas to current counseling issues. Highlighted below are some of the more recent areas of Adlerian application in the 1990s.

A number of recent Adlerian efforts have been made to combine Adlerian concepts with other approaches that are currently popular. For instance, Carish (1990a) explored hypnotic techniques and Adlerian constructs, and an entire special issue of the major Adlerian journal, *Individual Psychology; The Journal of Adlerian Theory, Research & Practice* (Carish, 1990b), was devoted to exploring the linkages between hypnosis and Adlerian application. Moreover, systems approaches in counseling and psychotherapy have become increasing popular (e.g., Bauserman & Rule, 1995) and efforts have been made, such in those of Nicoll (1993), to integrate these theories into an Adlerian perspective.

In regard to emerging counseling problems that have received popular and professional attention in the 1990s, Adlerian clinicians are again eager to explore the application of their concepts and techniques to contemporary problems. Entire special issues of *Individual Psychology: The Journal of Adlerian Theory, Research & Practice* have been devoted to the process of aging and working with special adults (Carlson, 1992), marriage and couples counseling (Evans & Dinkmeyer, 1993), and counseling homosexuals and bisexuals (Carlson, (1995). Recent empirical research lends support to various Adlerian life-style themes and provides a useful schema for eclectic counselors to assess clients' strengths and weaknesses and generate appropriate therapeutic goals (Ashby, Kottman, & Rice, 1998).

From the perspective of people with severe mental health disabilities, Mosak (1995) has explored and advocated drugless therapy with persons with schizophrenia, and Allers and Golson (1994) investigated Adlerian treatment of Multiple Personality Disorder. Slavick, Carlson, and Sperry (1993, 1995) have discussed the application of Adlerian concepts with adults with a history of childhood sexual abuse. Axtell and Newton (1993) studied the life themes of bulemic women. Adlerian thinking has also been applied to the pervasive present problems of alcoholism and substance abuse (e.g., Prinz, 1993; Keen & Wheeler, 1994).

The unifying focus in these applications of solid concepts to contemporary problems is the purposive nature of individual behavior within a social context. Expressed another way, personal problems are basically interpersonal problems–for all people, with or without disabilities.

Summary

The rehabilitation use of Adlerian life-style in the acceptance and adjustment to disability was discussed. This included a highlighting of Adler's background and contributions as well as review of the characteristics and assumptions of life-style understanding. Particular emphasis was further given to life-style creativity and behavioral implementation. An overview was provided of the life-style counseling process, which includes four phases: relationship, life-style analysis, life-style interpretation, and reorientation. Discussion was given to ongoing Adlerian efforts to overcome some of the contemporary problems of the 1990s and beyond as we move into the new millennium.

REFERENCES

Allers, C. T., & Golson, J. (1994). Multiple personality disorder: Treatment from an Adlerian perspective. *Individual Psychology: The Journal of Adlerian Theory, Research and Practice, 50* (3), 262-270.

Ansbacher, H. L., & Ansbacher, R. R. (Eds.). (1956). *The individual psychology of Alfred Adler.* New York: Basic Books.

Ashby, J. S., Kottman, T., & Rice, K. G. (1998). Adlerian personality priorities: Psychological and attitudinal differences. *Journal of Counseling & Development, 76* (4), 467-474.

Bauserman, J. M., & Rule, W. R. (1995). *A brief history of systems approaches in counseling and psychotherapy.* Lanham, MD: University Press of America.

Axtell, A., & Newton, B. J. (1993). An analysis of Adlerian life themes of bulimic women. Individual Psychology: *The Journal of Adlerian Theory, Research and Practice, 49* (1), 58-67.

Carish, M. S. (Ed.). (1990b). Hypnosis [Special issue]. Individual Psychology: *The Journal of Adlerian Theory, Research and Practice, 46* (4).

Carish, M. S. (1990a). Hypnotic techniques and Adlerian constructs. Individual Psychology: *The Journal of Adlerian Theory, Research and Practice, 46* (2), 166-177.

Carkhuff, R. (1980). *The art of helping IV.* Amherst, MA: Human Development.

Carlson, J. (Ed.). (1995). Counseling homosexuals and bisexuals [Special issue].. Individual Psychology: *The Journal of Adlerian Theory, Research and Practice, 51* (2) .

Carlson, J. (Ed.). (1992). The process of aging and working with special adults [Special issue]. Individual Psychology: *The Journal of Adlerian Theory, Research and Practice, 48* (4) .

Dreikurs, R. (1967). *Psychodynamics, psychotherapy and counseling.* Chicago: Alfred Adler.

Ellenberger, H. (1970). *The discovery of the unconscious: The history and evolution of* dynamic psychiatry. New York: Basic Books.

Ellis, A., & Dryden, W. (1997). *The practice of rational emotive behavior therapy* (2nd ed.). New York: Springer.

Evans, T. D., & Dinkmeyer, D., Jr. (Ed.). (1993). Marriage and couples counseling [Special issue]. *Individual Psychology: The Journal of Adlerian Theory, Research and Practice, 49*(3 &4).

Keen, K. K., Jr., & Wheeler, M. S. (1994). Substance abuse in college freshmen and Adlerian life-style themes. Individual Psychology: *The Journal of Adlerian Theory, Research, and Practice, 50* (1), 97-109.

Lazarus, R. (1969). *Patterns of adjustments in human effectiveness.* New York: McGraw-Hill.

Mosak, H. H. (1971). Life-style. In A. Nikelly (Ed.), *Techniques for behavior change.* Springfield, IL: Charles C Thomas.

Mosak, H. H. (1995). Drugless therapy with schizophrenics. Individual Psychology: *The Journal of Adlerian Theory, Research and Practice, 51* (1), 61-66.

Mosak, H. H. (1979a). Adlerian psychotherapy. In R. Corsini (Ed.), *Current psychotherapies* (2nd ed.). Itasca, IL: Peacock.

Mosak, H. H. (1977). *On purpose.* Chicago: Alfred Adler.

Mosak, H. H. (1979b). Mosak's typology: An update. *Journal of Individual Psychology, 35* (2), 192 195.

Nicoll, W. G. (1993). Multiple systems counseling: An integration and extension of Adlerian and systems theories. Individual Psychology: *The Journal of Adlerian Theory, Research and Practice, 49* (2), 132-152.

Prinz, J. (1993). Alcoholics and their treatment: Current Adlerian thinking. Individual Psychology: *The Journal of Adlerian Theory, Research and Practice, 49* (1), 94-105.

Roessler, R. , & Bolton, R. (1978). *Psychosocial adjustment to disability.* Baltimore: University Park.

Rule, W. (Ed.). (1984). *Life-style counseling for adjustment to disability.* Rockville, MD: Aspen Systems.

Rule, W. (1982). Life-style interpretation using imagination of the ideal social self. Individual Psychology: *The Journal of Adlerian Theory, Research and Practice, 38* (4), 339-342.

Rule, W. (1977). Corrective reactions to client negativism using a combined facilitative and Adlerian based approach. *Corrective and Social Psychiatry and Journal of Behavior Technology Methods and Therapy, 23,* 7-10.

Sechrest, L. & Wallace, J. (1967). *Psychology and human problems.* Columbus, OH: Charles E. Merrill.

Shontz, F. C. (1975). *The psychological aspects of physical illness and disability.* New York: Macmillan.

Shontz, F. C. (1977). Physical disability and personality: Theory and recent research. In J.

Stubbins, J. (Ed.) (1977), *Social and Psychological Aspects of Disability.* Baltimore: University Park.

Shulman, B. H. (1973). *Contributions to individual psychology.* Chicago: Alfred Adler.

Shulman, B. H. (1972). Confrontation techniques. *Journal of Individual Psychology, 28,* 177-183.

Shulman, B. H. (1977). Encouraging the pessimist: A confronting technique. *The Individual Psychologist, 14,* 7-9.

Slavick, S., Carlson, J., & Sperry, L. (1995). Extreme life-styles of adults who have experienced sexual abuse. *Individual Psychology: The Journal of Adlerian Theory, Research and Practice, 51* (4), 358-374.

Slavick, S., Carlson, J., & Sperry, L. (1993). An Adlerian treatment of adults with a history of childhood sexual abuse. *Individual Psychology: The Journal of Adlerian Theory, Research and Practice, 49* (2), 111-131.

Wright, G. N. (1980). *Total rehabilitation.* Boston: Little, Brown.

Chapter 12

RATIONAL EMOTIVE BEHAVIOR THERAPY (REBT): A COGNITIVE-BEHAVIORAL APPROACH TO ACCEPTANCE AND ADJUSTMENT TO DISABILITY

GERALD L. GANDY

This chapter is based on the pioneering work of Albert Ellis, a clinical psychologist, who combined humanistic, philosophical, and behavioral therapy to develop Rational Emotive Behavior Therapy (REBT) in 1955 (1962; 1994c). He was originally trained as a classical psychoanalyst but deviated from this background to initiate the cognitive-behavioral revolution in psychotherapy. Corey (1996) has noted that Ellis is rightly known as the grandfather of cognitive-behavioral therapy. "REBT is regarded as one of the premiere examples of the cognitive-behavioral approach" (Dobson & Block, 1988). Albert Ellis was born in Pittsburgh in 1913 and raised in New York City where he completed a bachelor's degree at the City College of New York and M.A. and Ph.D. degrees at Columbia University. He practiced psychotherapy, marriage and family counseling, as well as sex therapy, for over fifty years and continues this practice at the Albert Ellis Institute in New York. He also continues to give lectures and conduct workshops not only in the United States but in numerous foreign countries. He has now authored or edited over sixty books and monographs and seven hundred articles (Ellis & Dryden, 1997).

The primary purpose of this chapter is to discuss the application of REBT as a cognitive-behavioral approach to acceptance and adjustment to disability. An overview of the REBT model along with brief reference to related cognitive-behavioral models will also be presented. It should be noted that

---

Updated and adapted from Chapter 1: Overview of REBT and Chapter 2: Mental Health Rehabilitation and REBT in G. L. Gandy, *Mental Health Rehabilitation: Disputing Irrational Beliefs*, 1995. Courtesy of Charles C Thomas, Publisher, Springfield, IL.

REBT now includes many techniques that were developed by the newer cognitive-behavior therapies.

Overview of REBT

Ellis (1994c) originally called his approach Rational Therapy or RT to emphasize the cognitive element. He later changed it to Rational-Emotive Therapy or RET to reflect the emotive element. More recently, he has renamed it Rational Emotive Behavior Therapy because he thought it more accurately described his approach in terms of all three elements.

Basic Concepts

A basic philosophical premise of REBT is that, at least in Western society, people want to be happy (Ellis, 1994c). The extent to which people achieve their own individualized goals of happiness is greatly influenced by engaging in rational behavior and avoiding irrational behavior. The basic definition of rational in REBT theory "...means that which helps people to achieve their basic goals and purposes, whereas irrational means that which prevents them from achieving these goals and purposes" (Ellis & Dryden, 1997, p.4). The definition of rational utilized is based on the principles of the scientific method (Ellis & Harper, 1975).

An important concept in REBT is unconditional self acceptance (Ellis & Dryden, 1997). Healthy people are glad to be alive and accept themselves just because they are alive. They do not measure their intrinsic worth by their extrinsic achievements or by what others think of them. They avoid rating themselves–their totality or their being (Hauck, 1992). They avoid unconstructive guilt or blame, either of one's self or others (Ard, 1990). REBT also places a focus on constructive self-interest (Ellis and Dryden, 1997). Constructive self-interest demands social interest in order for an individual to help build the kind of society in which oneself would best live.

REBT theory hypothesizes that humans have a biological tendency to think irrationally but also have a biological tendency to think rationally (Ellis and Dryden, 1997). The biological tendency to think irrationally is based on the seeming ease with which humans think crookedly and the prevalence of such thinking even among people who have been rationally raised. However, REBT theory holds that humans also have a biological tendency to exercise the power of human choice and to work toward changing their irrational thinking.

When people become emotionally upset about an event, REBT postulates that their emotional reaction is caused more by their interpretation of the event rather than the actual event itself (Ellis, 1995). If they are rejected for a job, they may get depressed. They assume the rejection caused the depression. However, they probably silently verbalized to themselves that the event should not have happened and they are failures for being rejected. These ideas are highly irrational since there is no reason why they should not be rejected for the job, and there is no evidence why they will not have an opportunity to be successful in the future. More rational ideas could be that they wish the event had not happened and they do not like failing. These ideas would probably cause them to only feel annoyed and frustrated but remain determined to try again.

A distinction is made between inappropriate or disturbed emotions (anger, shame, anxiety, depression, etc.) and appropriate or nondisturbed emotions (displeasure, regret, concern, sadness, etc.) in REBT (Ellis, 1995). The distinction is not one of intensity but of quality. Intense levels of appropriate emotions tend to motivate constructive behavior whereas intense levels of inappropriate emotions tend to be disruptive and counterproductive. The goal is to change the quality of the emotion rather than lower the intensity; otherwise, clients may become indifferent about their problems.

REBT assumes that people are often indoctrinated with basic irrational ideas perpetuated by western culture (Ellis, 1995). Demandingness (an absolutistic should or must) is the core irrational belief that is responsible for human emotional disturbance. The main irrational ideas they learn and invent are: (1) I must do well and/or be approved by significant others or I am an inadequate person; (2) Others must treat me kindly and fairly or else they are rotten individuals; and (3) Conditions under which I live must be safe and comfortable or else the world is a horrible place in which to live and life is hardly worth living. An irrational absolutistic "must" is the basic premise. Three forms of thinking that are logical derivatives of a basic irrational "must" would be awfulizing, damnation, and I-can't stand-it-itis. There can be many variations and corollaries of the basic premise and its logical derivatives.

DiGiuseppe (1991) has noted that it is important to differentiate between inferences or automatic thoughts and core irrational beliefs that an individual may have about the world. A person may have a misperception or irrational idea about an event, which, if corrected, would be helpful to him or her. The more serious problem in REBT is a core irrational belief the person may have, such as that it should not be this way. A female client incorrectly perceives that some people do not like her. She will feel better to find out that her perception is not accurate. Nevertheless, she may still have a core irrational (demandingness) belief that people should never feel this way about her.

A distinction is also made in REBT between ego disturbance and discomfort disturbance (Ellis & Dryden, 1997). In ego disturbance a person makes demands on self, others, and the world, and if these demands are not met, the person becomes disturbed by damning self. In discomfort disturbance the person makes the same demands, but they are related to dogmatic commands that comfortable life conditions must exist (low frustration tolerance). When these demands are not met, the person damns the world.

Therapeutic Process and Methods

Dryden and DiGiuseppe (1990) describe the ABC framework in REBT as A = the activating event, B = the beliefs, and C = the emotional and behavioral consequences. They outline the following steps in the REBT treatment sequences: (1) Ask for a problem, (2) Define and agree upon a target problem, (3) Assess C, (4) Assess A, (5) Identify and assess any secondary emotional problems, (6) Teach the B-C connection, (7) Assess beliefs, (8) Connect irrational beliefs and C, (9) Dispute irrational beliefs, (10) Prepare to deepen conviction in rational beliefs, (11) Encourage the client to put new learning into practice, (12) Check homework assignments, and (13) Facilitate the working-through process.

Active-directive therapeutic techniques in REBT are generally considered the most effective way to change thoughts, feelings, and behaviors (Ellis and Dryden, 1997). Cognitive, emotive, and behavioral techniques include confrontations, probing, challenging, and disputing irrational beliefs, teaching procedures, giving emotive exercises, and assigning homework tasks. Behavioral methods such as relaxation, modeling, coping-skills, assertion, and self-management training are frequently utilized with clients. Expressive-emotive-experiential procedures adapted from Gestalt psychology are occasionally used to help clients get in touch with their feelings. Clients are then taught how they create most of their self-destructive emotions by what they are telling themselves.

"Shame-attacking" and "risk attacking" exercises are considered particularly effective in REBT (Ellis & Dryden, 1997). In shame-attacking exercises, clients deliberately act "shamefully" in public in order to accept themselves and to tolerate the ensuing discomfort. Clients are instructed not to harm themselves or other people, and only minor infractions of social rules are involved (e.g., calling out the time on a crowded subway, wearing bizarre clothes, going into a hardware store and asking if they sell tobacco). Risk attacking exercises involve clients deliberately forcing themselves to take risks in areas where they wish to make changes (e.g., people who experience shyness forcing themselves to attend social functions).

Ellis (Ellis & Dryden, 1997) believes that an ideal REBT therapist would give unconditional acceptance to a client. However, he encourages a very forceful style and believes that being too warm to a client could possibly be antitherapeutic. Not all REBT therapists concur with this latter view. Ellis admits that REBT can be combined with a "Rogerian" low key manner and still work, but he believes it is less effective that way and takes longer (Weinrach, 1980). He indicates that there can be different therapeutic styles as well as techniques borrowed from other therapeutic systems as long as one does not depart from the principles of REBT.

The therapeutic use of humor is considered helpful in REBT (Ellis, 1994c). REBT hypothesizes that almost all neurotic disturbances stem from taking things too seriously. Paradoxical intention, evocative language, irony, wit, cartoons, and rational humorous songs are all used as antidotes to irrational thinking. However, it humorously attacks the clients "beliefs" and not the "client."

Therapy is directed towards three forms of insight: (1) disturbance is primarily determined by absolutistic beliefs, (2) people remain disturbed by reindoctrinating themselves in the present, and (3) change comes about from diligent work and practice. The ultimate goal is not only removal of the clients' symptoms, but a change in their basic philosophy of life which will significantly lessen their tendency to disturb themselves. The most elegant and long-lasting changes are ones that involve philosophical restructuring of irrational beliefs.

Clients frequently have secondary emotional problems (and sometimes tertiary) problems about their primary emotional problems (Ellis & Dryden, 1997). A person may feel anxious about failing a test and then feel anxious about feeling anxious and eventually experience panic and hopelessness as a result of the secondary emotional disturbance. It may be necessary to work on the secondary or tertiary problem first if it is significantly interfering with work on the primary problem.

Ellis (1995) has noted that individuals who are out of contact with reality, in a highly manic state, seriously autistic or brain injured, and in the lower levels of mental deficiency are not normally treated in REBT. Nevertheless, because of its simplicity and clarity, he believes that REBT is more effective with less intelligent, poorly educated, economically deprived, and lower motivated clients than most of the usual psychotherapeutic approaches. Clients with borderline intellectual functioning, for example, may not be suitable candidates for rational restructuring, but they have been taught simple coping statements.

Although REBT can be presented at a very basic level as brief therapy, it is an approach that can become very complex as you work with clients with higher intelligence and education (Ellis, 1995, 1996). REBT becomes significantly more effective and complex with mildly disturbed individuals and those who have a single major symptom. It is a system with only a few parts, but one in which the interaction of those parts can become very complex.

REBT primarily follows an educational model of therapy (Ellis & Harper, 1975). A large variety of educational procedures are employed such as bibliotherapy, homework report sheets, tape recordings, cards with rational statements, diagrams, games, and so forth. Ellis and Harper (1975) suggested that the future of psychotherapy may well lie in the development of even better methods of emotional education and indicated that the terms "emotional education" or "tolerance training" may replace the term "psychotherapy."

Some helpful books that provide more practical detail on the application of REBT techniques include Bernard and Wolfe (1993), Grieger and Woods (1994), Dryden and DiGiuseppe (1990), Yankura and Dryden (1990), and Walen, DiGiuseppe, and Dryden (1992).

Research Considerations

Corey (1996) has noted that there are methodological shortcomings in REBT research but the recent reviews have provided evidence for the effectiveness of REBT. Most studies have focused on cognitive, not emotive and behavioral, methods. The cognitive disputing of irrational is what originally made REBT radically different from other psychotherapeutic orientations when it evolved. Nevertheless, REBT has always used cognitive, emotive, and behavioral techniques and is even more comprehensive in that combination in its contemporary form (Bernard, 1998).

Preferential REBT and Broad-Based Cognitive-Behavior Therapy

When clients are helped to make long-lasting philosophical changes in their irrational beliefs, Ellis considers that to be elegant or preferential REBT (Bernard, 1998; Ellis & Dryden, 1997; Kwee & Ellis, 1998). However, if it becomes apparent that clients are not able to change their irrational beliefs, the REBT therapist would endeavor to help them change the activating event directly or to change their distorted inferences about the situation. When therapeutic effort is directed in the latter manner, Ellis (Ellis & Dryden, 1997) considers that to be general REBT and to be synonymous with broad-based cognitive-behavior therapy.

In the 1970s, the behavior-therapy movement (Bandura, 1969; Eysenck, 1964; Krumbolt, 1966; Wolpe, 1958; Skinner, 1953) which had begun to flourish in the 1960s began to become largely cognitive-behavioral (Ellis, 1994). Ellis (Corey, 1996) is considered to have pioneered this cognitive-behavioral movement and now includes many techniques in general REBT developed by the newer cognitive-behavioral therapists. REBT therapists, for example, use rational-emotive imagery from Maxie Maultsby's (1984)

Rational Behavior Therapy, principles of correcting faulty inferences from Aaron Beck's (1976) Cognitive Therapy, rational coping statements from Donald Meichenbaum's (1977) Cognitive Behavior Modification, a focus on irresponsible behavior from William Glasser's (1965) Reality Therapy, an exploration of sensation from Arnold Lazarus's Multimodal Therapy (1989), and other methods and techniques (Ellis & Dryden, 1997). The main difference between preferential REBT and the newer cognitive-behavior therapies is their de-emphasis on core irrational beliefs and focus more on either correcting irrational inferences about the activating event or changing the activating event (Ellis, 1994). The newer cognitive-behavior therapies also tend to place more emphasis on the relationship, but this is also true of many REBT therapists, and, as noted above, Ellis has agreed that REBT can be practiced in that manner at a slower but effective manner (Ellis & Dryden, 1997).

Further information on the books, audiotapes, and videotapes as well as additional information on REBT can be obtained from the Albert Ellis Institute, 45 East 65th Street, New York, NY 10021, Ph. # (800)-323-IRET or Local (212) 535-0822.

Acceptance and Adjustment to Disability and Rational Emotive Behavior Therapy (REBT)

Ard (1968) initially introduced the idea of REBT in rehabilitation counseling in the therapeutic counseling of people with disabilities. The initial reaction was negative because of some major misperceptions of REBT (Gandy, 1985, 1994b). REBT was viewed as neglecting emotions, imposing values, neglecting the therapeutic relationship, and being effective only with highly intelligent and educated individuals. As indicated in the overview of REBT, this view was not accurate. Ellis (Weinrach, 1980) has noted that the film *Three Approaches to Psychotherapy* (Shostrum, 1965) with the client, Gloria, which is the impression that many people have of REBT, never accurately reflected his approach even then. A number of films and videotapes have been developed since then that are a more accurate reflection. A recent production, the *Master Therapists: Videotaped Sessions* (DiGiuseppe, 1993), depicts therapy sessions with four leading REBT therapists and trainers (Ray DiGiuseppe, Albert Ellis, Janet Wolfe, and Dominic DiMattia).

Weinrach (1982) noted REBT initially experienced a lack of acceptance in therapeutic counseling in general largely because of Albert Ellis' style, which entertains some and alienates others. He noted that there are many myths about Ellis and his life style. Two interview articles (Dryden, 1989; Weinrach, 1980) and a book of anecdotes by colleagues, students, and friends (DiMattia

& Lega, 1990) provide a more accurate perspective about Albert Ellis. As DiMattia notes "Is he the brusque individual of his public persona? Yes, he is that. But he is much more....Albert Ellis is, above all, a human being: sensitive, caring, funny, supportive, eccentric, energetic, dedicated; more interested in helping others than in being 'liked'" (DiMattia & Lega, p. 9).

As indicated in the overview, although REBT can become very complex, it is an approach that can be presented at a basic level as brief therapy (Ellis, 1996). Ellis and Abrahms (1978) have demonstrated that REBT encourages relatively short-term therapy by stressing directness, a high degree of activity by the therapist, bibliotherapy, and specific homework assignments for clients to perform in between the REBT sessions. They believe the basic principles and practice can be quickly learned and easily applied in the form of brief therapy by health care professionals.

An effective short-term approach to therapy is very helpful to rehabilitation counselors and related professionals performing therapeutic counseling functions in agency settings where they experience considerable time constraints (Martin and Gandy, 1990). Rehabilitation counselors and related professionals in the private practice of therapeutic counseling can also benefit from a brief therapy model because of the increasing emphasis on such procedures by third party insurance carriers.

As also indicated in the overview, REBT is primarily an educational model (Ellis & Harper, 1975). The educational emphasis is very compatible with rehabilitation counselor training as well as related disciplines involved with the therapeutic counseling of people with disabilities that operate from more of a behavioral or educational model (Gandy,1985; Gandy and Rule, 1983, Lassiter, 1983). The structured and organized problem-solving nature of REBT provides a clarity and specificity that is similar to methods and procedures that have been associated with the successful rehabilitation of people with disabilities.

Mental and Physical Disabilities

The fourth edition of the American Psychiatric Association's *Diagnostic and Statistical Manual of Mental Disorders* (DSM IV) (1994) notes that to make a distinction between "mental disorders" and "physical disorders" is a reductionistic anachronism of mind/body dualism. "A compelling literature documents that there is much 'physical' in 'mental' disorders and much 'mental' in 'physical disorders'" (American Psychiatric Association, 1994, p. xxi). The DSM IV further notes that the term "mental" disorders has been much clearer than its solution and the term persists because an appropriate substitute has not been found.

The above message of the *DSM IV* is important to keep in mind in the following discussion of the application of REBT to what are traditionally considered "mental" and "physical" disabilities.

REBT and Mental Disabilities. As noted previously, individuals who are out of contact with reality, in a highly manic state, seriously autistic or brain injured, and in the lower ranges of mental deficiency are not normally treated in REBT. However, Ellis (1995) also notes that most other individuals with difficulties are treated with REBT and include: clients with maladjustment, moderate anxiety, or marital problems; those with sexual difficulties; run-of-the-mill "neurotics"; individuals with character disorders; truants; juvenile delinquents and adult criminals, borderline personalities; overt psychotics, including those with delusions and hallucinations, when they are somewhat in contact with reality; individuals with higher grade mental deficiency; and clients with psychosomatic problems.

A considerable literature exists on the application of REBT to mental disorders; consequently, only selected and more recent references will be mentioned. Case studies and detailed discussions have been presented on the application of REBT to "neurotic" type reactions (especially anxiety and depression), psychotic conditions in partial remission, severe personality disorders, sexual difficulties, relationship concerns, and marriage and family issues (e.g., Bernard, 1991; Ellis 1988, 1994a, 1994b, 1994c, 1994d, 1995, 1996; Ellis, Sichel, Yeager, DiMattia & DiGiuseppe, 1989; Huber & Baruth, 1989; Warren & Zgourides, 1991, Wolfe, 1992)).

Ellis, McInerney, DiGiuseppe and Yeager (1988) report that alcohol abuse is the world's number one health problem. An innovative development in this area has been the development of Rational Recovery (RR) (Ellis & Velton, 1992; Trimpey, 1989, 1996). RR is a self-help program for people wanting abstinence from alcohol or other drugs that utilizes the Addictive Voice Recognition Technique (AVRT) and is offered as an alternative, not a competitor, to the traditional model of Alcoholics Anonymous (AA). A more recent self-help program development as an alternative to AA that uses REBT as more of a central component than RR is Self Management and Recovery Training (SMART) (S.M.A.R.T. Recovery Self-Help Network, 1996; Knaus, 1995). Although many members of SMART have spiritual beliefs, the main distinction between SMART and AA is that SMART is not spiritually focused. Further information on this alternative to AA can be obtained from SMART, 24000 Mercantile Road, Beachwood, OH 44122. For those who prefer AA, DiMattia (1991) has noted that many REBT concepts in themselves are very complementary to a spiritual focus. Ellis (1985) has pointed out that there are several steps in the AA 12-step program that help individuals significantly.

Although most of the REBT literature is devoted to adults with mental disorders, Bernard and Joyce (1994) have noted that REBT now has a long history of application with children and adolescents. REBT has been applied to a variety of childhood problems including conduct disorders, low frustration tolerance, impulsivity, academic underachievement, anxieties, fears and phobias, social isolation, obesity, and childhood sexuality. An active-directive, confrontational style of REBT has frequently been encouraged with adults, but an emphasis on relationship building has been the focus of REBT with children and adolescents.

REBT and Physical Disabilities. Sweetland (1990) has noted that people with physical disabilities are not necessarily more disturbed or irrational in their thinking than other people, but irrational attitudes can exacerbate physical disabilities. He believes there are at least three reasons why a cognitive approach is particularly appropriate when assisting people with physical disabilities: (1) the disability is permanent and only one's reaction to it, not the condition itself, can be modified; (2) many people hold extremely irrational attitudes toward physical disabilities; and (3) since people with a physical disability can rarely, if ever, attain a sense of physical mastery, a sense of cognitive mastery and control may be even more important for this population than the general population.

Sweetland (1990) further observed that a common irrational belief among people with severe or significant physical disabilities is that the disability is really awful, terrible, and catastrophic. Another common belief is the alternate belief sometimes referred to as reaction formation or denial, which is a defense against the underlying belief that having a disability is catastrophic. People with severe or significant physical disabilities also frequently have the unrealistic belief, "I have paid my dues." The corollary of the latter belief is that since something catastrophic has already happened in my life, nothing very bad should happen again. A similar belief is the idea that somehow the world should make up for the problems that the disability causes. A variation is the idea, "Since I have a physical disability, I can't be expected to do much."

Calabro (1990) has developed a three-phase cognitive-behavioral model for analyzing and facilitating the adjustment process which follows severe or significant physical disability. The "pre-encounter phase" is the first stage and immediately follows the onset of incapacitating disability. Shock and denial are characteristic of the first stage, and the individual has not acknowledged that an activating or impeding event has occurred. The second stage or "post encounter phase" involves acknowledgment of the impeding condition by the person, and periods of anxiety, depression, and expressed anger are common. Early treatment is better focused on managing the person's environment and on direct cognitive intervention with beliefs held by the rehabilitation team. The "rational re-encounter phase" or final stage is characterized by repeated re-encounters with various forms of the impeding activating event and anticipated activating events. During the final stage, the person is more able to benefit from direct cognitive intervention tailored to the specific pattern of irrational beliefs often associated with disability.

Calabro (1997) has further developed a framework for integrating Maslow's Hierarchical theory of human needs in identifying the psychological priorities of those who face severe or significant disability and hospitalization. A variety of behavioral and Rational-Emotive interventions have been proposed that are tailored to the most logical sources of the person's key emotional discomforts in each category of Maslow's hierarchy. There is a shift from a greater emphasis on addressing the staff-environment regarding the person's more basic and "prepotent" priorities to a gradually increasing focus on the patient belief system, as priorities at higher levels become more applicable to the person. Specific examples of cognitive distortions and disputations are given, but it is noted that there are numerous other variants as well. A thorough and flexible analysis of the person's report, behavior, affect, and the surrounding circumstances should be conducted in deciding the exact nature of interventions.

Wallace and Maddox (1978) have also discussed the usefulness of REBT with people with physical disabilities. REBT literature on some specific physical disabilities includes cancer (Golden & Gersh, 1990), chronic fatigue syndrome (Balter & Unger, 1997), coronary heart disease (Lohr & Hamberger, 1990), diabetes (Rubin, Walen, & Ellis, 1990), psychosomatic disorders (Woods & Lyons, 1990), renal disease (Fisher, 1976), stoke (Alvarez, 1997), and visual disabilities (Needham & Ehmer, 1980; Zaborowski, 1997). Oliver and Block (1987, 1990) have developed guidelines for the caregiver in coping with Alzheimer's disease patients, which is also helpful for dealing with any person who is chronically ill or has a severe disability.

Ellis (1981) applied REBT to thanatology many years ago. Recently, he has expanded on these ideas, in collaboration with Michael Abrams, and published a book entitled *How to Cope with a Fatal Illness: The Rational Management of Death and Dying* (Ellis & Abrams, 1994). They explain how people with terminal cancer, AIDS, or other death-dealing medical conditions can learn to cope and enjoy their remaining days. They note how friends and loved ones may have a harmful influence if they panic over impending death. Examples of well-known individuals as well as persons who are not well known are provided.

Ellis (1997) has published a journal article in a major psychological journal based on an invited address before the 1995 Annual Convention of the American Psychological Association on using REBT with disability derived from his coping with his own disabilities. His main disabilities include diabetes, deficient hearing, and chronically tired eyes. His diabetes has also created physical problems for him with his mouth, feet, and bladder. Regardless of these physical problems, Ellis maintains the heavy writing, therapy, lecturing, training and traveling schedule described at the beginning of this chapter. He uses REBT to accept what he cannot change and to avoid self-denigration. He has devoted himself to a philosophy of remaining happy and productive in spite of his disabilities and has been able to use himself as a model in working with clients.

Rehabilitation Counseling Applications

Some concepts and strategies in the rehabilitation counseling discipline that incorporate REBT principles and techniques have been developed over time. These concepts and strategies have been applied to mental and/or physical disabilities.

As previously mentioned, Ard (1968) initially introduced the concept of REBT in rehabilitation counseling in the therapeutic counseling of people with disabilities. He pointed out how it could be a helpful approach with rehabilitation clients whose disabilities have helped to exacerbate their frustrations with themselves, other people, and the world. Otsby (1985) later observed that REBT could be useful in rehabilitation counseling with a wide variety of clientele. He pointed out that REBT is appropriate for individuals who retain some ability to accurately perceive reality and who are able to understand the concept or the relationship between thoughts, feelings, and behavior (e.g., if I think this way, I end up feeling and acting in certain ways). Gandy (1985, 1994a, 1994b) has noted frequent misperceptions of REBT and how REBT can better be incorporated into the rehabilitation counselor education curriculum. Gandy (1995c, 1997) has also described the continuing value of rational restructuring or preferential REBT in rehabilitation counseling and how the newer cognitive-behavior therapies are used as an adjunct. Hardy's (1991) practitioner-oriented book demonstrated how cognitive-behavior techniques can be combined with Gestalt Therapy.

Lassiter (1983) developed a model that combined Adlerian life-style counseling with REBT as it related to work adjustment techniques with people with severe or significant physical disabilities. He noted that an important feature of REBT is that it incorporates a concept of closure or graduation from therapy to a continuing self-instructional program of learning. From a rehabilitation perspective, this is a beginning for clients to work toward independence now that they are equipped to deal effectively with unconstructive emotions they are bound to experience during work. Rule (1977) reported on how a self-modeled humor exercise involving a combination of the Adlerian and REBT approaches could increase self-awareness and self-acceptance.

Rule (1983) and Sweeney (1989) have developed practitioner-oriented books on Adlerian counseling techniques, which are useful resources for techniques that are highly compatible with REBT techniques in the rehabilitation counseling of clients with mental and/or physical disabilities.

Gandy's (1979) discussion regarding frustration with individuals who exploit other people is relevant to people with disabilities who are vulnerable to such behavior. Gandy (1987) has also discussed the application of REBT to clients with chemical dependency and their families. Gandy and Rule (1983) demonstrated how REBT can be applied to group counseling with clients with severe or significant physical disabilities. Rule (1980) also developed a rational apothecary, or brief guideline, for when to use various rational techniques. Gandy (1992; 1995a) described how a systematic written homework self-help technique of disputing irrational beliefs can be utilized as a brief therapy stress management technique in the emotional adjustment of clients with physical or mental disabilities. Gandy (1995b) has further elaborated on the use of the systematic written homework self-help technique in a practitioner-oriented book that includes several case studies.

References

Alvarez, M. F. (1997). Using REBT and supportive psychotherapy with post-stoke patients. *Journal of Rational-Emotive and Cognitive-Behavior Therapy, 15*(3), 231-245.

American Psychiatric Association. (1994). *Diagnostic and statistical manual of mental disorders* (DSM-IV) (4th ed.). Washington, D.C.: American Psychiatric Association.

Ard, B. N., Jr. (1968). Rational therapy in rehabilitation counseling. *Rehabilitation Counseling Bulletin, 12*(2), 84-88.

Ard, B. N., Jr. (1990). *Guilt and/or blame: Conscience, superego and psychotherapy* (2nd ed.). New York: Peter Lang.

Balter, R. & Unger, P. (1997). REBT stress management with patients with chronic fatigue syndrome. *Journal of Rational-Emotive & Cognitive Behavior Therapy,15* (3), 223-230.

Bandura, A. (1969). *Principles of behavior modification.* New York: Holt, Rinehart & Winston.

Beck, A. T. (1976). *Cognitive therapy and emotional disorders.* New York: New American Library.

Bernard, M.E. (Ed.) (1991). *Using rational-emotive therapy effectively: A practitioner's guide.* New York: Plenum.

Bernard, M.E. (1998). Albert Ellis at 85: Professional reflections. *Journal of Rational-Emotive & Cognitive-Behavior Therapy, 16*(3), 151-183.

Bernard, M. E., & Joyce, M. R. (1994). *Rational-emotive therapy with children and adolescents* (2nd ed.). New York: Wiley.

Bernard, M.E., & Wolfe, J.L. (Eds.). (1993). *The RET resource book for practitioners.* New York: Wiley.

Calabro, Louis E. (1990). Adjustment to disability: A cognitive-behavioral model for analysis and clinical management. *Journal of Rational-Emotive & Cognitive-Behavior Therapy, 8* (2), 79-102.

Calabro, Louis E. (1997). "First things first: Maslow's hierarchy as a framework for REBT in promoting disability adjustment during rehabilitation. *Journal of Rational-Emotive & Cognitive-Behavior Therapy, 15*(3), 193-213.

Corey, G. (1996). *Theory and practice of counseling and psychotherapy* (5th ed.). Monterey, CA: Brooks/Coles.

DiMattia, D. (1991). Using RET effectively in the workplace. In M. E. Bernard (Ed.), *Using rational-emotive therapy effectively: A practitioner's guide.* New York: Plenum.

DiMattia, D., & Lega, L. (Eds.). (1990). *Will the real Albert Ellis stand up?* New York: Institute for Rational-Emotive Therapy.

DiGiuseppe, R. (1991). Comprehensive cognitive disputing in RET. In M .E. Bernard (Ed.), *Using rational-emotive therapy effectively: A practitioner's guide.* New York: Plenum.

DiGiuseppe, R. (1993). (Series Ed.). *Master therapists: Videotaped sessions* (Videos). Mew York: Institute for Rational-Emotive Therapy.

Dobson, K. S. & Block, L. (1988). Historical and philosophical bases of the cognitive-behavioral therapies. In K. D. Dobson (Ed.), *Handbook of Cognitive-Behavioral therapies* (pp. 387-414). New York: Guilford Press.

Dryden, W. (1989). Albert Ellis: An efficient and passionate life. *Journal of Counseling and Development, 67*(10), 539-546.

Dryden, W., & DiGiuseppe, R. (1990). *A primer on rational-emotive therapy.* Champaign, IL: Research.

Ellis, A. (1962). *Reason and emotion in psychotherapy.* Secaucus, NJ: Citadel.

Ellis, A. (1975). *How to live with a neurotic: At home and at work* (rev.ed). Hollywood, A: Wilshire.

Ellis, A. (1981). The rational-emotive approach to thanatology. In H.J. Sobel (Ed.), *Behavior therapy in terminal care.* Cambridge, MA: Ballinger.

Ellis, A. (1985). Rational-emotive approach to acceptance and its relationship to EAP's. In S. H. Klarreich, J. L. Francek, & C. E. Moore (Eds.), *The human resource management handbook: Principles and practice of employee assistance programs.* New York: Praeger.

Ellis A.(1988). *How to stubbornly refuse to make yourself miserable about anything–yes anything!.* Secaucus, NJ: Lyle Stuart.

Ellis, A. (1994a). Rational-emotive behavior therapy approaches to obsessive-compulsive disorder (OCD). *Journal of Rational-Emotive & Cognitive-Behavior Therapy, 12*(2), 121-141.

Ellis, A. (1994b). Post-traumatic stress disorder (PYSD): A rational emotive behavioral theory. *Journal of Rational-Emotive & Cognitive-Behavior Therapy, 12*(1), 3-26.

Ellis, A. (1994c). *Reason and emotion in psychotherapy.* Revised and updated. New York: Birch Lane Press (Carol).

Ellis, A. (1994d). The treatment of borderline personalities with rational emotive behavior therapy. *Journal of Rational-Emotive & Cognitive-Behavior Therapy, 12*(2), 101-120.

Ellis, A., & Abrams, M. (1994). *How to cope with a fatal illness.* New York: Barricade Books.

Ellis, A. (1995). Rational Emotive Behavior Therapy. In R.J. Corsini & D. Wedding (Eds.), *Current psychotherapies* (5th ed.). Itasca, IL: F. E. Peacock.

Ellis, A. (1996). *Better, deeper, and more enduring brief therapy: The Rational Emotive Behavior Therapy Approach.* New York: Brunner/Mazel.

Ellis, A. (1997). Using Rational Emotive Behavior Therapy techniques to cope with disability. *Professional Psychology: Research and Practice, 28,*(1), 17-22.

Ellis A., & Abrams, E. (1978). *Brief psychotherapy in medical and health practice.* New York: Springer.

Ellis, A., & Dryden, W. (1997). *The practice of rational-emotive therapy* (2nd ed). New York: Springer.

Ellis, A., & Harper, R. A. (1975). *A new guide to rational living.* Englewood Cliffs, NJ: Prentice-Hall.

Ellis, A., McInerney, J. F., DiGiuseppe, R., & Yeager, R. J. (1988). *Rational-emotive therapy with alcoholics and substance abusers.* Needham, MA: Allyn & Bacon.

Ellis, A., Sichel, J. L., Yeager, R. J., DiMattia, D. J., & DiGiuseppe, R. A. (1989). *Rational-emotive couples therapy.* Needhamm MA: Allyn & Bacon.

Ellis, A., & Velton, E. (1992). *When AA doesn't work for you: Rational steps to quitting alcohol.* New York: Barricade Books.

Eysenck, H. J. (1964). *Experiments in behavior therapy.* Oxford: Pergamon.

Fisher, S. (1976). The renal dialysis client: A rational counseling approach. *Rehabilitation Counseling Bulletin. 19* (4), 556-562.

Gandy, G. L. (1979). An alternate approach to loving or hating your enemies. *The Humanist Educator, 17*(4).

Gandy, G. L. (1985). Frequent misperceptions of rational-emotive therapy: An overview for the rehabilitation counselor. *Journal of Applied Rehabilitation Counseling, 16* (4), 31-35.

Gandy, G. L. (1987). Rational-emotive therapy: A creative way to enhance emotions. *The Addiction Letter* (Manisses Communications Group, Inc.), 3(2), 1-2.

Gandy, G. L. (1992, September). *Disputing irrational beliefs in rehabilitation counseling.* Paper presented at the Fourth International Conference on Stress Management, Paris, France.

Gandy, G. L. (1994a, April). REBT and rehabilitation counselor education. In S. G. Weinrach (Chair), *Infusing REBT concepts into the counselor preparation curriculum.* Panel conducted at the annual meeting of the American Counseling Association, Minneapolis, Minnesota.

Gandy, G. L. (1994b, July). *Rational Emotive Behavior Therapy in Rehabilitation Counseling.* Paper presented at the 23rd International Congress of Applied Psychology, Madrid, Spain.

Gandy, G. L. (1995a). Disputing irrational beliefs in rehabilitation counseling. *Journal of Applied Rehabilitation Counseling, 26*(1), 39-40.

Gandy, G. L. (1995b). *Mental health rehabilitation: Disputing irrational beliefs.* Springfield, IL: Charles C Thomas.

Gandy, G. L. (1995c, July). *Rational restructuring with mental and physical disabilities.* Paper presented at the Fourth European Congress of Psychology, Athens, Greece.

Gandy. G. L. (1997, May). Disability and rational emotive behavior therapy. In B. Evraiff (Ed.), *Sixth International Counseling Conference Proceedings* (pp. 119-123), Beijing, China. San Mateo, CA: Northern California Graduate University.

Gandy. G. L., and Rule, W. R. (1983). The use of group counseling. In R. A. Lassiter, M. H. Lassiter, R. E. Hardy, J. W. Underwood, & J. G. Cull (Eds.), *Vocational evaluation, work adjustment, and independent living services for disabled people.* Springfield, IL: Charles C Thomas.

Glasser, W. (1965). *Reality therapy: A new approach to psychiatry.* New York: Harper & Row.

Golden, W. L., & Gersh, W. D. (1990). Cognitive behavior therapy in the treatment of cancer patients. *Journal of Rational-Emotive & Cognitive-Behavior Therapy, 8*(1), 41-52.

Grieger, R. M., & Woods, P. J. (1993). *The rational-emotive therapy companion.* Roanoke, VA: Scholars Press.

Hardy, R. E. (1991). *Gestalt psychotherapy: Concepts and demonstrations in stress, relationships, hypnosis and addiction.* Springfield, IL: Charles C Thomas.

Hauck, P. A. (1992). *Overcoming the rating game: Beyond self-love--beyond self-esteem.* Louisville, KY: Westminster/John Knox.

Huber, C. H., & Baruth, L. G. (1989). *Rational-emotive and systems family therapy.* New York: Springer.

Kwee, M. & Ellis, A. (1998). The interface between Rational Emotive Behavior Therapy (REBT) and Zen. *Journal of Rational-Emotive & Cognitive-Behavior Therapy, 16*(1), 5-43.

Knaus, W. (1995). *S.M.A.R.T. recovery: A sensible primer.* Longmeadow, MA: Author.

Krumboltz, J. D. (1966). *Revolution in counseling: Implications of behavioral science.* Boston: Houghton Mifflin.

Lassiter, R. A. (1983). Work adjustment techniques in life-style counseling. In W. R. Rule (Ed.), *Life-style counseling for adjustment to disability.* Rockville, MD: Aspen.

Lazarus, A. A. (1989). *The practice of multimodal therapy.* Baltimore: John Hopkins University Press.

Lohr, J. M., & Hamberger, L. K. (1990). Cognitive-behavioral modification of coronary-prone behaviors: Proposal for a treatment model and review of the evidence. *Journal of Rational-Emotive and Cognitive-Behavioral Therapy, 8*(2), 103-126.

Martin, E. D., Jr. & Gandy, G. L. (1990). *Rehabilitation and disability: Psychosocial case studies.* Springfield, IL: Charles C Thomas.

Maultsby, M. J. (1984). *Rational behavior therapy.* Englewood Cliffs, NJ: Prentice-Hall.

Meichenbaum, D. (1977). *Cognitive behavior modification: An integrative approach.* New York: Plenum.

Needham, W. E., & Ehmer, M. N. (1980). RET and adjustment to blindness. *Rational living, 15*(2), 27-32.

Oliver, R. & Block, F. P. (1987). *Coping with Alzheimer's: A caregiver's emotional survival guide.* North Hollywood, CA: Wilshire.

Oliver, R., & Bock, F. P. (1990). Alleviating the distress of caregivers of Alzheimer's disease patients: A rational-emotive therapy model. *Journal of Rational-Emotive & Cognitive Behavior Therapy, 8*(1), 53-69.

Otsby, S.S. (1985). A rational-emotive perspective. *Journal of Applied Rehabilitation Counseling, 16*(3), 30-33.

Rubin, R., Walen, S. R., Ellis, A. (1990). Living with diabetes. *Journal of Rational-Emotive & Cognitive Behavior Therapy, 8* (1), 21-40.

Rule, W. R. (1977). Increasing self-modeled humor. *Rational Living, 12*(1), 7-9.

Rule, W. R. (1980). What next after self-awareness?: A rational apothecary. *Rational Living, 15*(2), 24-25.

S.M.A.R.T. Recovery Self-Helf Network. (1996). *S.M.A.R.T. recovery coordinator's manual.* Beachwood, OH: Author.

Skinner, B. F. (1953). *Science and human behavior.* New York: Macmillan.

Sweetland, J. D. (1990). Cognitive-behavior therapy and physical disability. *Journal of Rational-Emotive & Cognitive Behavior Therapy, 8*(2), 71-78.

Trimpey, J. (1989). *Rational recovery from alcoholism: The small book.* New York: Delacorte.

Trimpey, J. (1996). *Rational recovery: The new cure for substance addiction.* New York: Simon & Schuster.

Shostrum, E. (Producer). (1965). *Three approaches to psychotherapy* (Part 3) .(Film). Wheeler, CA: Psychological Films, Inc.

Walen, S. R., DiGiuseppe, R., & Dryden, W. (1992). *A practitioner's guide to rational-emotive therapy.* New York: Oxford University Press.

Wallace, W. A., & Maddox, E. N. (1978). Rational-emotive theory. In W. A. McDowell & A. B. Coven (Eds), *Counseling theories applied to rehabilitation.* New York: Human Sciences Press.

Warren, R., & Zgourides, G. D. (1991). *Anxiety disorders: A rational-emotive perspective.* Des Moines, IA: Longwood (Allyn & Bacon).

Weinrach, S. G. (1980). Unconventional therapist: Albert Ellis. *Personnel and Guidance Journal, 59*(3), 152-160.

Weinrach, S. G. (1982). Confessions of a novice rational-emotive therapist. *Rational Living, 17*(1), 17-22.

Wolfe, J. L. (1992). *What to do when he has a headache.* New York: Hyperion.

Wolpe, J. (1958). *Psychotherapy by reciprocal inhibition.* Stanford: Stanford University Press.

Woods, P. J., & Lyons, L. C. (1990). Irrational beliefs and psychosomatic disorders. *Journal of Rational-Emotive & Cognitive Behavior Therapy, 8*(1), 3-20.

Yankura, J., & Dryden, W. (1990). *Doing RET: Albert Ellis in action.* New York: Springer.

Zaborowski, B. (1997). Adjustment to vision loss and blindness: A process of reframing and retraining. *Journal of Rational-Emotive & Cognitive-Behavior Therapy, 15*(3), 215-221.

Chapter 13

GESTALT THERAPY, HYPNOSIS, AND PAIN MANAGEMENT IN CANCER TREATMENT: A THERAPEUTIC APPLICATION OF ACCEPTANCE AND ADJUSTMENT TO DISABILITY

RICHARD E. HARDY

A major difference in treating cancer patients and others is the face of the life-threatening aspects of the disease, which generally requires the psychotherapist to produce definite change in a time-limited period. Cancer patients are inclined toward intense interest in understanding life and death issues as a result of their illness and are often eager to work in psychotherapy and hypnosis. Here and now concepts in Gestalt therapy can be extraordinarily useful in therapy of this type in that one can move away from predicting the future and blaming the past while focusing on the immediate problem solving versus catastrophic expectation (Perls, 1969b).

Soloman and Amkraut (1981) reported on psychoneuroendocrinological effects on the immune response which focused attention on the previously held thought that the immune system operated without central nervous system involvement. Innovative therapists and researchers such as Meares (1983), Newton (1983) and Simonton (1980) have reported successful treatment of metastatic disease through intensive meditation in Meares' case through hypnosis and psychotherapy by Newton and imagery and psychotherapy by Simonton. Since the early 1980s, hypnosis, imagery, and psychotherapy have been used in combinations as adjunct treatments for cancer patients. Shapiro (1983), for instance, has described the effective use of visu-

---

For a more detailed and comprehensive coverage of the use of Gestalt psychotherapy in various rehabilitation settings, see R. E. Hardy, *Gestalt Psychotherapy: Concepts and Demonstrations in Stress, Relationships, Hypnosis and Addiction*, 1991, Springfield, IL: Charles C Thomas. This book also focuses on the use of hypnosis in Gestalt therapy.

alization in keeping the white count acceptable even during treatments which usually deplete the white cell count.

Golden, Horwick, and Lockrich (1980) have discussed the toxic effect of chemotherapy used in the treatment of cancer which result in the common effects of immunosuppression, nausea, diarrhea, hair loss, sterility, and emesis during long-term treatment. The employment of deep muscle relaxation hypnosis and guided imagery to control pre and postnausea and emesis has been described in the literature (Redd, Rosenberger & Hendler, 1983).

With the diagnosis of cancer comes thoughts of and preoccupations with one's death and vulnerabilities as well as fears concerning pain and treatment (Hardy, 1983; Hardy & Cull, 1975). The importance of working toward constructively dealing with death as a possibility and involvement of the family has been described (Simonton, Matthews-Simonton, & Creighton, 1978; Oliver, 1983; Veach & Nicholas, 1998). The acceptance and adjustment process has similarities to other disabilities as reflected in various case studies (Gandy, 1995; Martin & Gandy, 1990).

The patient described in this report was a woman in her mid-thirties who was referred by a State Department of Rehabilitation Services for hypnotherapy and psychotherapy in that she had become vocationally dysfunctional as an instructor in a private school due to extreme nausea and emesis as a result of chemotherapy. She lived in fear and anticipation of the chemotherapy and often became nauseous at the thought of the treatment.

Ms. S. came into the office for the first time in December, just after Christmas. She was having chemotherapy treatment for the third time, having been told that she again had a tumor after two previous periods of extensive treatment. During the previous periods of treatment, she had received both chemotherapy and radiation. In addition, she had had a left radical mastectomy with axillary dissection. She stated that she reacted badly to radiation and she "hated chemotherapy." She further indicated that the mention of cancer on public television caused her to become ill.

Ms. S. was a former model, single, and lived alone in an apartment. Until just before entering therapy, she had an active social life which included dating a man whom she described as having "the power to control and manipulate me." She had seen this man for three years and lived with him for two of those years before he had moved to another state. She continued to be in regular touch with him.

Now, very ill again due to chemotherapy and in danger of losing her job if she did not return to work, she had become distraught and asked to see a therapist immediately on an emergency basis, in that she had been informed about hypnotherapy through her rehabilitation counselor at the State Department of Rehabilitative Services.

After describing her feelings about chemotherapy and radiation, she added "I give in to situations too easily." When she was questioned further, she stated, "I even let my boyfriend tell me what to do." She was a good hypnotic subject and an eager patient. The second session, which took place the following day, included the teaching of the self-hypnosis procedure. She developed, with the help of the therapist, several suggestions to give herself concerning self-regard, self-care, and stress and pain management. These included antinausea suggestions as well as approaches to viewing doctors, nurses, the hospital, and equipment as allies and a part of her team of helpers. She was encouraged to see herself as a general in control of an army of helpers.

She was experiencing pain at a level eight on a scale of zero to ten, with ten being most extreme pain. Sternback (1982) has reported on the reliability and helpfulness of such ratings. She was told to find the number in the corner of her mind and to notice the number as it changed. She found that she could decrease pain both by: (1) substitution of her painful sensation with one not so painful (sharp became dull) and (2) displacement of the locus of the pain (which was less successful). She was able to move pain from her chest cavity to her right shoulder, which gave her a feeling of controlling the pain. In addition, Rapid Induction Analgesia Procedure of J. Barber (1982) was very helpful as was a glove anesthesia technique. These in combination with progressive relaxation reduced pain in her judgment from a level eight to a level between two and three.

Psychological testing verified clinical judgment that she was well adjusted and had the potential for self-reliance, along with apathy, low energy, and the expected depression. She was experiencing substantial resentment as a result of self-imposed health demands.

After finishing psychological evaluation, she was commended for good work and given a dream suggestion. The therapist suggested that she could have a dream and that the dream would be related to her concerns. This suggestion was left basically open-ended and structured by indicating that she would want to write it down in detail after waking in the night and would sleep soundly after writing it.

In the next session, a dream interpretation was completed by Ms. S. and the therapist working it through together. The dream concerned her feelings of being controlled and dominated by her boyfriend and often giving into others at her own expense in order to please them.

Psychotherapy then centered on developing awareness of allowing herself to be a victim of circumstances and others' wishes and events outside herself. At this point, antinausea suggestions were reinforced and she went directly to the hospital for chemotherapy. The following day, she phoned to report that for the first time she had been able to enter the hospital with reasonably good feelings and confidence; and, more importantly, she had for the first time no nausea from chemotherapy. She was elated.

At this point, stimulus words and concepts (wellness, self-care, etc.) were used during several sessions while she was in trance as an intervention strategy for enhancing awareness. A program was taped for her on the subjects of deep relaxation, self-hypnosis imagery of the hospital, staff and equipment as friendly, positive and strong forces which were under her direction as commander of her mental health team and army. In addition, she was encouraged to develop her own anticancer imagery. She at first visualized a scrub brush covered with frothy white soap which she used to "wash the tumors." As she became more assertive in her outlook, the imagery became much stronger and included large and powerful sharks devouring small tumors.

The therapist at this point discussed with her some of the benefits of having her family (mother and father) involved in the therapy. She was in favor; however, neither mother nor father made an appointment. The mother indicated that she would come in at a later time.

One month after coming for therapy, sessions centered on the following: (1) her locus of control (being a pleaser and a victim), (2) developing creative imagery for increasing white cell count, (3) confronting fears and beliefs about death (it could be lingering and painful), (4) pain management, and (5) setting long-term and short-term goals for her life. In addition, she was taught and rehearsed in the use of ideomotor signaling in case this communication technique might be needed in the event of later treatment in a state of reduced communication. The importance of informing hospital or other health treatment team members that she was using self-hypnosis was explained to her from both the perspective of avoiding confusion of health care providers (Smith and Kamitsuka, 1984) and her own comfort in using self-hypnosis in the presence of others. She was seeing the therapist twice per week at this time.

After four months of chemotherapy and hypnotherapy, Ms. S's oncologist informed her that tumor activity was significantly decreased. Some tumors had decidedly shrunk and there seemed to be no new growth. Two weeks later she ended the relationship with her boyfriend and felt strong and positive in her decision to take this action. Having returned to work after an absence of four months, she discussed her situation with her students in a classroom setting and was able to talk somewhat comfortably about it with peers and colleagues. Her parents were supportive of her candor and openness but showed no interest in working with the therapist from a family perspective.

At this point the hypnotherapy centered on confronting recurrence and relapse possibilities, which she feared; positive imagery, dream work, and body feedback of health information. Her marching health army imagery was emphasized as well as the concept of an orientation in the present rather than attempting to predict the future.

In the second week of the sixth month of therapy, she made the following statement: "If I had come to you several months earlier, I would have never had a recurrence." The therapist saw this statement as a possible signal of change and asked her to stretch her imagery as she presently was using it. The imagery was oriented in power toward toxic or self-destructive elements versus life-sustaining ones. The next day she phoned complaining of difficulty with pain and a numbness in her left arm. Examination by her oncologist indicated new tumor growth along with further diminished activity of some tumors.

In the several weeks that ensued, her physical condition deteriorated and she was hospitalized. The therapist continued to work with her mental imagery and attitudes toward the imagery. Much of the imagery indicated a lack of assertiveness and feelings of weakness. In that she was confined to bed and could move about very little, disassociation was used frequently as a pain management approach and several additional recorded tapes oriented toward disassociation and also physical exercise imagery were made. She was able to substantially reduce her pain to the point that she felt little or no pain. Increased contact was accomplished by daily telephone sessions. Severe respiratory problems developed, and she required the use of oxygen. She died after reporting very pleasant restful imagery.

Initially this person had substantial fear of a long and lingering painful death, yet she died free of pain and without substantial fear. In fact, she claimed to have no fear. Hypnosis offered her an active part in taking some control of her symptoms and general health and, through hypnotherapy, she achieved real quality in both her life and death. When she was ready to give up the struggle against malignancy, she was able to talk of giving up freely with the therapist and to give comfort to her parents and friends. She told her parents, "I can see my way clear, and I'm all right." Approximately five weeks after her death, her parents began sessions with the therapist.

Ms. S. was making a healthy adjustment to a severe situation which had reached crisis proportions. In her work with the therapist, she attempted to protect herself by displacing feelings of vulnerability. For instance, she made the statement that her main problem in life was the mechanical condition of her car. She also, in her wish to avoid pain, attempted to disassociate herself from her body. This disassociation evidenced itself in statements such as, "If I could only leave." Later, she was able to successfully use her ability to disassociate in hypnosis.

In addition, she had considerable resentment in that she demanded health and wellness. This resentment coming from the health demands caused considerable guilt as well as doubts of self-worth. She denied her illness during the early stages of treatment and protected herself in fantasizing that she was totally healthy.

Especially since she had been a model, her ideal (desired body image) was quite different after a radical mastectomy than her actual body image. The therapist worked with her in order that she could see herself as a person of beauty, both within and beyond her physical body, and through this approach, she was able to accept an altered body image after several months of psychotherapy.

Initially she withdrew from her friends and colleagues in order to keep from being forced to face the acceptance of her newly acquired problem. She had become egocentrically oriented and her world had begun to revolve basically around herself and her mother. She had regression fantasies and wanted to return to an earlier day–and earlier age–a time when all was healthy and well. By adopting Gestalt concepts of here and now, however, she became able to enjoy everyday life to a significant degree.

Also, she began to take responsibility for her projections and be aware of the meaning of statements as, "the hospital staff is insensitive and does not care about me." She learned to "own" her feelings and projections and realized that she would have to be the one responsible for providing basic care and nurturance for herself and that the ingredients of this nurturance included self-concern and love for herself.

REFERENCES

Barber, J., & Adrian, C. (Eds.). (1982). *Psychological approaches to the management of pain.* New York: Bruner-Mazel.

Gandy, G. L. (1995). *Mental health rehabilitation: Disputing irrational beliefs.* Springfield, IL: Charles C Thomas.

Golden, S., Horwich, C., & Lockrich, J. (1980). *Chemotherapy and you* (DHEW Publication No. NIH 77-1136). Washington, D.C.: National Institute of Health.

Hardy, R. E. (1983). Hypnosis and pain management. *Brazilian Journal of Clinical and Experimental Hypnosis, 4,* 33-35.

Hardy, R. E. (1991). *Gestalt psychotherapy: Concepts and demonstrations in stress, relationships, hypnosis and addiction.* Springfield, IL: Charles C Thomas.

Hardy, R. E., & Cull, J. G. (Eds.). (1975). *Counseling and rehabilitation of the cancer patient.* Springfield, Il: Charles C Thomas.

Martin, E. D., Jr., & Gandy, G. L. (1990). *Rehabilitation and disability: Psychosocial case studies.* Springfield, IL: Charles C Thomas.

Meares, A. (1983). A form of intensive meditation associated with the regression of cancer. *American Journal of Clinical Hypnosis, 25,* 114-121.

Newton, B. W. (1983). The use of hypnosis in the treatment of cancer patients. *American Journal of Clinical Hypnosis, 25,* 104-113.

Oliver, G. W. (1983). A cancer patient and her family: A case study. American *Journal of Clinical Hypnosis, 25,* 156-160.

Redd, D. H., Rosenberger, P. H., & Hendler, C. (1983). Controlling chemotherapy side effects. *American Journal of Clinical Hypnosis, 25,* 161-172.

Shapiro, A. (1983). Psychotherapy as adjunct treatment for cancer patients. *American Journal of Clinical Hypnosis, 25*, 150-160.

Simonton, O. C., Matthews-Simonton, S., & Creighton, J. (1978). *Getting well again.* Los Angeles: J. P. Tarcher.

Simonton, O. C., Matthews-Simonton, S. & Sparks, T. F. (1980). Psychological intervention in the treatment of cancer. *Psychosomatics, 21*, 226-233.

Smith, M. C., & Kamitsuka, M. (1984). Self-hypnosis misinterpreted as CNS deterioration in an adolescent with leukemia and vincristine toxicity. *American Journal of Clinical Hypnosis, 26*, 280-282.

Solomon, G. F. & Amkraut, A. A. (1981). Psychoneuroendocrinological effects on the immune response. *Annual Review of Microbiology, 35*, 155-184.

Sternback, R. A. (1982). The psychologist's role in the diagnosis and treatment of pain patients. In J. Barber & C. Adrian (Eds.), *Psychological approaches to the management of pain* New York: Bruner-Mazel.

Veach, T. A., & Nicholas, D. R. (1998). Understanding families of adults with cancer: Combining the clinical cause of cancer and stages of family development. *Journal of Counseling & Development, 76*(2), 144-156.

Chapter 14

AN INTEGRATIVE COUNSELING AND PSYCHOSOCIAL APPROACH TO ACCEPTANCE AND ADJUSTMENT TO DISABILITY

GERALD L. GANDY AND E. DAVIS MARTIN, JR.

Acceptance and adjustment to disability is a highly individualized process. Severity of disability, on the surface, would seem to be a crucial factor. However, severity of disability or the perception of severity varies from person to person. Persons who have significant disabilities (blindness, cerebral palsy, mental retardation, paraplegia, and so on) will vary in their reaction(s) to their disability. The perception of severity among others–parents, siblings, loved ones, friends, work and schoolmates will, as well, vary considerably. The effect of paraplegia, for example, on one person may, from a psychological perspective, be completely devastating and for another be relatively insignificant. These two extremes certainly do not characterize all persons who have a paralysis disability. The majority of persons with disabilities probably fall somewhere between these two extremes. Disability for most persons, particularly those with physical disabilities as reported by Weinberg (1976) and Livneh (1982) and noted in Henderson and Bryan (1997), " . . . do not view their disabilities as the greatest tragedy in their lives . . . (but) considered their disability as a fact of life, an inconvenience and sometimes a cause of frustration but not the most terrible thing that has happened to them" (p. 80).

John Hockenberry's (1995) memoir, *Moving Violations,* is a superb reaction and analysis of Hockenberry's adjustment to his disability. This book was written from the perspective of an ordinary human being confronted with all the obstacles we all face in life plus the added frustrations of environmental and attitudinal barriers unique to persons who have a paralysis disability and who use a wheelchair for mobility. Similarly, books such as *Still Me* (1998) by Christopher Reeve, *The Body Silent* (1987) by Robert Murphy, *A Whole New*

Life (1982) by Renolds Price, *I Raise My Eyes to Say Yes* (1989) by Ruth Sienkiewicz-Mercer and Steven Kaplan, *Flying Without Wings: Personal Reflections on Being Disabled* [*sic*] (1989) by Arnold Beisser, and *Anger Until Sunset* (1991) by Louis Michaux (a semiautobiographical novel in which Michau writes of his experiences with disability, combined with fiction) all illustrate the highly individualized nature of adjustment to disability. Yet, each story, as well, leads the reader to a truth revealed in Harold Kushner's widely read *When Bad Things Happen to Good People* (1981); that is, the "why" questions we ask and often focus upon when disability occurs are largely counterproductive to adjustment.

Disability can affect personality. The manner in which personality may be affected, however, varies with the particular circumstances and life patterns of an individual (Wright, 1980). Disability, it should not be assumed, will always result in psychological turmoil. Disability, of course, will present frustration, inconvenience, and grief to the person with a disability, but the disability may, as well, present the person with a " . . . potentially powerful stimulant to psychological growth (Vash, 1981, p. 130)"

> I have been disabled [*sic*] since I was sixteen, yet hardly a week goes by, nearly thirty years later, that I don't make some discovery or improvement that in one way or another makes my disability less handicapping. Since I hope that happy process never stops, I have to say that I hope I am never fully "rehabilitated." My physical abilities are still increasing. When, with age, they begin to decrease, I fully expect to continue or accelerate in the psychological and spiritual discoveries that make my disability not only less handicapping, but a matter of trivia compared with the nonphysical realms of discovery and improvement I am experiencing. Each in its own age, but all part of my own human growth . . . or psychological development . . . or rehabilitation . . . or whatever you prefer to call it. Sometimes I'm not sure what my disability is. Is it being paralyzed, or does that add a laughably small increment to the primordial handicap of being mortal human? The core of psychological development is realistic acceptance of one's limitations–be they physical, intellectual, spiritual, or of some other realm. We are not perfect; we are never what we would wish to be–however beautiful, good, gifted, serene, or strong we appear. These imperfections must be accepted without rancor before we can get on with the real and simple business of psychological development–doing the best we can with whatever we've got [Vash, 1976, pp. 2,3].

More recently Vash (1994) has noted that re-framing attitudes and enlarging perspectives regarding the perception of adversity can be a very positive factor in adjustment (pp. 201-202):

> The common social view is that lacks, losses, pain, and suffering are adverse and undesirable; and that anyone who thinks differently is a masochist or some

> other kind of nut. To be about 80% paralyzed is generally considered to be a tragic catastrophe. I shared this view before I became 80% paralyzed. The cultural evaluation fell apart afterward in the face of persistent refutation. Paralysis and all, I kept having fun, successes, and general feelings of life satisfaction that belied expectations. Adverse experience changed my attitudes and three decades' work as a rehabilitation psychologist, plus conscious dedication to evolving a communicable philosophy of life, helped me formalize the process.

Reynolds Price (1994) revealed in his memoir *A Whole New Life* that the advent of disability and its consequences for him and, by extension, to others led him to the following "facts" regarding adjustment (p. 182):

> 1. You're in your present calamity alone, far as this life goes. If you want a way out, then dig it yourself, if there turns out to be any trace of a way. Nobody–least of all a doctor–can rescue you now, not once they've stitched your gaping wound.
> 2. Generous people–true practical saints, some of them as boring as root canals–are waiting to give you everything on Earth but your main want, which is simply *the person you used to be.*
> 3. But you're not that person now. Who'll you be tomorrow? And who do you propose to be from here to the grave, which may be hours or decades down the road?

Moreover, Price noted that these first two facts take care of themselves (acceptance of reality), but it is the third fact that a person may exert a measure of control over; that is, the ability to adjust to a new way of accomplishing tasks and a new way of living. Price's advice (p. 183) is to "(g)rieve for a decent limited time over whatever parts of your old self you know you'll miss" . . . and by implication get on with the business of life–living, growing, and becoming.

Similarly, those persons who share in the life of a person with a disability may also experience difficulty in coping or relating to the person with a disability. This arises not so much from the reality of the disability but more likely because the disability has introduced a new element into the relationship; it has, in essence, changed the relationship. The ability to cope with the changes brought about as a result of the disability then portends the future relationship. Beatrice Wright (1983) has written that " . . . the burden in interpersonal relations will be borne by the person who has the disability. Although the pathology may lie with the group, the person with the disability is the one who is annoyed or hurt most directly. It is he or she who has to 'take it', who has to handle the ineptitudes of others in the ordinary affairs of getting along" (p. 335). Accordingly, it is the person with the disability that must help those persons who are close to them and, as well, to those persons who are strangers deal with and adjust to their disability. While this may seem to be an overwhelming or at least unfair responsibility that has been placed upon the person with a disability, it is, nevertheless, a reality that must be faced.

Integration of Major Theoretical Approaches

Two of the previous chapters have presented Adlerian and psychodynamic orientations. Considering that Sigmund Freud viewed Alfred Adler as a heretic, it would seem that it would be difficult for the two orientations to be compatible (Corey, 1996). However, the psychodynamic chapter actually represents more of a neo-Freudian point of view. The neo-Freudians were later psychoanalysts who deviated from Freud's orthodox position. Mosak (1995) observed the some authorities have suggested that it would be more appropriate to refer to them as neo-Adlerians. The latter point of view is based on the fact that these psychoanalysts (such as Horney, Sullivan, and Fromm) moved away from Freud's biological and deterministic point of view and toward Adler's social-psychological and nondeterministic view of human nature.

The psychodynamic orientation chapter certainly gives more importance to the effects of environmental events and learned responses than the original theoretical point of view expressed by Sigmond Freud. However, a major contribution of the psychodynamic chapter is the discussion of intrapsychic dynamics and its manifestation in outward behavior. Although Freud's concept of a deeply repressed unconscious may be questionable, rehabilitation counselors and related professionals have found it useful to hypothesize about some unconscious processes in regard to people with disabilities. The psychodynamic orientation chapter, therefore, with an emphasis on intrapersonal dynamics, provides an appropriate complement to the Adlerian orientation chapter which focuses more on interpersonal behavior. The Adlerian concept of life-style which evolves from the individual's subjective perceptions and interactions within the early family certainly contributes to a broader social psychological understanding of human behavior. The chapter on a personal experience of acceptance and adjustment to disability well represents a neo-Freudian point of view consistent with a broader Adlerian social psychological perspective.

The psychodynamic chapter also briefly described the ingredients of genuineness, nonpossessive warmth, and accurate empathetic understanding as defined by Truax and Carkhuff (1967) and Truax and Mitchell (1971, p 11) as necessary interpersonal skills no matter what counseling or therapeutic intervention strategy is used by the counselor. The extensive research supporting these variables has been further elaborated upon by Carkhuff and Berensen (1977). It should be noted that the emphasis on these variables was derived from the work of Carl Rogers (1942; 1951; 1961; 1980). He is credited with originating and developing the humanistic movement in psychotherapy which developed out of the existential tradition and eventually influenced all fields related to psychotherapy (Corey, 1996). He initially called his approach nondirective counseling, later changing it to client-centered counseling, and eventually to person-centered counseling. Rogers's basic assumption was that people have a vast potential for understanding themselves and resolving their own problems without direct intervention on the therapist's part and that they are capable of self-directed growth if they are involved in a trusting and accepting therapeutic relationship.

As mentioned above, Rogers's approach developed out of the existential tradition (Corey, 1996). The existential point of view emphasized such concepts as freedom, choice, values, personal responsibility, autonomy, purpose, and meaning (Frankl, 1963; Kierkegaard,1944; Laing, 1965; May, 1983; Tillich, 1952; Yalom, 1980). The existentialists, however, focused more on ideas, and Rogers developed more of a humanistic-existential position that focused on the relationship. May and Yalom (1995) noted that the main aim of the founders of existential therapy was that its key concepts and themes would become integrated into all therapeutic schools rather than existential therapy's being a separate school.

Contemporary counseling and therapy approaches have generally incorporated existential concepts and themes as well as Rogers's humanistic-existential emphasis on the therapeutic relationship but have also emphasized that active procedures are necessary to bring about cognitive, emotional, and behavioral changes in people (Corey, 1996). The Rational Emotive Behavior Therapy (REBT) chapter has well illustrated this contemporary viewpoint in combining behavioral and cognitive-behavioral strategies along with existential concepts and themes and a trusting and accepting client/therapist humanistic relationship to help clients deal with specific problems. As also noted in the REBT chapter, the behavior therapy movement which had begun in the 1960s had become largely cognitive-behavioral by the 1970s. Corey (1996) has further elaborated on how these approaches have become integrated with existential themes and principles.

A limitation of cognitive-behavioral approaches, however, is that they can promote intellectualization of feelings on the part of clients. As also noted in the REBT chapter, expressive-experiential procedures adapted from Gestalt therapy are occasionally used to help clients get in touch with their feelings. The chapter on the therapeutic application of Gestalt therapy, hypnosis, and pain management in cancer treatment is an excellent example of expressive-experiential procedures combined with cognitive-behavioral techniques.

The value of Gestalt therapy is it is existential in that it is grounded in the here and now and promotes direct experiencing rather than the abstractness of talking about situations.

Although the purpose of all the previous counseling and psychosocial chapters was to emphasize a particular orientation through discussion or application, they have all reflected an eclectic viewpoint in representing how techniques from one orientation can be combined with another orientation to effectively bring about change in human behavior. Corey (1996) has noted that the trend in counseling and psychotherapy is toward an integrative approach or the process of selecting concepts and methods from a variety of systems.

Unless, however, an eclectic approach is based on a synthesized conceptual framework (as represented in the previous chapters in this section), the choice of techniques can become haphazard and not susceptible to scientific evaluation. Of particular help to beginning students of counseling are several texts that have emphasized conceptual models for a more comprehensive understanding of the counseling process as well as an approach to integrating various concepts and techniques (Carkhuff, 1992; Egan, 1994; Ivey, 1994; Young, 1992). The terminology varies, but an integrative comprehensive conceptual model of counseling and psychotherapy usually addresses the following aspects: (1) attending to the client verbally and nonverbally; (2) responding to the client at an empathetic level; (3) assisting the client in understanding the problem; and (4) helping a client to set goals and achieve their completion.

Corey (1996) has observed that the acceleration of public funding for all types of human service programs has pressured researchers and practitioners to demonstrate the effectiveness of counseling and psychotherapy by using scientific methods. In the era of managed care, it has become essential for mental-health providers to demonstrate the degree to which their interventions are both clinically sound and cost effective. Moreover, as Gandy (1988, 1990) has noted, this evidence needs to be presented in a manner that is understandable and convincing to the public and the implications better incorporated into the counselor education curriculum. VandenBos (1986) observed that by 1980 a consensus had emerged that counseling and psychotherapy was demonstrably more effective than no treatment. He concluded it appears that future research should be focused on exploring the relative advantages and disadvantages of alternative treatment strategies for different psychological and behavioral problems. This research should include factors such as the relative cost, the length of time necessary to effect change, and the nature and extent of change. A guideline for improving the global question of the effectiveness of counseling and psychotherapy was provided many years ago by Paul (1967): "*What* treatment, by *whom*, is the most effective for *this* individual with *that* specific problem, and under what set of circumstances?"

A Psychosocial Approach

Beatrice Wright (1983) best illustrates the psychosocial approach to acceptance and adjustment to disability in her seminal work *Physical Disability–A Psychosocial Approach.* An understanding of how disability affects the person with a disability as well as those who come into contact with that person is a basic tenet of the psychosocial approach. The concept of spread originally introduced by Dembo, Leviton, and Wright (1956), and noted by Wright (1983), provides an understanding of the dynamics that occur when a disability imposes more than a handicap. Spread " . . . refers to the power of single characteristics to evoke inferences about a person" (Wright, 1983, p. 32). For example, a person whose disability is blindness may be perceived by others as being "totally disabled." Quite frequently persons with limited or no vision are assumed by others to be unable to hear or to communicate and, as such, are not spoken to directly but are communicated to through persons who are with them. Similarly, persons with disabilities may look at themselves as being "totally disabled" because of the handicap that has been imposed by the disability. Wright (1983) has stated that "because of the spread, the degree of disability is often perceived as more severe than it actually is" (p. 32). Attitudinal handicaps are imposed not as a result of the disability but result from the effects of spread and may prove to be more limiting than the effects of the disability.

Acceptance of one's disability is facilitated when the person with a disability accepts the disability in a nondevaluating manner (Wright, 1983). "The disability . . .," as noted by Wright (1983), " . . . may still be seen as inconvenient and limiting" (p. 159). Acceptance, if it is to be psychologically healthy, must be from a perspective of nondevaluation; that is, the person with a disability must view their disability (and its effects) not from a comparative-status value orientation but from an asset value orientation.

A comparative-status value is based on the comparison of some attribute of the person and judged to be either more or less of some standard (Wright, 1983). For example, a person with a mobility impairment may have considerable difficulty in walking. Judged from a comparative-status value, this person will not measure up to the accepted standard of walking. If, however, the judgment of this person is made from an asset-value orientation, walking is seen not from a comparative perspective but is seen as the effort of this person to be their best. It is an evaluation " . . . in terms of usefulness or internal value. The focus is the value of the attribute, not the person's position relative to that of others" (Wright, 1983, p. 179).

Change in the value system of the individual must occur in order for full acceptance of the disability to be accomplished. Wright (1983) identified the following "... changes within the value system of the person that are important in overcoming the feeling of shame and inferiority resulting from disability as a value loss . . . (1) enlarging the scope of values, (2) subordinating physique relative to other values, (3) containing disability effects, and (4) transforming comparative-status values into asset values" (p. 163).

Enlarging the scope of values refers to a realization of values other than a preoccupation with the loss (value loss) associated with the disability. "It represents an awakening interest in satisfactions that are accessible and facilitates coming to terms with what has been lost" (Wright, 1983, p. 163).

An important concept to be understood in connection with enlarging the scope of values is that of "period of mourning." Wright (1983) refers to the period of mourning as the person's preoccupation with the disability or the loss of function that has been imposed by the disability. Mourning, as stated by Wright (1983), may be thought of as being "all inclusive suffering" or dealt with by the person with a disability as a slight bump in the road of life. Mourning is an important time for the ". . . person (to) prepare himself or herself before taking the leap to meet the challenges that lie ahead" (Wright, 1983, p. 170). All persons with a disability, regardless of the degree of preoccupation with the loss, need the time (regardless of duration) to come to the realization that life is worthwhile and that other values do exist for them (Wright, 1983).

The subordination of physique relative to other values is extremely important as the person progresses from the period of mourning. Values which hold significance and satisfaction to the person begin to widen and become more important (Wright, 1983). The effects of spread become less if the person accepts the existence of other values.

Containing disability effects refers to an understanding by the person with a disability that the effects of disability are not to be generalized but are to be contained to the actual effects of the disability. Wright (1983) put it best: "Not all of life is influenced, let alone determined, by disability. Moreover, not all effects are negative. The view emphasizing containment of disability argues that disability is but one among an array of factors that determine the nature and direction of life" (p. 178).

Transforming comparative-status values into asset values, as noted earlier, is essential for acceptance. A shift in perception to a more healthy psychological perspective is the desired result. Moving from judgment based on comparison to judgment or evaluation based on the intrinsic value of an attribute is required. This is not to say that comparisons are always bad, but rather " . . . the problem . . . is to eliminate the use of status comparisons when they are unnecessary and harmful" (Wright, 1983, p. 179).

Summary and Conclusions

The process of coping with the effects of disability affect not only the person with a disability but those who share in the life of that person as well. As we have seen throughout this section of the text, accepting and adjusting to disability is not a lock-step process but is highly individualized and is not related to severity of disability. Handicaps associated with a disability result not only from the disability but from societal attitudes as well. These latter perceptions often are more limiting than the disability itself.

Parents and siblings of persons with disabilities often find themselves limited by their attitudes and a myriad of feelings and emotions regarding the son, daughter, brother or sister who has a disability. Parental reaction to a child's disability, for example, is often " . . . some combination of shock, disbelief, guilt, and an overwhelming sense of loss" (Batshaw, 1997, p. 746). Siblings often mirror the behavior and attitudes of their parents (Batshaw, 1997). Within families where positive attitudes are the norm, effective adjustment and interaction within the family and community is the result and where ambivalent or negative attitudes are present, physical and emotional withdrawal is often the outcome. Parents and siblings of persons with developmental disabilities, in particular, will come into contact with many human service workers throughout their lifetime. Because disability is a dynamic phenomenon, it is essential that human service workers know and understand their own attitudes, both positive and negative, and work toward the elimination of stereotypical responses to persons with disabilities and toward family members as well. Attitudes are subtle and difficult to determine; we do not carry a three by five card listing of our attitudes or values. To be an effective rehabilitation practitioner, a person must know, understand, and appreciate the value systems or philosophies that rehabilitation rests upon and those of the consumer or consumer's family. To do so allows the rehabilitation practitioner to empower persons with disabilities and, similarly, to empower others who share in the life of the person with a disability.

Rehabilitation practitioners must be cognizant of the dynamic nature of disability and must be willing and able to provide an environment that is conducive to success for the person with a disability and for those close to that person. The rehabilitation practitioner must assist not only the person with a disability but others whose lives are intertwined with that person move from a perspective that is dominated by a comparative-status value orientation to that of an asset value orientation.

REFERENCES

Batshaw, M. L. (1997). (Ed.) *Children and disabilities.* Baltimore: Paul Brookes.

Beisser, A. E. (1990). *Flying without wings.* Bantam: New York.

Carkhuff, R. R. (1992). *The art of helping* (7th ed.). Amherst, MA: Human Resources Development Press.

Carkhuff, R. R., & Berenson, B. G. (1977). *Beyond counseling and therapy* (2nd ed.). New York: Holt, Rinehart and Winston.

Corey, G. (1996). *Theory and practice of counseling and psychotherapy* (5th ed.). Monterey, CA: Brooks/Coles.

Egan, G. (1994). *The skilled helper: A problem management approach to helping* (5th ed.). Pacific Grove, CA: Brooks/Cole.

Frankl, V. (1963). *Man's search for meaning.* Boston: Beacon.

Gandy, G. L. (1988). *Practice oriented research: A bridge to increase the public's understanding of the benefits of counseling/psychotherapy.* Based on a paper presented at a Soviet-American Psychology Conference, Leningrad, USSR, October, 1987. Richmond, VA: Center for Public Affairs Publication, Virginia Commonwealth University.

Gandy, G. L. (1990). *Rehabilitation counselor education and public policy.* Based on a paper presented at the Twenty-Fourth International Congress of Psychology, Sydney, Australia, August, 1988. Richmond, VA: Center for Public Affairs Publication, Virginia Commonwealth University.

Henderson, G. & Bryan, W. V. (1997). *Psychosocial aspects of disability* (2nd ed). Springfield, IL: Charles C Thomas.

Hockenberry, J. (1995). *Moving violations: War zones, wheelchairs, and declarations of independence.* New York: Hyperion.

Ivey, A. (1996). *Intentional counseling and interviewing: Facilitating development in a multicultural society.* Pacific Grove, CA: Brooks/Cole.

Kierkegaard, S. (1944). *The concept of dread.* Princeton, NJ: Princeton, University Press.

Kushner, H. S. (1981). *When bad things happen to good people.* New York: Avon.

Laing, R. D. (1965). *The divided self.* Baltimore: Pelican.

May, R. (1983). *The discovery of being: Writings in existential psychology.* New York: Norton.

May, R., & Yalom, I. (1995). *Existential psychotherapy.* In R. J. Corsini & D. Wedding (Eds.), Current psychotherapies (5th ed.) (pp. 262-292). Itasca, IL: F. E. Peacock.

Mosak, H. H. (1995). Adlerian psychotherapy. In R., J. Corsini & D. Wedding (Eds.), *Current psychotherapies* (5th ed.) (pp. 51-94). Itasca, IL: F. E. Peacock.

Murphy, R. (1987). *The body silent.* New York: W. W. Norton

Paul, G. L. (1967). Outcome research in psychotherapy. *Journal of Consulting Psychology, 31*, 109-188.

Price, R. (1982). *A whole new life.* New York: Atheneum.

Reeve, C. (1998). *Still me.* New York: Random House.

Rogers, C. (1942). *Counseling and psychotherapy.* Boston: Houghton Mifflin.

Rogers, C. (1951). *Client-centered therapy.* Boston: Houghton Mifflin.

Rogers, C. (1961). *On becoming a person.* Boston: Houghton Mifflin.

Rogers, C. (1980). *A way of being.* Boston: Houghton Mifflin.

Sienkiewicz-Mercer, R. & Kaplan, S. B. (1989). *I raise my eyes to say yes.* West Hartford, CT: Whole Health Books.

Tillich, P. (1952). *The courage to be.* New Haven, CT: Yale University Press.

Truax, C. B., & Carkhuff, R. R. (1967). *Toward effective counseling in psychotherapy.* Chicago: Aldine.

Truax, C. B., & Mitchell, K. M. (1971). *Research on certain therapist interpersonal skills in relation to process and outcome.* In A. E. Bergin & S. E. Garfield (Eds.), Handbook of psychotherapy and behavior change: An empirical analysis. New York: Wiley.

Vandenbos, G. R. (1986). Psychotherapy research: A special issue. *American Psychologist, 41*(2), 111-112.

Vash, C. L. (1981). *The psychology of disability.* New York: Springer.

Vash, C. L. (1994). *Personality and adversity: Psychospiritual aspects of rehabilitation.* New York: Springer.

Wright, B. A. (1983). *Physical disability: A psychosocial approach.* New York: Harper and Row.

Wright, G. N. (1980). *Total rehabilitation.* Boston: Little Brown.

Young, M. E. (1992). *Counseling methods and techniques: An eclectic approach.* New York: Merrill.

Part Four

SPECIAL TOPICS IN REHABILITATION

Chapter 15

REHABILITATION COUNSELING CREDENTIALING AS A PROFESSIONAL COUNSELING SPECIALTY

RICHARD S. LUCK

The profession of Rehabilitation Counseling has for over 75 years been recognized as one of the original counseling professions (Leahy & Szymanski, 1995). Jenkins, Patterson, & Szymanski (1992) note :

> Although the central role of the rehabilitation counselor has remained quite consistent over the years, the functions and required knowledge and skill competencies of the rehabilitation counselor have expanded. Regardless of their employment setting and client population, most rehabilitation counselors (a) assess client needs, (b) develop goals and individualized plans to meet identified needs, and (c) provide or arrange for the therapeutic services and interventions (e.g., psychological, medical, social, or behavioral) needed by clients that may include job placement and follow-up services. Counseling skills are considered an essential component of all of these activities. (pp. 28-29)

However, with the growth and development of professional counseling credentialing, largely promoted by the American Counseling Association, the question has arisen as to whether rehabilitation counseling is a counseling specialty or a separate profession. Some authors maintain that this question remains unresolved (Leahy & Szymanski, 1995); however, the position is taken here that it has always been a specialty area of professional counseling and will remain as such with the probable continued development of subspecialties such as rehabilitation substance abuse and addictions counselors, rehabilitation counselors for the deaf, psychiatric rehabilitation counselors, and others. This position adds to the solidarity of the professional counseling movement and helps to alleviate the fragmentation of the discipline. It furthermore provides a solid foundation for the continuation of the several credentialing and accreditation processes existing in rehabilitation counseling.

As one of the foundation blocks of professional counseling, rehabilitation counseling holds an important position in the history and development of professional counseling credentialing. Some authors (Bradley, 1995; Forrest and Stone, 1991) credit the beginnings of counselor credentialing with the teacher certification movement in the 1940s and 1950s which also included guidance counselors. This was the case until two events occurred in the middle 1970s. From a national perspective, the first and most significant was the credentialing of Certified Rehabilitation Counselors (CRC) in 1974 by the Commission on Rehabilitation Counselor Certification (CRCC). The second was in 1976 by act of the General Assembly of the Commonwealth of Virginia which established the nations's first Board of Professional Counselors. Earlier legislation was enacted in Virginia which was a precursor to professional counselor regulation. This was in 1975 and dealt with the registration and licensure of guidance personnel. Subsequently, the first state regulations governing the regulation of professional counselors were adopted by the Virginia Board on August 29, 1977 to become effective October 19, 1977 (Va. Board of Professional Counselors, 1993). As early as 1978, the American Rehabilitation Counseling Association (ARCA) was supportive of rehabilitation counselor specialty certification with generic licensure by the states (Hardy & Luck, 1980; Hardy, Luck, & Chandler, 1982). The ARCA Licensure Committee surveyed the membership in 1979 and found that an overwhelming majority (86%) were in favor of licensure (Hardy & Luck, 1980).

Interestingly enough, Virginia recognized specialty areas of professional counseling in its early regulations which were later dropped in favor of the prevailing generic approach to counselor licensure. It recognized and provided requirements for the specialties of Marriage and Family Counselors; Pastoral Counselors; Substance Abuse Counselors; Career Counselors; Research Counselors; and Rehabilitation Counselors. However, Virginia did not accept the CRC as meeting the requirements for the rehabilitation specialty of the license. These early developments in Virginia were especially prophetic of the current debate which rages in the profession over the recognition of counseling specialties.

Bradley (1995) summarized the history of counselor certification and licensure succinctly by stating (after the aforementioned developments) that:

> ... in 1979 , the first mental health counselors were certified by the American Mental Health Counselors Association. Established in 1983 to provide national certification for counselors, the National Board for Certified Counselors (NBCC) emerged (Brooks and Gerstein, 1990). In 1985, the certification of career counselors was given to NBCC, marking the beginning of specialty certification by NBCC. (p. 185)

According to Rhodes (1996), "NBCC has approximately 24,000 active certified counselors and offers specialty certification in addictions, career, gerontological, school and mental health counseling" (p. 1).

Regarding the development of licensure, Bradley (1995) goes on to say that:

> Counselor licensure traces its beginnings to the early 1970s. Awakened by the restrictions proposed by the 1967 American Psychological Association (APA) Committee on legislation, the counseling profession began to mobilize. In 1973, the Southern Association for Counselor Education and Supervision established the first counselor licensure committee. One year later , the Board of Directors of the American Personnel and Guidance Association, now the American Counseling Association (ACA) adopted a position paper titled, "Counselor Licensure: Position Statement." (p. 185)

According to the American Association of State Counseling Boards (AASCB), there are counseling regulatory boards existing in 43 states, the District of Columbia, and the possession of Guam, for a grand total of 45 boards that govern the practice of professional counseling in the United States (AASCB, 1996). Counselor credentialing has literally exploded in the 1990s. According to Bloom (1996), in 1990, there were 61,868 total counselors credentialed either by states (45,968) or professional organizations (15,900) in the United States. In 1995, only five years later, these figures had soared by an approximate 80 percent increase to 73,154 state-credentialed counselors, and 38,028 professionally-credentialed counselors for a total of 111,182 credentialed counselors in the nation. According to the Foundation for Rehabilitation Education and Research (1997), there are over 13,500 Certified Rehabilitation Counselors practicing in the United States and several foreign countries.

Distinctions Between Types of Credentials

What exactly is meant by the term "credential" in professional counseling? A closer examination of this and the types of credentials that apply to rehabilitation counseling and the other professional counseling areas appears to be in order. First of all, a credential is an official written documentation that an individual possesses some title, competency or skill, quality, right, or privilege. For example, the possession of a valid driver's permit is a credential that affords the individual the privilege to operate a motor vehicle. A passport, on the other hand, is a document which provides official international recognition of citizenship, a right. The driver's permit is issued by the state government and the passport is issued by the federal government.

Another type of credential is a diploma which evidences graduation from an educational institution after the completion of all the requirements of a particular curriculum and implies some competency.

In professional regulation and credentialing, there are three recognized levels and types of credential: licensure, certification, and registration. According to the Council on Licensure, Enforcement and Regulation (CLEAR) (1993), these three types of credential are defined as follows:

> **Licensure** is the most restrictive form of state regulation. Under licensure laws, it is illegal for a person to practice a profession without first meeting state-imposed standards. Under **certification**, the state grants title protection to persons meeting predetermined standards. Those without title may perform the services of the occupation, but may not use the title. **Registration** is the least restrictive form of regulation, usually taking the form of requiring individuals to file their names, addresses and qualifications with a governmental agency before practicing the occupation. (p. 1)

There is not, however, universal consistency in the application of these definitions to professional counseling, and consequently there exists a great deal of confusion in their practical use. Before the explosion in the credentialing of mental health professionals of the 1980s and 1990s, most professions went through the orderly progression of least restrictive to most restrictive regulation in a developmental fashion. A professional group would be listed on a register, then as the group grew in numbers, influence, and complexity, it would certify its members so they could be recognized by their title and not be confused with other occupational or professional groups. Then later in the process as the group further defined its unique skills and competencies through their application or practice, it would seek licensure to prevent others with lesser skills and competencies from engaging in the unique practice of its members. In the 1990s, however, this orderly developmental progression is the exception rather than the rule. Due to the pressures from third party payors for mental health services, most professional groups have escalated the credentialing process and have sought licensure. This is due, in large part, to the requirement of the third party payors that service providers be licensed as a condition for receipt of financial reimbursement.

Adding to this confusion and complexity is the fact that the process of credentialing can be provided by several different types of agencies or organizations. Licensure, as mentioned earlier, is entirely the province of the states, while certification can be done by a state authority, a federal authority, or a national organization. The number of professional organizations which provide certification credentials has expanded exponentially in the last twenty years. Some of the organizations are well known and reputable, while others may be or appear to be marketing schemes to make money for the "board of directors" of the certifying agency. In order to provide assurances that certifying organizations are bona fide, the National Commission for Certifying Agencies (NCCA) was developed. This is a commission which operates under the auspices of the National Organization for Competency Assurance (NOCA) which is an organization that certifies the certifiers. It promulgates standards for approval of certification programs and jointly publishes with CLEAR "Principles of Fairness: An Examining Guide for Credentialing Boards" (Gross & Showers, 1993). Thus the development of oversight agencies has occurred in order to protect both the professional and the public from bogus and/or unfair credentialing practice.

Persons holding a national certification such as a CRC or NCC, for example, can use that title but may not practice in the private sector in their state of residence if they are not licensed by the state. Certification, therefore, is generally national in scope and documents that the professional has achieved a certain level of competency. As such, it benefits the practitioner in helping the public to become aware of one's skills and competencies but does very little to protect the consumer of services because practitioners cannot be legally required to seek certification. According to Clawson (1995), the number of complaints and cases adjudicated by the NBCC has been steadily increasing over the course of the past few years. In 1994, 91 calls, complaints, or letters were received; of these, 5 were accepted as valid complaints and 61 official investigations were conducted. On average, NBCC has approximately 25-30 ongoing ethics investigations at any given time. Additionally, the NBCC cooperates with state licensure boards and reports to them complaints regarding NCCs.

Licensure, on the other hand, even though traditionally criticized as guild membership (Young, 1987), exists with the expressed purpose to protect the safety, health, and welfare of the public. This is more the case in the 1990s than in the past and is especially so due to the fact that many state counseling boards require that nonprofessional citizen members serve on the regulatory boards. The AASCB Disciplinary Information Network, in May 1997, reported an aggregate total of 155 counselors disciplined by 21 states. By contrast, the NBCC had 7 cases listed on the same report. It is apparent from this data that the state boards are much more active in receiving complaints and levying disciplinary sanctions than the NBCC. During this same time period, the CRCC reviewed 18 cases of alleged violations of the Code of Professional Ethics but did not report any disciplinary action taken (CRCC, 1997). Certainly, one way the public is protected can be ascertained by the examination of disciplinary data such as these, using the underlying principle that the more cases that are disciplined the more aggressive the protection of the public.

Requirements for Licensure and Certification

Both certifying agencies and state counseling boards generally have the same levels of regulatory authority. A major distinction between the two in the exercise of this authority is that certification is generally seen as voluntary, while licensure is mandatory. Otherwise, they both require passing a written competency examination; have requirements for education, training, and experience; and investigate violations of ethics or standards of practice. If violations, either of ethics or standards of practice, are committed then both can be used to impose sanctions upon the practitioner. These sanctions can range from a formal reprimand to revocation of certification or license, and in the case of many states, monetary fines can be imposed as well.

While state regulations, either for certification or licensure, will always mandate only the minimal competency required for practicing the profession, national certifying agencies usually require more than minimal proficiency. National certifying agencies generally certify at the specialty level as opposed to the general level of competency. An obvious exception to this is the NBCC which began and continues to certify persons as nationally certified counselors (NCC), a generalist and not a specialist designation. With this exception noted, consider the CRCC's Certified Rehabilitation Counselor credential. This certification requires more than minimal counselor competencies and denotes knowledge, skills, and abilities (KSAs) in excess of those required to be a generalist. The person holding the CRC is recognized as possessing special KSAs dealing in the following 10 knowledge domains as identified by Leahy (1993): (a) vocational counseling and consultation services; (b) medical and psychological aspects; (c) individual and group counseling; (d) program evaluation and research; (e) case management; (f) family, gender, and multicultural issues; (g) foundations of rehabilitation; (h) worker's compensation; (i) environmental and attitudinal barriers; and (j) assessment.

As mentioned earlier, the CRC was the first counseling specialty designation. Since that time a great deal of effort has been placed on the identification and certification of other counseling specialties and subspecialties. An excellent presentation of this debate was made in a special issue of the *Journal of Counseling & Development* (Myers, 1995). This review of the history, specialization areas, and advantages and disadvantages of speciality credentialing describes in detail the many issues and conflicts regarding this discussion.

Added to this rhetoric is *accreditation* which is yet another process which must be defined regarding the credentialing of rehabilitation counselors. Sweeney (1995) reported that specialties within counseling are synonymous with the process of accreditation. Accreditation is defined by the Council for Accreditation of Counseling and Related Educational Programs (CACREP) as the process of granting recognition to an institution or program of study that meets established guidelines and evaluation procedures. This process, according to the Council of Post-secondary Accreditation (COPA) involves:

1. a clear statement of educational objectives;
2. a directed self-study focused on these objectives;
3. an on-site evaluation by a selected group of peers;
4. and, a decision by an independent commission that the institution or specialized unit is worthy of accreditation (CACREP, 1994, p.99).

The accrediting body for rehabilitation counseling education programs is the Council on Rehabilitation Education (CORE), which was begun as a joint effort between the National Rehabilitation Counseling Association and the American Rehabilitation Counseling Association in 1972. There were 84 accredited master's programs and one in-candidate status for the 1996-97 academic year (Council on Rehabilitation Education, 1996).

Cooperation between certifying bodies and accrediting agencies is perhaps nowhere better illustrated than in the example which exists between CRCC and CORE. Graduates with a master's degree from a CORE accredited rehabilitation counselor education program are eligible to sit immediately upon graduation for the CRC examination. This eliminates the cumbersome process of credentials review of the individual candidate through a process better known as program approval. Many graduate programs require some type of exit examination from the degree program prior to graduation. It seems a plausible idea that those programs that require such an exit criteria could possibly utilize the CRC exam for such a purpose. This has obvious advantages for all involved, namely, expediency. The new graduate after passing the exam has not only the master's degree but the specialty certification respected by the profession. The education program is assured that their product is up to industry standards as measured by the competency examination. And finally, the accrediting and certifying bodies are assured that the educational program is maintaining its quality assurance through a national examination of its graduates.

Managed Care Considerations

Certification, licensure, registration, and accreditation can all be viewed as regulatory processes internal to the profession of counseling. However, when third-party payors and managed health care organizations enter the picture, a formidable external process begins to influence the credentialing of rehabilitation and other professional counselors.

The following is a brief description of third-party payors and managed care processes involved in the credentialing of rehabilitation counselors.

These factors do not come into play in the provision of rehabilitation services unless there is an insurance company or other entity to which payment for services rendered will be made on behalf of the client. An insurance company, a state, or the federal government is the payor and, more often than not, an independent management company retained by the payor administers the reimbursement program. In the case of Medicare and Medicaid, the federal or state government can be the payor and the managed care entity.

What, then, is managed health care. According to D'Alessandro (1992), the term "managed health care" is:

> applied to any system committed to providing high quality and cost- effective health care that is focused on evaluating results and procedures by monitoring medical, psychiatric, and psychological practices. Such programs utilize treatment guidelines, peer review, financial incentives and penalties to influence providers, payors, and financial intermediaries to manage the cost, financing, utilization, and quality of the health care delivered. (pp.2-3)

The document which drives the participation of a counselor in a managed care program is known as the provider agreement. This document is a contract which details every aspect of the services provided including which ones are and are not reimbursable. Additionally, the amount to be reimbursed for services and the conditions under which the services will be provided are also specified.

The major document of concern relative to the insurer or payor is the insurance policy. This is a document which is rarely seen by the counselor and seldom seen by the insured. It most often is issued to an employer, who in turn publishes an employee handbook that explains the benefits available to the employee. The most significant concept and condition in the policy is the requirement of "medical necessity." Services will not be reimbursed that do not constitute medical necessity. This means essentially that the service is necessary to slow down, halt, or eliminate a condition which threatens the life or functional ability of the patient, or if left untreated would substantially result in the deterioration of the general health of the patient or the patient's ability to function at generally acceptable levels.

Most policies contain language which specifically excludes coverage for certain conditions. Examples of some of these exclusions are: marriage counseling, vocational counseling, educational services, mental retardation, experimental treatments, and personality disorders (DSM-IV Axis II disorders).

To complicate this issue further, many policies do include coverage for services which the managed care company may not authorize due to their appraisal of the need for the service. This occurs in two ways: one, by a reduction in the quantity of the service; and, two, by a refusal to authorize the service as necessary. An example of the former is the authorization for fewer individual counseling sessions than requested by the counselor and provided for in the policy; and, of the latter, a refusal to authorize psychological testing to establish a diagnosis.

Types of Managed Care Organizations

Within the managed care industry there exists a variety of differently structured organizations that seek to accomplish the same goals but through different organizational structures. The following is a brief description of several of these different types of organizations.

HMO is the acronym for Health Management Organization. A traditional HMO has a closed panel of providers that are responsible for all care delivered to the member, usually at discounted fees. These services are coordinated by a primary care physician. The providers are paid by capitation which is a prepaid, fixed cost system of health care, where the provider is paid according to a fee for each patient per contract period as opposed to a fee for service each time a service is provided. The primary care physician is the gate keeper and makes all decisions regarding referral for specialty examinations and services (D' Alessandro, 1992; Strosnider & Grad, 1993).

IPA stands for Independent Practice Association which is a subtype of HMO based upon community physicians banding together to form a central administrative organization. In this type of organization, the individual member can retain choice of primary care physician; however, the financial savings are lower and the risks higher for participating physicians according to D'Alessandro (1992).

PPO, Preferred Provider Organization is still another type of structure that is designed to deliver cost effective health care services. The PPO is a group of hospitals, physicians, and other practitioners who contract with employers, insurance companies, or other third-party groups to provide comprehensive medical services for a fee which is usually discounted, and specified in a formal contract (D' Alessandro, 1992; Strosnider & Grad, 1993). This type of structure has emerged as the most popular, because they are easier to start, encompass more providers, and can cover a larger area. Most mental health managed care organizations fall into this category and according to D'Alessandro (1992), there are advantages for providers and patients alike. Providers retain fee for service, autonomy in treating patients, and larger patient volume, with limited provider financial risks. Patients like this type of organization due to flexibility to go outside the network, minimal fears of being undertreated, lower insurance premiums, occasional expanded benefits and no claims to file.

Quality Assurance and Treatment Outcome

A major responsibility of the managed care organization is the oversight of the delivery of services and the outcome of treatment. This is done through a process known as Utilization Management (UM). UM encompasses a process called Utilization Review (UR) which according to D'Alessandro (1992) is designed to "reduce the incidence of unnecessary or inappropriate hospitalization. UR involves the use of criteria to establish guidelines for appropriate admission, hospital lengths of stay, and course of treatment"(p.8). This process has been applied to outpatient counseling and psychotherapy services as well. It is intended to reduce the inappropriate delivery of services and to insure that clients receive only those services which are necessary to alleviate or ameliorate the current source of distress.

Treatment outcome evaluation is a process designed to measure the effectiveness of an individual practitioner or group of practitioners. It is a system which can either be imposed by the payor or by the provider. Outcome indicators such as length of time in treatment, cost of services, client satisfaction, and client improvement are measured. These are often stated as averages for a given period of time, usually a year. A provider with the shortest length of treatment time, at the lowest cost with the highest client satisfaction and greatest improvement could be said to be an effective provider within the PPO or HMO. Providers are evaluated and those who don't measure up to whatever standards are set may run the risk of being dropped from the provider network.

Treatment outcome evaluation is not only found in the private sector but is applied to public agencies as well in a variety of forms. There is certainly insufficient space here to fully discuss all of the ramifications of the impact of managed care on the rehabilitation counseling profession, but suffice it to say that even counselors who work in the state-federal program of rehabilitation are no longer immune to such influences. This is especially true as states begin to creatively search for ways to pay for the cost of services to citizens with disabilities. Medicare and Medicaid are reimbursable programs that provide coverage, and counselors will need to be qualified providers if the cost of their services is to be reimbursed from these sources. As this development continues to gain momentum, rehabilitation counselors will find themselves scrutinized anew by the managed care industry and required to be additionally credentialed by it.

Managed care companies retain the right to bestow provider status only onto those practitioners who in their estimation measure up to the standards of quality set by them. Each managed care company maintains its own group of providers, sometimes referred to as preferred providers. In order for these practitioners to be paid for services rendered, they must measure up to the standards set by each individual managed care company. Unfortunately, there is no central certifying body in managed care for professional counselors. If there were, it would eliminate an extraordinary amount of unnecessary and duplicative paperwork and wasted time and money by the counselors and the companies as well. No managed care company accepts any of the nationally recognized certifications or state licenses mentioned earlier as sufficient evidence of provider competence. Instead, lengthy applications on forms which contain no consistency from one company to the other must be filed and refiled periodically in order for the counselor to keep provider status.

The situation in the credentialing of professional counselors and the specialty of rehabilitation counseling is a morass of disconnected, duplicative, costly documentation procedures which have no meaning to consumers and have little value to practitioners. The current situation is far too complex, costly, confusing, and time consuming. The current system contains too many agencies, with too many credentials, none of which is interconnected. It is expensive to the counselor, with many of the credentials costing upwards of $150.00 to obtain and as much as $50.00 a year to retain on an annual basis. Nobody, especially the consumer, understands all the acronyms after a counselors' name, and they probably don't care. The proliferation of all the certificates in specialty and subspecialty areas has cheapened the more desirable and easily understood ones. And finally, the time spent maintaining credentials and recredentialing is excessive and, for many persons, onerous. There has to be a better way! Perhaps a commission or coalition could be formed composed of such groups as CRCC, NBCC, CORE, CACREP, and others to study this situation and make recommendations for the unification of counselor credentialing. Such a group could decipher all the different credentials and interpret them to the insurance and managed care industry. The managed care industry could eliminate the costly and time-consuming method it currently uses by adopting a posture of accepting verification of one set of credentials from a central entity along with evidence of state licensure in good standing. This should greatly simplify the credentialing process at least in the managed health care industry.

Professional Counselor Liability and Ethical Considerations

No discussion of rehabilitation counselor credentialing would be complete without an explanation of the impact of the profession's ethical standards and the counselor's liability when failing to adhere to those standards. Every organization, be it a state government or independent private commission that issues any type of credential imposes standards of conduct upon the recipient as a condition of bestowing the credential. These standards of conduct or codes of ethics are numerous and, with few exceptions, rarely are they ever mutual between organizations. One notable exception was the adoption of a code of ethics jointly subscribed to by the American Rehabilitation Counseling Association, the National Rehabilitation Counseling Association, and the Commission on Rehabilitation Counselor Certification in 1987 (Leahy & Szymanski, 1995).

A major tenet of any professional code of conduct is to insure that practitioners practice in such a way that does not harm the client, patient, or consumer. The cardinal rule of "Do no harm" is imposed, and the codes are put in place for the protection of the public, and to insure that practitioners are prohibited from any professional conduct that would be harmful. Counselors are held liable for their conduct, and complaints can be made and sanctions imposed for infractions of the standards of practice. This process will be discussed in more detail in the following section, but the point needs to be made that the practitioner needs to protect him or herself in legal and ethical situations where professional liability may become an issue due to malpractice.

Malpractice is defined (Stronsnider & Grad, 1993) as " the failure of a health care practitioner to act in a professional situation in the same manner as a reasonable, prudent practitioner of a similar specialty. The way in which a reasonable, prudent practitioner deals with a client in a set of circumstances is called the standard of care" (p. 59).

Liability is defined as being legally obligated; responsible by the *American Heritage Dictionary*. Counselors are legally and ethically responsible to provide services in accordance with the standard of care or codes of ethics to which they have sworn allegiance. A consumer who believes a counselor has failed to uphold the standards in the provision of services or in professional conduct may file a formal complaint against the counselor. It is here that the counselor needs to have professional practice liability insurance coverage. This coverage will provide protection for the costs of defense and damages if complaints are found to be valid. Professional liability insurance is available from most professional organizations such as the American Counseling Association, the American Psychological Association, and others. This is group insurance, relatively low cost, and comprehensive. This insurance is designed to protect the practitioner in civil proceedings where litigation for monetary damages is threatened. It does not necessarily provide protection for defense against complaints to state licensure boards. The policy should be carefully checked for the extent of coverage as well as any exclusions. Examples of exclusions are that damages will not be paid for sexual assault, abuse, molestation, or licentious, immoral or amoral acts; infringement of copyright laws or actual plagiarism; and any fraudulent or criminal or malicious acts or omissions. Coverage is usually provided, however, for defense against allegations such as these and others.

There are several very troubling areas for most professional counselors practicing in the managed care arena. These are, according to Strosnider and Grad (1993), as follows: failure to identify the suicidal patient who completes a suicide, inappropriate sexual contact between the counselor and client, violation of confidentiality or counselor-client privilege, dual relationships not of a sexual nature, and inappropriate third-party payment billing practices. In support of this contention, the Virginia Board of Professional Counselors reviewed five years of disciplinary cases in 1990, and found that of the 71 cases involving 85 complaints, 54 percent resulted in findings of a violation. The cases where violations were found were divided into the following categories: 38 percent unlicensed activity, 26 percent dual relationships, and sexual misconduct 8 percent (Anderson, Luck & Stenzhorn, 1990). The ACA has published an excellent series titled "The Legal Series" that provides a more complete review of these and other legal practice issues (ACA, 1993).

As certified or licensed rehabilitation counselors become involved in the provision of services either within or outside of managed care, they become vulnerable to claims and complaints against them for malpractice and unethical conduct. The next section contains a brief description of the complaint and disciplinary process as it applies to the professional rehabilitation counselor.

The Complaint and Disciplinary Process

The complaint and disciplinary process will vary according to state law and other organizational procedures; however, the following components of the process are generally involved. This process involves only those instances where a counselor is licensed by a state government or certified by a professional organization or certifying agency. It does not pertain to counselors working in the public sector. Complaints made against public employees are usually handled in an administrative manner as a personnel matter. The process which follows is condensed from the Adjudication Manual of the Virginia Department of Health Professions, 1987 (Stenzhorn, 1993). It begins with a **complaint** being made to the board or department of state government that regulates professional counseling. Complaints can be made by clients, employees, administrators, other professionals, associations and insurance companies.

The **investigation** of a complaint is initiated most often by an intake officer who screens it and makes an initial determination as to whether the allegation comes within the jurisdiction of the board. After the jurisdictional determination is made, the complaint may be assigned a priority designation for investigation. Practitioners are usually notified of the complaint shortly after it is received; however, silence from the board does not mean that the case has gone away. The practitioner will always be notified in writing of the status of the investigation even though this may involve a considerable passage of time.

The complaint will be assigned to a field investigator who is usually a trained investigator and most often a licensed health care professional although not necessarily a licensed professional counselor. The investigator will gather information regarding the complaint and will usually begin by interviewing the individual who made the complaint. The investigator is empowered to review client records and can obtain them if necessary by subpoena. Investigators can and often do use undercover techniques and may pose as a client to gather information during the investigation. The investigator will write a complete report of the results of the investigation and turn it over to the board for action. The investigator's role is to collect information and not to make recommendations or interpretations regarding the information.

The next step in the process is the convening of an **informal conference** where usually three board members meet with the counselor and any representative to review the complaint and the result of the investigation. This three board member panel has the authority to determine whether the information they have received is without foundation, or that, if true, does not merit a formal hearing. The panel also has the authority to exonerate the practitioner, issue a reprimand or censure, or place the practitioner on probation with stipulations for supervision and or counseling.

As a result of the informal hearing when the panel has determined that the allegations are true, the practitioner will be offered a **consent order**. This stipulates the complaint, the findings of fact, conclusions of law, and the terms and conditions of the sanction or discipline that is to take place. The licensee, referred to as the **respondent**, has the option to accept the order or take the complaint to a hearing before the entire board.

A **formal hearing** is convened before the entire board with the Chairperson of the board serving as the presiding officer. The findings from the formal hearing are issued as an order and can only be appealed to civil court. Formal hearings are usually required for license revocation; however, other less serious sanctions can also be made.

A **sanction** is defined as the penalty for noncompliance specified in a law or decree (*American Heritage Dictionary*, 1982). The sanctions which can be imposed consist of only four possibilities with infinite variations decided upon by the board. The four sanctions listed in order from least to most serious are: reprimand, probation, suspension, and revocation. Boards are also usually empowered to levy monetary fines in addition to the above sanctions. A respondent can usually apply for **reinstatement** after the sanctions have been satisfied.

It is important for practitioners to be aware that a domino effect is initiated when a board sanctions them. Most all state boards and many professional organizations report practitioners who have been disciplined to national data banks. In the case of professional counselors, most state boards as well as national counselor certifying agencies report disciplined counselors to the American Association of State Counseling Boards (AASCB) Disciplinary Information Network. The AASCB publishes the counselor's name, infraction, and sanction, and distributes the list quarterly to interested parties such as insurance companies, state regulatory boards, and other interested parties. This usually results in further inquiries and penalties such as restrictions in managed care provider status, hospital credentialing, and adjustments in liability insurance.

The counselor has many rights and remedies in this process which are too numerous to mention here. Suffice it to say though, a counselor who has a complaint filed against him or her would be very wise to obtain legal counsel to protect those rights. The selection of an attorney skilled in administrative law and the professional complaint and discipline process is critical. Many counselors make the mistake of obtaining the services of the lawyer who handled the real estate closing on their house or some other unrelated matter to assist them in this process. This can be a very costly error in selection. Most state bar associations operate free referral services and they should be contacted for an appropriate selection.

While limited space prevents a complete discussion of the full range of ways counselors can protect themselves from having sanctions levied against them, there is one area which warrants mention even if ever so briefly. This is the area of counselor/client boundary violations. While this is generally not the most frequently occurring complaint made against counselors, it is the one which can be the most devastating.

At the American College of Legal Medicine Seminar on Sexual Misconduct and the Physician in 1992 (Communication from C. R. Russek, October 7, 1992), the profile of the client who is most likely to become a victim of sexual misconduct by therapists was identified as:

- clients who were sexually abused as children;
- persons who are mentally retarded;
- adults who as children had undergone extensive medical procedures;
- clients with borderline personality disorder.

Counselors need to recognize and appreciate the special dynamics which may come about as a result of the emotional needs of the types of clients listed above. One way is to pay attention to the following list of suggestions offered at this same seminar:

- maintain relative neutrality;
- foster psychological separateness of the client;

- interact verbally with the client only, minimizing physical contact;
- avoid all types of present or future dual relationships;
- provide a consistent private setting for counseling;
- be consistent regarding length and time of sessions.

Summary and Conclusion

This chapter has engaged in a discussion of the broad spectrum of rehabilitation counselor credentialing including licensure and certification and the ramifications imposed by them. Counselors are cautioned that they should choose their certifications carefully and select only those that help them to define their competencies and specialities appropriately. In the 1990s, there has been a veritable explosion of all types of professional certifications, some which are reputable and some which may be questionable. The adage of " more is better" may not hold true in this case; more is most likely to be more costly and make the counselor more vulnerable to sanctions in the event of infractions of the various standards of conduct.

A requirement, in most states, if the counselor is going to engage in private sector practice and seek third-party reimbursements, is licensure. Certification, on the other hand, is voluntary and is viewed as a way to publicly demonstrate special competencies as a counselor.

While one can become a rehabilitation counselor by many routes, the standard in the profession is to obtain a masters degree from a CORE accredited program, obtain certification as a rehabilitation counselor (CRC) and become licensed as a professional counselor in the state of residence. Specialty certification can be added to the CRC, such as the Master Addiction Counselor (MAC) designation depending upon the desires and professional inclination of the individual.

REFERENCES

American Association of State Counseling Boards (AASCB). (1996). *The liaison, 3.* 1-9. Baltimore, MD: Author.

Anderson, D. , Luck, R. S. & Stenzhorn, R. B.(1990). Analysis of board discipline: A summary of general findings. Reported in Anderson, D.(1991) A letter from the chairman. *Professional counselor news. 2,* 3-6. Virginia Board of Professional Counselors, Richmond, VA.

Bloom, J. W. (1996). *Credentialing professional counselors for the 21st century.* ERIC Counseling and Student Clearinghouse, Greensboro, N.C.

Bradley, L. J. (1995). Certification and licensure issues. *Journal of Counseling and Development, 74,* 185-186.

Brooks, D. K. & Gerstein, L. H. (1990). Counselor credentialing and interprofessional collaboration. *Journal of Counseling and Development, 68*, 477-485.

Clawson, T. (1995). Untitled communication. The National Board of Certified Counselors, Greensboro, N.C.

Council on Licensure, Enforcement and Regulation (CLEAR).(1993). *The directory of professional and occupational regulation in the United States and Canada.* Lexington, KY: Author.

Commission on Rehabilitation Counselor Certification (CRCC) (1997). *CRC: The counselor*, Fall. Chicago: Author.

Council for Accreditation of Counseling and Related Educational Programs.(1994). *Accreditation standards and procedures manual.* Alexandria, VA: Author.

Council on Rehabilitation Education. (November, 1996). *Core news*, 8(1).

D'Alessandro, A. (1992). *Managed behavioral health care.* Clearwater, FL.

Forrest, D. V., & Stone, L. A. (1991) Counselor certification. In F. O. Bradley (Ed.), *Credentialing in counseling.* (Pp. 13-23). Alexandria , VA: American Association for Counseling and Development.

Gross, L. J. & Showers, B. (1993). Principles of fairness: An examining guide for credentialing boards. Council on Licensure Enforcement, and Regulation & National Organization for Compliance Assurance. Lexington, KY and Washington, D.C.

Hardy, R. E. & Luck, R. S. (1980) The American Rehabilitation Counseling Association position paper on licensure and certification. Department of Rehabilitation Counseling, Virginia commonwealth University , Richmond, VA.

Hardy, R. E., Luck, R. S., Chandler, A. L. (1982). Licensure of rehabilitation counseling and related issues: Results of a national survey. *Rehabilitation Counseling Bulletin, 25*(3), 157-161.

Jenkins, W. M., Patterson, J. B., & Szymanski, E. D. (1992). Philosophical, historical, and legislative aspects of the rehabilitation counseling profession. In R. M. Parker & E. M. Szymanski (Eds.), *Rehabilitation counseling: Basics and beyond* (2nd Ed.). Austin, TX: PRO-ED.

Leahy, M. J. & Szymanski, E. M. (1995). Rehabilitation counseling: Evolution and current status. *Journal of Counseling and Development, 74*,163-166.

Leahy, M. J., Szymanski, E.M.,& Linkowski, D.C. (1993). Knowledge importance in rehabilitation counseling. *Rehabilitation Counseling Bulletin, 37*, 130-145.

Myers, J. (Ed.). (1995). Professional counseling: Spotlight on specialities. (Special issue). *Journal of Counseling & Development, 74*(2).

Rhodes K. K. (1996). NBCC completes research on counseling and managed care. *NBCC News and Notes, 13*, 1-2.

Russek, C. R.(1992). Written communication. Richmond, VA.

Stenzhorn, R. B. (1993). How complaints are handled: Sequence of disciplinary actions. *Professional Counselor News, 3*, 7-9. Virginia Board of Professional Counselors, Richmond. VA.

Strosnider, J. S. & Grad, J. D. (1993). *Third party payments.* ACA Legal Series Vol. 9. American Counseling Association, Alexandria, VA.

Sweeney, T. J. (1995). Accreditation, credentialing, professionalization: The role of specialties. *Journal of Counseling and Development, 74*, 117-125.

Virginia Department of Health Professions. (1987). *Adjudication manual.* Richmond, VA: Author.

Young, S. D. (1987). *The rule of experts.* Cato Institute, Washington, D.C.

Chapter 16

SUBSTANCE USE DISORDERS IN REHABILITATION

CONSTANCE CORLEY SALTZ, MARCIA J. LAWTON, AND MURIEL GRAY

The abuse of and dependence on recreational, medicinal, and otherwise harmful substances have been noted historically for centuries, accompanied by a wide range of explanations of causality. Although a discussion of etiology is beyond the scope of this chapter, awareness of the impact of harmful substances on persons presenting in health care settings (whether due to the consequences of one episode of using crack or a long-term addiction to tobacco) is essential for practitioners. The thrust of this chapter is to help those in a gatekeeper role to identify addiction and to know how to refer the client to an appropriate component of the continuum of care.

The chapter begins with an overview of the prevalence, cost, and consequences of chemical abuse and dependency, with a brief presentation of definitions and terminology. The chapter then focuses on addiction, using the substance of alcohol to explore the addiction process, screening, intervention, treatment, and recovery. Relevant considerations pertaining to several other major addictions (especially cocaine and nicotine) are addressed. Implications for treatment on both the practice and policy levels are discussed in the concluding section of the chapter.

Prevalence

The most recent national survey on drug abuse (Substance Abuse and Mental Health Services Administration [SAMHSA], 1996) found that overall drug use has leveled off since 1995. However, a substantial number of persons in the United States continue to abuse one or more of the following sub-

Adapted from C. Saltz, M. Lawton, & M. Gray, Chapter 26: Substance Use Disorders in M. G. Eisenberg, R. L. Glueckauf, & H. H. Zaretsky (Eds.), *Medical Aspects of Disability A Handbook for the Rehabilitation Profession*, 1999. Copyrighted and used by permission of Springer Publishing Company, Inc., New York, N.Y. 10012.

stances: alcohol, tobacco, marijuana, cocaine/crack, heroin, hallucinogens, inhalants, and psychotherapeutic drugs used for nonmedical purposes (e.g., sedatives, tranquilizers, stimulants, analgesics, and anabolic steroids).

According to the National Household Survey on Drug Abuse (SAMHSA, 1996), legal drugs are the most used and abused. Although per capita alcohol consumption has declined, alcohol continues to be the most commonly used and abused substance. It is used by approximately 51 percent of the U.S. population age 12 and older. Of those users, about 16 percent engaged in binge drinking, and 5.4 percent were heavy drinkers. An estimated 7 percent of adults have an alcohol use disorder (either abuse or dependence), and 45 percent of the traffic crash deaths in the United States are attributed to alcohol consumption (National Institute on Alcohol Abuse and Alcoholism [NIAAA], 1997). Alcohol in combination with other drugs was mentioned in 39% of deaths reported in medical examiner cases (SAMHSA, 1995). The prevalence of substance use disorders in general and alcohol disorders in particular is difficult to determine. Data gathered from the National Hospital Discharge Surveys concluded that hospital discharge records may underrepresent the extent of disorders related to alcohol use. It found that, whereas 7.4 percent of hospital patients had an alcohol-related diagnosis, when screened specifically for alcohol problems, 22 percent screened positive (NIAAA, 1997). Substance use disorders also lead to myriad social, legal, and job-related problems.

Tobacco, like alcohol, is a highly addictive legal substance. It is used regularly by 29 percent of the U.S. population age 12 and older. According to the Monitoring the Future study (National Institute on Drug Abuse [NIDA], 1996), tobacco use was slightly down for adults, whereas use among adolescents increased.

Approximately 6 percent of the U.S. population 12 years of age and older reported current use of an illicit substance in the 1996 National Household Survey on Drug Abuse (NIDA, 1997). Marijuana is the most commonly used illicit substance. Of current illicit drug users, 77 percent reported marijuana use (SAMHSA, 1997). The director's report to the National Advisory Council on Drug Abuse (NIDA, 1997) reports a resurgence in marijuana use among adolescent emergency department mentions, treatment admissions, and arrests. The rate of marijuana initiation is at the highest level ever among U.S. youth between the ages of 12 and 17 (SAMHSA, 1997). Along with tobacco and alcohol, marijuana is considered to be a "gateway" substance to other drug use (NIDA, 1991).

The proportion of the population age 12 and older who are current cocaine users remains stable at approximately 0.8 percent (SAMSHA, 1997). However, cocaine was the most frequently reported substance in drug abuse deaths. According to data from the Drug Abuse Warning Network (SAMSHA, 1997), it was reported in 46 percent of drug-related deaths.

According to 1995 medical examiner data, heroin is the second most often mentioned substance in drug abuse deaths (SAMHSA, 1997). Preliminary results from the 1996 National Household Survey on Drug Abuse report decreasing overall heroin use but an increased number of new users between the ages of 12 and 17. They also show that most new heroin users are under the age of 26 (SAMHSA, 1997).

Consequences and Costs

Regular use of harmful drugs (and sometimes even a single incident of use of a drug such as crack) can have major adverse medical, psychological, psychiatric, economic, and social consequences. The medical complications resulting from alcoholism (Kinney & Leaton, 1991) perhaps best illustrate how one widely available substance can affect almost every body system; cardiovascular, gastrointestinal, genitourinary, endocrine, nervous, musculoskeletal, and immune systems. Major nutritional deficits can result from chronic alcoholism, as well as changes in the skin and hair (Kinney & Leaton, 1991). Hematological disorders are more common in alcoholics than in the population at large, and at least 10 percent of all cancer occur in sites affected by heavy drinking (Kinney & Leaton, 1991).

In terms of psychological/psychiatric consequences of misuse of alcohol and/or most other harmful substances, the following may result: intoxication, craving, depression/mood swings, anxiety, paranoia, hallucinations/delusions, organic brain syndromes (both acute and chronic), and flashbacks (Kinney & Leaton, 1991). Suicide is a major risk among alcoholics: an estimated 7 to 21 percent of alcoholics commit suicide (Kinney & Leaton, 1991).

Although calculating the economic costs of substance abuse and dependence is more difficult than for other illnesses, the costs of alcohol, tobacco, and other drugs are estimated as close to or in excess of $400 billion (Center on Addiction and Substance Abuse [CASA], 1993).

Although the primary costs are those of health care expenditures, such figures also take into account lost productivity from employee substance abuse and social losses from premature deaths, substance-induced psychiatric disorders, and family disruption. The impact of substance use disorders on the family will be discussed below.

Definitions and Terminology

Several concepts are important in defining and identifying maladaptive effects of harmful substances. These include abuse, dependence, tolerance, withdrawal, and addiction.

Two diagnostic categories that broadly cover chemical misuse are included in the *Diagnostic and Statistical Manual of Mental Disorders* (4th edition; herein referred to as DSM-IV): psychoactive substance abuse and psychoactive substance dependence (American Psychiatric Association [APA], 1995).

Criteria for Substance Dependence

A maladaptive pattern of substance use, leading to clinically significant impairment of distress, as manifested by three (or more) of the following, occurring at any time in the same 12-month period:

(1) tolerance, as defined by either of the following:
  (a) a need for markedly increased amount of the substance to achieve intoxication or desired effect
  (b) markedly diminished effect with continued use of the same amount of the substance

(2) withdrawal, as manifested by either of the following:
  (a) the characteristic withdrawal syndrome for the substance (refer to Criteria A and B of the criteria sets for Withdrawal from the specific substances)
  (b) the same (or a closely related) substance is taken to relieve or avoid withdrawal symptoms

(3) the substance is often taken in larger amounts or over a longer period than was intended

(4) there is a persistent desire or unsuccessful efforts to cut down or control substance use

(5) a great deal of time is spend in activities necessary to obtain the substance (e.g., chain-smoking, or recover from its effects)

(6) important social, occupation, or recreational activities are given up or reduced because of substance use

(7) the substance use is continued despite knowledge of having a persistent or recurrent physical or psychological problem that is likely to have been caused or exacerbated by the substance (e.g., current cocaine use despite recognition of cocaine-induced depression, or continued drinking despite recognition that an ulcer was made worse by alcohol consumption) (p. 181).

Criteria for Substance Abuse

A. A maladaptive pattern of substance use leading to clinically significant impairment of distress, as manifested by one (or more) of the following, occurring within a 12-month period:

(1) recurrent substance use resulting in a failure to fulfill major role obligations at work, school, or home (e.g., repeated absences or poor work performance related to substance use; substance-related absences, suspensions, or expulsions from school; neglect of children or household)

(2) recurrent substance use in situations in which it is physically hazardous (e.g., driving an automobile or operating a machine when impaired by substance use)

(3) recurrent substance-related legal problems (e.g., arrests for substance-related disorderly conduct)

(4) continued substance use despite having persistent or recurrent social or interpersonal problems caused or exacerbated by the effects of the substance (e.g., arguments with spouse about consequences of intoxication, physical fights)

B. The symptoms have never met the criteria for Substance Dependence for this class of substance (pp. 182-183).

Tolerance occurs with the regular consumption of a substance over an extended period and is one of the defining characteristics of alcohol addiction (Kenney & Leaton, 1995). Withdrawal results in the development of adverse physical symptoms when the use of a substance is stopped (Beasley, 1990).

Addiction, the primary emphasis of this chapter, is a physiological process in which the person with an addiction craves one or more substances, used the substance(s) compulsively (daily and/or in binges), and continues using the substance(s) despite a range of adverse consequences (Beasley, 1990). Tolerance and withdrawal occur with many forms of addiction (e.g., alcohol). Denial of the addiction itself is usually also a hallmark of addiction.

Given the multifactorial nature of addiction, the following factors must be taken into account during assessment, intervention, treatment, and recovery: biological, psychological, social/economic, and spiritual. This will be referred to as the biopsychosocial-spiritual approach. The process of addiction to alcohol through the steps to recovery is now presented to exemplify this approach.

Alcoholism as an Example of Addiction

The nature of the addiction process has been most extensively studied and is best understood with alcoholism. Therefore, alcoholism is used here to demonstrate the highlights of the addiction process–screening, recovery, intervention, and treatment.

Addiction Process

Alcoholism has generally been accepted, since the American Medical Association (AMA) declaration in 1956, as a primary, chronic, progressive, fatal, family disease. The most notable aspect of alcoholism (or any addiction) is the development of the denial system. This is not simply a psychological defense used to cope with anxiety but a complex system composed of multiple mechanisms (blaming, minimizing, rationalizing, intellectualization, humor, and others, depending on the individual), which becomes an unconscious way to protect a life-style focused on alcohol. One of the best practical resources on understanding denial, from Hazelden ("Dealing with Denial," 1975), describes it as follows:

> The development of a denial system is a cardinal and integral feature of chemical dependency. It is one of the major symptoms of this disease and develops along with the more visible symptoms, i. e., harmful consequences. To a greater or lesser extent, it can be found in all chemically dependent persons [*sic*]. Denial is the fatal aspect of alcoholism and other drug dependencies. It impairs the judgment of affected individuals and results in self-delusion which keeps them locked into an increasingly destructive pattern. It is the denial system which, for example, permits a chemically dependent person [*sic*] to ignore a physician's advice or "stop or you will die." (p. 9)

In addition to the denial system, alcoholism is characterized by certain predictable signs and symptoms that manifest themselves as the illness progresses. There are some discrepancies as to what constitutes alcoholism or at what point one crosses the imaginary line. There does appear to be a fairly wide acceptance that once a person reaches a stage where there are physical consequences (tremors, liver damage, etc.) and loss of ordinary willpower, alcoholism is in the picture. Other consequences may occur earlier in the process: psychological (e.g., guilt), mental (e.g., preoccupation with alcohol), and spiritual (e.g., moral deterioration) signs; these deserve as much attention as do the physical consequences.

A very important aspect of this chronic illness is relapse; it is later addressed in more detail. What triggers this relapse or resumption of use varies. Gorski (Miller, Gorski & Miller, 1982) and Marlatt (Marlatt & Gordon, 1985), coming from different philosophical orientations (the former, from a disease orientation, and the latter, from a learned-behavior one), both stress the significance of relapse in addiction. Among the 37 signs of relapse that Gorski lists are several indicating that the addiction is being activated even before the person with an alcohol addiction resumes drinking: recurrence of the denial system, tendencies toward loneliness, a feeling that nothing can be solved, progressive loss of daily structure, thoughts of social drinking, and unreasonable resentments.

The role of the family in maintaining or returning to addiction to alcohol has been increasingly studied (Wegschneider, 1981). Alcoholism has been described as a hanging mobile; as one member changes, the others have to make adjustments to acquire an equilibrium. Jackson (1954) spells out the seven adjustment stages through which family members go as the person with an alcohol addiction progresses in his or her disease: attempts to deny the problem, social isolation, disorganization of family structure, efforts to reorganize in spite of the problem, attempts to escape the problem, reorganization of part of the family, and , finally, recovery and reorganization of the whole family.

In understanding the significance of the family, it is important to address two concepts, enabling and codependency. Enabling is any behavior on the part of anyone that protects the denial system of a person with an alcohol addiction. Codependency is a term full of confusion in the addiction field today. It currently has a variety of meanings, many of which focus on it as an addiction in its own right, whereby the person with codependent behavior is addicted to having someone else provide emotional support and in fact defines his or her own identity by that relationship. Probably the best and most useful definition of codependency is the following: "Codependency is a pattern of painful dependency upon compulsive behaviors and on approval from others in search for safety, self-worth and identity. Recovery is possible" (Lawton, 1990, p. 1).

Screening for Alcoholism

An overall recommendation is that the practitioner work with an individual to examine at a conscious level the client's relationship with alcohol. If the client is comfortable in that relationship and does not let alcohol control behavior and the ability to deal effectively with life stresses and problems, then he or she is probably not a person with an alcohol addiction. To assist further in the decision about drinking behavior, Alcoholics Anonymous (AA) has prepared a brief pamphlet that includes 12 questions such as (a) do you wish people would mind their own business about your drinking–stop telling you what to do? (b) have you ever switched from one kind of drink to another in hopes that this would keep you from getting drunk? (Alcoholics Anonymous, 1973). As a guideline, if the client answers yes to 4 or more of the 12 questions, then there is probably trouble with alcohol. The counselor can review this material with the client along with information on the progressive signs of alcoholism (e.g., using the chart developed by Glatt in 1957, based on Jellinek's research published in 1954). Additional tools are available in the form of the Trauma Scale (Skinner, Holt, Schuller, Roy, & Israel, 1984), the CAGE (Ewing, 1984), the Michigan Alcoholism Screening Test (MAST) (Seizer, 1971), and formalized interviews such as the Addictions Severity Index (ASI) (McLellan, Luborsky, Woody, & O'Brien, 1980).

The CAGE is composed of four simple questions:

1. Have you ever tried to cut down on your drinking?
2. Do you get annoyed when drinking is criticized?
3. Do you feel guilty about your drinking?
4. Do you use alcohol as an "eye-opener"?

A score of two "yes" answers constitutes concern.

The MAST is a self-report test with 25 items regarding the consequences of problem drinking; a positive answer of 12 or 13 deserves taking some action. The ASI is a structured clinical interview suitable for use with persons with either an alcohol or drug addiction. It can be administered by a technician in about 20 to 30 minutes and provides a problem severity profile reflecting six areas: medical, psychological, legal, family/social, employment/support, and chemical abuse. Each area is measured independently, and the severity is derived from two kinds of information, the client's subjective judgment and objective data (e.g., lab reports).

There are some clinical lab tests available (serum gamma-glutamyltransferase and aspartate amniotransferase) that can indicate an alcohol problem, but unfortunately they lack diagnostic specificity and are not positive until later stages of addiction when denial is strongest (NIAAA, 1990). Sometimes particularly negative consequences of alcoholism (e.g., citations for driving under the influence) can be indicators of alcoholism; the helpful role these can play in presenting the reality of the illness will be discussed in the intervention section.

Recovery from Alcohol

On the Jellinek chart referred to earlier (Glan, 1957), recovery is pictured as a mirror-image representation of the addiction process. However, more research done by Brown (1985) on a dynamic, developmental model of recovery belies this description. Brown discovered a process whereby the individual undergoes a second-order change regarding the ability to control drinking. The stages are (a) drinking: "I can control my drinking." "I am not an alcoholic [*sic*]"; (b) transition: "I cannot control my drinking." "I am an alcoholic [*sic*]"; (c) early recovery: same as transition but with a beginning awareness of the environment and a slight interpersonal focus; (d) ongoing recovery: same as transition but with increased awareness of environment and relationship between self and others.

Brown (1985) acknowledges the role of AA in accomplishing these changes. Since its inception in 1935, AA has been beneficial to many persons with an alcohol addiction as a support system that recognizes the internal healing that occurs in recovery. This self-help movement emphasizes self-responsibility and surrender to a higher power. The focus is on spirituality, the energy force within each one, rather than on religion, an institution created by people with a set of rules (Lawton, 1991a). This is the spiritual component mentioned in the biopsychosocial-spiritual approach discussed in the introduction and in Kuhn's (1988) article, which provides a spiritual inventory for the person with a medical illness. It should be noted that recovery is an internal healing process with its own developmental stages and is distinct from the external treatment given to an individual.

Intervention with the Alcoholic

Because the denial system is the most crucial aspect of addiction, it is essential that it be addressed to stop the cycle and promote recovery. Johnson (1980) found that, by involving significant others (or concerned persons) in the planning part of the intervention and helping break through their denial, there was increased likelihood of reaching the person with an alcohol addiction. A trained professional teaches the concerned persons about alcoholism as a disease, helps them collect factual data about the consequences of the drinking of an individual with an alcohol addiction and works through the concerned person's anger and judgmental attitudes through attendance at counseling meetings and Al-Anon support groups. The group then formalizes a concrete plan with clear alternatives, such as "go to treatment" or "accept my having to leave the family."

Following a real crisis (such as arrest for driving under the influence), when the guilt of the individual with an alcohol addiction is the highest and defenses are the weakest, the group meets with the individual with an addiction and presents the prepared choices. When done in a factual, nonjudgmental, caring manner that taps into the core being of the person with an alcohol addiction, it is most likely to achieve changes.

Treatment for Alcoholism

Since its inception in 1948, the Minnesota Model (developed at Hazelden by Dan Anderson) has gained widespread recognition as the treatment of choice for the person with an alcohol addiction and family. It focuses on the holistic nature of alcoholism and is best described as having the following components:

1. Philosophy of treatment: assumption that alcoholism/chemical dependency exists; it's a multiphasic illness; focus on the phenomenon of addiction as the major presenting problem; denial is part of the illness.

2. Goals of treatment: improved mental and physical health achieved through total abstinence.

3. Content of treatment: help people take better care of themselves by understanding chemical dependency as well as the strategies that will help maintain sobriety.

4. Quality of interdisciplinary staff: trained people who meet professional standards to address the physical, social, family, spiritual, and psychological areas; important that recovering chemically dependent people are part of the staff.

5. Duration of treatment: length of stay based on the average time it takes a typical patient to complete primary care; treatment duration must remain individualized.

6. Intensity of treatment: living in a therapeutic community that includes lectures, group meetings, individual meetings with professionals as needed, aftercare planning.

7. Context of treatment: atmosphere conductive to self-evaluation; environment in which people are treated with dignity and respect by staff who are caring and concerned–a caring community.

8. Quality assurance measures: process and outcome quality measurements (Engleman, 1989).

Although the Minnesota Model focuses on a therapeutic community to provide services, earlier detection of alcoholism and limited insurance coverage for treatment have led to a broader and more varied choice of options, with emphasis on utilizing outpatient services initially if not exclusively in some instances. A diagram of the current continuum of care in the addiction field is depicted in Figure 16-1.

Although this picture appears somewhat confusing to the uninitiated, efforts are underway to help clarify placement criteria. In particular, the American Society of Addictive Medicine (ASAM) and the National Association of Alcohol Treatment Programs (NAATP) cooperated in developing a set of guidelines that has been well accepted by the field (Lawton, 1991b). Four different levels of care are highlighted: outpatient, outpatient with partial hospitalization, medically monitored intensive inpatient, and medically managed intensive inpatient. The assignments are not limited to "medical necessity" but include biopsychosocial considerations.

Figure 16-1. Continuum of Care

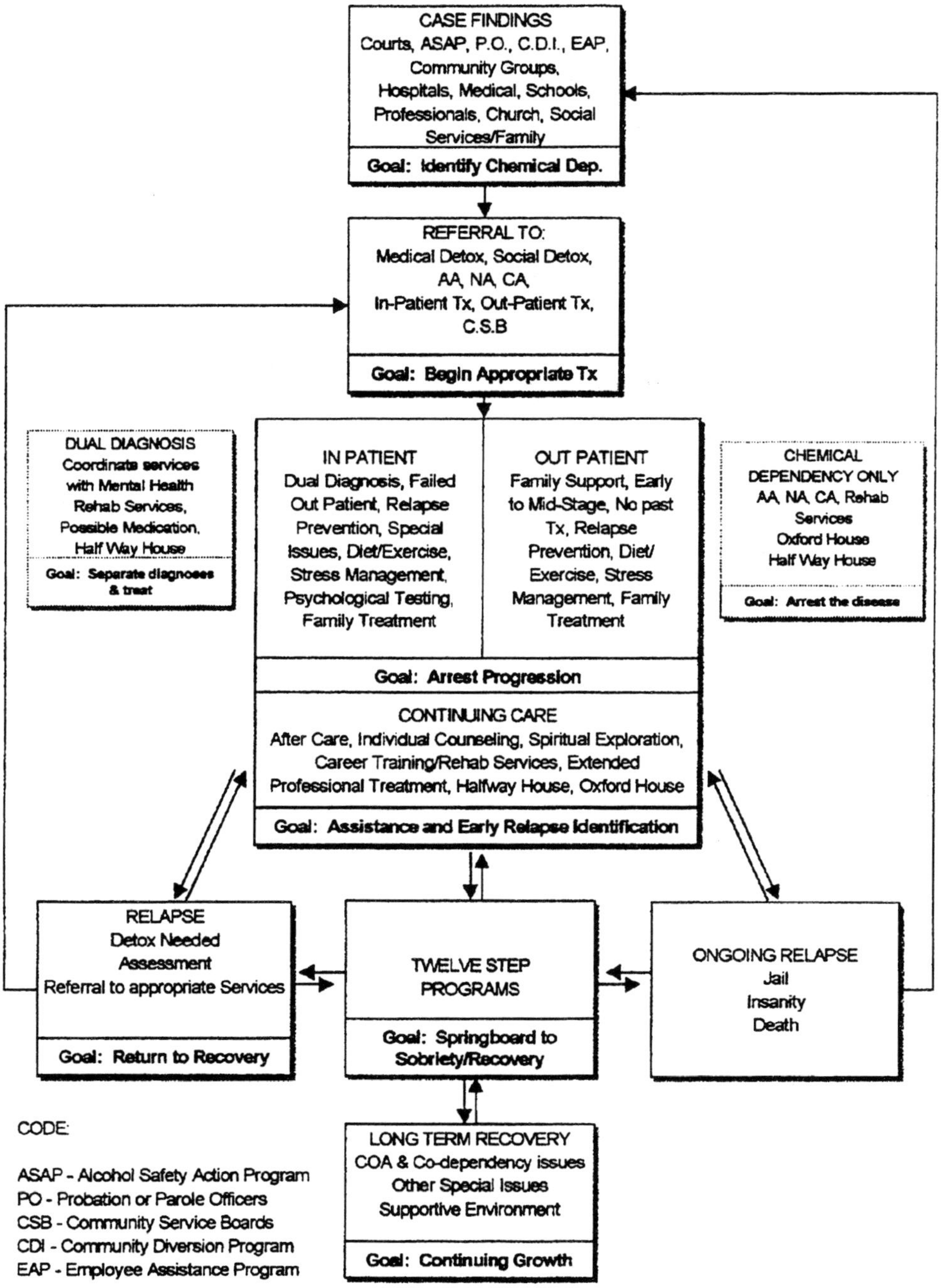

CODE:

ASAP - Alcohol Safety Action Program
PO - Probation or Parole Officers
CSB - Community Service Boards
CDI - Community Diversion Program
EAP - Employee Assistance Program

Special Considerations with Other Addictions

Cocaine

Although cocaine is a stimulant rather than a depressant, the person with a cocaine addiction (like the person with an alcohol addiction) nevertheless manifests the characteristics common to addiction, such as the denial system, preoccupation, and loss of control. "Coke" addiction has its own distinctive signs and symptoms (e.g., weight loss, chronic runny nose, frequent upper respiratory infections, loss of interests, auditory hallucinations, and repetitious compulsive acts such as tapping fingers or playing with hair). They occur in a sequence of three phases: crash, withdrawal, and extinction.

The fatal nature of cocaine may more likely be played out in heart failure rather than in liver or pancreatic diseases as seen in alcoholism (Nuckols, 1989). One substantial difference encountered in cocaine addiction is the problem of intense cravings, which serve to perpetuate the use of cocaine. This appears to be the result of the vivid euphoric memories associated with cocaine binges. Also, with cocaine addiction there is the issue of illegality, which can intensify the isolation because of the perceived need to keep the use secret for fear of the legal consequences. Finally, a further complication resulting from cocaine addiction is the situation in which intravenous needles are used, leading to an increased possibility of acquired immune deficiency syndrome (AIDS).

In treating cocaine addiction it appears that simply using the standard addiction approach of breaking denial is not sufficient. Additionally, pharmacological nonaddictive antidepressants (e.g., imipramine) are being tried, along with psychotherapeutic treatment focusing on the systematic desensitization of persons with an addiction to craving-loaded cues like razor blades or syringes (Gawin, 1990).

Nicotine

Although nicotine follows the benchmarks for addiction in its own right, it is mentioned here because of another interesting aspect; it can be a gateway and/or trigger to another addiction, especially alcohol. Evidence is mounting to suggest that it plays a part in preventing quality sobriety or in fact even abstinence from other substances. Treatment is increasingly moving away from dealing with one addiction at a time and including trigger addictions as part of the initial treatment. For example, hospital units use decaffeinated coffee and have "no smoking" rules (Henningfield, Clayton, & Pollin, 1990; Pletcher, Lysaght, & Human, 1990).

Other Addictions

So far, except for codependency, which appears to be in a class of its own, the discussion has been on drug addictions (primarily alcohol, cocaine, and nicotine). It is also possible to demonstrate the same major characteristics of addiction (denial system, loss of control, preoccupation, and moral deterioration) with other compulsive behaviors, such as overeating and gambling. It is not within the scope of this chapter to address the many details associated with a specific addiction. Two general resources that cover the substance addictions in more depth are *Concepts of Chemical Dependency* (Doweiko, 1996) and *Visions of Addiction* (Peele, 1988).

Misuse and abuse of prescription and over-the-counter medications also is receiving increased attention. Older persons "are at a particularly high risk for addiction due to their more frequent use of medications to treat a variety of acute and chronic medical conditions, to economic stability for the majority, and to a high prevalence of depression and anxiety disorders" (Lowinson, Ruiz, Millman & Langrod, 1992, p. 849). Polyaddiction among persons who are older may be masked by the greater prevalence of multiple medical conditions.

Relapse Prevention

Regardless of the substance, primary intensive treatment alone is not sufficient for these disorders. Relapse prevention as a biopsychosocial strategy to maintain abstinence and a healthy life-style is critical (Gray, 1993).

Although relapse prevention is individualized to address client needs, most such treatment plans include social support approaches, life-style change approaches, cognitive-behavioral approaches and pharmacological approaches (USDHHS, 1995; Wormer, 1995).

Research studies (NIAAA, 1997) cite that the availability of social resources following primary intensive inpatient treatment increased the rate of abstinence among people. Special resources may include psychosocial therapy, relationship enhancement, aftercare groups, family networks, and many types of support groups. The most prevalent type of support groups associated with abstinence from substance use and the prevention of relapse are 12-step programs such as AA and Narcotics Anonymous. Rational Recovery, a support group utilizing the Addictive Voice Recognition Technique (AVRT) (Trimpey, 1996), and SMART (Self Management and Recovery Training) Recovery, a support group using a cognitive-behavioral approach based on Rational Emotive Behavior Therapy (REBT) (Knaus, 1995), are relatively new support groups offering alternatives to the spiritually-based 12-step programs. Other support groups, like Women for Sobriety, are population-specific, and still other approaches (e.g., One Church One Addict) are religion- and church-based.

Approaches addressing life-style changes focus on breaking ties with people who use drugs and teaching ways of coping with negative behaviors while acquiring a new social identity as a person who does not use drug substances. Many of these approaches utilize the cognitive-behavioral approach to teach self-efficacy and avoidance skills, using such instruments as Situational Confidence Questionnaire (Annis & Graham, 1988) and workbooks such as the *Staying Sober Workbook* (Gorski, 1989) to identify warning signs and internal and external cues associated with cravings.

According to *Effectiveness of Substance Abuse Treatment* (USDHHS, 1995), many pharmacotherapies are not available for the treatment of substance use disorders and the prevention of relapse. For opiate addiction such drugs as buprenorphine, clonidine, methadone, naltrexone, and LAAM (levo-alpha-acetyl methanol) are approved as opiate-craving blockers. Some of these also have been found effective in the treatment of alcohol use disorders, specifically, disulfiram (Antabuse), an alcohol-sensitizing agent for avoidance of alcohol consumption, and naltrexone for alcohol craving and opiate addiction. Some antidepressant medication trials have found mixed results in reducing cocaine abuse. The efficacy of these therapies continues to be studied.

Implications

Greater societal awareness of the multidimensional impact of chemical abuse and dependency has led to increased prevention efforts as well as awareness of the need for early recognition and treatment. Health care professionals are in a critical position (as gatekeepers to a range of services and programs) to provide and/or refer those at risk to educational, diagnostic, intervention, and treatment options. Addiction per se must be considered a primary illness in health care settings. If overlooked or inadequately treated, it will continue to take its toll on individuals, their families, and society at large. Identifying and managing triggers (e.g., caffeine and nicotine) for other chemical use and addiction, especially among persons who are younger and those who are compromised by health problems or are otherwise vulnerable because of changes in social status (such as unemployment or homelessness) are essential. Building support for persons at risk may require community-based treatment and referral, with long-term follow-up and services to pertinent family members and significant others. Although they are beyond the scope of this chapter, there are additional considerations in working with persons who abuse or are addicted to multiple substances and in addressing those persons who may also have a psychiatric history. Access to care and follow-up for those with multiple treatment needs is often inadequate and sometimes inappropriately provided.

Addiction, like other chronic disorders, is a lifelong illness requiring a comprehensive approach. Given the rapid and confusing changes in the organization and financing of health care services, treatment for persons with addictions and/or their families may be compromised. This is particularly evident with the introduction of managed care and cost-containment approaches intended to control cost in the traditional medical acute-care setting, where treatment is based on medical necessity and physician's orders. These same criteria are not always applicable to the rehabilitation model needed for addiction, a chronic, multidimensional illness for which family support and aftercare services are critical (Spicer, 1991). Managed care will undoubtedly have an impact on the current role of employee assistance programs (EAPs), which serve as an identification/referral arm for industry in the area of chemical abuse and dependency. EAPs could be considered as duplication of, replacement for, and/or supplements to managed care programs. In any event, the trend is toward reduced reimbursement of fewer services, which will profoundly affect access to essential treatment and follow-up for addicted persons and their families.

In spite of the negative aspects of addiction, with its stigma and pervasive prevalence, there is a very positive aspect to be considered. Since the beginning of AA in 1935 there has emerged increasing hope for converting the crisis of addiction into an opportunity to improve the overall quality of one's life. With the advent of the Hughes Act in 1970 (Comprehensive Alcohol Abuse and Alcoholism Prevention, Treatment, and Rehabilitation Act), the chances to capitalize on these opportunities were enhanced as the stigma was decreased and appropriate resources were developed. Although currently there seems to be a loss in momentum and a shift backward toward an emphasis on controlling drug use through supply and/or punishment, the progress and gains of the past several decades are still available for those who have the motivation and access to services. Using the biopsychosocial-spiritual approach, it is the role of those with professional credentials to identify the addiction, challenge the denial system of the person, and work with the person and his or her family to find the resources necessary for treatment and recovery. With appropriate and adequate care, persons who abuse or are addicted to harmful substances can return to and/or maintain healthy and productive lives.

REFERENCES

Alcoholics Anonymous (1973). *Is AA enough?* New York: Alcoholics Anonymous World Services.

American Psychiatric Association (1995). *Diagnostic and statistical manual of mental disorders* (4th ed, rev.). Washington, D.C.: Author.

Annis, H., & Graham, J. (1988). *Situational Confidence Questionnaire (SCQ-39) user's guide.* Toronto: Addiction Research Foundation.

Beasley, J. (1990). *Diagnosing and managing chemical dependency.* Durant, OK: Essential Medical Information Systems.

Brown, S. (1985). *Treating the alcoholic: A developmental model of recovery.* New York: John Wiley and Sons.

Caring Community Series (1975). *Dealing with denial.* Center City, MN: Hazelden.

Center on Addiction and Substance Abuse (1993). *The cost of substance abuse to America's health care system: Report 1: Medicaid hospital costs.* New York: Columbia University Press.

Doweiko, H. (1996). *Concepts of chemical dependency.* Pacific Grove, CA: Brooks/Cole.

Dube, C. E., Goldstein, M. G., Lewis, D. L., Meyers, E. R., & Zwick, W. R. (Eds.). (1989). *Project ADEPT: Curriculum for primary care physician training.* Providence, RI: Brown University, Center for Alcohol and Addiction Studies.

Ewing, J. A. (1984). Detecting alcoholism: The CAGE questionnaire. *Journal of the American Medical Association, 252,* 1905-1907.

Gawin, F. (1990). Cocaine addiction: Psychology and neurophysiology. *Science, 251,* 1580-1585.

Glat, M. M. (1957). Group therapy in alcoholism. *British Journal of Addiction, 54,* 21-28.

Gorski, T. (1989). *The staying sober workbook.* Independence, MO: Harold House Press.

Gray, M. (1993). *Relapse prevention in L. Straussner clinical work with substance abusing clients.* New York: Guilford Press.

Haverkos, H., Genser, S., Grace, W., & Smeriglio, V. (1991). Complications of drug misuse. *Current Opinion in Psychiatry, 4,* 454-459.

Henningfield, J., Clayton, R., & Pollin, W. (1990). Involvement of tobacco in alcoholism and illicit drug use. *British Journal of Addiction, 85,* 279-292.

Jackson, J. K. (1954). The adjustment of the family to the crisis of alcoholism. *Quarterly Journal of Studies on Alcoholism, 15,* 562-586.

Jans, P. (1991). *Delivery of services: Continuum of care.* Unpublished manuscript, Virginia Commonwealth University, Richmond.

Jellinek, J. K. (1954). *The disease concept of alcoholism.* New Haven, CT: College and University Press.

Johnson, V. E. (1980). *I'll quit tomorrow.* New York: Harper & Row.

Kinney, J., & Leaton, G. (1995). *Loosening the grip: A handbook of alcohol information.* St. Louis: Mosby-Year Book.

Knaus, W. (1995). *S.M.A.R.T. Recovery: A sensible primer.* Longmeadow, MA: Author.

Kuhn, C. C. (1988). A spiritual inventory of the medically ill patient. *Psychiatric Medicine, 6* (2), 87-100.

Lawton, M. J. (Ed.). (1990). Codependency: The search for definition. *Addiction Letter, 6* (8), 1.

Lawton, M. J. (Ed.). (1991a). A thread in the tapestry of life. *Addiction Letter,* 7 (11), 8.

Lawton, M. J. (Ed.). (1991b). Two provider groups propose patient placement criteria. *Addiction Letter,* 7 (2), 3.

Lowinson, J., Ruiz, P., Millman, R., & Langrod, J. (1992). *Substance abuse: A comprehensive textbook* (2nd ed.). Baltimore: Williams and Wilkins.

Marlatt, G., & Gordon, J. (1985). *Relapse prevention.* New York: Guilford Press.

McLellan, A. T., Luborsky, L., Woody, G., & O'Brien, C. (1980). An improved diagnostic evaluation instrument for substance abuse patients: The Addiction Severity Index. *Journal of Nervous and Mental Diseases, 168,* 26-33.

Miller, M., Gorski, T., & Miller, D. (1982). *Learning to live again.* Independence, MO: Independence Press.

National Institute on Alcohol Abuse and Alcoholism (1990). *Alcohol and Health.* Washington, D.C.: U.S. Government Printing Office.

National Institute on Alcohol Abuse and Alcoholism (1997). *Alcohol and health.* Washington, D.C.: U. S. Government Printing Office.

National Institute on Drug Abuse (1991). *Drug abuse and drug abuse research.* Washington, D.C.: U.S. Government Printing Office.

National Institute on Drug Abuse (1996). *The Monitoring the Future Study, 1975-1995.* Washington, D.C.: U.S. Government Printing Office.

National Institute on Drug Abuse (1997). *Epidemiologic trends in drug abuse* (Volume 1: NIH Publication No. 97-4204). Rockville, MD: National Institutes of Health.

Nuckols, C. C. (1989). *Cocaine: From dependency to recovery.* Blue Ridge Summit, PA: TAB Books.

Peele, S. (Ed.). (1988). *Visions of addiction: Major contemporary perspectives on addiction and alcoholism.* Lexington, KY: Lexington Press.

Pletcher, V., Lysaght, L., & Human, V. (1990). *Treating nicotine addiction.* Center City, MN: Hazelden.

Selzer, M. L. (1971). The Michigan Alcoholism Screening Test: The quest for a new diagnostic instrument. *American Journal of Psychiatry, 127* (12), 89-94.

Skinner, H., Holt, S., Schuller, R., Roy, J., & Israel, Y. (1984). Identification of alcohol abuse using laboratory tests and history of trauma. *Annals of Internal Medicine, 101,* 847-851.

Spicer, J. (1991, May). The rehabilitation concept in managed care: Uneasy partners. *Professional Update,* P.3.

Substance Abuse and Mental Health Services Administration (1995). *Drug Abuse Warning Network annual medical examiner data 1995.* Washington, D. C: U.S. Government Printing Office.

Substance Abuse and Mental Health Services Administration (1997). *Preliminary results from the 1996 national household survey on drug abuse.* Washington, D.C.: U.S. Government Printing Office.

Trimpey, J. (1996). *Rational recovery: The new cure for substance addiction.* New York: Simon & Schuster.

U.S. Department of Health and Human Services (1995). *Effectiveness of substance abuse treatment* (DHHS Publication No. SMA95-3067). Washington, D.C.: U.S. Government Printing Office.

Wegschneider, S. (1981). *Another chance: Hope and health for the alcoholic family.* Palo Alto, CA: Science and Behavior Books.

Wormer, K. (1995). *Alcoholism treatment: A social work perspective.* Chicago: Nelson-Hall Publishers.

Chapter 17

AN INTERNATIONAL AND MULTICULTURAL PERSPECTIVE ON DISABILITY AND REHABILITATION

GERALD L. GANDY AND RICHARD E. HARDY

The purpose of this chapter is to provide our personal perspectives on rehabilitation as a global phenomenon. Therefore, it is not a representative survey of rehabilitation in the various countries of the world. Instead, it is based on our reading, writing, and editing in regard to international rehabilitation and on international consultation and conference visits by the authors. We believe this type of approach will help to "move" the reader to become more interested in international rehabilitation. Rehabilitation is a global and not just local phenomenon. We hope to encourage the reader to do more thinking about rehabilitation on an international scale as we continue to move toward a global economy and society.

Far East

Beijing, China, the capital of the largest and most powerful communist country in the world, was the site of the Sixth International Conference on Counseling in the 21st Century (Evraiff, 1997). The conference featured a theme that has much relevance for the 21st Century, "Caring in an Age of Technology." Zheng, Zhang, Tan, and Zhang (1997) provided insights about the rapid development of counseling and therapy in China in the past ten years. Unemployment has become a serious problem, and vocational adjustment counseling for people with mental as well as physical disabilities is in great demand. The rapid development of a market economy has created stresses that have promoted other counseling problems such as adjustment issues for children in schools, instability and separation in families, and mental and physical health symptoms among those who are older. The presenters noted, however, that China, as measured by scientific criterion, is considered to be in a primary stage in regard to counseling and therapy.

The authors, being Westerners, continue to find the languages and customs and traditions of the Far East to be unusual and fascinating. While Tokyo, Japan, has a very Westernized appearance and is very similar to New York City, Chicago, or any other major city in the United States, the flavor of the orient and ancient Japan is well represented in nearby Kamacura, a city of temples and shrines. As Meyers (1983) noted years ago, Japan cannot be fully understood and appreciated until it is experienced. Japan is not only a recognized leader among developing nations throughout Asia but also seeks to provide technical assistance and training to other nations. Japan's rehabilitation programs are worthy of study, but one must consider the totality of Japan's unique and complex culture (Nosek, 1991).

Tension among the political powers of Asia continues in Panmunjom, Korea, where United Nations and Communist representatives negotiate in an open forum at the center of a designated DMZ (demilitarized zone). Ironically, some refer to Korea as the "Land of the Morning Calm" suggesting an exotic, peaceful Shangri La. However, it is a country which has experienced war and destruction for centuries. Rehabilitation has been a continuing theme.

The authors continue to be impressed with the scenic beauty of Hong Kong. The view of the harbor and surrounding city is an inspiration. However, the overcrowded conditions and need for additional resources are soon apparent. There have been many productive rehabilitation projects such as the Home for the Aged in Kowloon and the Happy Life Psychiatric Rehabilitation Farm. Experts await the opportunity to evaluate the impact of Hong Kong's recent reunification with China.

Near and Middle East and Africa

In spite of an increase in terroristic activity at the time, the 21st International Congress of Applied Psychology was held in Jerusalem, Israel, in July, 1986 (International Association of Applied Psychology, 1986). Although tensions were high, visitation to nearby Cairo, Egypt, by congress participants was accomplished without incident. Terroristic activity is the norm in this part of the world, only varying in intensity even to the present day. Nevertheless, as evident in contemporary news events, many Israeli and Arab efforts have been and are directed toward solutions of peaceful coexistence, and rehabilitation endeavors are part of these efforts. Feigin's (1995) article on the need to better clarify and understand the changing role of the vocational rehabilitation counselor is a manifestation of these efforts. These efforts have been greatly influenced by the Keren, a public nonprofit organization of the vocational rehabilitation centers in Israel, sponsored by the Israeli Ministry of Labor & Social Affairs.

One of the great challenges of rehabilitation workers today is fulfillment of the role of universal negotiator from the perspective of rehabilitation of people with disabilities as a concept and goal in which many persons in every country of the world are intensely interested and willing to cooperate to achieve. The concept is well demonstrated by the work of James F. Garrett of the World Rehabilitation Fund, who was involved in operating training programs for health and human service workers from Lebanon. Professionals from all sides of the conflict were willing to meet with him and his coworkers on neutral ground in Cyprus, where rehabilitation of people with disabilities is seen as a unifying goal and concept.

Continuing educational development of rehabilitation practitioners internationally should be a priority. The problems of disability will never be mitigated unless there are people with the qualifications and ethical values to tackle the problems. The authors are reminded of a sign in Monrovia, Liberia, advertising the work of a high-level rehabilitation practitioner. The sign reads as follows:

> UNIVERSAL PRAYER HOUSE. MEET THE PROPHET ASTROLOGER: FOR YOUR PROBLEMS, MARRIAGE AND FAMILY, HARD LUCK, ETC., SICKNESS, MADNESS, SPELLS, STROKE, BLOOD PRESSURE, CONVULSION, BARENESS [meaning emptiness], HEADACHE, CREEPY CRAWLY FEELINGS, WEAKNESS. READING OF THE STARS, OBSERVATION OF THE CELESTIAL BODIES IN THE SOLAR SYSTEM, INTERPRETATION OF THE INFLUENCE OF HEAVENLY BODIES ON HUMAN AFFAIRS.

Interestingly, on one side of the street near the sign was the Nixon Institute of Technology and across the road from it stood the Watergate Inn.

Europe

Peters (1976) observed many years ago that there is a greater humanitarian emphasis in European countries as compared to the United States. Rehabilitation is considered to be more of a right than a privilege. He suggested that the greater appreciation for the needs of people with disabilities may be because the problem is closer to home. Men, women, and children were injured in war as well as soldiers, and families were uprooted. Vulnerability and suffering seem to have had an enlightening effect upon people of Europe and their national governments.

At least prior to the confounding effects of their current economic crisis, Szuhay (1987) and Gandy (1987) noticed how most medical care was free to the citizens of Russia and that workers did not lose pay during hospitalization. There was no need for Worker's Compensation as in the USA. Goldberg (1989) observed how the Federal Republic of Germany provides comprehensive, coordinated educational, vocational, medical, social, and recreational services within one institution, whereas the American system is fragmented among different federal and state regulations. However, the American system does provide more opportunity to integrate persons with disabilities into society via community-based programs. Visitation to post "Wall" Berlin continues to reveal a country with a strong rehabilitation system; and combined with the heritage of centuries of substantive cultural contribution, it is almost difficult to comprehend that a tragic era such as the "Third Reich" ever existed.

Although Germany could improve its rehabilitation system by emulating the USA community-based feature, there are excellent examples in Europe of the integration of people with disabilities in the community. Sweden has developed a system of mental health care that is aimed at providing the most comprehensive and integrated care possible (Ljungberg, 1987). The shift to more local community settings has been a trend in overall health services in the United Kingdom since the beginning of the twentieth century (Shepherd, 1987). Numerous longitudinal studies in the United Kingdom have verified improved life satisfaction and subjective well-being of individuals with mental disabilities who have been deinstutionalized (Barry, 1995).

Eysenck (1989) noted at the First European Congress of Psychology in Amsterdam, Holland, that the USA and Europe are becoming more similar in regard to clinical therapeutic orientation. There are many innovative rehabilitation projects involving cooperation between the USA and European countries. One of the earliest projects involved the postoperative fitting of prostheses in Warsaw, Poland (Garrett, 1980). The surgeon, Marion Weiss, used carpenters to train his surgeons to carve bone. Electrical engineers were also used in the project. Research efforts have included the electrical potential of muscles, sight substitutes, joint replacements, functional electrical substitution, the person-machine interface, personally licensed vehicles, and personal hygiene technology.

The prestigious Pitie-Salpetriere Hospital at Pierre et Marie Curie University in Paris, France, was the site of the Fourth International Conference on Stress Management in September, 1992 (International Association for Stress Management, 1992). This facility is also noted as the place where Freud first met Charcot and, sadly, more recently, as the place where Princess Diana was brought after her tragic and fatal automobile accident. F. J. McGuigan (1992), Director of the Institute for Stress Management at the United States International University in San Diego, California, was responsible for bringing together a distinguished group of therapists and behavioral scientists from all over the world to share information on stress management research and techniques that have helped to prevent or eliminate hypertension, coronary heart disease, colitis, anxiety, excessive fatigue, bruxism, headaches, and other conditions that can have a temporary and often permanent impeding effect on human beings. Such conferences in Europe underscore the valuable contribution of international collaboration on issues of disability and rehabilitation (Gandy, 1995).

Canada and Mexico

Most of the Canadian pioneers in the professional counseling movement in Canada received their training in the United States, and developments in Canada paralleled those in the USA until the 1960s (Robertson & Paterson, 1983). A cursory review of counseling-related professional journals in recent years will indicate that Canadian counselors have contributed to and have been influenced by international ideas and sharing of information, as indicated by the international conferences such as the International Round Table for the Advancement of Counseling and the World Congress of Psychology that have been hosted in Canada. A visit to contemporary Quebec province approaching the year 2000 will sensitize one very quickly to the separatist political climate in Canada. Although the latter phenomenon has its disadvantages, it also has potential for unique developments in the counseling field independent of influences in other parts of the country. Stalikas, Peternelli, and Fitzpatrick (1994), with their discovery-oriented change process research at McGill University in Montreal, designed to explain therapeutic change in counseling and therapy, represent some of the creative work being done in this country.

Mexico is an attractive vacation spot for many USA citizens not only because of paradise beach and entertainment locations such as Acapulco and Cancun but also because of the favorable monetary exchange rate. However, it doesn't take long for one to see that economics are far more favorable to a reasonably financially comfortable USA visitor than the average citizen of this country. Sanchez-Escobedo (1993) has noted that the economic situation has prompted the government to assign a meager pension to a person rather than finance a full rehabilitation program for the individual. There are centers specializing in the treatment of persons with perceptual problems, motor limitations, physical rehabilitation, and mental retardation; however, the focus is on medical rehabilitation. There is a lack of professionals trained in counseling and related rehabilitation service areas. Recent efforts have been made to promote a change of focus, but better monetary support will be needed to fully develop this trend.

Caribbean and Central and South America

Hardy (1992) authored a fictional novel, *Hispaniola Episode: A Mental Health Allegory*, that reflects nonfictional aspects and insights about the culture of the Caribbean islands. Voodoo, for example, has features similar to spiritualistic aspects of more recognized religions, as well as psychological aspects of the behavioral sciences. In spite of poverty and malnutrition, there is a very low suicide rate in Haiti and a very high respect for life. Alternative medicine, which is just now gaining interest in the USA, is well developed in the Caribbean culture where natural foods, hypnotic trance phenomena, and self-responsibility have been the norm for a long time.

The willingness of people to work cross-culturally is demonstrated through programs of the U.S. Agency for International Development Partners of the Americas, which aligns states and locations in the United States with similar and sister states throughout the Americas and which cooperates in fields including rehabilitation, agriculture, arts and culture, education, emergency preparedness, communication, health, medicine, rural youth, sports, tourism, women in development, and others. Through the active involvement of this organization, a new rehabilitation center was built in Guatemala City for the citizens of Guatemala after a devastating earthquake. The splendor and beauty of Rio de Janeiro, Brazil is impressive but the poverty and health problems of Brazil necessitates intervention efforts. US Agency for International Development Partners of the Americas' projects with people with mental and physical disabilities have been active throughout Brazil, especially in the Santa Caterina area. More information on the activities of this organization can be obtained by writing to their address located at the end of this chapter.

Australia and New Zealand

By air from the east coast of the USA, with a couple of stopovers, it can take as long as 24 hours (with a "lot" of time over water) to get to what is both the largest island and smallest continent in the world–Australia. Although it is some distance from other regions of the world, Australia is a very advanced country in many respects, especially in the nature of counseling and related rehabilitation and health activities. The latter was very apparent in programs at the 24th International Congress of Psychology held in Sydney, Australia, August/September, 1988 (International Congress of Psychology, 1988). One of the international symposiums at this congress demonstrated not only the advanced treatment approach that Australia has made in the area of alcohol abuse with moderate drinking programs but how the USA is behind the major industrialized countries of the world in this endeavor. Dunlap (1990), in a later study through the International Exchange of Experts and Information in Rehabilitation (IEEIR) of the World Rehabilitation Fund, demonstrated how the community-based psychosocial rehabilitation project in New South Wales, Australia, is a helpful model for the USA and other countries of the World. More recently, Barreda-Hanson (1995) described an innovative multimodal treatment approach with attention deficit disorder with short-term groups using specific behavioral objectives to assess success.

While New Zealand is a much smaller geographical area, it is separated from Australia by 1200 miles of water and is an independent nation. Although there is some affinity between the two countries, they are quite distinct, each having an individual character and landscape. However, they share a commonality in their involvement with counseling and related rehabilitation and health activities (Newsome, 1988). Such organizations as the New Zealand Disability Resource Centre, the Rehabilitation League NZ (Inc), and the New Zealand Rehabilitation Association have been active and involved in the disability scene in New Zealand over the years. Involvement with nontraditional disability groups such as persons with eating disorders (Bushnell, 1995) and persons with AIDS (Brady, 1994) is evident.

Concluding Perspectives

The authors were coeditors with other colleagues on a major publication, *International Rehabilitation: Approaches and Programs* (Cull, Hardy, Peters, Peters, & Gandy, 1980). It included contributors from 23 countries from most of the major regions of the world. The contributors were leaders in the rehabilitation movement in their countries and many were prominent internationally. A variety of professional disciplines were represented. Gandy (1980) made some summary observations in the overview chapter that appear to be highly relevant to the contemporary international rehabilitation scene. Rehabilitation in many of these countries generally seems to be available to anyone who is in need rather than placing an emphasis on eligibility as in the USA. Many countries have made admirable progress in the development of their rehabilitation programs in spite of massive obstacles. Although not a problem in some countries, many face problems similar to the USA in regard to complex organizational and administrative problems in the delivery of rehabilitation services. There is evidence of enlightened concepts and attitudes regarding rehabilitation in many countries.

Some findings of a United Nations study conducted in the International Year of the Disabled Persons [*sic*] in 1981 also continues to have relevance

(Hammerman & Maikowski, 1981). They found that when the sum of all the categories of production is compared to the total costs of rehabilitation service production, it is possible to demonstrate a very positive benefit to cost ratio for services for people with disabilities. Repayment to society of the costs of rehabilitation occurs over a much shorter period than the productive period of the worker with a disability. A nation may regain the costs of rehabilitation services through benefits such as returned tax income, reduced transfer payments, and added production output, in a period of three to five years, whereas the worker with disability may be productive for an average of 12-16 years after completing the rehabilitation process. The availability of social benefits may serve as an important stimulus to the success of rehabilitation. A pattern of dependency which may have existed for generations within a family, can be altered through early intervention. This study also found that at least 10 percent of the population of any country experiences some form of mental or physical impairment. Considering that disability may produce secondary effects on the work force participation of those close to the person with a disability, a large proportion of the population can be adversely affected. Estimates based on average family size indicate that the proportion of the population affected by disability could be at least 25 percent.

One of the most important concepts concerned with rehabilitation on an international scale is that of nonapplicability of some specific information and techniques on a cross-cultural basis. When one thinks of a concept or technique that will "float" in terms of usability, one is often greatly disappointed in that generalizations and specific approaches are often not universally applicable even within the same country. In some countries where stop signs differ on different sides of the mountain, so-to-speak, applicable concepts have to be keenly evaluated in terms of their effectiveness. The use of local norms is of utmost importance.

A rehabilitation specialist must be attuned to folkways and attitudinal differences. Living with a disability in some cultures can be seen as building strengths and credits for advancement in the next life. Disability can also be seen as a way of identifying an individual as special, and a condition through which an individual may get attention from a government or voluntary agency. Children in some areas of the world are mutilated in order that they can have an occupation–that of begging, first for their parents, then themselves. These extreme examples give indications as to why broad and sweeping generalizations about rehabilitation philosophy and approaches cannot work in many areas of the world.

The dedication and interest in people with disabilities in some countries, considered to be totalitarian and society-oriented rather than individually-oriented, can be quite eye-opening. There is little bureaucracy in some of these countries in reference to service to people with disabilities. All social services, and often, medical services, are offered within one system, frequently within one building, which might serve a certain area of the country. A person walks across a hallway to apply for various services rather than journeying many miles and dealing with multiple agencies as is true in the USA. People with disabilities in some communist countries have a much stronger role in operating and managing their rehabilitation programs and in setting directions for themselves and other people with disabilities than has been generally true in the USA. They are the program directors and policy makers for their specific program.

Attitudes among professional persons, including physicians, psychologists, social workers, and lay persons differ enormously cross-culturally. This has been further verified by a study by Hardy, Cull, and Campbell (1987) which indicates significant differences in the ways these professionals view various disability groups in terms of being fortunate or unfortunate. Attitudes among approximately 500 different subjects in various groups were compared. Results indicated significant differences in cross-cultural orientations toward mental illness, physical disability, and general health problems.

Worldwide, rehabilitation practitioners need to give more attention to the problems of drug abuse and poly-substance abuse of children in reference to the effects of drugs on entire family units. These effects include those that are obvious in reference to children growing up in families in which drugs are a predominant force but also extends to profound disability of children born as a result of parental drug abuse and use. Rehabilitation practitioners are concerned about this worldwide situation, which is creating a large group of children with mental and physical disabilities.

As indicated at the beginning, the approach taken with this chapter was to provide our own personal perspectives rather than to present a representative survey. We feel this approach will better motivate practitioners to become interested and do more thinking about rehabilitation on an international scale. Rehabilitation is a global and not a local phenomenon. The problems of disability are universal, and people with disabilities can only benefit from international cooperation and sharing of information. A valuable reference for practitioners to consult, along with their further study of international and multicultural rehabilitation is Pederson's (1994) *A Handbook for Developing Multicultural Awareness* (2nd. ed.). The authors, as reflected in the Rational Emotive Behavior Therapy (REBT) and Gestalt chapters in this book, have developed practitioner books that focus on the nuances of thinking and feeling and thus help one to become more sensitive to cultural differences (Gandy, 1995; Hardy, 1991). A better understanding of disability and improved rehabilitation practices internationally cannot be accomplished without becoming more sensitive to the cultural differences and complexities throughout the world (Mays, Bullock, Rosenzweig, & Wessells, 1998; Pawlik & d'Y dewalle, 1996).

Organizational Sources of Information

The following are organizations which could provide additional information about international and multicultural rehabilitation activities.

U.S. Agency for International Development
Partners of the Americas
1424 K Street, N.W., #7
Washington, D.C. 20005

World Rehabilitation Fund
International Exchange of Experts and Information
In Rehabilitation (IEEIR)
Institute on Disability
University of New Hampshire, 6 Hood House
Durham, New Hampshire 03824-3577.

Rehabilitation International, USA 25 East 21st Street
New York, NY 10010.

REFERENCES

Barreda-Hanson, M. C. (1995, July). *Life is worth living after all–The ASHD child.* Paper presented at the Fourth European Congress of Psychology, Athens, Greece.

Barry, M.M. (1995, July). *Well-being and life satisfaction as components of quality of life in long-term psychiatric clients.* Paper presented at the Fourth European Congress of Psychology, Athens, Greece.

Brady, E. C. (1994, July). *A survey of potential caregivers and managers in the workforce: Attitudes towards AIDS sufferers.* Poster session presented at the 23rd International Congress of Applied Psychology, Madrid, Spain.

Bushnell, J. (1995, July). *Impulsivity and eating disorders: A community study.* Poster session presented at the Fourth European Congress of Psychology, Athens, Greece.

Cull, J. G., Hardy, R. E., Peters, , II, J. S., Peters, M. F., Gandy, G. L. (Eds.). (1980). *International rehabilitation: Approaches and programs.* San Antonio, TX: Clinical Prediction Press.

Dunlap, D. A. (1990). Rural psychiatric rehabilitation and the interface of community development and rehabilitation services. *Psychosocial Rehabilitation Journal, 14*(1), 67-90.

Evraiff, B. (Ed.) (1997, May). Counseling in the 21st century. *Sixth International Counseling Conference Proceedings*, Beijing, China. San Mateo, CA: Northern California Graduate University.

Eysenck, H. (1989, July). *Clinical psychology in Europe and in the United States--development and future.* Paper presented at the First European Congress of Psychology, Amsterdam, Holland.

Feigin, R. (1995). Trends and directions in the role of the vocational rehabilitation counselor in Israel. *Journal of Rehabilitation, 61*(4), 16-19.

Gandy, G. L. (1980). An overview of international rehabilitation. In J. G. Cull, R. E. Hardy, J. S. Peters, II, M. F. Peters, G. L. Gandy (Eds.), International rehabilitation: Approaches and programs. San Antonio, TX: Clinical Prediction Press.

Gandy, G. L. (1987, October). *Accountability in counseling/psychotherapy and the public interest.* Paper presented at a Soviet-American Psychology Conference in Leningrad (now St. Petersburg), Russia.

Gandy, G. L. (Chair). (1995a, July). *Counseling for minorities and special populations.* Thematic Session, Fourth European Congress of Psychology, Athens, Greece.

Gandy, G. L. (1995b). *Mental health rehabilitation: Disputing irrational beliefs.* Springfield, IL: Charles C Thomas.

Garrett, J. F. (1980, September). *Perspectives on disability and international rehabilitation.* Paper presented at the twenty-fifth year anniversary of the founding of the Department of Rehabilitation Counseling at Virginia Commonwealth University, held in conjunction with the annual Virginia Rehabilitation Association conference in Fishersville, VA.

Goldberg, R. T. (1989). Comparison of the German and American Systems of Rehabilitation. *Journal of Rehabilitation, 55*(1), 59-62.

Hammerman. S., & Maikowski, S. (1981). *The economics of disability: International perspectives.* New York: Rehabilitation International.

Hardy, R. E. (1991). *Gestalt psychotherapy: Concepts and demonstrations in relationships, hypnosis and addiction.* Springfield, IL: Charles C Thomas.

Hardy, R. E. (1992). *Hispaniola episode: A mental health allegory.* Needham, MA: Simon & Schuster Higher Education.

Hardy, R. E., Cull, J. G., & Campbell, M. E. (1987). Perception of selected disabilities in the United States and Portugal. *Journal of Human Behavior and Learning, 4*(3), 1-12.

International Association for Applied Psychology. (1986, July). *Program: 21st International Congress of Applied Psychology.* Jerusalem, Israel: Author.

International Congress of Psychology. (1988, August/September). *Program: 24th International Congress of Psychology.* Sydney, Australia: Author.

International Stress Management Association. (1992, September). *Program: Fourth International Conference on Stress Management.* Paris, France: Author.

Ljungberg, L. O. (1987). The Swedish system of mental health care: An integrated approach. In M. A. Jansen (Ed.), *An international perspective on community services and rehabilitation for persons with chronic mental illness.* (Monograph No. 36) New York: International Exchange of Experts and Information in Rehabilitation.

Mays, V.M., Bullock, M., Rosenzweig, M.R., & Wessells, M. (1998). Ethnic conflict: Global challenges and psychological perspectives. *American Psychologist, 53*(7), 737-741.

McGuigan, F. J. (1992). *Calm down: A guide to stress and tension control.* Dubuques, IA.

Myers, J. (1983). Rehabilitation in Japan: Impressions and reflections. *Journal of Rehabilitation, 49*(4), 80-85.

Newsome, L. R. (1988). *Disability in New Zealand: A study of rehabilitation and disability organizations* (2nd ed.) (Monograph No. 43). New York: International Exchange of Experts and Information in Rehabilitation.

Nosek, M.A. (1991). Relationships between personal assistance and productivity among Japanese adults with severe physical disabilities. *Rehabilitation Counseling Bulletin, 35*(2), 105-118.

Pawlik, K., & d'Ydewalle, G. (1996). Psychology and the global commons: Perpectives of international psychology. *American Psychologist, 51*(5), 488-495.

Pederson, P. (1994). *A handbook for developing multicultural awareness* (2nd ed.). Alexandria, VA: American Counseling Association.

Peters, II, J. S. (1976). Vocational rehabilitation in Western Europe, Yugoslavia and the United States 1971-72. *Rehabilitation Counseling Bulletin, 19*(3), 476-481.

Robertson, S. E., & Paterson, J. G. (1983). Characteristics of guidance and counseling services in Canada. *Personnel and Guidance Journal. 61*(8), 490-493.

Sanchez-Escobedo, P. (1993). Rehabilitation and special education in Mexico. *Rehabilitation Psychology News, 21*(2), 13-14.

Shepherd, G. (1987). Community mental health services in Great Britain: A personal view. In M. A. Jansen (Ed.), *An international perspective on community services and rehabilitation for persons with chronic mental illness.* (Monograph No. 36). New York: International Exchange of Information in Rehabilitation.

Stalikas, A., Peternelli, L., & Fitzpatrick, M. (1994, July). *How does client change occur?: A discovery oriented, process research strategy answer.* Paper presented at 23rd International Congress of Applied Psychology, Madrid, Spain.

Szuhay, J. A. (1987). One view of rehabilitation medicine in Russia. *Journal of Rehabilitation, 53*(2), 71-76.

Zheng, R., Zhang, S., Tan, L., & Zhang, C. (1997, May). The development of counsling and psychotherapy in China. In B. Evraiff (Ed.), *Sixth International Counseling Proceedings,* (pp.313-319), Beijing, China. San Mateo: Northern California Graduate School.

AUTHOR INDEX

SUBJECT INDEX

E